Cast A Grudge

Rhoan Flowers

Cast A Grudge

Navan, Ontario
Canada

Published by: Rhoan Flowers Books
Released: November 2022

Genre: Drama

ISBN 978-1-989995-09-9 (SC)
ISBN 978-1-989995-10-5 (EB)

Library & Archives of Canada
395 Wellington Street
Ottawa, Ontario
K1A-0N4

Special Recognition

Jurnay Spence (Female Cover Model)

Shakeem Philips (Male Cover Model)

Jahvon Flowers (Photographer for Rhoan's pic)

Clyde Williams (Front Cover Designer)

Introduction

Following all the abuse that Celine suffered at the hands of her ex-boy-friend, she decided against telling him about the daughter he fathered. A wonderful man entered her life who offered to help and be there for her, therefore she made him her child's father and started a family. When her fiancé got killed, she returned to the town where she and her ex-boy-friend ran away from as teenagers. She was then the mother of two, to a rebelling teenage daughter and an adoring younger son. Finding out about a history they never heard about, was educational for her children, who got to meet their grandmother and uncles. The town itself was a bit older than the place the children grew up, even though it was a major hub where people around the territory got most of their supplies.

Some of the police officers across the southern territories of the province were corrupt. The department itself was undermanned, therefore the officers had to work long hours. Celine's brother owned and operated the mechanic shop in town. One of his employees got into a relationship with a policeman's wife, who went to the shop for a repair. When the officer found out about his wife's cheating, he decided to eliminate the side-man, who had dark complexion. The mechanic shop's employee went missing and became the second of several racist incidents across the territory. The police department was believed to be protecting its officers, therefore an outside agency had to get involved to investigate the story. There were protests and unrest when evidence was discovered to prove the officer committed the crime.

The decision Celine made would come back to haunt her, when her ex-boyfriend's younger brother developed a crush on his niece. The mother hated Celine since she was younger and was not happy about her returning to town. Her husband was the town's bank manager, who was an undercover bigot despite his position. When their son who was a regular church attendee chose to start following some racist tyrants in town, he changed and stopped going to church. To appease his brother the young bigot committed an unforgettable crime. Fearing the police were zeroing in on him, the young man decided to commit a mass shooting and thereby reacted on his impulses.

This is the story of Robin Walker, who became an activist in the war against racism, when her boyfriend and she chose to avenge the slaying of their loved ones, who were killed during a brutal church massacre.

Chapter 1

Lloyd Walker Jr. was physically tired when he rang the bell on the number 29 city bus, to demand a stop at the next intersection. The bus had a moderate number of passengers onboard, so everyone was comfortably seated with extra available seats. As the bus approached the stop at Connaught Avenue and Bayers Road, the African Canadian male rose from his seat and walked to the rear exit door to disembark. Mr. Walker Jr. had high toned complexion and was the son of a Caucasian female and a dark complexion Bajan from Barbados. Once the driver brought the vehicle to a stop on Bayers Road, he stepped off the transport bus and extracted his cellular phone from his pocket. The season was changing from Automn to Winter therefore, the temperature was beginning to get chilly. The traffic signal was green and indicated the pedestrian crossing, so Lloyd ran to catch the signal before it changed. It was very easy to distinguish that he was a construction worker, with his hard yellow hat, lunch box, steel toed shoes, and dirty clothing. There was a black male crossing the street headed in the opposite direction, with whom Lloyd bumped fist as they went by each other. After a short scroll through the callers' list on his cellular, Lloyd pressed a button to phone his girlfriend who was at home.

"Hey honey! You on your way," Celine asked?

"Yes, I'm just stopping by the corner store to pick somethings up," Lloyd answered!

"OK, see you when you get here! And bring me some chips or something," Celine stated, as she disconnected the call?

The couple's daughter who was almost fifteen walked into the kitchen, where Celine was preparing dinner for the family. The young lady went over to the fridge, opened the door, and stood there looking inside. From inside another room a little boy's voice shouted, "mom is dinner ready yet?"

"I thought you said dad would be home by now? Was that him on the phone," Robin asked?

"I told you he gets home at about this time, it depends on where he worked," Celine responded!

"Well, if you know that I need his help, why did I hear you asking him to pick you up something," Robin argued?

"Will you relax? Your father will be home in a few minutes, OK! Then you can get whatever you want from him," Celine answered!

"Fine," declared Robin as she took a bottle of water from the fridge and walked back to her room, where she closed the door behind her.

"Young lady I told you about closing doors in my house! The only door you allowed to close is the bathroom, whenever you in there," Celine shouted!

Their young son Julien who was seven years old, walked into the kitchen as Robin's bedroom door squeaked while she slid it open. The little boy had his Play Station console controller in his hand and a sad look on his face.

"Mom isn't dinner ready yet," Julien asked?

"In a few minutes Julien," Celine answered.

"You said that twenty minutes ago mom," Julien argued.

"OK son, it's coming right up," Celine stated!

After getting off the phone with Celine, Lloyd walked into the corner store at the Canadian Tire Gas Station, where he headed directly to the refrigerator in the back. There was an Asian cashier behind the counter reading a magazine and a black female standing at the ATM machine doing a transaction. As Lloyd went by the bread in isle two, he grabbed a white loaf from the counter, then a two-litre bottle of Ginger Ale at the end of the isle. The father of two wanted a tub of milk, so he stood by the glass door looking for their favorite grade to purchase. The three-bag package of milk was a good price, so he opened the door and began reaching in for one. Suddenly the front door to the convenience store swung violently open and three armed men rushed inside barking orders.

"Everybody keep your hands where we can see them," yelled the first man through the door as he looked around to see who was inside the store!

"Hey you, open the register now bitch," shouted the second thief, who went behind the counter and shoved the cashier to the ground!

All three robbers wore masks and had different types of handguns. The third thug through the door moved to securing the customers, so the female by the ATM machine threw her hands in the air. The money she had just taken from the machine was dangling in her right hand, along with her bank card. The third robber walked over to the female with his 9mm Taurus G2C pistol aimed at her stomach, then grabbed the money and bankcard from her hand. As the robber moved away from the female, he threw her bankcard on the floor and placed the cash inside his pocket. The first two men through the door had the cashier secured and were busy taking whatever they wanted. The third robber began looking around the store and saw Lloyd standing by the refrigerator. Without any hesitation the robber strutted towards Lloyd, whose hands were filled with the products he went to purchase. Lloyd did not expect to be hassled once the thief saw his attire, so he began reasoning with the man to disclose more about himself.

"Hey bro, I'm just a construction worker heading home to my wife and kids! I really ain't got shit man," Lloyd stated!

When the thief reached halfway down isle three, he lifted the mask halfway over his face to show Lloyd his facial features. The construction worker's eyes lit wide open with surprise once he saw who the thief was. With his Taurus G2C aimed at his victim's chest, the robber callously fired three shots which struck Lloyd and propelled him backwards through the refrigerator's glass door.

"Oh shit, holy shit," the female customer yelled!

"What the hell man," shouted the first robber who was stacking the cigarettes from the showcase into a bag.

The second robber had removed all the money from the register and was tampering with a business safe that was underneath the counter. When the thief lifted his head and realized his partner had killed a customer, he immediately began running for the front door with the first robber. The scared female had no idea if the shooter planned to execute everyone inside the convenience store, so she took off running towards a rear exit door. Instead of continuing his malicious assault, the robber ran directly through the front door behind his companions, who all jumped into an awaiting Nissan Altima and drove away.

Soon as the store clerk realized that the thieves had left, he slowly rose to his feet and began looking around. There was blood trickling from a cut on his forehead, so the clerk grabbed for some napkins and placed it over the wound. The female customer stopped at the exit once she realized the thieves had gone, then walked over to check on the injured customer.

"Call the police! My god, that guy killed this man for no reason at all," the female declared!

The store clerk picked up the phone and called 911, as he walked down isle two to check on the assaulted male.

"It was like they got history or something, because that dude just shot him down for nothing man," the female declared!

"Why would anyone want to kill this guy," said the clerk?

"Do you know who he is," the female asked?

"He is a family guy! He comes in here all the time with his kids, or when he is going home from work. This is really horrible," said the clerk!

A police cruiser arrived at the location four minutes later, with Officers Lafountain and Hibberts. The two officers were not exactly sure if danger still lurked, so they withdrew their service weapons and slowly approached the door. When they reached the entrance Officer Lafountain opened the door, at which they looked inside but saw nothing.

"Is everything OK in here," Officer Hibberts shouted?

"Yes, yes, hurry come on in! This guy has been shot," the clerk shouted?

When the officers entered the convenience store, they observed signs that the business had been robbed, as they made their way to the victims. Officer Lafountain went directly to examining the victim, while his partner took the two survivors aside to acquire information. As they walked away the female survivor remembered her bank card on the floor and began fussing about her stolen money.

"May I know your guys' names," Officer Hibberts asked, as he removed a note pad and pen from his upper pocket, then began writing?

"I am Puk Zu," the clerk stated!

Officer Hibberts fought to hold back his chuckle at the man's name, as he jotted it down on his note pad. The female, however, was not as thoughtful as she busted out into laughter.

"Ha-ha-ha-ha! That sounded like screw you," said the female!

"And what would your name be ma'am," Officer Hibberts questioned?

"I am Beverly Johnson!"

"Thank you both for that! Are you both OK, no other injuries," asked the officer as he wrote down the information!

"Apart from this cut on my head, I am fine officer," Puk answered!

"Those damn thieves stole the money I just got from the machine! How the hell am I going to get my money back," the female argued?

"If we are able to catch them soon, maybe you'll get your money back," Officer Hibberts exclaimed!

"I thought that son of a bitch was going to steal my bank card too," the female cursed!

"You mean he held your bank card in his hand," Officer Hibberts asked?

"Yes! Then he tossed it on the floor over there," said the female!

"Maybe we might be able to get a fingerprint off that card. If you don't' mind us taking it for a while, you can phone your bank and explain what happened and have them issue you another one. Aside from the bank card, is there anything any of you can tell me about the thieves? How many of them were there," Officer Hibberts explained?

4

"There was three of them! Aside from that I can't say, because they wore masks and shoved me to the ground, then kept their foot on me! I thought they were going to kill me," the clerk stated!

"How about you Miss Johnson," asked the officer?

Three other cruisers and an ambulance arrived on the scene, at which four new officers entered the store with the pair of paramedics. Two officers stayed outside the store and began managing the gathering crowd, which was eager to find out who had gotten shot.

"Excuse me for a second! Officer Molino there is a bank card over there on the floor, can you photograph it and bag it for evidence please," Hibberts said?

"No problem Hibberts," Officer Molino answered!

"The guy who shot that construction worker, lift up his mask and showed his face before he shot him," Beverly stated!

"Are you saying they knew each other," the officer asked?

"It seems like it! That construction guy's face looked scared when he saw the shooter," Beverly said!

"Where was the shooter when he fired the gun," Officer Hibberts asked?

"He grabbed the money from my hand over there, then walked down that isle towards the other guy," Beverly answered.

At that the interrogating officer began looking around the store and realized there was a camera directly ahead of the shooter, as he walked towards the rear of the store.

"Can we watch the security footage inside the store, especially from that camera" Officer Hibberts enquired?

"Yes, you can, but I will need to get the manager down here, because he is the only person with the code for the video recorder," Puk responded.

"Can you call your manager and ask him to come down please," Officer Hibberts asked?

"I will get him on the phone right away," Puk answered!

"We are going to have to close the store, due to the fact this is now an ongoing murder investigation! It would be helpful if you also compile a list of the things stolen, after you speak with your manager." Hibberts responded?

"No problem officer," Puk responded!

Officer Lafountain walked over with Lloyd's wallet, which contained his personal identification. The officer tried his best to keep the victim alive and eventually gave way to the paramedics, but he knew there was very little chance to save him. Officer Hibberts took out Lloyd's driver's license and looked at the photo, then looked at his partner who shook his head, to signal the victim's slim chance of surviving. The paramedic technicians did their utmost to save Lloyd, hence, they rushed from the store with the patient securely strapped to the gurney, and an intravenous needle attached to his arm.

"We need to contact his next of keen," Officer Hibberts declared as he passed back the wallet.

"It appears he only lives down the street, so I'll get on it right away," Officer Lafountain stated!

"Sorry about that Miss Johnson! What did you do after the robber shot the victim," Hibberts asked?

"I thought they, I mean he might be getting ready to kill us all! So soon as I saw daylight, I took off running for that back exit," Beverly explained!

"That was very brave of you," Officer Hibberts stated!

"You damn right! Shiiittt! I ain't gonna just stand around waiting for some asshole to come shoot me! That bitch better chase me down and shoot me in the back! Shiiittt, you better believe that," Beverly lamented!

There were detectives arriving on location, officers taking pictures, and putting up crime scene yellow tape, when Officer Lafountain drove a few meters down the street to Lloyd's address. The convenience store front had become a busy atmosphere with a news team on site to capture and broadcast the story. The local news reporter spoke with several eyewitnesses, but none bigger than Beverly who gave him a play-by-play description of what happened. The police had not yet notified Lloyd's family of his injury therefore, the reporter could not mention his name during the broadcast. Celine had heard the emergency sirens going by her window, but never thought they were because of her mate, so she went about her chores preparing to feed her family. When Officer Lafountain knocked on the door, Celine knew that something terrible had happened before Julien ran to open it. As she stood listening to the officer ask to have a word with her by the door, her feet became heavy and felt like they would not carry her to the entrance.

"Mom, there is a police officer here to speak with you," Julien yelled, before he ran away from the door!

Robin overheard her brother and walked out from her room to investigate. Celine finally reached the door and was extremely nervous to hear what the officer had to say.

"Hello, may I help you officer," Celine asked?

"Good evening, ma'am! Would this be Lloyd Walker's residence, and are you his partner," Officer Lafountain asked?

"Yes, to both your questions! Is something wrong? Did something happen to Lloyd," Celine demanded?

"I am terribly sorry to inform you that he was shot and injured inside the convenience store down the street! The ambulance just rushed him to the hospital, but it honestly doesn't look too good for him," Officer Lafountain informed!

"Oh my God no," screamed Celine as she broke out in tears!

"What the hell did you say happened to my dad," Robin yelled from across the room, before she stormed back into her room crying?

"I am terribly sorry to inform you about this ma'am! Do you have a ride to the hospital? If you need one, I would be delighted to carry you there," Officer Lafountain declared?

"Please, please! Oh my lord, no," Celine cried!

Little Julien noticed his mother in tears and ran to her side. "Are you OK mommy? What happened?"

"It's your father Julien, the officer said someone shot him in the corner store," Celine said!

"I'll give you a few minutes to get ready and wait for you downstairs in the car," Officer Lafountain lamented!

Back at the convenience store the manager arrived within half an hour of being summoned. The Asian supervisor was terribly shaken to discover that someone was shot inside the store, so he gave his clerk the rest of his shift off. The video surveillance machine was kept inside the business office, therefore, Detective Laddimer, Officer Hibbert, and another squad officer accompanied the manager to watch the footage. The manager rewound the captured footage to the beginning, where they watched the robbers barged into the store and held everybody at gun point. When the footage reached the point of interest, everyone drew closer to the screen to try and identify the shooter. At the angle from which the camera caught the shooter, his hand slightly blocked some of his face, but the officers believed they could get a better view of him if they expanded the picture. The recording machine did not allow for photo enlargement, so the officers confiscated the device for their technicians to evaluate and identify the suspect. Outside the convenience store the residents had begun creating a makeshift memorial for the deceased father, by placing flowers and teddy bears along a fence, a few yards away from the location. Word had gotten around that Lloyd was the victim shot, so those who knew him and many others went by the scene to pray for his family.

Chapter 2

Once inside their get away vehicle, the Caucasian thieves removed their masks while their driver sped along Connaught Avenue, on the west end of Nova Scotia, Canada. Contrary to the driver who was eager to uncover what his comrades had gotten, one of the other thieves was furious at his companion who had committed the crime. The shooter was seated in the rear of the Nissan beside the second robber that entered the store, who behaved rather nervous and kept looking through the rear glass for pursuers. Through all the excitement that surrounded him, the shooter remained calm and simply inspected his firearm, which was still warm. The thieves were heading to one of the men's residence in the Westmount Subdivision, where they sought to lay low for a few hours. All three thieves were involved in several other armed robberies, but their levels of violence had always been minimal.

"What's wrong with you guys? What did we get! I hope you fellows cleaned that bitch out," declared the driver!

"Damn it! What is wrong with you man? We agreed that no one should get hurt, yet still you shot that dude three times," argued Eddie!

"Wait, who got shot? What the hell happened in there," asked the driver?

"Don't look like we being followed! Drive easy Nickle," Quest declared!

"This dumb ass cousin of yours shot some guy who was only buying some groceries and shit," quarrelled Eddie!

"Who did you shoot Cuz," Nickle asked?

"That punk Lloyd, who stole my girlfriend when I was doing time," Aaron declared!

"So, you see this guy in a store and shoot him? What are you, a damn idiot," Eddie argued?

Aaron shoved his right hand around the headrest section of the front seat and placed Eddie in a choke hold. The shooter then jammed his 9mm Taurus against his accomplice's temple, at which Nickle immediately began begging for Eddie.

"Cousin, cousin! I'm sure he didn't mean nothing by that! Take it easy man," Nickle pled!

"I told you I don't take disrespect from anybody," Aaron threatened!

"Sorry Aaron, sorry man! I don't mean anything by it, I'm just running off my mouth," Eddie said!

"Well next time keep your opinion to yourself! Before the same thing happen to you," Aaron warned!

When they reached Nickle's apartment building, they parked the car in an outdoor slot and entered the building through the main entrance. There was a Caucasian female named Elenna Rose waiting for the elevator, who turned and watched the robbers as they entered the lobby. Instead of riding the elevator to the third floor, the four thieves chose to take the stairs and walked up to their destination. Quest, Aaron, and Nickle were all in a festive mood and joked about as they went up the stairs, but Eddie felt embarrassed and was less social after the car incident. Despite their friendship, Quest, Nickle, and Eddie feared Aaron, who had a lengthy criminal history and had done prison time on three separate occasions. Even though the other thieves felt similarly and knew that the murder would increase their chances of getting caught, none of them objected with Eddie, fearing Aaron's reaction.

Elenna went home and had three of her girlfriends over that evening for their weekly game of Bridge. The ladies ended their game night around 10:49 PM, after which they departed and Elenna got ready for bed. Before going to sleep she decided to watch the night's newscast, while she laid tirelessly in bed. A few minutes into the broadcast the anchor aired the convenience store robbery, at which they showed pictures of the three robbers inside the business. The instant Elenna saw the men's outfits, she knew exactly who they were and quickly telephoned the police station. Elenna was connected and transferred to a Detective Laddimer, who took all the information she had to provide. One of the ladies who played Bridge with her lived on the third floor, two doors away from Nickle's apartment, therefore, she also provided the suspects' possible location.

By the time the information was received by Detective Laddimer, the day shift officers had already signed off duty. The night shift did not have a substantial number of officers to spare for the raid, therefore, the detective phoned some of his colleagues individually with his request. The murder of such a well respected and hardworking father shook the entire community, so none of the involved officers felt comfortable to sleep that night. Remarkably enough, every officer who Detective Laddimer phoned and asked to join the raid team accepted and were at the precinct within half hour of the call. There was no motive or cause for the killing, so residence throughout the city felt nervous knowing there was a crew of killers roaming their streets. It had only been a few hours since the senseless killing, yet the police force was already under scrutiny for not apprehending the shooters.

A police cruiser was sent to the apartment building, where they found the make and model of the escape vehicle they sought. With all the information they received, the officers were confident in the research done and thus acquired the necessary search warrant to enter the premises. The raid team met inside the tactical room at the local police station before they headed out to apprehend their suspects. Detective Laddimer who lead the team, briefed the others on their apprehension strategy with the use of a blueprint copy of the building. Some of the chosen officers wanted to ensure they were headed to the right location, therefore, they asked important questions about the information gathered. When the concerned officers learnt that their eyewitness not only described all the clothing worn by the thieves, but included the getaway driver, they grew more satisfied with the detail.

Officers Hibberts and Lafountain were a part of the raid team and were the first two members contacted by Detective Laddimer. Their police chief was notified about the raid by the detective yet was at his residence resting comfortably while his officers conducted the apprehension. All the officers took their task seriously and wanted to return home safely to their spouses, so there was none of their routine comical blunders as they prepared. Everyone ensured their teammate's tactical uniforms were correctly installed before they checked their weapons and departed from the station. The undercover officer who was sent to investigate the suspect's vehicle, was instructed to keep watch, and remain on the scene until the raid team arrived. Detective Laddimer did not want any of the suspects to leave the location or they would have had to postpone their plans.

At 2:41 AM the raid team arrived on location, driving unmarked vehicles to avoid early detection. The officers parked along the left side of the building close an emergency exit, then had one of their comrades make his way inside and allowed them entry. Once inside the building the team quietly made their way up to apartment 311, where Nickle lived with his girlfriend and a small child. All the bandits were drinking beer and smoking Marijuana, but while his accomplices played Dominos, Arron sat watching a movie with Nickle's girlfriend. The couple's young son was asleep inside their bedroom with the door closed, yet they disturbingly carried on as if he was not present.

The raid team was all dressed in their tactical uniforms, with helmets, a protective shield, and bullet proof vests for added protection. The officers were warned that the four wanted men were armed and considered dangerous, so they had no idea if they would be walking into a shootout situation. Moments after they gathered by the front door, Officer Breeland who was 6ft. 4in tall, weighed three hundred and seventy pounds and bench pressed over five hundred and fifty pounds, swung their battering ram, and knocked the door off its hinges. As soon as the door flew open, the officers barged in behind their protective shield, which startled everyone inside the residence.

"This the police, we have a warrant! Get down on the ground now," the lead officer yelled before his companions repeated his warning!

Aaron grabbed for his 9mm pistol, stood tall and aimed it at the intruding officers, while Nickle's girlfriend dropped to the floor, curled into a ball, and cried out, "Aaron my son is in the bedroom, please don't shoot!"

Even after the female's plea Aaron refused to drop the weapon, with several officers aiming at him and shouting orders. The only thing Nickle heard aside from the thumping sound of his heartbeats was his terrified girlfriend's voice, so he slowly dropped to the floor with his hands extended away from his body.

"Eddie, Quest, my son is in the next room man," Nickle pled!

The officers moved into the apartment without further resistance and arrested everyone inside. Detective Laddimer and his team recovered the three handguns used during the store robbery and other merchandise that were stolen. The Child Care Unit was also called in to retrieve the little boy and transfer him to their facilities, while his parents went through their legal troubles. CJCH a local news station in Halifax got word of the raid and sent a video team to record the arrest, which they knew would be a huge relief to many citizens. A paddy wagon arrived several minutes after the arrests to transfer the suspects to the precinct, where they would get booked and charged for their many crimes. Despite the late hour, by the time the officers began walking their suspects out to the paddy wagon, a small crowd had gathered to watch the spectacle. Most of those who gathered cheered and applauded the officers for the arrests, knowing the group was responsible for a loving father's death. All the arrested suspects tried to hide their faces while they were led out from the building and placed into the back of the paddy wagon.

The news team was still present when Detective Laddimer and his colleagues exited the building with several brown paper bags filled with evidence. The reporter begged the detective for an update on their raid and was granted an interview by the leading investigator.

"Detective Laddimer thank you for your time! Sir can you tell our viewers what your team did here tonight," the reporter asked?

"Well after some grueling investigative work we learnt that the shooters from the convenience store robbery were held up inside this building, therefore, we dug further and uncovered their exact location, at which we came here and made the arrests," Detective Laddimer stated!

"Was it a violent apprehension," the reporter questioned?

"Surprisingly it was not! We learnt earlier that this was a violent bunch, so we did not know what to expect. But the suspects had a young boy inside the apartment, so that may have played a role in their peaceful surrender," the detective answered!

"How many persons were taken into custody," the reporter asked?

"We arrested five adults, the four males involved in the store robbery, a female who lives at the location and a little boy who also was taken by Child Services," Detective Laddimer stated!

"Are the police confident these are the persons responsible," the reporter questioned?

"According to the evidence so far, I believe we have the correct persons," the detective said!

"Thank you for this detective," the reporter responded, before they ended the interview!

Chapter 3

Celine was laying in bed holding a picture of her boyfriend across her chest. Her son was sound asleep on her other arm; however, she was unable to find a moment's rest and wept constantly. The family lived comfortably, so she had no idea how they would cope without Lloyd. Despite all her attempts to fall asleep, her memories of Lloyd on the gurney inside the morgue, disturbed her ability to relax her thoughts. The scent of her boyfriend was imbedded into the pillow on which he slept, so Celine hugged it tightly, closed her eyes, inhaled deeply, and envisioned Lloyd in the bed beside her.

The officer who brought them to the hospital had very little information to comfort Celine, but he did mention that 'the shooting was an ongoing investigation'. Officer Lafountain believed they might be able to solve the case with help from the public, but there was also a strong chance their evidence might lead them to the perpetrators. The officer understandably did not want to pressure Celine, but to help solve the case he enquired, "if she knew of anyone who would wish to harm Lloyd?" They spent a few hours at the hospital, where Lloyd was pronounced dead moments after he arrived. Robin was incensed when the doctor related the message, therefore, she cursed at her mother and said, "You got what you wanted, you can move on with your life now!" After she made her accusation, Robin took off running down the hallway and headed towards the exit.

Instead of chasing her daughter, Celine held tightly onto Julien's hand and focused on their reason for being at the hospital. The grieving mother wanted to see Lloyd's body, so the doctor offered to bring her to the morgue. Officer Lafountain offered to watch Julien until she returned, instead of forcing the young lad to experience such an innerving sight. Julien was teary eyed and felt afraid, but he agreed to go with the officer until his mother returned. The officer understood how stressful such a time must have been for a young boy, so he brought Julien to the cafeteria and bought him a slice of pizza and a bottle of soda. After they bought the food the officer brought Julien back to the cruiser, where he allowed him to eat in the front cabin while he showed him the operations of the vehicle.

The doctor brought Celine to the basement where the hospital kept the bodies of the deceased. Once inside the morgue, the doctor spoke with the pathologist, who then walked over to Lloyd's body that was covered on a gurney. Celine thanked the doctor for his assistance, as he abandoned her to return to his duties. The pathologist uncovered Lloyd's face and left the covering just below his neck, to prevent Celine from seeing his wounds. At the sight of her partner's body, Celine bravely fought back her tears as she slowly walked over to him. Lloyd's body was cold to her touch, nevertheless she lovingly caressed his face without a care. After she spent several minutes speaking to her deceased partner, Celine kissed him on the lips with tears running from her eyes before she moved away.

The morgue's policy was to return the items that belonged to deceased victims to their family members, so the pathologist handed Celine two bags that contained Lloyd's belongings. Even though Celine was presented as Lloyd's girlfriend, she still had to provide identification and sign for the items before, both bags were given to her. The grieving mother thanked the pathologist for allowing her to spend time with her lover, as she then made her way to the emergency exit, where the officer parked his cruiser. Officer Lafountain was kind enough to drive them back home, under the assumption that the single mother might experience tough times ahead without her primary money earner. The officer was also worried about Robin, so Celine tried assuring him she was confident her daughter would eventually make her way back home, thus she was not concerned. Should Robin failed to return at a decent hour, Officer Lafountain did not want her to fret, thus he gave the grieving common-law wife one of his cards and offered to help locate her.

From the moment Celine returned home and placed the paper bags that contained Lloyd's belongings inside her coat closet, she ignored them while being on the phone with his family members, discussing what they heard happened, and his funeral arrangements. Robin came home an hour after they arrived, but went directly to her bedroom, without acknowledging Celine or getting something to eat. At 2:50 AM her girlfriend Donette phoned and instructed Celine to turn her television on and tune into the CJCH Nightly Newscast. Donette was a registered nurse who worked at a local old age home, so she had to get back to her duties and ended their call. Celine figured the newscast might have an update on Lloyd's death, so she reached for the remote control and powered on her TV set. The latest development on the case was being discussed by the reporter and the news anchor, who wanted more clarity on what led to the arrest. The station began showing pictures of the five people arrested, but when they featured Aaron's photo Celine gasped for air, before she covered her mouth to prevent from screaming. The sight of her ex-boyfriend's picture was innerving, therefore she quickly pressed the power button and turned off the television.

There was no way she could fall asleep once she discovered who the shooter was, so Celine crept out of bed and wondered around the apartment, worried about what people might think should word got out. To relieve some of her tension Celine fixed herself a cup of coffee, but inserted a shot of Grey Goose Vodka for added stimulation.

It was 6:48 AM when Robin exited her bedroom and went directly into the bathroom. Celine was sitting at the dinner table inside the kitchen having her third mug of coffee, while she looked through their family photo album. The memories from each picture brought tears to the mother's eyes, yet Robin expressed no emotions towards her. Moments after Robin entered the bathroom, Celine overheard the shower running and started preparing the items for her children's breakfast. The mourning mother took a box of Kellogg's Cereal from the cupboard, along with two bowls and spoons, then milk from the refrigerator and placed them on the table. There were some essential errands for Celine to handle concerning Lloyd's burial preparation, so she went back to her room to assort her outfit.

Julien usually woke up by 7:15 to begin getting ready for school and was out the door before 8:20. Her murdered partner would have already left for work, considering they began working at 8 AM on site. After Celine laid out her clothes across her side of the bed, she opened a drawer that contained several envelopes and papers. When she found the paper for which she sought, she sat close to the phone and dialed a number written on it. Instead of calling the company directory to advise them of her partner's passing, Celine phoned his boss directly on his cellular. Lloyd's boss Mr. Edge had no idea about his murder, but was overtaken with emotions and extremely empathetic about losing one of his best employees. They spoke briefly during which the construction foreman expressed their willingness to assist with some of the funeral costs and wanted information on the procession details whenever that became available. Mr. Edge expressed that Lloyd was well liked; therefore, the entire construction team would want to attend his funeral.

At the end of their conversation Celine woke Julien, who was groggy and wanted to go back to sleep. Julien had an uncanny resemblance to his father and expressed his sorrow over their loss the instant he wiped his eyes clear. They hugged each other tightly for the first few minutes as they reminisced about Lloyd, who was a loving and genuine provider. Celine eventually got up and walked Julien into the kitchen, where she left him at the table and continued to the bathroom. Robin had finished taking her shower and was back inside her bedroom getting dressed, therefore Celine went into the vacant facility and closed the door. Moments after her mother went into the shower, Robin exited her room with her school backpack and stopped in the kitchen, where she shoved her brother in the back of his head. Julien smiled at his sister's gesture and grumbled, yet continued eating. The young teenager ignored the cereal her mother placed on the table, opened the fridge door, and took out an apple. As she passed by Julien, Robin gave him a kiss on the forehead, picked up her bag, and headed for the front door.

"See you later Jules! And tell mom I left for school," Robin stated as she walked through the door!

Julien finished eating his cereal and placed the bowl and spoon in the sink. He then walked into his bedroom and turned his television onto his favorite cartoon channel. The young lad knew that he was supposed to get ready for school, but the action caught his attention and distracted him. Moments later Celine exited the bathroom wearing her robe and peeked into his room, where Julien was sitting on his bed fascinated with the program.

"Julien, get in the shower now! You're going to be late for school," Celine commanded!

"Oh, oh, I forgot mom sorry! Robin said she gone to school," Julien declared as he got up and moved towards the bathroom!

The instant Robin stepped through their apartment door, she shoved her ear-bugs into her ears, pulled her hoodie over her head, and began playing music from her phone. When she ran away from the hospital, she went by her girlfriend Eve to kill some time and relieve her stress. The convenience store where Lloyd was shot was several street blocks away, so Eve suggested they went by to witness all the ongoing activity. As soon as they reached and Robin saw the news crew, the law enforcement investigators, and the gathering crowd, she quickly pulled her hoodie over her head. Watching strangers drop off flowers, notes, and teddy bears at the make-shift memorial outside the store, was truly a heartwarming feeling for Robin who began crying. They stayed around the area until the special unit officers left, at which the manager closed the store and went home. The two friends lived in the same direction, so they walked along until they separated and went their own ways.

The crisp morning breeze gave Robin a slight chill, therefore, she zipped up her jacket and moved briskly. The bus stop was a short distance away, wherein she had to walk a block and a half to the main road, then another street block before she reached. Robin was slightly early for the scheduled transit bus, which was expected to pass in the next eighteen minutes. As she stepped from the building into the cool morning dew, she received a phone call from her Aunty Tamara, who called to see how she was coping with her loss. The saddened young teenager quickly answered the call and was happy to hear her aunt's voice, knowing how empathetic she was.

"Hi, my little Robin Bird, how are you holding up this morning honey," Tamara asked?

"Hi Aunty Tamara, I'm not bad," Robin answered!

"Are you on your way to school or you staying home today," Tamara enquired?

"I'm going to school. I can't bare the sight of my mother right now," Robin stated!

"Why? What happened? Tell me honey!" Tamara continued?

"Ah, to you it may be nothing, but one day last week I overheard mom on the phone talking to some guy, who was telling her that he is going to get her back, even if he had to kill dad! Then yesterday some robber randomly shot and killed my father! I don't know, but all I know is I can't stand her right now," Robin complained!

"What did your mother say to this guy after he said all that," Tamara asked?

"Oh, she was like, I'm not leaving my man for you! But I know that was only because she probably heard me on the phone," Robin stated!

"If you want to come by my apartment for a few days, I could pick you up from school later if you want," Tamara offered?

"Oh Aunty, could you please, please, please," Robin begged?

"Say no more my Robin Bird, I will pick you up after school OK! Mom and I are supposed to bring your mother to a funeral home later this morning to make arrangements for Lloyd," Tamara responded!

"Do you want me to take the bus over to your place," Robin asked?

"No, that's fine, I'll pick you up! I'm off from work for a few days anyways, so I got nothing but free time," Tamara said!

"OK! I'll text you before my last session starts," Robin exclaimed!

"Alright my little Robin Bird, I'll see you later," Tamara lamented!

Robin was half a block away from her bus stop when she finished her conversation with Tamara. There was already a lineup of people waiting for the bus, so she walked up and joined the line. While patiently standing in line she received a text from Eve which read, "I'm on the bus 3 stops to your stop. Hope you not running late again?" A smirk slid across Robin's face, thus she responded, "LOL, already here genius!"

Chapter 4

None of the arrested store robbers chose to speak with the investigating officers and instead requested their phone calls to acquire public defendants. While the men decided to play hardball with the cops, Suzie Hawkins who was Nickle's girlfriend grew remorseful and tried to save herself. When the officers asked if Miss Hawkins wanted to disclose her recollection of the events, she thought solely of her child and accepted. Detective Laddimer had all the evidence they needed to formally charge all the accused, but they needed to know more about Suzie's involvement, before they laid any charges against her.

Officer Lindle led the handcuffed female from her holding cell to an interrogation room, where she sat and awaited the overseeing detective. The officer had removed her restraints and closed the door behind himself, thus allowing the detainee the option to freely move around. There was a table in the middle of the room, with two chairs on one side and a third chair on the opposite side. Moments after Suzie entered the room, a tall and well-groomed gentleman walked in with a folder and a tape recorder under his arm. The detective had his service weapon holstered to his right hip, wore a dress shit with his tie loosely hanging, no jacket, beige khaki pants, and brown leather shoes. Despite his elegant attire the detective kept a straight face, to reintegrate the seriousness of the moment. Suzie had barely stopped crying since they were arrested and had tears gushing from her eyes.

"Hello, I am Detective Laddimer, here to take your statement and ask you a few questions! I must make you aware that I will be recording you and taking notes while we speak, so please be precise and honest with your answers? Can you state your full name for the record please," the investigator declared?

"I am Suzie Ann Hawkins! Can you please tell me what happened to my son," the female responded?

"Your son is presently being held by the social services department, so if you want to get him back, I suggest you tell me everything you know, and I'll try to help you get your child back," Detective Laddimer stated!

"But I really don't know anything," Suzie argued!

"I'll be the judge of that! Did you participate in the robbery with your boyfriend and his friends," Detective Laddimer enquired?

"No, I did not! I was home with my son all evening," Suzie stated!

"Did you know that they had robbed a convenience store and shot someone," Detective Laddimer continued as he scribbled information on his note pad?

"What! They shot someone? Whoever shot the person could not be my Nickle, he is not capable of that," Suzie argued, to which her tears stopped running!

Detective Laddimer could sense the rage that overcame Suzie, who was quick to defend her boyfriend. "Approximately what time did Nickle and his friends return home," the detective asked?

"About five! I was cooking and watching my show," Suzie answered.

"What did they do when they got home," Detective Laddimer enquired as he wrote some more notes?

"They emptied the bags they had on the living room floor and were talking about getting into some action. I wasn't paying much attention because I thought someone gave them some merchandise to sell, plus I was more focused on my show," Suzie stated!

"Did you at any point hear them talking about a shooting," Detective Laddimer asked?

"I know Eddie was mad at Aaron for something and did not say anything when they returned for a few hours. But they all scared of him because he is a lunatic, so that was nothing new," Suzie declared!

"Is Aaron the leader of their little crew," the detective enquired?

"Maybe because he is older than them and been to jail many times before, they look up to him! But they damn sure act like he the boss," Suzie exclaimed!

"Which of them is more likely to injure someone," Detective Laddimer asked?

Suzie looked down at the recorder on the table and paused before she responded. The detective could see her reluctance to answer, fearing that she might be indicting one of Nickle's partners. Despite her straightforward answers, she would sniffle and wipe away tears occasionally, so the detective allowed her time to gather herself. With each passing second Detective Laddimer wondered if Suzie was also scared of Aaron; and might substitute someone else's name to avoid retaliation.

"Are you OK to continue Miss Hawkins? Would you like a drink of water or a soda or something," Detective Laddimer continued?

"My throat is a little dry. Maybe I would take a soda, like a Sprite or something," Suzie requested?

"No problem, I will get you something to drink and be right back," the detective stated!

Detective Laddimer paused the recorder, got up from his seat, and exited the interrogation room. Suzie looked up at the huge one-sided glass on the wall and thought of the many police shows and movies she had seen, where officers would stand and observe from the other side. The detective's notes and the recorder were on the table across from her, yet the thought of tampering with them never entered her mind. The detective's last question would be his first, therefore, Suzie geared up to respond without hesitation. Within six minutes Detective Laddimer returned with the can of Sprite and slid it across the table to his interrogatee. To give Suzie the incentive to answer his questions freely, the detective allowed her to drink most of the soda before he proceeded.

"I spoke with my superiors outside a moment ago and because of your clean record plus your corporation, we might be able to release you with conditions and a promise to appear in court sometime within the near future. But you must be honest about everything you know," Detective Laddimer stated to ease the female's nerves!

Freedom without facing the news circus and the judge was all the sweetening to the deal Suzie could ask for. She took one last gulp from the can of soda and rested it on the table before her. The female took a deep breath, as if she were an auctioneer readying to pitch the item up for bid to the crowd.

"Ah, when I mentioned that I did not know about the shooting, I was not quite telling the truth. When Nickle got home, he met me in the bedroom and was almost freaking out; but tried his best to calm down! To avoid being heard, Nickle whispered every word like he was telling me a secret. He told me that his cousin Aaron had just killed his Ex-girlfriend's man, because the guy stole her from him while he was locked up in prison," Suzie revealed!

"So that was the reason why Arron shot the victim," Detective Laddimer questioned, as he scribbled down notes quickly?

"Yes, apparently so! Nickle said that he is still crazy in love with this woman, he even tracked her down and calls her all the time," Suzie declared!

"Did Nickle say if they had been involved recently or have plans to get together," Detective Laddimer asked?

"No, he never said anything else after that. He just walked out into the other room and started acting like nothing was bothering him," Suzie exclaimed!

"What else have you lied to me about," the detective asked?

"Nothing else I swear! I didn't want Nickle to get in any trouble, but I have to get back my son," Suzie revealed as tears once again began running down her face!

"Did the guys know that the victim would be at this specific location at this time," Detective Laddimer continued, as he wrote down more notes?

"I can't say! I don't think so! I wished Nickle had told me they were planning some stupid shit like robbing that store, so I could have told him to stay out of it," Suzie lamented as she wiped away the tears again!

"It is a tough situation, but thank you for answering my questions. Officer Lindle will be back shortly to transfer you back to your holding cell," Detective Laddimer reasoned, while gathering his note pad and recorder.

After the detective left the room Suzie finished the can of soda and sat back looking around the room. The officer who led her into the interrogation room returned a few minutes later and reattached the pair of handcuffs, before he led her back to the female's holding cell area. Suzie caught a peek at a clock against a wall during the transfer and noted that it was 3:43 AM. Time felt as if it was at a standstill once she returned to her cell, where she paced across the six-foot floor open space. There were no windows attached to the cell and the overhead light was kept on constantly. The cell was not built for comfort, therefore, the steel toilet and bed made her decision to pace about rather easy.

An hour and forty minutes later Officer Lindle again returned and brought Suzie to the fingerprint room, where he collected her prints and had her sign the document. The station was practically empty along the route they walked, and Suzie looked for a clock wherever they went. Officer Lindle brought her back to the holding area, but that time she had no clue what the hour was. It was 7:25 when the female officer who replaced Officer Lindle opened Suzie's cell door.

"Come this way please! You are being released with a promise to appear and several restrictions with which you must comply. There are some documents you must sign before your release, I have them prepared and waiting," Officer Buchanan explained!

The officer brought Suzie to the booking area where she passed her a manilla envelope, that contained all the belongings she had on her person when they brought her in. Suzie removed her rings and chain and put them back on, then placed her money and identification into her pocket. While Suzie relaced her Nike Air sneakers Officer Buchanan gathered some documents and coupled them together. By the time Suzie finished lacing her sneakers, there were two piles of documents awaiting her signatures.

"Now you will need to sign these release papers, stating that you agree to all the terms listed here," Officer Buchanan stated!

Suzie scanned through the list of eight restrictions, most of which prohibited her from associating with Nickle or any of his friends, thus it took her five seconds before she signed. She noted the date listed for her to attend court, which was scheduled four months away from that day. In all her haste to vacate the jailhouse's walls of confinement, Suzie began signing documents without even reading what she was autographing. After she finished signing the first pile of documents, Officer Buchanan piled them together and placed them inside a folder. The officer then slid the second pile of papers to Suzie, who looked confused at the first page.

"These are the documents you will need to file to get back your child. I arranged them all in the sequence you need to follow, so I'll place these inside this envelope," Officer Buchanan explained.

"Thank you, for your help," Suzie stated as tears again began running down her face!

Once they were through Officer Buchanan led Suzie to an exit door, where she walked out to freedom. Suzie looked around once outside to determined what direction to take, then headed towards the public transport which drove pass her dwelling. It was early in the morning and the streets were relatively quiet, therefore, she was eager to get home before anyone recognized her from the newscast. The instant Suzie walked around to the front of the building, she got spotted by a team of reporters who were out covering the biggest story ongoing in Nova Scotia. When the reporters saw Suzie, they immediately ran toward her and swarmed her with questions.

"Is it true that the shooter who killed the victim from the convenience store yesterday, did so because he wanted to get back his old sweetheart," the reporter asked with his cameraman running into position?

Suzie wished she could disappear from there and started looking around to determine how could she escape.

"What was your boyfriend's role in all of this Miss Hawkins," the reporter continued? "Word is he was the shooter's chauffeur! Even when he went to see his Ex!"

"Nickle was not anybody's chauffeur, understand! He was just, in the wrong place at the wrong time," Suzie shouted!

"Then why is it, he is one of the four men being charged with murder," the reporter argued?

"I don't know! Why don't you tell me since you have all the answers," Suzie exclaimed, before she walked away and ignored them?

"Miss Hawkins, are you going to be in court later this morning supporting your boyfriend," the reporter questioned?

Suzie extended her middle finger at the reporter and continued walking away.

Chapter 5

Tamara and her mother Roslyn pulled up in front of Celine's building and parked in an available visitor's slot. Moments later Celine exited the residence and climbed into the back of Tamara's Lexus RX, before they drove out for their appointments. It was indeed a turbulent time for the family; therefore, they were all teary eyed and saddened while they individually mourned. Nobody said a word after Celine entered and they acknowledged each other's "hello", but Lloyd's mother continuously sniffed her runny nose! Lloyd was Roslyn's only son, and her only offspring who produced grand children, while Tamara preferred and dated women. None of the ladies wanted to be in the same vehicle with each other, however, they had Lloyd's business to handle, therefore, none of them had a choice in the matter. Roslyn originally migrated from Portugal and spoke very little English, so people would often have to try and deciphered what she meant whenever she spoke.

"How Robin with Julien coming," Roslyn asked as their vehicle drove pass the third street block?

"Julien and Robin miss their father, but we will get through this as a family," Celine stated!

"Make a sure you bring a them to house! We spend time! You do what you try," Roslyn exclaimed!

Despite losing her partner, Celine was never asked about how she personally felt, but she knew Lloyd's family members never liked her, so none of that was a surprise. They first drove to Lloyd's bank at the RBC branch in the plaza at Dutch Village Road and Bayers Road, where Tamara waited inside the vehicle while Celine and her mother went inside. The bank had just opened, and an employee was packing away their security grill inside its holding area. Celine

23

asked to speak with Miss Luss, whom they had dealt with several times prior. Both ladies took a seat in the waiting area in case they had to wait for a long period of time. Their wait thereafter was rather brief, as the person who Celine requested walked out of her office carrying a mug that contained hot beverage and went directly over to them.

"Oh Celine, it's you! Good morning, how are you," Miss Luss declared?

"Not too good this morning I'm afraid Miss Luss! Can we speak inside your office, please," Celine asked?

"Oh, but of course! Come on in," Miss Luss stated!

The banker showed them into her office and closed the door behind them. Celine allowed Roslyn to sit on one of the three chairs available, before she selected her seat, as Miss Luss made her way across to her side of the desk. Instead of sitting on the middle seat to be closer to Roslyn, Celine sat on the furthest chair away from her boyfriend's mother.

"Excuse my rudeness, but this is Lloyd's mother Roslyn! She speaks very little English, but she understands quite well," Celine stated!

"Hello Roslyn, welcome! What can we do for you this morning," Miss Luss asked? Roslyn nodded her head in recognition of the banker's comment.

Celine took a deep breath and exhaled slowly before she began speaking. "Lloyd was shot and killed yesterday…"

"Oh, my lord that is terrible! I am sincerely heartbroken for your family right now! I know what a wonderful man Lloyd was, and he will absolutely be missed," Miss Luss sympathized as she stood up from her seat with her right hand rested across on her heart!

"Which is why we are here…" Celine began.

Miss Luss walked around her desk and stopped beside Celine, then placed her hand on her client's shoulder. "You don't have to say another word, Celine. I am going to get the paper to file to close Lloyd's account! We can't just let the government hold onto your family's funds, during this time when you will need it more!"

As soon as Miss Luss walked out of her office, Roslyn turned to Celine and said, "Good banker!"

Celine had gotten choked up talking about Lloyd, therefore tears began running from her eyes. While checking about for something to wipe away the tears, Celine was stunned when Lloyd's mother handed her a piece of Kleenex. Instead of declining and ruining the gesture, Celine simply took the Kleenex and said, "Thank you!" The bank employee went to their document's station and collected the necessary papers, then returned to her office. When Miss Luss returned, she was surprised to find both Roslyn and Celine sitting closer together, holding each other's hand, and crying. Without disturbing her clients' interactive moment, Miss Luss sat back at her desk and began filling out the paperwork. After she had completed her requirements, the bank employee slid Celine the papers with a pen for her to sign. Miss Luss tried to make the process less conversational and more relaxing for her clients, so she inserted the information into her computer and completed the termination of Lloyd's account. When asked, "how she would like the funds from Lloyd's account," Celine handed Miss Luss her personal bank card and instructed her "to transfer the amount." At the completion of their business affairs, Miss Luss wished both ladies the best, before they exited the bank with additional engagements to attend.

Tamara drove to their second appointment at the Atlantic Funeral Home on Bayers Road, where they sought to transfer Lloyd's body and hold his funeral church service. Contrary to Celine and Tamara, Roslyn forgot her handkerchief at home and had to use a box of Kleenex to wipe away her sniffles, tears, and sneezes. Before they exited the Lexus at the funeral home, Roslyn removed several sheets of tissue from the box and shoved them into her purse. Regardless of how she felt about Lloyd's family members, Celine knew that he cared deeply for them and never tried to alienate his children from them. Having his mother and sister assist with his burial would have been a requisition of Lloyd's, so she welcomed them along during the procedure, regardless of their personal dealings.

Their appointment was set for 10:45 AM with the funeral director, who had a range of topic to discuss. Upon their arrival at 10:37, the secretary offered them coffee, tea, a glass of wine, or a bottle of water, while she had them wait inside the main office. At 10:43 Mr. Boulangerie the funeral director exited his office and greeted the ladies. He invited them into his office with whatever they were consuming, and provided them with comfortable seats, before they got down to discussing business. Mr. Boulangerie asked, "what happened to Lloyd," at which Celine disclosed that "he was shot and killed inside a convenience store!" After covering the reason why his clients' loved one was killed, Mr. Boulangerie proceeded to disclose what services they provided, which was always welcomed news to families.

The funeral home covered every aspect of a burial, from preparing the body, to placing the tomb stone at the head of the grave. The funeral director stood amid his clients while they spoke, but paused to retrieve three pamphlets off his desk, which he passed to each female. The pamphlets contained photos of caskets, which ranged from pine boxes to quality of the expensive type.

"If you ladies don't mind following me, I will show you to our showcase room where you can see some of these models! We will also be able to discuss the type of fabric you wish to have inserted into the casket, plus whatever additions you may wish to add," Mr. Boulangerie exclaimed!

The funeral director then led all three ladies across the hallway to their casket showcase area. Roslyn continued flipping the pages of her pamphlet to determine which of the lot she preferred.

"Mama-mia," said Roslyn at the price of some of the caskets!

"Look at this one mammy! This is really nice eh," Tamara responded, as she held the photo for Celine to see?

"I like that one! Really nice," Celine answered!

"What no nice, the Denario," Roslyn argued, to which Tamara and Celine began giggling!

Mr. Boulangerie had sensed the tension among the females when they entered, but for the first time watched them interact caringly. As he listened to them find humor during their time of grief, Mr. Boulangerie had no idea what Roslyn said whenever she spoke, therefore, he would simply smile and nod his head. The instant they entered the showcase room and Roslyn saw the casket models, she grabbed her head and shouted, "Oh Lord, my son no run for this a bed!" Tamara had to hold her mother, who nearly tumbled to the ground with hurt and sorrow. Following her extravagant reaction, Roslyn reached into her purse and removed two plies of Kleenex, which she used to blow her nose and wipe her eyes. It took the ladies several minutes to finally agree on a casket that was elegant and well priced. They were also given the chance to select the type of fabric and color they wanted inside the casket, but Celine was stern with her decision to select the color purple, which was Lloyd's favorite. Lloyd was well insured so none of the proceedings had to be paid out of pocket, thus they all wanted a memorable send-off for him.

Following the casket selection, Mr. Boulangerie showed his clients back to his office. As they went by the secretary's station, she offered them beverage refills, but they declined. After the ladies re-entered the office and reclaimed their seats, the funeral director retrieved three maps of their burial grounds off his desk, then passed them along. To provide his clients with a better understanding of the space, he walked over to a projector machine he had already set up and picked up the remote. Once he pressed play, a video of their burial ground which was five miles away from their location, began showing. Roslyn again threw her hands into the air and dropped them on top of her head, as she yelled, "my boy should live he house, no there!" Mr. Boulangerie paused the video often to point out the available slots, and each time he did Lloyd's mother yelled as if she was in pain. Following his presentation, the funeral director uninterruptedly allowed the ladies to choose the resting place, they found more desirable for Lloyd. With the business arrangement between his clients and the funeral home engaged, Mr. Boulangerie wanted the ladies to feel confident that their loved one would be well taken care of, therefore, he phoned his secretary and instructed her 'to prepare the transfer papers for their mortuary transporter to collect Lloyd's body from the hospital'.

While Mr. Boulangerie spoke on the phone, Celine's cellular rang inside her purse. Believing it might be for one of her children at school, she quickly retrieved the device and looked at the screen before she answered it. The caller identification said Nova Scotia Police Service, which puzzled the grieving mother. Tamara and Roslyn neglected the funeral director and began looking at Celine, who politely got up from her seat and walked to the back of the room.

"Excuse me Mr. Boulangerie, I must take this!... Hello," said Celine! The funeral director waved his consent as he continued speaking with his secretary.

"See what I told you mom! She have something hiding," whispered Tamara to Roslyn!

"Good morning, Miss Walker, I am Detective Laddimer from the police department! Is this a good time to talk," asked a low-pitched male's voice on the phone?

"I am presently at the funeral home taking care of my boyfriend's final resting. Can I phone you back or something," declared Celine?

"It would actually be much better if you came down here to the police station. I have some questions I would like for you to clear up for me," exclaimed Detective Laddimer?

"Ah, sure! Why not! I will have my in-laws drop me off there after our next appointment," responded Celine.

"Do you know where we are located," asked the detective?

"Yes I do! I have been there before," stated Celine!

"OK then, I look forward to seeing you! Just ask for Detective Laddimer at the front and I will be right out," explained Detective Laddimer!

By the time Celine got through and returned to the conversation, Mr. Boulangerie was showing her companions the types of head stones they provided, from an album of pictures. The funeral home also provided different types of packages to care for the graves, such as placing flowers regularly, grass treatment, etc. Mr. Boulangerie felt nervous when introducing any other service they provided, fearing Roslyn's extravagant reactions. There was a cap placed on the amount of money payable for funeral expenses by the insurance company, so the head stone they finally chose was not as big as the one Roslyn and Tamara preferred.

None of the ladies realized there were so many items associated with burying someone, but the funeral director had everything covered. They dealt with every aspect necessary for the burial, from the viewing dates and times to the actual funeral procession, which they scheduled for the third following week. The meeting lasted nearly two and a half hours, but Celine, Roslyn, and Tamara left the funeral home confident Lloyd would get a decent burial. On their way from the facility the ladies began discussing what Lloyd should get buried in. Tamara thought they should purchase a new suit for her brother, but Roslyn was the first to disagree with that idea. At the end of their debate, it was decided that Lloyd should get buried in his favorite suit, rather than them spending unnecessary money.

Their next appointment was only a few blocks up the street, at a convention hall which the owners rented occasionally to hosts of local events. It was evident that they had recently conducted an event, with the tables and chairs scattered across the floor and out of place. There was a maintenance employee mopping the floor when they entered, hence they asked him for the person in charge? The employee pointed them in the right direction and returned to his chores, which seemed like it would take all day to complete. The manager for the hall was Mr. Herd, who was inside his office when the ladies walked approached and knocked the door.

"Hello! Come on in folks, what can I do for you lovely ladies," Mr. Herd exclaimed!

"We would like to rent your hall to have a repas for my boyfriend," Celine asked?

"What date would you like?"

"Three weeks from now," Celine stated.

Mr. Herd looked through his scheduling book and shook his head. "I'm sorry but we have a late-night event on that date."

"Late night event! What time does that start," Tamara asked?

"Ah! Their event goes from 8:00 until 3:00 AM."

"We just need a few hours in the afternoon! Our funeral runs from 10:00 until midday, maybe 12:30, so we could be out of here by six, seven latest," Tamara argued!

"If you people promise to clean up after you get done, then we have a deal? Because I won't have time to get my cleaner in here between both events to prepare for the next!"

"You have a deal Mr. Herd! We will make sure this place is just like we found it when we leave," Celine declared!

"Great," Mr. Herd stated as he reached into a drawer and withdrew a rental form! "We also provide catering, have a great DJ, and provide liquor service, if that would interest you ladies."

"We would like to have that package please," Celine requested?

Mr. Herd went back into the drawer and withdrew some other papers. "Here is a list of the pricing and the different meals you could have, from Kosher to Japanese, whatever your flavor our chefs will prepare it! Plus, what kind of bar do you want? An open one or should clients buy their own drinks"

"I think we will go with this package," Celine declared.

"Lovely! Lucky guests getting treated to free liquor," Mr. Herd joked!

"I think we are going to find out what everyone eats before we fill in the menu," Celine exclaimed!

"No problem, Ma'am, you can easily do that on the internet from home once you find out!"

Celine gave Mr. Herd her credit card to charge for the bill, which concluded all the requirements to bury Lloyd, and ensured that those who attended his funeral ate, drank, and partied well. It meant great prosperity for families which honored the friends of their deceased in Roslyn's culture, thereby she was pleased with Celine's selection. After she signed and finalized the contract, Celine looked at Roslyn who for the first time all day had a smile on her face. They had accomplished all that they sat out to do that morning, therefore they shook hands with Mr. herd and left the facility.

Roslyn wanted to drive directly to the grave site to see where her son would be buried, but Celine asked to be taken to the police station instead. When Celine made the request Tamara looked at her mother and rolled her eyes, as if she knew what the outcome of the visit would be. Although she refrained from speaking her mind, Tamara expected the police to charge Celine for conspiring to have her brother killed. The drive to the police station was innerving, during which everybody kept to themselves and stayed quiet as if they were total strangers once again.

When they pulled up out front the police station and Celine exited the vehicle, Tamara sped away so viciously that her tires squealed and burnt the asphalt. Celine felt a bit nervous walking into the police station and wondered if she should have contacted a lawyer first. The desk officer knew who she was the instant she requested Detective Laddimer, therefore, he asked her to wait while he summoned his peer. Several moments later a 'Personnel Only' door opened, and the detective walked out with a folder underneath his arm.

"Hello Miss Devers, I am Detective Laddimer! Thanks for getting here so quickly! I understand that you have two younger children to get home to, so I'll try to make this as quick as possible," Detective Laddimer said!

"What may I ask is this pertaining to," Celine asked as she followed the detective inside towards an interrogation room.

"This has to do with the murder of your boyfriend Lloyd Walker Junior," Laddimer answered as he led her into the room. "You may have a seat, Miss Walker!"

Celine sat across from the detective who opened his folder, which consisted of several photos of Lloyd and other papers. Detective Laddimer retrieved his pen from his inner pocket and began writing down information, such as the time and date of their meeting.

"I am not sure if you are aware that we charged four men with Lloyd's killing. One of these men was Aaron Adams, who was the actual shooter caught on camera."

"I know, I saw the news coverage of them being arrested last night."

"Ah, do you personally know Aaron Adams?"

"Yes, I do!"

"How do you know Aaron?"

"He was my first ever boyfriend."

"According to your phone records he contacted you several times over the past few months. Why?"

"He was trying to get back with me, but I turned him down and told him to stop calling me!"

"Did he know where you live?"

"No, I don't think so!"

"What was the relationship between Lloyd and Aaron?"

"Lloyd took the phone one time when Aaron called and told him to stop harassing me. They argued and that was that, I didn't hear from him for many years after that."

"So, was there a situation between them before all of this?"

"No, they didn't even know each other."

"Were you in any way leading Aaron to believe you would be with him sometime in the future?"

"No! Why would I want to be with someone who beat me, over a man who treated me like a real woman?"

"Thank you for your answers today, Miss Devers. That is all I required. I'll show you out!"

The detective smiled at Celine as they finished the questioning, then jotted down his final thought and closed the folder. Detective Laddimer again placed the folder underneath his arm as he rose from the chair, then led Celine back through the pathway they entered and allowed her to leave freely. Once outside the building Celine walked down the street to the bus stop, where she waited for the first of two public transits home. After Laddimer led Celine out the building, he passed by their coffee machine and fixed himself a fresh cup. While preparing the beverage, Laddimer removed a paper from the folder, which had four names written on it and looked at all the contacts' information. The only person who could simplify his investigation refused his request for an interview, so the detective had no option than to rely on old police work to close the case. Moments after returning to his post, the desk officer contacted him with an informant on the line, who believed they knew something relevant to Lloyd's murder case. When Laddimer accepted the call and got connected with the caller, he was shocked to hear that the informant was Lloyd's sister Tamara.

"Hello! You are speaking with Detective Laddimer!"

"Are you the detective in charge of investigating my brother Lloyd's murder?"

"Yes, that would be me!"

"Then I am Tamara Walker, Lloyd's sister! I believe I might have some important information regarding the people involved in his killing!"

"You mean Aaron Adams and his friends?"

"No Detective Laddimer! The true mastermind behind the killing, his girlfriend Celine!"

Detective Laddimer nearly fell off his chair, as he grabbed for his pen and notepad and began taking notes. "Celine! Why would you believe she had something to do with the shooting?"

"Because when my brother met that tramp, she was pregnant with that bastard Aaron's child! My brother told me how he used to phone her from prison; and they got into it over the phone one time! But I know that bitch wanted to leave my brother and go back to that worthless low life!"

"So, you're saying that Celine's daughter Robin is actually Aaron's child?"

"That is exactly what I'm saying detective!"

"Whose idea was it to give Celine's daughter Lloyd's name?"

"Who do you think? That tramp of course!"

"Why did you say that Celine would want your brother dead and get Aaron to do the killing?"

"Because she wants his life insurance policy cashed! What better way than to get your criminal ex-lover to kill my brother, while you play the mourning victim?"

"Did your brother tell you anything regarding the discussion he had with Aaron?"

"Yes, he did! He told me that bastard told him that he was going to shoot him dead wherever he saw Lloyd! And that was exactly what he did! All because that bitch probably promised him her rotten ass couchie, if he got rid of Lloyd!"

"Did Lloyd tell this to anybody else?"

"Hell, no he didn't! He thought of telling mom, but I didn't want him to give her a heart attack! If you knew my brother, he was a proud man, so he didn't even tell any of his boys! Probably too embarrassed about how they would laugh at him!"

"So, how would you describe your brother's relationship with Celine?"

"Lloyd was weak in love with that bitch! But she was only with him for comfort! Celine never loved my brother! So, I have no doubt she orchestrated all this bullshit from Aaron was locked up!"

"Thank you for the information, Tamara!"

"No problem, Detective Laddimer! Just don't let that bitch get away with killing my brother," declared Tamara before she disconnected the call.

Chapter 6

Celine and Julien were inside the Atlantic Superstore walking through the produce section slightly after darkness came across the evening's sky. As they began inspecting the grapes, the Asian shelf stacker who tended to that isle walked by and whispered, "you murdering Bitch", then continued on! Even though Celine clearly overheard the female, she thought the woman was having an unpleasant day and ignored her. Julien wanted apples for lunch at school, so they walked over into the other isle and picked up a packaged dozen. A Caucasian female was passing along the main isle and abruptly changed her course the instant she saw Celine, and marched directly toward the mother and son. The woman seemed intent on saying whatever she had on her mind and there was no one else in the isle, so Celine moved Julien to the inside of her and stood her ground.

"You know something! It is people like you who make me sick to my stomach! I don't know why God gave you people the ability to have children," said the woman who spat on the floor close to Celine's Nike Air sneakers and stormed away!

"Lady, I don't know what your problem is, but you need to go see a doctor," responded Celine!

"Mommy, what is that lady's problem," asked Julien?

"Some people are just rude son! Let's go," said the enraged mother who quickly moved away from the produce area!

Celine knew something definitely had to be wrong when she stopped by the fridges and began removing three packs of her favorite yogurt off the shelf. A

Caucasian lady who had her young daughter seated in the grocery cart's child seat and a full basket of items, came down an isle and saw Celine. The woman developed a disgust look on her face as she stopped her cart, lifted her daughter from the seat, and began walking away from the groceries.

"Come on honey, we don't shop in places that allow murderers like that inside their establishments," the woman said as they turned and walked away!

There was a male employee bringing a box of milk to restack the shelf, who saw the female shopper abandon the items. The employee was confused by the shopper's actions, so he called out to her to enquire about the issue.

"Excuse me madam! You can't leave your grocery cart in the middle of the isle," the shelf stacker yelled!

"Then sue me! I'll never shop in here ever again anyways! Seeing that you people allow all sorts of murderers to shop here," the female shouted!

"God damn it," mumbled the employee who realized he would have to empty the cart!

Celine's heartrate began increasing, not knowing why or what was fuelling the locals rage against her. As the mother and son walked through the juice isle, they stopped to pick up two six packs of mini fruit punch for the boy to bring to school. There was a black male picking up grocery items for his family, who saw when the female shopper abandoned her cart and created the scene. The man walked up and began putting kids' juices inside his shopping cart, but gently whispered to Celine.

"I think she saw that news footage earlier tonight, where some woman was telling the reporter that she knows you conspired with the shooter who killed that construction guy inside the convenience store."

"What! Who the hell could have said something like that? Thank you for telling me," Celine exclaimed!

The embarrassed mother thought of leaving the shopping cart like the other lady, but she needed the items for her home. Therefore, Celine lowered her head and held tightly onto Julien's hand as she quickly moved toward the cashier. One of the cashiers' station was open, but an old man was slowly making his way over, so Celine ran ahead of the elderly customer and nearly knocked him over. In her haste to get out of the store, the female was willing to break all the rules rather than being subjected to the scrutiny by customers. As she exited the Atlantic Superstore, Celine wondered if there might be someone hiding in the dark to harm her or her son, so she watched from the door for anything suspicious before she held Julien tightly and walked briskly to the bus stop. To avoid being recognized, Celine kept her head lowered while they waited for the bus to arrive. The jolting experience inside the supermarket gave her the need for clarification that her daughter was safe, so Celine phoned Robin to check on her.

"This is Robin! Sorry I missed you, but please leave me a message and I will call you back," said the voice mail after the ringer stopped ringing!

"Why the hell doesn't that little girl ever answer her phone when you want her to," Celine argued as she looked out and saw their bus coming?

After they mounted the bus with their bags of groceries and sat close to the driver for increased protection, Celine's cellular rang inside her purse. When she removed the phoned and looked at the screen and saw the caller was Tamara, she immediately thought to ignore the call, yet answered at the last second.

"Hello!"

"It's me Celine! I forgot to call you before to let you know that Robin will be sleeping over by me tonight!"

"Oh! So why didn't she phone and tell me that when she left school? And why didn't you tell me she was sleeping over at the funeral home?"

"I was too concerned about Lloyd this morning; and later I must have forgot! Sorry about that sis!"

"Well, she doesn't have school tomorrow so that's fine. But tell her I need to talk to her, so make her call me!"

"OK, I will! Have a good night!"

"Yeah, I will," said Celine! "That bitch," she then thought to herself!

They dismounted the bus at the stop across from their building on Bayers Road and waited for the traffic to pass, before they briskly walked toward their home. While waiting for the cars to pass Celine noticed a group of six ladies standing closer to the sidewalk in front their building. None of the ladies appeared to be doing anything threatening, so Celine was not initially concerned for their safety. As they crossed the street one of the females shouted, "there goes that bitch," at which the others retrieved their protesting signs and began yelling all sorts of derogatory comments. Celine could not believe they were being hounded and had no choice but to press ahead, so she held Julien's hand tightly and walked through the shaming.

"You're a murderer," shouted one female!

"Conspiracy to commit murder is just like pulling the trigger bitch," another female kept repeating!

"I can't wait to see them lock you away," declared a third woman!

"How dare you bitch! How dare you," repeated another woman!

It was a struggle to get to their apartment building door, but Celine quickly pulled it open and went inside. Following such a tremoring experience, the startled mother stood by the entrance and looked out at the group of protestors, while she read some of their degrading signs. When they finally reached indoors, Celine threw the bags on the floor, brought Julien to his room, powered up his television, and turned on his favorite cartoon station. The enraged mother immediately fixed herself a shot of Grey Goose Vodka, then a second, and a third, before she began preparing something for Julien to eat. It was imperative that she calmed her nerves after feeling threatened several times, without knowing why total strangers reacted as they did. Her phone rang with an unidentified phone number and again she hesitated to answer; but responded just before the call went to voice mail.

"Hello!"

"You're going to get what's coming to you for what you did, you whore!"

"Who is this?"

The male caller disconnected the call and all Celine heard thereafter was the dial tone.

"Who was that mommy," asked Julien, who had wondered from his room to check on his mother?

"Just some bill collector honey," lied Celine!

The phone rang again, and the caller identification showed the same unidentified caller. Instead of responding to the call Celine turned off the ringer on the phone and threw it on the table. She had an irresistible urge to watch the news feature and find out what everyone was all heated about, but she wanted to protect Julien from as much of the madness as possible. The protective mother wanted to wait until her son was in bed before she watched the news coverage, to keep him from seeing whatever new revelation had been aired. Once the Chicken Nuggets and French Fries meal was prepared, Celine gave Julien his food and sat watching him eat. As soon as Julien went to bed Celine closed most of the lights inside their apartment, then ran into her bedroom and turned on the television. The family's PVR cable box enabled her to watch previously aired programs whenever she wanted, so she rewound the CJCH Evening Newscast and replayed it.

The senseless murder of the construction worker inside the gas station convenience store was the biggest story across the province since the news broke. As a result, citizens on the island wanted to know everything about the latest developments in the case. At the commencement of the newscast the anchor revealed that they had an exclusive witness, who knew relevant information about the players involved. When the news anchor brought their field reporter into the conversation, the female was broadcasting from outside the courthouse building and informed their audience, 'that all the accused murderers had been remanded into custody by Judge Harper'. To provide the news viewers with an idea of what the atmosphere was like inside the courtroom, the reporter showed drawings of each accused and described their mannerism before the judge. It was important that the reporter pointed out the type of overseer

Judge Harper was, therefore, she described him as 'a stern, no-nonsense, yet fair judge'. The reporter read out the different charges laid against the robbers, spoke about their court appointed lawyers, and finally disclosed their next court dates. Following her courthouse updates, the reporter announced that she spoke with someone earlier that afternoon who knew everything about the case. Before they showed the interview, Celine's heartrate began beating rapidly not knowing who the informant was going to be.

The interview was recorded with the female reporter speaking to Aaron's girlfriend Trudy Greenfield, who despised Celine by the manner with which she spoke about her. Celine never knew of Trudy, so to listen to someone depict an unpleasant picture of her was very disheartening. The interview was short and only lasted a few minutes, but the damage caused was irreparable and Celine knew they would face tough times ahead because of it.

"Today we have the pleasure of speaking with Trudy Greenfield, who has come under heavy scrutiny since her boyfriend Aaron Adams was charged with first degree murder in the killing of Lloyd Walker. We are here to find out why she does not believe that she deserves the treatment she has been receiving; and why people should be more compassionate towards her. So, Trudy can you tell us more about your relationship with Aaron?

"Well, I met Aaron three years ago at a party and he was always the gentleman, until a year and a half ago, when he found out that his ex-girlfriend still lives somewhere here in Nova Scotia!"

"How long ago did he date his ex-girlfriend?"

"I believe more than fifteen years ago."

"What have been happening since Trudy?"

"Since then, he began beating me and threatening me that he was going to shoot me dead if I ever tried leaving him like she did..." Trudy began sniffling as if she wanted to cry.

"And when you said she, you are referring to his ex-girlfriend Celine?"

"Yeah, Celine Devers! It was like he became someone different whenever he started thinking about her!"

"So was Aaron still in love with Celine?"

"Yes, he was! And I think that she wanted him back too! Aaron has a tattoo of her face on his chest and said they have an undying love for each other, so one day they were bound to be together!" Trudy used a piece of tissue to wipe her tears away.

"So, you believe that they would be together again?"

"Aaron surely believed so! He hasn't wanted me since, he just beats me then forces me to have sex! People have no idea what I have been going through! I tried leaving him and he finds me! I can't keep any friends because they think my man is crazy! He already pulled his gun on three of my old girlfriends, then threatened them he would blow their heads off! They all so scared not one a them told the police; and they rather stop talking to me to avoid dealing with his crazy ass! They just don't know," chuckled Trudy as she began crying!

The technicians ended the recording at which the reporter began speaking with the news anchor back at the CJCH news station.

"Well, that was our brief conversation with Trudy Greenfield, who wanted to clear her name around this whole Aaron Adams mess, and to let people know that she was essentially a victim in this entire ordeal, so she would appreciate not being called all sorts of names whenever she went out in public," stated the reporter!

"So, she puts the blame on me, like I want this shit," Celine yelled as she pressed the remote to power off her television!

Celine stormed from her bedroom and out into the days room where she looked through her blinds to see if the protesting women were still outside. To discourage the protesters and send them home, Celine had turned off most of the lights throughout their residence. Most of the women had left except for two busybodies who walked in circles holding their signs high. The clock on the wall showed it was 9:41, so Celine walked into her kitchen and grabbed the bottle of liquor and a glass.

"When are those bitches going to go home," Celine said to herself as she poured herself a glass and added ice from her fridge dispenser?

Celine walked back into her days room and turned on the light so the protesters below could see she was still awake. The stressed-out mother of two turned on her stereo and adjusted the volume to not disturb her son, while she laid on her sofa covered in a warm blanket, with a picture of Lloyd on her stomach and soothing RNB music playing. Even though her volume was not adjusted loud, Celine could still faintly hear the protesters shouting, while she calmly sipped on her Vodka. The protesters discarded the late hour and the fact there were other people living in the building and continued hollering, until they innerved Miss Gooding who lived beneath Celine's apartment. To disperse the protesters, Miss Gooding telephoned the police department and reported the disturbance. Within five minutes two squad cars pulled up at the location, at which the officers escorted the remaining troublemakers from the premises.

Celine sat quietly and did not even watch the interaction between the officers and the protesters. It had been years since she drank so much liquor at once, but the more she consumed was the less concerned she felt about the entire situation. The bottle was nearly empty and as much as she rarely drank, she knew she would need a lot more liquor before it was all said and done. The clock on the wall had raced to 11:58 and Celine thought of expiring to bed for the night. As she attempted to get off the sofa, she realized the improbability of making it to her bedroom, so she grabbed her cellular phone off the center table and laid back on the sofa. The thirty-three missed calls were the first notification Celine noticed, before she saw she had also missed nine text messages. Most of the calls originated from private callers, but Celine only looked through the list to find Tamara's phone number. There was no doubt that Robin and Tamara would be up that late, therefore, the intoxicated mother felt no way about calling.

"Hey Sis," Tamara responded after the phone rang several times!

"You don't have to put on the act bitch, everybody knows we don't like each other! Just make sure you get my daughter back here early in the morning," Celine exclaimed then hung up the phone!

Tamara and Robin had been lying in bed watching girl's movies on stream, since earlier that evening. Robin had just dozed off after a long day at school, after which she went shopping with her aunty, but Tamara did not notice she was asleep. Following the brief exchange with Celine, Tamara looked over and realized her niece was asleep, thus she angrily slammed her phone on the mattrass.

Chapter 7

Aaron, Nickle, Quest, and Eddie were all transported to the Central Nova Scotia Correctional Facility, where they were remanded by Judge P. Harper. While Quest and Nickle felt elated about their debut trip to one of the province's premier criminal confinements, Eddie felt betrayed by Aaron's callous action and grew increasingly bitter. When they reached the central lockup, the guards transported all the new incoming inmates to holding cells, while they were being processed for housing. Each inmate went through the process of a thorough body search, where they had to strip all their clothing, then were instructed to expose areas where it might had been possible to hide items. Inmates were instructed 'to lift their arms above their heads, open their mouths, lift their tongues, flap their ears, bend over and squat, and showed the bottom of their feet,' by the inspectors. The guards had to ensure that the inmates did not bring in any contraband or weapons, so they tried diligently to find and confiscate illegal items being smuggled. All street clothing were taken and placed in Ziplock bags, then stored away until the inmate's release or transfer.

The detainees were then given province issued clothing, which was worn by every criminal in custody. Once each inmate got assigned a pod, they were given a role that contained two sheets, a blanket, and a towel, along with an additional change of clothes and underwear. Inmates were then given miniature form of supplies such as toothbrush and a toothpaste yet, had to purchase other necessities such as soap/body wash, shampoo, deodorant, and extra food. Their transporter arrived at the jailhouse during supper hours, so each detainee received a cold Bologna Sandwich with an Oatmeal Cookie attached, and a small box of milk.

The Central Nova Scotia Correctional Facility was a place where Aaron had been twice before, so many of the guards and a few inmates knew him. Because Arron had been to the facility before, he was the second newcomer housed once the administration department found him a bed in B-Pod. Each time Aaron returned to the jailhouse they sent him to the same housing unit, hence before the guards transferred him, he advised his co-defendants to request the B-Pod. Eddie was starting to separate himself from the crew and sat inside the holding cell listening to others described what the environment was like inside the prison. There was one young thug who revered going to any pod where there were none of his homies, who described having to fend against numerous combatants if you were alone. When Eddie's name got called for processing and the guard assigned him to B-Pod, instead of refusing the housing unit he chose to be around his co-defendants. The entire pod was under lockdown when the guard transferred Eddie to his cell, so he had no idea if Quest and Nickle were assigned there. The inmate already assigned to the cell was an old man named Marcus, who was quite pleasant to his new roommate. Marcus' bed was on the bottom bunk, so Eddie unraveled the mattress and made up the top bunk with the sheets provided to him.

The unit was under lockdown until 7:00 pm, before the inmates were allowed back out into the general area for the remainder of the evening. The final lockdown was at 11:00, when the sergeant on duty would enter the pod with several guards, who went throughout and locked the doors. Eddie spent most of the lockdown standing at the metal covered wooden door, which had a small thick pane of glass in the middle for viewing. Each cell was 6X10 and quite cramped for two men, due to the additional metal bunk beds, a metal table with two seats, and a metal toilet attached to a sink. The pod was shaped like a triangle with high wall on both sides that led to the only entrance. There was a volume-less television on one wall and three telephones on the opposite wall. The guards had a circular post of operations just outside the pods, from which they monitored all the happenings throughout the prison. All five pods were similarly built with two tiers that had sixteen cells on each floor. Both floors had two individual showers that allowed inmates to bathe during general hours. When the guard finally walked by and unlocked the doors, Eddie was stunned to watch detainees rushing out to claim the metal tables, on which they played various games.

Marcus had a chess game lined up with another inmate, so he dashed through the door once the guard opened it. It was not mandatory for inmates to leave their cells during general hours, but everyone usually spent the last three hours before lockdown, out in the population. Eddie was one of the last persons to leave his cell, after he stood and watched his co-defendants reunited with other inmates they knew. Everyone appeared excited to see Aaron, therefore Nickle and Quest stood close to him for the acknowledgement. The attention being paid to the man who caused their incarceration angered Eddie, who instead of joining his comrades decided to join the phone line. Quest called to him from across the room and signalled him over, but Eddie indicated he needed to make a phone call.

After forty minutes of waiting for a phone, Eddie finally got his opportunity and dialed his girlfriend's number. The female was blunt and advised him that, 'she would not be waiting around for him if he was convicted and sentenced for the murder that which they were charged!' The frustrated girlfriend disconnected the call after she spoke her mind, therefore Eddie was left feeling embarrassed, hurt, and angered. With the call lasting less than a minute, Eddie telephoned his mothers house, but nobody responded. The last number he thought to call was his father, with whom he had a strenuous relationship. Eddie's father accepted the charges and immediately began chastising his son once they were connected, for his decision to commit theft with murderers. The heartwarming feeling that Eddie felt when the call got accepted quickly vanished, as he stood and listened to the scrutiny. With his frustrations mounting, Eddie slammed down the receiver and hung up the phone.

"Hey, buddy take it easy with the phone! Other people need to use it," said the next detainee in line!

Eddie walked away and began pacing around the outer edges of the pod. There were two other inmates circling the pod who inspired him to do the same, thus he tried to walk off his frustration. Nickle noticed his friend pacing the floor instead of joining them, so he ran over and strolled alongside his co-defendant.

"What's happening Bro," Nickle questioned?

"Bro, I'm like stressed man! My girl threatening to leave me! My family acting like they don't want nothing to do with me! This legal aide lawyer talking about I could get up to twelve years for this shit! Man... all this could have been avoided if Trigger Happy McCoy over there, could control his damn self," Eddie argued!

"Bro, see that's why I don't be calling anyone! I already know they aren't going to accept the charges anyways, so why should I waste my time," Nickle reasoned!

"Man, that's you, I can't see myself doing all that time," Eddie decreed!

Nickle then realized they were talking about two different things, so he changed topics to discuss his reason for coming over. "Come hang with me, Aaron and the boys?"

"I'm sorry Bro, but I can't do that right now," Eddie emphatically responded!

Eddie was no longer enthused about being around Aaron like much of their other associates. Nickle sensed there was a bit of resentment towards Aaron, so he allowed Eddie to continue pacing around the pod and rejoined the group of thugs. When Nickle returned to the group Aaron wanted to know why Eddie refrained from coming amongst them? Nickle told Aaron that he believed 'Eddie still held a grudge, from the happened inside the convenience store.'

The atmosphere inside B-Pod remained tranquil for most of the evening, with all the inmates behaving civil to each other. After Eddie finished pacing about, he went over and sat beside his cell mate Marcus in the middle of the floor, who was still on the chess board reigning supreme. Eddie had never played the game and found it interesting, so he began enquiring about the objective of the game and the movements of the pieces. Marcus found the time to tutor the young learner while he played and told him, "He would bring the chess board to the cell that night and provide him with additional lessons."

At 10:38 Eddie felt the urge to urinate and walked into the lower-level toilets to relieve himself. Aaron and the group of thugs were still interacting, when he noticed Eddie moving toward the restroom. Neither Nickle nor Quest noticed when Aaron nodded his head at two of the thugs, who then walked away towards the bathroom. Eddie walked up to a urinal and began urinating but remained alert by constantly looking over his shoulders. When the two thugs who Aaron signalled walked in, Eddie felt safer and began focusing more on his task. Without any warning both men rushed Eddie and slammed his head into the wall behind the urinal. The impact knocked him woozy and sent him crumbling to the floor, thus the two thugs started stumping him with their shoes. The spectators built quickly and blocked the bathroom entrance, so nobody could get in or out of the restroom.

A surveillance camera inside the unit caught the crowd buildup before the guards realized there was an ongoing incident in the bathroom. The security operator sounded the alarm and sent a security team to B-Pod, therefore within two minutes there were twenty guards at the pod entrance prepared to enter. The guards were all armed with batons and two of them carried transparent shields for protection, as they stormed into B-Pod. Many of the inmates began moving away from the incident and retreated to their cells, knowing that they were all about to get locked down for some time. An associate of the antagonists alerted them that the guards were coming in, thus the two attackers quickly ran from the bathroom, while pretending they were innocent. By the time the guards rushed into the pod and entered the bathroom, Eddie was battered, bleeding, and unconscious, therefore one of the guards provided medical treatment until the doctor arrived. The guards immediately locked down the entire unit, as they began their investigation to uncover who committed the assault. Eddie was led out laying on a stretcher immobilized, after he was diagnosed with a sprained vertebrae, possible brain injury, broken limbs, and numerous lacerations. The jailhouse doctor and his aide rushed the critically injured patient to the medical office, where they did their best to keep him alive. An ambulance had to be used to transport the patient to the hospital, where doctors did several X-Rays to determine the scope of his injuries, before they rushed Eddie into surgery.

When Eddie awoke four days later, both of his arms and his right leg were hoisted in stabilizing positions and almost every part of his body ached. One of his attackers had kicked him in the mouth and severely broken his jaw, therefore Eddie could not speak or eat, as his jaw had to wired shut. The nurses at the hospital tried to understand his grumbling, but without his hands and mouth they could not. Eddie had to get fed through a straw and was laid up for the next six weeks, before he could scribble with his right hand. The first words that Eddie scribbled was a request for Detective Laddimer to pay him a visit, despite his inability to communicate fully. Doctor Lue who treated Eddie during his recovery did not believe that he was ready for such an accord, yet he contacted the detective and advised him of his patient's status and wishes.

Despite the doctor's advice, Detective Laddimer went to see Eddie two days after they spoke to make his own determination. Eddie was inside the Intensive Care Unit in a private room, being held as a prisoner of the province with one of his injured hands handcuffed to the bed rail. Laddimer walked into the room where a nurse was attending to Eddie and went over to his bedside. The detective showed both the nurse and Eddie his badge before he began addressing the recovering patient.

"How are we doing this morning? I'm Detective Laddimer, the person you requested to speak with," introduced the detective!

Eddie's mouth was wired shut therefore he could not speak properly. He barely could write with a pen yet, began pointing and grumbling at the notepad and pen on his bedtable. The nurse retrieved the items, then placed the pen in Eddie's hand, but had to hold the notepad close to the tip of the pen for him to write on it. Detective Laddimer began trying to uncover what he thought Eddie wanted to discuss, therefore, at the first sight of what resembled an A, he yelled out "Aaron Adams"! The patient nodded his head in agreement hence, Detective Laddimer began asking him questions relevant to the reasons why prisoners would contact law enforcement personnel.

"Is this relating to the killing of Lloyd Walker?"

Eddie nodded his head in agreement.

"Did you invite me here to tell me that Aaron Adams pulled the trigger?"

Again, Eddie nodded his head.

"Will you be willing to testify to that fact in a court of law?"

Eddie unhesitantly nodded his head despite the pain he still felt.

"Listen Eddie, I appreciate you calling me to do this! Even though the prosecution team have a very solid case, hearing from you at the trial will go a long way to getting that guilty verdict against Aaron, plus you may have just helped your own case!"

Eddie tried smiling but one could see the pain in his eyes.

"I need you to rest up and as soon as you are abled to talk, I will have you speak with the prosecutor on the case. Until then, I will inform them that you have decided to come aboard and help their case! Thanks, we'll talk soon," Detective Laddimer stated before he made his leave!

Following the bathroom incident in which Eddie got assaulted, the on-duty sergeant and two of his team members watched the recordings from the camera, that was pointed in that direction. There was one other inmate inside the bathroom when Eddie entered, but that person exited seconds after the victim went in. The video showed when Samuel Yatti and Bernard Harris entered the bathroom seconds later, followed by the spectators who gathered at the entrance. It was a violation of inmates' civil rights to place cameras inside the bathrooms, so the guards had to determine what happened and who committed the assault. They watched the entire footage up until the officers came into view and regained control of the pod. From what the guards saw there were only two people who entered the bathroom after Eddie went in to urinate, therefore, they returned to B-Pod and retracted Samuel Yatti and Bernard Harris from their cells. It was nearly 1:00 AM when the correctional officers returned for the attackers, so most of the detainees were asleep and did not see them get taken away. When Nickle and Quest learnt that the two thugs who assaulted Eddie were men from their crew, they realized Aaron was a cutthroat friend who could not be trusted. Bernard and Samuel were carried away handcuffed, nevertheless the entire pod remained under lockdown for an additional five days. Over those five days, no one was allowed any recreational time, meal trays were passed through the slots in the doors, no phone calls were allowed, every inmate had to remain inside their cells, except for the trustees who passed out the food, showers every other day were done one cell at a time, and the only people who left their cells were court appointees.

The two attackers were removed from the pod and brought to the Segregation Unit, where they were formally charged with assault, and placed in solitary cells for five weeks. Two days later both Samuel and Bernard had separate video hearings before Magistrate Q. Royse, who listened to the charges being laid and had to determine their punishments. The presiding magistrate needed more time to learn about Eddie's prognosis before he could reach a decision', therefore he rescheduled the hearing for four weeks later. At the time of the hearing Eddie was still under the "critical condition" diagnosis at the hospital after getting slammed against the wall and kicked in the head several times.

Chapter 8

Detective Laddimer drove to Lloyd's job site in Greenfield, N.S, where the Flint Construction Company was building town homes. The detective wanted to find out more about 'Lloyd the man' and knew the best information would only come from his friends. To locate the men he should speak with, Detective Laddimer first went to the foreman's office and knocked the door, which was attended to by the onsite boss Mr. Edge. The foreman was in a meeting with some of his employees but took time to speak with the detective.

"Yes, what can I do for you," Mr. Edge asked?

"Morning, I am Detective Laddimer investigating what happened to your employee Lloyd Walker," Detective Laddimer stated!

"Oh, come on in! Lloyd was my best worker and everybody around here loved the guy," Mr. Edge boasted!

"I was told I should talk with Elvis Mayfair about Lloyd. But who else could I speak with to gain an idea of how Lloyd was with his relationship and family," Detective Laddimer asked?

"Then you definitely need to speak with Kerby and Garth also, those guys are like nuts and bolts," Mr. Edge joked!

To summon the workers the foreman picked up his communication radio and pressed the link button.

"Yes Mr. Edge, Neil here," the worker responded!

"Neil, can you tell Elvis, Kerby and Garth to come by my office right away please," Mr. Edge requested?

"No problem boss, right away," the worker stated!

"You can wait around until the boys get down here, but I got some work to get back to," Mr. Edge explained.

Mr. Edge was busy inspecting some blueprints with two other engineers when the detective knocked the door. Detective Laddimer had noticed the boss was busy, so he thanked him for his assistance and stepped outside. Elvis, Garth and Kerby came walking toward the office minutes later, thus the detective stopped them and introduced himself.

"Are you guys Kerby, Elvis and Garth?"

"Yes, we are! Who are you," Garth asked?

"I am Detective Laddimer from the Nova Scotia Police Department, and I'm here regarding Lloyd Walker's death. I was told that you guys are very close to Lloyd, so I hoped you guys can tell me a little about him," Detective Laddimer stated as he took out his notepad and pen to take notes?

"That was my best friend detective! One of the best people you would ever meet," Elvis declared!

"Super awesome guy detective! Loved his family, loved life, loved his friends! Nobody like Lloyd," Garth added!

"He got me this job, helped to get me back on my feet! I loved that guy man! I owe him everything I got today," Kerby stated!

"So how was his family life?"

"You kidding! That's some garbage they talking on the TV about Lloyd and Celine! That man was a family man, one hundred percent," Garth declared!

"Listen detective, Lloyd bought a wedding ring for Celine over a month ago, but he was waiting for the right time to pop the question," Elvis stated!

"But who knows what their home life was like, maybe they started having problems?"

"My wife Donette and Celine are best friends, and all my wife tells me is how much they love each other! Donette made me laugh the other day when she told me that Celine planned on asking Lloyd to marry her, because she loves him that much," Elvis exclaimed!

"Would it be OK if I spoke with your wife Donette?"

"Fine by me! She has been working extra shifts at the old home as of late, so you might have to phone her," Elvis explained. The construction worker did not know Donette's telephone number by memory, therefore he scrolled through his contact list, selected the number, and showed it to the detective. Detective Laddimer wrote down the number on his notepad, then looked around at the work being done on the site.

"How long have you guys been working together?"

"Elvis and Lloyd have been together the longest, something like fourteen years, then Garth joined the crew two years later, and I came on three years after that," Kerby explained!

"Did Lloyd speak with any of you regarding the threats made by Aaron Adams?"

"He told me that fool had been bothering Celine from jail, but it was nothing to worry about because he had no idea where they lived," Elvis stated!

"How about Tamara, Lloyd's sister, how would you describe her relationship with Celine?"

"Oh, those people hated Celine! And that bothered Lloyd so much, because he was going to marry Celine and wanted them to get along," Elvis answered!

"I must thank you fellows for clearing up some issues I had with this case! Thanks for your time, and I'm sorry that you all had to lose your friend this way," Detective Laddimer declared as the construction workers went back to work!

The detective walked back to his car and sat inside the vehicle looking over his notes. Aside from a few jealous players everybody had something positive to say about the couple, but the detective had to work the case and followed every lead. Laddimer reached for his cellular phone and dialed the number given to him by Elvis, whose wife was an alleged good friend of Celine. Donette answered her phone through her vehicle's Bluetooth link while she drove herself home from work.

"Hello," Donette responded!

"Hello Donette, this is Detective Laddimer from the Nova Scotia Police Department, and I am investigating the Lloyd Walker murder," the detective introduced himself!

"OK, how may I help you detective?"

"I was just speaking with your husband Elvis, and he told me that you could clear up a few details I needed to know about Celine Devers."

"If I can help I sure will!"

"Wonderful! Would you say that Celine and Lloyd made a good couple?"

"Those two human beings were made for each other Detective Laddimer!"

"Your husband seemed to think so. He mentioned that Lloyd was looking forward to proposing to Celine. Do you think Celine would have accepted his offer?"

"I had been holding onto that secret for weeks and could not tell my girl, now unfortunately she will never hear those words from Lloyd. But yes detective, Celine definitely would have accepted! She already warned me that I would be her best lady whenever they decided to tie the knot!"

"What sort of relationship did Celine have with Aaron?"

"That lunatic wanted Celine back after all those years, but she wanted nothing to do with him! Lloyd stood his ground against that criminal, that's why that coward killed him!"

"How long have you been friends with Celine?"

"Almost thirteen years."

"Do you know if Celine knows a Trudy Greenfield?"

"Celine does not keep much friends Detective Laddimer! But no, I don't recall ever hearing her speak of this Trudy Greenfield!"

"What sort of relationship would you say Celine had with Lloyd's mother and sister?"

"Roslyn and Tamara hated Celine and did everything they could to break those two up! But no matter what they did it backfired, because those two were meant for each other!"

"Thank you for your time today, Donette! Should I have any further questions, may I contact you?"

"If it's to clear my girl's name and change people's perspective about her, then phone me anytime Detective Laddimer," Donette stated before she disconnected the call!

The detective was intent on speaking with all his persons of interest before the weekend ended, so he drove to his second and final destination that day. Trudy Greenfield was not one the people who Detective Laddimer originally had on his list as someone of interest. Following her appearance on the CJCH Evening Newscast, Laddimer thought she might present a different angle on the case and drove to her legal address. After parking his vehicle on the street, the detective made his way to the left side of the family house, which was Trudy's entrance to her rented basement apartment. Laddimer did not make any prior arrangement to speak with Trudy, yet he stepped to her door and rung the bell. There was no answer to his first alert, so the detective rung the bell a second time, at which Trudy presented herself at the door. The female peeped through the glass pane on the side of her door, to check who the caller was, before she opened the door. Trudy was struggling to cover herself beneath her robe, and looked like she had just woken, with her hair scattered in every which direction, and her eyelids shuttering to adjust to the light.

"Yes, may I help you?"

"Are you Trudy Greenfield?"

"Yes, who is asking?"

"Miss Greenfield I am Detective Laddimer with the Nova Scotia Police Department, and I would like a few words if I may?"

"I'm sorry... but this is not a good time right now, I have someone over."

Trudy began hesitating then, turned to look back inside her apartment, when her male companion appeared behind her. Ruddy was rushing to get dressed and barely had his trousers on, yet grabbed his Reeboks sneakers from the front door, as he made his way pass Trudy. Detective Laddimer stepped to the side to allow her companion to pass, thus Ruddy shoved his feet into the sneakers and quickly went by without acknowledging either of them. The male guest tried to abstain from making any visual contact with the detective, as if he was a wanted criminal trying to conceal his identity. Even though the detective was there on official business, he knew how nervous the man must have felt, getting caught in another man's dwelling while he was incarcerated. After her guest left, Trudy made the detective stepped to the frame of her door, rather than fully inside the apartment.

"So, what can I do for you detective?"

"I was putting together a profile of your boyfriend Aaron, and wanted to know if you could help me fill in some information about him?"

"What sort of information?"

"I heard you said during your TV interview, that Aaron was a violent person. To the extent that he would beat you for different reasons?"

"Yes, that's true!"

"Why did you never report him to the police?"

"Because I was afraid that the only thing some judge would do was release him back into society, then he would surely beat the hell out of me, maybe even killed me!"

"I take it, Aaron carried weapons from time to time?"

"No, more like all the time!"

"So, you were afraid of him?"

"Yes sometimes, other times he made me feel safe like no one could touch us!"

"Was that because people knew that he was a dangerous man who carried weapons?"

"That had something to do with it! Plus, his macho style and guys respected him! You know?"

"So, that was why you stayed with him?"

"I guess so!"

"Did you ever meet his ex-girlfriend, Celine?"

"No!"

"Do you have any children?"

"No, but I did have three miscarriages courtesy of Aaron!"

"Were you aware that Aaron's ex Celine has two children?"

"No, I did not know that," demonstratively answered Trudy, whose facial expression grew serious!

Detective Laddimer could see that Trudy was becoming increasingly agitated with his line of questioning. However, he was already able to distinguish that she used Celine's bad fortune to clear her reputation, from dating a heartless criminal and did not care who the other woman was. To avoid being considered pro Celine, Detective Laddimer quickly pivoted to discussing Aaron, who Trudy obviously was elated to get rid of.

"How often did Aaron go on these robbery schemes of his?"

"Oh, Aaron went on the hustle every day! Every now and then he would have to lay low for a few days, but he was bred for the streets, so he made money doing all the illegal shit he did!"

"Have you ever seen Aaron shoot someone?"

"I saw him shoot at someone! That guy was lucky we were driving down the street, when Aaron suddenly rolled down the window and began shooting!"

"Were you the driver of the vehicle?"

"Yeah, we were on our way to get some Mary Brown's Chicken when that shit happened! Scared me and my girlfriend Joann half to death! Then all Aaron kept saying was how that guy owed him money!"

"I don't know you, but you seem like a very smart person! You need to get away from this guy Aaron before, you possibly end up dead!"

"I know I need to! So many people have told me that," stated Trudy who began crying!

"Now that he is off the streets for a while, you need to move on from him!"

"You're right Detective Laddimer," sobbed Trudy.

"I must thank you for helping me with my profile! I hope you take my advice and think about your personal safety," Detective Laddimer stated before he took his leave.

Chapter 9

Tamara and Robin sat quietly inside her Lexus RX, as they drove along Interstate 101. Both females normally sang and danced to music inside the vehicle wherever they commuted, but Aunty Tamara decided against any entertainment. Robin felt there was a problem from the moment she woke, at which the very first instruction Tamara gave her was to "pack her belongings to go home," but she did as ordered without further agitating her aunt. Once they left Tamara's apartment and Robin noticed there would be no music playing inside the vehicle, she popped her Ear-bugs into her ears and listened to her personal tunes. A song began playing which made Robin began thinking about Lloyd, therefore she pulled one of the devices from her ear and said, "you know what the worst thing about losing dad will be, never getting to see those quirky dance moves he does!"

Tamara broke out laughing and responded, "I know! Lloyd had two left feet and couldn't dance for shit!"

Both females began laughing at the thought of their deceased relative dancing. Discussing Lloyd transformed the entire mood inside the Lexus, therefore, Tamara became more social and pleasant to speak with. Despite the way she felt about Robin's mother, Tamara knew her niece considered her brother her father and nothing would change that fact.

"You remember when he got drunk at his birthday party and tripped over his own feet while dancing," Tamara joked?

"Ha-ha-ha-ha! The best one had to be at Uncle Kerby's wedding, when dad, Uncle Elvis, and Uncle Garth all rehearsed that RNB song to dance to, and dad forgot the dance moves halfway through the song! So, he started improvising; and messed the whole dance routine up!"

"Ha-ha-ha-ha-ha, that had to be funny to see! I used to always tell him that he can't dance, but he went to some white punk rock party one night with some other friends, and everybody was like, dude you got some awesome moves! Totally blew Lloyd's mind and since then, he swore he is the king of the dance floor!"

"I can't just have you like completely riff on my dad, he did have some pretty ingenious moves! Remember when he did that break dance stuff; and broke the table he was windmilling on?"

"OK, I must give him that, he was popping it then! Until he messed up and broke the table," laughed Tamara!

As they drove up to the buildings and turned into the parking area, they noticed the group of female protesters walking in front the building holding up signs. The ladies refrained from causing any loud disruptions, yet they walked up and down the courtyard displaying their anger. Tamara had no idea that Celine had been under constant pressure, until she saw the protesters and realized what may had sparked her rage the night prior.

"What the hell is going on here," Tamara said as she parked in a visitor's slot!

"Why are those women holding up those signs about my mother," Robin asked?

"I don't know baby, but let's get inside and see how your mother is holding up," Tamara answered!

They both exited the vehicle and started walking toward the building, during which Tamara held onto Robin's hand. One of the female protester's saw Robin and knew enough about the family to realize she was Celine's daughter. Instead of allowing the young lady to safely enter her dwelling, the woman rushed over towards Robin and Tamara and began shouting disrespectful slurs.

"There goes that tramp Celine's daughter," shouted the female protester as she approached! "Tell your whoring mother she is going to get what's coming to her!"

By then, the other eight ladies had begun running over to make their voices heard.

"We have no place in Nova Scotia for people with no morals like your mother," shouted another female!

"They should lock her ass up for using sex to entrap men from prison," shouted another!

Tamara attempted to cover Robin's ears, but it was impossible to shut out the degrading comments. As they moved closer to the door the first protester tried to block the path, thus Tamara stepped in front of Robin and held her behind her.

"You better get out of our way before I knock your teeth in Bitch," Tamara threatened at which the woman stepped to the side!

Robin and Tamara entered the building and raced up to Celine's apartment. Once Robin used her key to open the door and entered the dwelling, she began franticly searching about for her mother and brother. They were surprised to find Celine and Julien in bed comfortably wrapped underneath the blanket watching an animation movie. Despite all the protesting taking place outdoors, both mother and son seemed undisturbed while they lounged in bed. Celine was rather stunned when Robin rushed over and leapt onto the bed, before she started kissing both Julien and her.

"Where is all this coming from? Good morning to you too Robin Walker," Celine lamented!

"I am just happy to see you guys safe," Robin declared!

Tamara stood between the doorframe looking at the family members with a smile on her face. Celine expected her to be less cordial after the manner with which she dealt with her, but Tamara was rather forgiving.

"Celine, why don't you leave the kids to watch the movie and come outside let's talk," Tamara reasoned?

Celine could see that Tamara had something important to discuss, so she wrapped both Robin and Julien into the blanket and left the room. Both ladies walked out into the days room, where Tamara walked over to the window and looked out at the protesters marching about with their signs.

"What's up," Celine asked?

"I want you guys to come over to my place for a while, until this shit blows over," Tamara offered?

"You know there ain't enough space inside that little apartment of yours for all of us," Celine argued!

"Yes, I know, but anywhere else is better than this right now," Tamara said!

"Thanks, but we will be all right. Those people have nothing else to do, that's all," Celine commented!

"You never know what people like that are liable to do! We had to just force our way through, because one of those women tried to block us," Tamara declared!

"I'm not afraid of any of those bitches," Celine insisted!

"OK, then at least let me take the kids for a few days, so they don't have to hear or see that bullshit," Tamara suggested?

Celine walked over to the window and looked through at the women walking about down below. As she considered Tamara's request, she walked back to the kitchen and picked up the bottle of Grey Goose Vodka, which was almost empty. There was no point in arguing because Tamara was genuine and wanted the best for the children, therefore Celine uncorked the bottle and drank the remaining liquor.

"OK, you are right! I need to keep the kids from seeing that garbage outside! But you have to bring me to the liquor store before you take them, and you have to bring them by your mother for a day or two," bargained Celine?

"Let's go," stated Tamara!

"Robin and Julien! You guys get to go chill with Aunty Tamara for a little while, so go pack a few things in your bags, so we can get out of here," Celine shouted!

"Yes, I get to go by Aunty Tamara's place too," Julien cheered as they walked to their rooms.

Celine also returned to her bedroom to search through her drawers for the matching hoodie to complete her ensemble. She expected to get hassled wherever anyone recognized her, therefore she wrapped her hair and threw on a baseball cap, then added a pair of dark sunglasses. Once Celine got ready to leave, she went into her son's room and helped him select what to carry. Within ten minutes they were all prepared to leave the premises; thus, Celine locked the door behind them, then they walked down to the front entrance. A police cruiser had appeared on the scene and was parked just inside the parking area, but none of the family members could tell if the officer was inside the vehicle. The Lexus RX was parked a few rows over from the police cruiser, so the ladies felt confident the protesters would show restraint. Tamara went ahead of the group before they exited the building door, while Celine held her children between them and manned the rear.

The instant they exited the building and the gang of protesters recognized that their party of four had to be Celine's entourage, the sign wavers moved to intercept them. It was impossible for them to reach their vehicle without colliding. The officer was inside his cruiser speaking with his girlfriend on the phone and did not expect any altercation when assigned to the scene.

"… could not believe there," spoke the female on the phone.

"Holy shit, Vanessa I have to call you back, I have a developing situation here," declared Officer Miller as he threw the door open and moved to exit the cruiser; before he realized he did not unbuckle his seatbelt! Knowing he would probably need back up to control the ladies, the officer got on his radio and alerted their dispatch of the escalating danger, as he moved toward the quarrel.

The gang of protesters caught up with Celine's company, primarily because Julien could not quicken his pace. Instead of trying to block the family members' path however, the protesters walked alongside them shouting and waving their signs. Officer Miller wanted to prevent any injuries or having to arrest anyone, hence he forgot to close his vehicle door and ran toward the dispute. Neither party were being physical, but the protesters had gotten close enough to be considered harassing the family members.

"You ladies stop right there," Officer Miller shouted as he ran toward the altercation.

Tamara was persistently pressing forward regardless of the filthy remarks being uttered by the protesters. Even though the protester who Tamara threatened to 'punch her tooth out' had one of the biggest mouths in the group, she wisely kept her distance, yet invigorated her protesting companions. Celine covered Julien's ears and looked extremely serious, knowing her daughter had to listen to the profanity and degrading comments by the misinformed protesters. While slowly moving toward their transportation Officer Miller came sprinting along the walkway and stood between the female protesters and Celine's group. The officer began threatening the protesters with arrests as he guarded the four family members to the Lexus RX and had them safely climbed aboard. Robin hopped into the front of the vehicle with her aunty, while Celine sat clutching Julien inside the back.

They sped out from the parking lot onto Bayers Road with Officer Miller left arguing with the protesters. The shock from their experience had everyone stunned, so no one said a word for the first two blocks. Julien looked around the vehicle and realized that everyone seemed scared, so he tugged on Celine's sweat top and emphasised, "Mommy, those women were crazy!" Everybody inside the Lexus busted out laughing at the youth's comment, knowing that was exactly what they thought of the protesters.

"Mom, you should have seen when we were going into the building and that one woman stepped to Aunty Tamara! Aunty was like, you better get out of my face before I punch your teeth out; that woman moved so fast! I had no idea Aunty was a badass," Robin joked!

"Oh, she did, did she," Celine stated?

"That woman was so scared, even just now she made sure she stayed way in the back," Robin added!

"I mean hey, don't be stopping me and my niece with some bullshit," Tamara declared!

"Where the hell did you get a fight game," Celine jokingly asked?

"I throw down when I need to! Dang! Sometimes all I got to throw down are words, but you can't let some bitch know you scared of her," Tamara exclaimed at which they all laughed!

When they reached the Liquor Store, Celine decided to go in alone, therefore Tamara told her what she wanted and stayed with the kids. Celine pulled her hoodie over the top of her hat and placed her sunglasses on her face before she stepped out of the Lexus. To avoid eye contact with anyone she held her head down toward the ground and walked briskly into the store. Normally she would have refused a cart, but Celine felt she needed the support with the amount of liquor she wanted. The moment she began walking around the store one of the employees noticed her and thought she might be a shoplifter, so the worker unknowingly started following her. The disguised shopper went through two of the wine isles, where she selected three bottles of various wines. After selecting the bottles of wine, Celine went by the refrigerator and picked up a six pack of Heineken, which she added into her cart. The liquor isles were several places over, therefore she discretely made her way to the Vodka section. Once she had selected all the alcohol she desired, Celine walked through three more isles looking at different brands. The store worker thought she was either moving about to hide the bottles on her person, or getting ready to make a quick dash through the door, so she continued watching Celine closely. The female customer decided against purchasing any of the liquor she looked at and moved toward a cashier with all the bottles she had picked up inside the cart. At that point the employee realized she had made a bad judgement and went back to her regular duties.

Celine had no idea she was being followed even though she went in and out of the Liquor Store without any altercation. The customers inside the liquor store seemed more focused on getting their correct beverage of choice, rather than antagonizing other clients. During Celine's absence her children spoke with their Aunty Tamara and begged her to offer their mother a place to stay. Both Robin and Julien knew that neither their aunty nor their mother cared much for each other, thus they thought that the riff between them was the reason why their mother could not join them. Tamara was indeed scared for the entire family yet, told Julien and Robin that "their mother would not abandon her dwelling, regardless of what she asked!" Following their talk, the kids became increasingly worried about their mother's safety and were extremely silent once she returned into the Lexus.

It did not take Celine very long to realize there was an issue after she rejoined her family members. The vibrant atmosphere she left inside the Lexus had changed, thus everyone was less interactive as they focused their attention elsewhere. Robin had reinserted her Ear-bugs into her ears and listened to music, while she gazed through the window. Julien had taken out his Sony PSP and was playing his video game with his back turned toward Celine on the rear seat. The instant Celine climbed back into the vehicle, Tamara tried to focus her attention on the roadway, as she pulled out of the parking lot.

"OK, Tamara your bill is exactly eighty-six dollars! This is your bag right here, I'll leave it on the floor after I get out," Celine explained!

"Thank you," Tamara answered as she fought to avoid looking back at Celine!

They drove up to a red traffic light that led from the shopping plaza. As soon as the Lexus RX came to a stop, Tamara reached into her blouse pocket and handed Celine ninety dollars. With her children attempting to ignore her, Celine sensed there was a problem and patted Julien on the head.

"Are you OK Jules," Celine asked?

"Just leave me alone mom," Julien answered as he shook off her hand!

"What's wrong son? Robin, what's going on," Celine enquired?

"I am scared that those women are going to hurt you! Why don't you come stay with us by Aunty Tamara," Julien cried?

"Don't worry about me Jules! I'm not afraid of those women, and now that I don't have you guys to worry about, it might be better if they went somewhere else, because mommy is not having it," Celine responded yet her son continued brushing her off!

"I told them that you can come over and spend a few days with us, but it was your choice and you said no," Tamara declared!

"You need to come stay with us mom," Robin argued!

"I know that I can stay by your aunty with you guys, but I prefer to be in our home right now! I miss your dad; and the only place I feel his presence is inside our apartment, so I can't leave," Celine explained!

Tamara already had tears bobbled in her eyes from the discussion she had with the children about their mother staying over. Hearing Celine's comment about her brother was heartbreaking, therefore the flow of tears increased. Robin became emotional after hearing about her father and, also began crying, thus before long everybody inside the Lexus were sheading tears. Julien paused his game and hugged his mother, while Robin and Tamara held hands for comfort. When they got back to the apartment building Celine instructed Tamara to leave her at the rear of the building, from which she entered through the back exit.

The group of protesters were dispersed by the police officers who came on the scene after Celine left, so having to sneak back into her building was unnecessary. For the first time in days Celine felt a calm not seeing the protesters outside waving their signs. Instead of having a drink she began scrolling through her caller's list and redialed Detective Laddimer's number. The detective had just finished speaking with Trudy and was walking to his car when his phone rang.

"Detective Laddimer here!"

"Hi Detective Laddimer, this is Celine Devers!"

"Hey Celine, nice to hear from you! What can I do for you?"

"I have had a group of women protesting outside my apartment now for a few days!"

"I am sorry to hear that! I heard the report two days ago."

"Ah, is there any way I can get an officer or someone to watch out for me or my children whenever they are out there?"

"Unfortunately, they have a right to protest, but they must stay off private property and follow some other guidelines, so if we are to restrict them from protesting, you need to get proof of them breaking any of these laws! I will send you a website with all the protesting regulations once I get back to the office. But I will have a cruiser pass by more often to ensure that they don't break the law!"

"So, there is no way to get those women to stop the name callings, degrading signs, and profanity?"

"Not as long as they follow the law. But if all this is stressing you out and causing you depression, I say file a lawsuit against the people who put you in this position! Might as well get some money if you have to go through all that!"

"Thanks for the information, Detective Laddimer, and remember to send me that website link?"

"Soon as I get to the station, Celine!"

They disconnected the call and Celine was left staring at the bottles of liquor, but she walked away and went over to their desktop computer, where she began searching for private attorneys' information. If she was going to get hounded by certain citizens whenever she went out in public, Detective Laddimer's suggestion to get compensated made sense. Instead of doing any drinking for the remainder of the day, Celine searched through dozens of lawyers to find the perfect representative to handle her lawsuit. When she came across Baren Igby Private Practice that evening, Celine thought his qualifications and win/loss record were impressive, so she phoned his law firm to arrange a consultation. There was no response to her call, therefore she left a voice mail and hung up the phone.

Chapter 10

A court appointed inmate named Patrice Huller from B-Pod, returned after he was refused bail during his appearance. Patrice rode to court in a patty wagon filled with detainees, two of which had since been sent home. One of the men Patrice rode to court with was Bernard Harris, therefore he returned with a message from their old pod mate. B-Pod was back to its regular operations, so all the inmates were in the days room when Patrice returned. Aaron had just gotten on the phone and dialled someone's number, when Patrice and another detainee walked into the pod. Quest and Nickle were a few feet away from Aaron, along with the group of thugs they always assembled with. Despite their personal sentiments toward Aaron, Nickle and Quest remained as members of the crew to avoid the same treatment that Eddie received. The crew of thugs dominated the pod hence, it was of greater convenience to both men siding with them.

Patrice had some court documents to put away inside his cell, but he passed closer to the phone area to address Aaron. "Hey Aaron, I went to court with Bernard this morning! He said to tell you, he is getting transferred and Samuel got sent to D-Pod," shouted Patrice!

Aaron casually nodded his head and went back to his conversation, while Patrice continued to his cell. Three of Aaron's associates started trailing Patrice with questions about Bernard and Samuel, none of whom were being sent back to B-Pod. Nickle and Quest caught Aaron's neglectful gesture and looked at each other, then shook their heads knowing he instigated everything that happened. It was a rare sight to see Aaron on the phone, because he had very little contacts beyond the detention center's walls. However, one of Aaron's main contacts was the person on the line named Ruddy, with whom he had committed numerous criminal offenses. Ruddy and Aaron were the same age with similar traits, except Ruddy was a single child who had never moved out of his parent's house and was always sheltered by his mother. Therefore, whenever they got into trouble, Ruddy's parents always acquired the best representatives who would either get him acquitted or community service.

"So, what's happening in the streets since I been down," Aaron asked?

"Nothing much bro, it's quiet out here," Ruddy answered!

"Listen, I'm going to need you to go pick up those coins from Old Boy for me and put it on my books," Aaron instructed!

"Yeah bro, I got you man! Consider that handled," Ruddy stated!

"Yow, I'm going to need you to link a call for me," Aaron asked?

"No problem go ahead, give me the number," Ruddy insighted!

Aaron began giving Ruddy the phone number while speaking code, to avoid being understood by the correctional officers.

"The area code is where Sunny goes for vacation every year."

Ruddy grasped what Aaron meant and wrote down the 782-Area Code and said, "OK, got that!"

"Your birthday without the zero before the month."

Again Ruddy understood what Aaron meant and wrote down the first three digits.

"How many dogs did your mother have the first time I went to your house?"

Ruddy quickly jotted down the number.

"What balcony did we have to jump from when those biker dudes chased us the time?"

Ruddy chuckled as he wrote down the number and said, "Got that!"

"Do you remember that awful looking pink fuzzy sweater you wore with the big number on the front?"

"Yeah, yeah I remember," chuckled Ruddy as entered the number then he pressed the call button, at which the phone began ringing in his ear! "Hey Bro, I got something to handle real quick! So, once I link you up, I won't be on the line. Whenever y'all get done talking, just hang up!"

The phone rang until a female came on the line, thus Ruddy connected Aaron and placed the receiver on a table. Celine screened every caller who dialled her phone and only responded to Ruddy's call, because his number was not private. Even though she had no reservations about who the caller might be, she never expected to hear the voice on the other end of the line.

"Hello," pleasantly Celine greeted!

"Hi baby it's me Aaron," Aaron answered softly.

Celine was so surprised to hear Aaron's voice that she froze and could not utter a word for the first few seconds. The pleasant glare that glistened across her face when she answered quickly vanished; and was replaced with a displeasing snarl.

"Listen, before you say anything, I never expected things to happen like they did! But it must have been faith why I ran into Lloyd that day, like I told you we were meant to be together! I know you might be a little upset right now, but in time you will see this was all for the best! No matter what you say, I know you still love me, and I love you too! I was the first man you were ever with; and I should have been the only man that ever got to touch you! That fool you were with was a joke, he can't love you and take care of you..."

"And you can? You have been in and out of prison for more than half your life! What can you do for me and my children? Eh! You used to beat the crap out of me and had me believing that was love!"

"Don't act like I was the only one throwing punches! You throw a pretty mean combination when you get heated!"

"I was raised with two brothers, don't forget!"

"Yeah, but you chose to come run away and live with me!"

"Despite all that years later, you killed my man and think that I would ever come back to you! The Celine you knew, is not the person I am today! So if I were you, I would hope they lock me away for the rest of my life, because if I ever see you again Aaron, I'm going to be the one doing time for murder!"

"I know you don't mean any of that Celine! Remember the good times we used to have?"

"You're delusional! Don't you ever call back my number," Celine threatened before she hung up!

Hearing Aaron's voice added insult to the injury he already caused, therefore as soon as Celine disconnected the call she went and retrieved Officer Lafountain's card. The grieving female dialled the officer who was still on duty, yet found time to assist her thoroughly. There was a watermain busted underground at the corner of Titus Street and Main Avenue, which was squirting water into the air earlier that evening. A crew of workers from the city were sent to block off the roadway, dig up the asphalt and soil, fix the damaged pipe, and finally repair the roadway for motorists. Officer Lafountain was assigned to traffic duty, therefore he simply had to sit inside his cruiser with the emergency lights flashing, to alert drivers of the danger.

"Hello, Officer Lafountain, this is Celine Devers, Lloyd Walker's girlfriend!"

"Oh! Hello Celine, how are you doing? Didn't your daughter come back home yet?"

"Yes, she did, this is not about her though! Listen, I need some information regarding what I can do to stop someone from harassing me from inside a Correctional Facility?"

"Is there someone bothering you from jail?"

"Yes, Aaron phoned me and was boasting about killing Lloyd to get me back! I think he is delusional for the things he believes!"

"If Aaron is calling you that is a violation, that might result in added charges against him! So, I will personally contact the right people and let them know!"

"Do you think I will need to change my phone number to get him to stop harassing me?"

"Eventually you might have to! You might even have to move if you wish to totally get away from this guy!"

"Thank you for all your help, Officer Lafountain!"

"Just doing my job Miss Devers. Someone should get in touch with you over the next few days, to verify your story! But take care of yourself and those kids and you have my number if you need anything!"

Celine came off the phone thinking about what the officer said. She loved living in Nova Scotia and wanted her children to grow up around their family members. Even though what Officer Lafountain said made sense, Celine eventually brushed the thought to the side and went back to watching her television program. Officer Lafountain wanted to ensure that as a victim Celine was not made to be scared, hence he began probing to find the prosecuting attorneys on Aaron Adams' case. With a quick call into the station, the officer was able to uncover the information he wanted thus, he telephoned the number he retrieved but it rang unanswered.

Officer Lafountain was determined to get Aaron charged with harassment, in order for the correctional facility to place tighter restrictions on all his calls. As a result, he began calling the prosecution office from 8:59 AM the next morning, to get the ball rolling on the case. After having to phone back three times, Rick Schultz the main prosecuting attorney working the Lloyd Walker Murder Trial, answered the telephone in his office. Lafountain told Schultz about what happened to Celine and reasoned with him about informing the Correctional Facility. While the prosecutor could not guarantee that Mister Adams would never be allowed to contact Miss Devers, he did agree to alert the institution and bring the matter before a judge to try and get charges laid.

To get the correct assessment of what happened, Mr. Schultz telephoned Celine to hear her story in her own words, and to find out if she was willing to testify if needed. Celine was stunned when she saw the Prosecution Bureau's phone number calling her that morning, which was evidence that Officer Lafountain had done as he promised.

"Hello good morning! May I speak with Celine Devers please?"

"Yes, this is Celine!"

"Miss Devers I am Prosecutor Rick Schultz, and I received a complaint you made to Officer Lafountain regarding Aaron Adams! Is this true?"

"Yes, it is!"

"When did this incident occur?"

"Just yesterday."

"So, this is pretty fresh in your memory?"

"Yes, it is!"

"Do you care to describe or tell me what happened around this phone call made to you from Aaron Adams?"

"Well, I received a call where the name on the caller ID said Judith Rutherford, so I knew it wasn't from a prison and I did not think of any reason why I should not answer! Anyways, I was floored when I heard Aaron's voice on the line..."

"Pause for a second please? Did you mean that he did not contact you through the conventional means?"

"No, there was no secretary or recording letting me know the call was from a prisoner, so I was shocked when I realized the person I despise was on the other line!"

"What did you guys talk about or what did he say to you?"

"He said that he never expected to run into Lloyd that day, but when he did it must have been faith because we were meant to be together! He said I belonged to him, and no other man should have ever touched me! Then he started getting weird saying he knows I still love him, and he still loves me, and we are going to be together, because Lloyd could not please me and he knows how to please me!"

"So, he has been fantasizing about you all these years?"

"I guess so!"

"Did he say anything else to you?"

"Not really, I called him a lunatic or something, told him to stop calling my phone, then hung up on him!"

"Thank you for coming forward with this information Miss Devers! I will see to it that Mister Adams pays for violating you," Prosecutor Schultz declared before they ended their call.

Before the prosecutor acted on the information he received, he contacted the Correctional Facility that housed Aaron and requested a diagnosis of the calls the detainee made the day prior. Within fifteen minutes a correctional officer from the jail phoned back with their analysis, after they listened to the entire call. The prison guards were able to determine that Aaron indeed had his friend Ruddy connect a three-way link; and presented the transcripts of that call to Celine. Once Prosecutor Schultz obtained all the information he required, he had a member of his team write up the formal harassment charges for a judge to sign and made binding. When his secretary brought him the list of new charges, Mr. Schultz took the document and brought it to see Judge Q. Royse at his office.

The judge was indisposed for a few minutes when they arrived, so Rick had to wait until he was finished in the bathroom, and ready to entertain visitors before he got allowed in. When the prosecutor was finally allowed into the judge's chamber, he entered to find Judge Royse buckling his belt and adjusting his attire. After they warmly greeted each other, the prosecutor presented their findings to the judge and proposed why Aaron should be assessed additional charges. Judge Q. Royse was not about to have a possible witness threatened or tampered with in any means, therefore, he signed the documents which officially charged Aaron with harassment. A copy of the document was sent to the Correction Facility were Aaron received it by mail the following evening. Even though Aaron idiotically felt that Celine cared for him, he did not anticipate or appreciate the additional legal infractions, for which he would have to answer to in court.

Sergeant Gibbs was the on-duty senior officer that dreadful evening when Eddie got beaten to within inches of his life by Bernard and Samuel. Following the incident, the correctional officers watched the entire video and observed who gave the order for the attackers to strike. The correctional officers also knew who ran each pod, the most dominating crew of individuals, and those less likely to cause disruption. Since the incident Sergeant Gibbs had sought the right opportunity to repay Aaron for unleashing his thugs, so discovering that he violated the prison's telephone rules gave him just that. During lockdown that night, the sergeant brought two of his male correctional officers to Aaron's cell, where they placed the two cellmates in handcuffs. After subduing the inmates, the guards led them from the room and had them stand by the entrance, while they determined what items inside the cell belonged to whom. The guards packed Aaron's belongings then led him from the pod and brought him to the Segregation Unit, where he spent the next six weeks for the telephone violation he had committed. Instead of allowing Aaron to return to B-Pod after he finished serving his sentence, Sergeant Gibbs transferred him to A-Pod which had way fewer of his friends.

Chapter 11

Throughout the coming days Celine remained indoors without leaving her apartment building. Early one morning before the light barely brightened the sky, she awoke and began contacting the guests to uncover what food allergies they had. To ensure that the chef made everything they requested, Celine emailed their requirements for the menu before the due date, to provide them with ample time to prepare. Even though they had lost the pillar of their family, the mourning mother would have still sent her children to school if it were not for the agitating demonstrators. Education was an important factor in the life of both parents, who wanted their children to acquire the highest levels of schooling. When Celine was only a teenager she dropped out of high school and ran away from home to live with her ruthless boyfriend; but have since returned and acquired her diploma, through the Adult Education Program. Contacting the children's schools was on her agenda that morning, however she forgot to call initially until she received the notifications of their absence on her cell. The alert reminded the mourning mother she had to notify each school's principal, thus she contacted them and explained their predicament. Both school principals were extremely understanding and sympathetic, hence they allowed the children to take all the necessary time they needed to heal.

Celine had many missed messages and unattended calls indicated on her display screen, which she continued ignoring and attended to the necessary business. Lloyd and her, had a carton box in which they stored all their bills for tax purposes, therefore she went through the pile of receipts, and phoned the creditors they owed money. They had recently purchased some furniture on a payment plan, so Celine phoned the furniture store and warned them 'their payment may arrive late due to Lloyd's death'. With her children safe at their relatives, she used the time to finalize the business with Lloyd's insurance company and their debt collectors, most of whom were paid in full. There was no need for her to leave her apartment with the capability to have whatever she wanted delivered, not to mention her cooking lasted longer without the children home to devour it.

The protesters did not return the evening after they were dispersed by the police, but they were back the next morning thereafter to continue their demonstrating. After managing the schools and their bills affairs, the lonely mother felt the urge to talk to her children at Roslyn's apartment, but neither of them had awakened, thus the phone rang without a response. Celine felt the urge for Lloyd's favorite breakfast and went into her kitchen, prepared a Western Vegetarian Omelet, with Waffles, Strawberries, and a mug of Hot Chocolate. There were two things missing from her nutritious and tasty meal, which was her children and Lloyd, still she imagined they were there seated in their individual seats while she ate. The only person Celine felt genuinely cared about her was her girlfriend Donette, so she picked up her phone to dial her number. The phone display indicated that she had missed forty-three calls, so she began scrolling through the numbers to see who the callers were. Most of the calls were from private numbers, but shortly thereafter she noticed that she had missed three calls from Donette, so she immediately redialed the number.

"Hey girl, I've been trying to call you but no answer," responded Donette!

"Sorry about that girl! I've been getting some weird crank calls from people threatening me and shit! Not to mention the protestors walking around with signs out on the corner, shouting all sorts of garbage whenever we go by!"

"Are you serious?"

"Yeah girl, some people got no idea what is what, yet they think they got an opinion!"

"Don't let them bother you Celine, you have those two kids to still raise! Plus, you know we here for you!"

"I know! They haven't broken me yet, so don't worry! Who the hell is this now, on my phone?"

"Sounds like you need one of them crank caller detectors, to let you know if it's safe to answer!"

Celine chuckled at the joke while looking at her caller ID to see who the caller was. "Girl let me phone you later, this that lawyer I called to handle some business for me!"

"OK girl, talk to you later! If not see you at the viewing!"

Attorney Baren Igby returned Celine's phone call after she had contacted his office the day prior. If her caller identification had not featured his name and number, the female would not have responded to the call, especially after the conflict with Aaron. The high volume of crank callers and bigots phoning her throughout the day had not stopped, therefore she kept the phone volume off and only attended to callers she recognized.

"Hello," Celine responded!

"Yes, good morning! May I please ah, speak with Miz Celine Devers," asked the French accent speaking lawyer on the line?

"Yes, this is Celine!"

"Hello Miz Celine, I am so sorry for miss your phone call yesterday, it has been crazy past seventy-two hours for me! Even so, how may I ah, help you?"

"Can I facetime you or get you on a conference call? I have to show you exactly what I have been putting up with outside my home!"

"No problem! Will you ah, wait for little while, I send to you the link!"

Attorney Igby sent Celine a Facetime link, which she connected to and immediately turned her video camera onto the demonstrators outside. There were eight females holding aloft signs that defamed Celine, as they walked back and forth along the sidewalk where they were free to associate and protest. The officers had driven the demonstrators several yards away from the property to appease the tenants, yet they never wavered and continued their protesting.

"I hope you can see those people outside my window, because that is the level of harassment, I have been experiencing for days now!"

"How did ah, all a this begin?"

"This guy I dated years ago shot and killed my boyfriend recently. After that happened people started hounding his girlfriend about being with such a heartless demon! The critic and pressure led her to do a TV interview, where she made a number of false claims about me! Since then, all I have gotten is bitches who don't even know me, saying all sorts of shit about me and my children! So, I would like to know if I have a case against the news station, for not guaranteeing their story before they ruined my life?"

"You definitely do Madam Celine, a very strong case against a them I believe!"

"Will you take my case then?"

"Mais Oui! It will be ah, my pleasure to assist you manage this problem!"

"Thank you, Mr. Igby!"

"Before you go I ah, just want you to ah, do one thing for me! Can you make video of protestors outside, please? This will ah, be very useful in court!"

"I'm one step ahead of you Mr. Igby! I already recorded enough footage of them to make a movie!"

"This is good! I shall phone you as I proceed and ah, get more information if I need!"

"Thank you!"

"Pas problem madam!"

Celine came off the phone with a renewed sense of purpose. Suddenly the demonstrators mattered less and no matter what they said, advertised, or did, it would have no impact on her. She stood by the window looking out at the mis-informed women, walking around with their signs held high. According to the weather forecast on her phone it was 9 Degrees Celsius across the island of Nova Scotia that day; and some of the protesters were not adequately dressed. The temperature outside was chillier than normal, therefore after watching some of the protesters rubbing their hands together to get warm, Celine went into her kitchen and made a pot of coffee. She searched inside a cupboard and found some Styrofoam Cup, then poured the hot coffee into a pitcher and brought the warm beverage out to the demonstrators. When Celine exited her building with the steaming pitcher of coffee and the protesters saw it was her, they began shouting all sorts of degrading comments. Instead of turning around and bring-ing her coffee back to her apartment, she walked over toward them and placed the container with several other items on the grass. The kind gesture surprised and silenced most of the demonstrators, whilst Celine simply turned around and returned to her dwelling without saying a word.

There were a few packets of sugar and several mini cups of crème provided with the cups and coffee, for whosoever desired. The demonstrators had mixed reactions towards the pitcher of coffee, thus some saw no issues in drinking it, while others were against taking anything from Celine. With some of the fe-males debating what course of action they should take, two of the demonstra-tors went over and fixed themselves warm beverages with the items donated. By the time Celine reached upstairs, poured herself a warm mug, and went to the window to peep at the protesters, they were all sipping on the warm bever-age she had provided. The kind-hearted female smiled to herself and retreated to her bedroom, where she went back to looking through the picture albums.

A few days later Celine felt bored while standing in the middle of her apart-ment, looking around at her spotless dwelling. To keep from constantly remi-niscing about Lloyd, she tried to keep occupied by exercising with trainers on the internet, surfing through unnecessary sites, plus physical chores around the house. She had cleaned, then recleaned every crevice and corner of the apart-ment, until there was nothing left to clean. All the laundry had been washed, folded, and placed in their proper places. Her meal for the evening had already been prepared, thus Celine felt as if she had absolutely nothing else to do. Since the day she came home with the bags that contained Lloyd's belongings, she left them inside the closet closest to the front door, because she did not have the strength to look through them. The grieving mother thought of the items and slowly walked over and retrieved them, then walked into her living room with them.

Even before Celine reached into the first paper bag tears were rolling down her face, yet she conjured up the strength to proceed. The first item she pulled from the bag was Lloyd's yellow hard hat, which she hugged tenderly before she placed it on top of her head. The second piece of clothing she pulled out was Lloyd's dirty blue jeans, which she hugged dearly, then folded gently, before she laid it across her lap. When next she reached inside the bag, Celine withdrew Lloyd's underwear and socks, that were tucked into each other. There were too many tears to wipe away, so Celine ignored them while she folded the underwear and socks. The last piece of clothing inside the bag was the most difficult to look at because, Lloyd's shirt was soaked with his blood. Despite being able to control herself thus far, Celine broke out loudly bawling, as she hugged the shirt against her broken heart.

The next large paper bag contained Lloyd's lunchbox, his jacket, and a smaller plastic bag, in which they placed his jewelry, his watch, his sunglasses, his belt, and his wallet with most of his identification cards. There was only twenty-five dollars inside the wallet, but each card Celine removed and tossed on the sofa brought more tears to her eyes. After she removed all the cards and money Celine shoved her finger inside a small compartment and felt a piece of paper. When Celine extracted the paper, she saw that it was a ticket for an item from a jewelry store, that she had visited with Lloyd many years before. The ticket intrigued Celine who wanted to know what Lloyd had purchased, therefore she went back to searching through his pants pockets to see if she had missed anything. Lloyd's pants pockets had already been emptied, so after finding no resolution to her quest, the weeping mourner went back to assorting her deceased boyfriend's belongings. The watch was a present she had given to him two Christmases prior, thus she intended on passing it to their son as a memorabilia, of his father. It was incredibly difficult for Celine to hold and look at Lloyd's gold chain with its golden cross, which she knew that her boyfriend loved dearly. Even though she intended to give the gold chain to Robin, the thought of never seeing Lloyd wearing it, reignited her outburst bawling.

Several minutes passed before Celine was able to regain her composure, at which she walked into the kitchen and retrieved a garbage bag and a pair of scissors. When she returned to the days room, she used her phone and took pictures of all the Identification Cards, before she used the scissors and began cutting them into small pieces. There was no way she could allow her children to see and interact with the bloodied clothes Lloyd was killed in, so she placed them inside the garbage bag, along with the wallet and other unwanted items. Celine knew that she would have to go through Lloyd's things and throw away some stuff, donate other items, and keep whatever she found too personal to part ways with. Since she had already started with the items they brought home from the hospital, Celine decided to continue with Lloyd's clothes inside their closet. The first piece of clothing the mourning female came across, was a dinner jacket Lloyd wore to a school function, where Robin received a plaque for her excellent work. The jacket was hung on the inside of the closet door, but once Celine saw it, memories of that pleasant day flooded her thoughts. Instead of proceeding with her plans to sort out Lloyd's clothes, Celine began crying again, therefore she took down the jacket and wrapped herself in its warmth.

To Celine the jacket felt as if she was being hugged and caressed by Lloyd, thus she went into her living room and retracted their photo albums from the cabinet. Instead of making herself comfortable inside their family room, Celine walked into her kitchen, where she grabbed a glass and an open bottle of wine. Everything inside the apartment reminded her of Lloyd at that instant, hence the tears continued flowing the more she thought about him. With the albums in hand, the jacket over her shoulders, and the other items held secured, Celine returned to her bedroom and crawled under the blanket. The tears were already flowing heavier as she turned the cover to the first page, where she stared at the four pictures of her entire family. The pictures were taken several years prior during a trip to Marine Land in Niagara Falls, when her children looked much younger. Each photo she diligently looked at brought smiles and tears to her face, as she reminisced on the time that picture was taken. Before long, five hours had crept by, yet Celine had only scanned through three of their four albums. The bottle of wine had only yielded two glasses, due to the different approach she took to drinking. As she was about to open the last photo album her cellular rang and featured Tamara's information, hence she paused and answered the call.

Tamara was driving and had Celine on the vehicle's Bluetooth Connection, to abstain from being distracted while she sped along the highway. The reason for Tamara's call was to inform Celine that she intended on picking up the children, rather than allowing them to spend the night at her mother's residence. Roslyn and her were also having a family feud over where Lloyd's father would stay when he went to the funeral, so Tamara wanted to discuss that issue also. Robin and Julien were at their grandmother's, where they spent the entire day because Tamara got called into work unexpectedly. Grandmother Roslyn expected to keep the kids for at least two days, after demanding for more than a week that Tamara brought them by. Both households were equally supposed to share the children, yet Tamara intended on reclaiming them regardless of what her mother said. It was pleasing to Celine to know that her children's relatives genuinely cared for them, should anything unforeseen happened to her.

Lloyd had taught the children to speak Portuguese from they were babies, therefore Roslyn loved having them over because she did not have to embarrass herself speaking English. Robin spoke Portuguese more fluently, while Julien was rather shy and would grumble his words. It was a tradition for Roslyn to either bake or prepared meals with children, which was something she had done with both Lloyd and Tamara. Roslyn and Robin were baking a pound cake, while being overseen by Julien, when Tamara arrived and thought she could intimidate her mother into surrendering the kids. By then Tamara had terminated the call with Celine, who was assured that the kids would leave their present location. Julien opened the door for his aunty to enter, before they both walked back into the kitchen where the sweet aroma of Pound Cake filled the room.

"Mama, I come to take the kids," Tamara stated in Portuguese!

"You better get out of my house, before I throw you out in the street," Roslyn responded!

"Mama, I no bring them here to stay long time with you..."

"I no care what you say, my granddaughter and I bake cake! They stay tonight here, that's it! Finish!"

Contrary to her tough talk, Tamara saw the determination in her mother's face and knew she stood no chance at succeeding. Instead of arguing any further, she went into the living room, got cozy on the sofa, and turned the television channel to a program of interest. An hour and forty minutes later, Tamara sent Celine a test message stating that, "they would be spending the night at her mother's, what time were they to meet for the mall?" When Celine received the message, she laughed to herself knowing how stubborn Lloyd's mother was, before she replied, "around 11 AM."

The next morning Tamara and the children arrived at 10:49 to pick up Celine. Everyone inside the Lexus vehicle held their breath in advance of the unknown, with the demonstrators circling the sidewalk like vultures. Celine had to purchase new clothes for Robin and Julien to wear to the funeral, thereby they intended to visit the mall to find the perfect dress and a suit. When Celine finally exited her building and started walked toward the vehicle, Tamara and the children watched nervously. Instead of any of the hostilities, they were all surprised when both parties simply nodded their heads at each other, while Celine approached the Lexus.

"Hey guys! Missed having you at home," Celine stated!

"Hi mom," Julien said!

"Wow! What the hell happened," Tamara asked?

"Long story! Let's just leave it at we came to an understanding! But what were you saying about you guy's dad? When is he coming," Celine asked?

"First thing is, mom don't even want me to bring him over there, much less have him stay there for the five days he'll be in town!"

"So, keep him at your apartment."

"I don't have a problem with that, but I'll be working that week, so I don't want him being bored not having anything to do!"

"Sounds like your mom trying to keep something else from your dad! But he is a big man, plus he used to live here, so he must still have two friends to go see!"

"Dad said he keeping as far as possible from those old crooks he used to hang with!"

"I thought your mom and dad got along?"

"Yeah they did, but I think mom still loves him deep down!"

"And I'm sure your dad wouldn't mind tapping that ass one more time!"

"Stop it, those are my parents you talking about!"

"So, what do think your dad was doing when you got made?"

"Shut up, whatever," Tamara joked!

The family drove to the Park Lane Mall and parked their vehicle closest to the South Park Street exit. Celine did not enter the Lexus wearing her baseball cap, glasses, and other disguises, but by the time they reached the mall she was fully decked out. They walked into the mall and began visiting stores they might find the clothing they sought. Even though they were primarily there for the children, both ladies occasionally dipped into a store and bought themselves something that caught their eye. Julien and Robin needed entire outfits, so they went to several stores to find the right clothes and shoes. The were able to find the perfect little suit for Julien inside a gentlemen's store and an adorable black dress for Robin in a small boutique. By the time they finished acquiring all the items it was lunchtime, so they decided to purchase food to eat at the Food Court.

When they reached the Food Court everybody wanted something different. To hasten the ordering process, Tamara offered to buy Julien what he always ordered, which was a burger and fries from his favorite restaurant. While they went off Celine followed Robin to fetch a cup of her favorite health juice from Just Juices. Watching the attendant prepare the health drink for Robin convinced Celine to get her own, therefore she ordered a Fruit Smoothie. After they bought the juices Robin and Celine walked over to a Szechuan restaurant, where they selected the platter combinations they wanted and paid. With their meals at hand, they began searching for Tamara and Julien, who had already ordered and held a table for them. They made their way over to the table and began preparing to eat, by removing their jackets and excessive items. A Caucasian woman from halfway across the dining hall noticed it was Celine, and completely ignored her food, shopping items, and purse, to walk across the hall just to speak her mind.

"The audacity of you! How dare you sit out in public around good Christian folks, after what you did to your partner! You should be locked away for what you and that lover of yours did to that man…"

Celine tried ignoring the woman who got more agitated the more she spoke. A mall security guard who overheard the argument was rushing over toward the scene, while she yelled for backup in her two-way radio. The customers seated next to Celine's table began moving away, sensing there might be a fight between the two ladies.

"So, say something bitch!? I thought so, you nothing but a coward!"

Celine nodded to Tamara indicating they should leave and started getting up off her chair, when the female spat on her, then grabbed a half cup of soda from a neighboring table and threw the contents on her. The security guard had arrived on the scene by then and began subduing the female vigilante, who was behaving as if she wanted to attack Celine. There were three other guards rushing toward the scene, while the onlookers present either filmed the event with their phones or murmured to each other. Tamara, Robin, Julien, and Celine got up and got dressed, then collected all their belongings and walked out of the mall. In all the confusion a thief stole the vigilante's purse and made away with her money, identification cards, and car keys, due to her meddlesome ways. Each of those assaulted felt degraded as they walked out the mall with a male security guard chasing them.

"Excuse me! Excuse me! Please, wait a minute," shouted the male guard as he chased behind them?

Celine neglected him and walked directly to the Lexus, where she began packing the items they bought inside. Robin had tears bobbled up in her eyes and looked at her mother's stern expression, therefore she wiped them away and climbed into the vehicle.

"What the hell do you want man," Celine finally shouted?

"I saw what happened to you and your family in there! Even though I don't know the specifics of what happened, I just want to say I'm sorry your children had to see that! And if you wish to press charges against that woman, you have all rights to pursue that option! Here is my card if you need someone to testify or anything," said the Caucasian guard.

"Thank you, Willy," said Celine while looking at the name on the card!

With everyone aboard the Lexus safely, Tamara pressed gas and sped away angrily from the mall. The incident was immediately uploaded onto the internet by several spectators and went viral, wherein it racked up millions of views in the first few hours.

Chapter 12

The secretary from the Atlantic Funeral Home contacted Celine and requested that she bring the suit they intended Lloyd to get buried in, as well as provided the pictures necessary for the viewing event. The home wanted the pictures preferably on a Memory Stick, with which they could insert into their screen device for easy viewing. Tamara wanted to assist with everything that related to her brother's burial, so they had her come over to the apartment to help. Celine asked Robin to upload the pictures because she had more knowledge and skills on the computer. While Robin sat and scrolled through the thousands of pictures they had taken over the years, Julien, Tamara, and Celine stood behind her crying, while they selected the photos to upload. There were so many pictures to choose from that they spent nearly an hour choosing their favorites, which included many with Lloyd and his friends.

When they finished uploading the pictures, they went into the bedroom to select the suit they felt Lloyd should get buried in. Celine's first choice was the jacket she had been wearing around the house, before the children returned from Tamara's. Everyone loved the jacket until they noticed a small wine stain that was accidentally caused by Celine. Lloyd only had four suits, so with the favorite out they would have to select one of the final three. Celine started bringing the suits out from their clothes closet individually, to see which would bring out that lasting cheer from the judges. The first blue suit drew a modest round of applause, therefore Celine laid it on the bed and went back in. The second brown suit drew a higher cheer and slipped into first place with one final outfit to go. When Celine emerged with the last Double-Breasted black suit, the judges went wild and cheered the loudest, hence they selected number three.

Celine placed the third suit beside the others on the bed and went back into the closet for their Lint Remover. With everyone joyous about the selections they had made, Celine began wiping the pants to remove any excess fuzz. After cleaning the pants, she picked up the jacket and felt something inside the inner breast pocket, therefore she reached inside for the contents. There were four train tickets that went from Nova Scotia, Canada to Dominion City, Canada. Everybody was surprised when Celine withdrew the items from the jacket, but once she looked at the tickets' destination, Celine became the only person crying. The tickets were not the only items inside the pocket, so Celine reached back in and withdrew a small jewelry box. With her heart pounding ever faster, Celine frightfully looked at everyone inside the room. Julien, Tamara, and Robin were all nodding their heads saying yes, indicating that she should open it and check the contents.

When Celine slowly opened the jewelry box and looked inside, there was a sparkling ring which said everything it needed to say. She looked directly at Tamara to see if Lloyd's sister knew anything about the ring, but the female merely shrugged her shoulders in awe. The kids were so happy for their mother that they hugged her and cheered, while Tamara shook her head in disbelief, then moved in and joined the group hug. Following the celebrations, Celine removed the ring and placed it on her marriage finger. Robin noticed a piece of paper underneath the train tickets on the bed and picked it up, then gave it to her mother. There was an address on the piece of paper which Celine knew quite well, even though it had been fifteen plus years since she last saw the place.

"Why did daddy buy us tickets to that place mom? Is that where Disney World is at," Julien asked.

"No son, that's not where Disney World is. That is where I grew up, before I ran away to live here in Nova Scotia," Celine calmly responded.

"Do we still have more family living there," Julien continued?

"Yes, we do son! Matter a fact, I think it is time I brought you guys to meet your other grandmother!"

Tamara knew they would hate to see them leave the province, but she wholeheartedly supported the decision. After observing the reactions of many Nova Scotians toward her sister-in-law, Tamara would rather them relocate elsewhere than have her niece and nephew suffered through the humiliation. Even though Celine neglected to mention that she took actions against the woman who assaulted her, once they returned home from the mall that day, she immediately contacted her lawyer Mr. Igby and had him file assault charges. There was no way she was going to let that woman have the last laugh over her, after nationally embarrassing her and her family.

They all got dressed and left the apartment to bring the requested items to the funeral home. When they exited the building and began passing by the demonstrators, Celine unexpectedly turned off and walked over to the protesters. There was an unmarked police cruiser parked along the driveway, from which an officer leapt and began running toward the demonstrators. The mourning mother stopped a few feet away from the group of females and calmly spoke to them.

"I respect what you ladies are doing, but that woman lied about me on national TV! With all that aside, me and my family are getting ready to bury my late dear fiancée, so during this time we would appreciate if you people could just stop this, so we can bury Lloyd in peace," pled Celine who then turned and walked away?

When the approaching officer realized that the assailants were behaving civil, he stopped before he reached the group. Celine calmly dealt with the protesters then climbed into the Lexus RX with her family members, before they drove away from the area. Robin, Julien, and Tamara were flabbergasted at her actions; and praised her thereafter for taking such a courageous stance against the demonstrators. They drove directly to the funeral home which was a few miles away and met with Mr. Boulangerie, who collected the suit and Memory Stick from them. It was difficult for any of them to fully accept that Lloyd was forever gone, until the visit to the funeral home with his burial clothing made everything seemed official.

Once they had concluded at the funeral home, Celine and the kids accompanied Tamara to the Via-Rail Train Station. Lloyd's father was arriving from Toronto, Ontario, for the funeral, but had never physically met Celine or the kids, therefore they thought it would be a nice welcoming gesture. They reached the station twenty minutes before the train was scheduled to arrive, therefore they waited inside the Lexus until they heard the whistles of the train getting closer. Tamara had not seen her father in almost eight years, so she was very excited to see her old man. Both Tamara and her father had been texting each other throughout the trip, which took forty-eight hours and fifteen minutes before he arrived.

They all stood in the middle of the station looking around for Tamara's father. Celine saw a baldheaded man stepping off the train from a distance and got hypnotized by his facial features, which reminded her of someone she had lost. The resemblance was so striking that she could barely utter a word, instead she tugged on Tamara's jacket to gain her attention. When Tamara spun around and looked at Celine, she thought her sister-in-law was experiencing a heart attack, until she nudged her head directly ahead. There was no denying that the person headed towards them had to have been Lloyd father, because he had the same looks, body type, and walked similarly.

"Dad," Tamara shouted before she took off running like a little girl!

Tamara ran into her father's arms, and they gently embraced each other. All across the station hall were travellers hugging their loved ones, with whom they were reuniting after time spent apart.

"Mom, is that our grandpa," Julien asked?

Celine who was overtaken by emotions from watching Tamara and her father responded, "Yes son, that is your grandfather!"

When Tamara told her father that her companions were Lloyd's family, he immediately broke down into tears. They had spoken a few times over the years on the telephone, but never actually met in person. The introductions came at a bitter time in all their lives, yet it was also sweet, because of the positive energy they engineered.

"Dad, this is Celine, Robin and Julien!"

"Mr. Walker it is truly wonderful to finally meet you," Celine stated as she moved in to shake hands!

Instead of formally shaking Celine's hand, Mr. Walker moved in and gave her a huge hug, followed by a kiss on her left cheek.

"You may call me Marston! Boy you is beautiful! Lloyd found himself a beautiful woman, no wonder these kids are so beautiful! Hello, Miss Robin! Come give granddad a hug?"

Robin walked over and gingerly hugged her grandfather, who reached into his inner jacket pocket and gave her an envelope.

"I know you is around fifteen or sixteen right now, but I don't know what your age group is into these days, so I put the money in the envelope! You now go and buy what you want!"

Hearing there were funds inside the envelope excited Robin, who affectionately hugged her grandfather. "Thank you Grandfather, thank you," Robin exclaimed!

"What's going on Mr. Julien, you don't remember Grandpa or what?"

Julien moved to Lloyd's father with more enthusiasm than his sister did. As he drew closer to Marston, his grandfather bent down to one knee and gave him a huge hug. Before he rose to his feet, Marston unzipped his luggage and reached inside a side compartment. When he withdrew a classical Spiderman figure still unwrapped and gave it to Julien, the boy's face lit up like a Christmas tree. To show their gratitude for the gifts, both Robin and Julien took charge of their granddad's luggage and pulled it to the vehicle. Tamara drove Celine and the kids home first, before she headed home with her father.

The undertakers at Atlantic Funeral Home scheduled two viewings for Mr. Lloyd Walker. The first was supposed to take place from 1:00 PM until 3:30 PM, and the second from 7:00 PM until 10:00 PM. Mr. Boulangerie scheduled the viewing and the burial three days apart, therefore visitors were allowed to see Lloyd's body and spent all the time they wanted with him on the Wednesday. The religious ceremony was to be held that Saturday at the funeral home, before they transferred the body to the graveyard for burial.

Celine and the Walker family arrived at the 1:00-3:30 PM viewing at 12:38. Their party which consisted of Roslyn, Tamara, Robin, Julien, and Celine, were the first to arrive. Marston wholeheartedly wanted to see his son but decided to attend the evening viewing for two reasons. The Lexus was technically at its capacity without him and if Roslyn did not want to be around him, then he certainly would try to avoid her. There was another service ongoing in a separate hall, so there were people going in and out of the building. Celine, Tamara, and Roslyn had no idea there was another service scheduled, therefore they thought the other visitors were there for Lloyd. Once they entered the building and spoke with the attendant, he relieved their worries and pointed them to their function. The hall was already arranged with flowers, chairs, huge photos, and the looping video tribute to Lloyd on a huge screen. They had not yet transported the body into the room, but he was well dressed and waiting to receive his audience.

At 12:58 the mortician rolled the casket with Lloyd's body into the viewing hall. The mere sight of the casket affected every family member present, each of which started crying profusely. Roslyn was always prepared for the moment, therefore, she had her handbag loaded with serviettes to wipe her tears. Julien and Robin wanted to see their father, so they held each other's hand and walked ahead of everyone, while the others conjured up the strength to look at Lloyd. The mortician had opened the casket to allow the guests to see Lloyd's face, therefore Robin and Julien could see him quite clearly. Celine bravely walked up to the casket and hugged her children, as they all wept and stared at Lloyd.

It took Tamara a moment to conjure up the strength she needed to approach the casket, therefore she held onto her mother's hand and brought her along. As they drew closer to the casket and Lloyd`s body came into view, Roslyn began overexaggerating and tried throwing herself into the casket. Tamara had to physically restrain her mother from leaping into the casket, as Roslyn flared her arms and began behaving as if she were about to faint.

"My son, my son! My a only son! Why they take he? Why," exclaimed Roslyn, who had a handful of tissue that she used to wipe away the tears?

"It will be alright Mom! Calm down," Tamara pleaded!

After thoroughly looking at Lloyd and criticizing the job the morticians did to put him on display, Roslyn slowly walked away with Tamara. Both ladies took seats along the front row of chairs, that were reserved for the family members. Celine and her children were still standing at the casket speaking with and touching Lloyd, as they corrected any discrepancies they observed. The attendant opened the doors when the viewing officially began, to allow for any flow of traffic to move about freely. Julien stood by his father's side long after everyone else had taken up a seat in the hall. There were zero visitors for the first eighteen minutes which led the family members to wonder if anyone would show up.

The first person to pass by and pay his respects was Lloyd's foreman, who again gave his condolence to Celine and the other members of the family. Once Mr. Edge came in and stood by the casket expressing to Lloyd what losing him meant, it became as if the flood gates opened, as visitor after visitor started passing by. There were more strangers than actual people they knew, despite all the negative publicity that Celine had been receiving. Celine was surprised to see a few of the women who had been demonstrating outside her building, yet she showed them no malice. Many of the visitors were people who had interacted with Lloyd in one way or another, and were left with such admiration for him, that they had to pay their due diligence. With such a generous community in many ways, many of the viewers only heard of the tragedy; yet went to show their support. Most of the viewers stopped and expressed their sympathies to Celine and the other family members, who sat along the front row of chairs. At one point the lineup was through the door, which made Lloyd seemed like a celebrity in the province. By the time 3:30 rolled around Celine saw so many people passed by that she completely lost count. Luckily the attendant was keeping count and provided a total number of six-hundred and eighty-one visitors. According to the attendant, he had never seen so many visitors during one session, then to imagine there was a second viewing scheduled later that evening.

Despite losing her son, Roslyn was elated with the viewing he received. She felt proud as a mother to see the outpour of support from the community, which was excluded from the private burial ceremony, thus they attended his viewing. Apart from Lloyd's foreman, Celine did not see any of his friends or his workmates, but she understood that they would just be finishing work at that hour. They stayed at the funeral home until 3:58, due to the amount of people lingering behind to chatter about everything, from gun control laws to the criminals' using weapons. By the time Celine reached home she was exhausted physically and emotionally, moreover she only had a short time to gather herself and redo everything.

Roslyn asked to keep the children rather than have them return to the funeral home for the second viewing. It made sense allowing them to stay by their grandmother's, so Celine went home alone and made Tamara dropped them off. As soon as she reached home, Celine fixed a mug of hot coffee then went into her living room, where she sat in the dark and drank the beverage. She had developed a tendency to speak with Lloyd, even though he was not there to respond.

"I know you liked seeing all those people come and pay their respects to you earlier! But honestly baby, you deserve it all! Those people said some beautiful things about you! What am I telling you any ways, you were right there to hear for yourself! That was so tiring though, but I really can't wait until tonight to see your friends; and see how many more people coming out to see you!"

It was a little over a month until Christmas and Celine felt rather conflicted about continuing to reside in Nova Scotia. Without Lloyd in her life, she had very little reason to remain in the province, thus she reached for her cellular and dialled her landlord. Instead of prolonging the inevitable, Celine spoke with the landlord about terminating her rental agreement at the end of the month. They had been amazing tenants for more than ten years and the landlord knew of the demonstrations and public harassments she had endured, so he accepted the foreclosure of their lease without applying any penalties.

The clock said 4:56 when Celine finished the coffee and placed the mug on the side table. She rested her head back on the sofa and closed her eyes, where she began envisioning Lloyd as she fell asleep. Celine was so tired that she did not feel or hear her cellular vibrating on the sofa next to her, as a result, Tamara nervously drove to her apartment, after she tried several times to phone her. The buzz of the doorbell frightened Celine, who jumped from her sleep and looked at the clock. The time had elapsed to 6:44 and the second viewing was to begin at the top of the hour.

"Oh shit," Celine exclaimed as she leapt off the sofa and went to buzz Tamara in!

With Tamara heading upstairs, Celine unlocked the door and ran into her bedroom while she undressed herself. Her outfit for the evening was already prepared on the bed, so she threw on the dress and ran into the bathroom to check her face. There was no time to redo her makeup, so Celine touched up where possible and picked up her shoes. Tamara reached the apartment and entered as Celine ran from one room to another.

"Oh girl, you had everyone so worried! I tried calling you..."

"I know, I know, I fell asleep and did not hear the phone beside me!"

"Well, come on we're going to be late!"

"Let's go I'm right behind you! Where is Pops?"

"Outside in the truck!"

They reached the funeral home eleven minutes late and there was a lineup of people already there. Neither Celine nor Tamara felt concerned about who the people were there to see, so they took their time getting ready before they entered. An attendant from the funeral home went out to Celine and told her that they were waiting for her to commence the viewing, therefore they had to make haste and hurried inside. Lloyd's father had heard about the afternoon crowd, but he was astonished to see the number of people already waiting to see his son. As they went by the viewers, everyone began offering their sympathies and were eager to see Lloyd. Everything was already arranged, therefore the viewing ceremony started within three minutes after they entered the hall.

Marston was in good humor until they entered the hall and he saw the casket holding his son's body. Celine wanted them to get there earlier to allow him private time with Lloyd, but her unscheduled nap wrecked those plans. Once Marston saw the casket his legs became wobbly and could not keep him upright, thus he crumbled to the carpet near the back row of chairs. Tamara, Celine, and the attendant helped him onto a chair to sit and collect himself. Even though they had a lineup of viewers waiting to see Lloyd, Marston's health was more important, but he assured them that "the stress of the moment affected him!" With people waiting outside in the cold they decided to begin the viewing, so Celine and Tamara took their places in the designated area for family members.

Once they began allowing the viewers in, people began orderly paying tribute to Lloyd. Due to the late start and the frigid outdoor temperature however, viewers were not allowed to spend too much time by the casket. Lloyd's friends and coworkers who wanted more time with him were angered by the decision, but they understood the situation and abided. All the employees from the construction site who missed the afternoon viewing showed up to see their co-worker for possibly the last time. When Donette arrived with Elvis, she left him standing in line with some of his coworkers and went inside to loan her support to her friends. Tamara and Celine's closest girlfriend had become tight family friends throughout the years, therefore during their embrace, Donette offered her condolence. Celine was excited to see her dear friend, whom she hugged and offered a seat beside them. Each of Lloyd's workmates stuck around after they saw him, wherein they reminisced and joked about interactions they had with him. Marston sat at the back row of chairs until some of Lloyd's friends started gathering after they had paid their tributes. Garth was rather shaken up after he saw his close friend and was walking to join their workmates with tears in his eyes, when he noticed the facial likeness between Marston and Lloyd.

"Excuse me Sir, would you happen to be Lloyd's father," Garth asked with tears running down his face!

"Yes, I am! Marston Walker, pleased to meet you!"

"No Sir! The pleasure was all mine! I am your son's friend Garth. You had a great son! One of the best people I ever met," Garth stated as they shook hands! "Hey fellows, you all come meet Lloyd's father, Mr. Marston Walker!"

Each of the construction workers rushed over and almost fought to shake Marston's hand. They all expressed 'the wonderful type of character that Lloyd was, and how much they would miss having him around'! Just listening how sad the men were to have lost such a dear friend, motivated Marston to stand by the casket, therefore he thanked the workers for their testimonies. To get next to Tamara, Celine, Donette, and his son, Marston apologised to everyone in line as he walked by and made his way to the front row. Tamara and Celine were happy to have him join them as they greeted the viewers, who all passed by the family members to offer their sympathies. Celine introduced Marston to Donette, as he sat beside them with tears running from his eyes and a huge grin on his face. The female minister who was scheduled to do the eulogy at the funeral, passed by and introduced herself to show her support.

The lineup of viewers seemed like they would never end, thus they accepted visitors until 10:28 PM. Mr. Boulangerie and his employees were kind enough to stay later and allowed all those in line to pay their respects, instead of terminating the viewing at the designated hour. By the time Celine, Marston, and

Tamara left the funeral home it was 10:40 PM, moreover they had seen an additional nine-hundred and seventy-one viewers that night. Everyone was surprised by the number of people who went to see Lloyd that day, which was not the funeral home's record, but Mr. Boulangerie had to put the subtotal in their record book.

Tamara had to work over the next few days, as a result none of the family members saw each other until the morning of the funeral. When Marston learned that the ladies' plan was for Tamara to be their designated chauffeur on the day of the funeral, he decided to surprise everyone and rent a limousine. Lloyd's father called around town and found an affordable rate for a stretch limousine, therefore he booked it on his credit card to chauffeur them around town that Saturday. On the morning of the funeral, Tamara was overwhelmed with the amount of things she had to do, that she ended up being pressed for time and had to rush to pick up Roslyn, then get over to Celine and the kids. The limousine arrived on time, yet Marston said nothing about it until they stepped through the front door of her building, and there stood the chauffeur holding the door open. The gesture was so affectionate that Tamara nearly began crying and had to quickly dap the tears, before they started flowing and ruined her makeup. It was Tamara's first-time stepping foot inside a limousine, hence despite the occasion she was quite excited. The Lincoln Continental Limousine was quite roomy and came with all the amenities, such as glasses, ice, complimentary liquor, disco lights, massaging seats, sunroof, snacks, sodas, bottled water, movie screen, surround sound, and many other gadgets. Before they departed for their first location, the chauffeur opened the privacy parting between both compartments, introduced himself, and offered his sympathies for their loss.

When they reached Roslyn's apartment the chauffeur stepped out of the driver's seat and went around to the clients' entrance. Instead of letting her mother know on the phone they were being chauffeured, Tamara made Roslyn exit her building and stood looking around for the Lexus. Before her mother reached her boiling point, Tamara stepped from the limousine and called to her. Roslyn knew nothing of the transportation arrangements and seldomly spoke her mind, so even though she felt pleased with the limousine, she would have never disclosed it. As she entered the vehicle Roslyn hugged and greeted her daughter. She smirked and nodded her head at Marston yet, was rather dismissive toward him thereafter. Instead of behaving uncivil Marston pleasantly greeted Roslyn, however she refrained from looking in his direction and focused on her cellular phone. They were almost an hour early for the ceremony because, Celine made arrangement with Mr. Boulangerie to have Marston spend some time with his son. After picking up Roslyn, Greg drove directly to Celine's residence, where his passengers were already waiting for them inside the lobby.

Julien was ecstatic when he saw the limousine, knowing that meant he would not have to sit on anyone. The limited seat availability in the Lexus would have confined him to sit on his mother's lap, which he was never comfortable doing. Robin climbed into the Lincoln first and slid over beside her grandmother, before Celine and Julien entered. Once his passengers were all aboard, Greg reintroduced himself and reoffered his sympathies, before he departed for the funeral home. Following their pleasant greetings, the vehicle's occupants went silent as if they were total strangers. Julien sat looking around at everyone wondering why they were so quiet, instead of them encouraging each other to get through the day. Without them interacting the Atlantic Funeral Home seemed much further away, and every red light impeded their progress, hence Julien wanted to know if that was to be expected throughout the day?

"Mommy, is everyone going to ignore everyone like this at the funeral," Julien whispered?

Despite the lad's attempt to avoid being heard, everyone inside the Lexus caught his whisper. Marston reached for a glass and began fixing himself a shot of Scotch, to calm his nerves.

"Funerals are hard for some people to deal with son! Burying your relative is hard," Celine stated!

"Your mom is right Lil Nephew, right now my heart feels like it is beating a million miles per minute, because this is the day we bury my brother," Tamara declared!

"No man is ever supposed to bury his son, so as much as we still have you and your sister Robin, your father is gone forever," Marston added before he started crying!

"You all say true, but Julien more! We family of my son Lloyd, we need act like this," Roslyn exclaimed!

By the time they reached Atlantic Funeral Home there was thirty-seven minutes remaining until the scheduled start of the burial ceremony. They were all elegantly dressed underneath the warm jackets, as they made their way into the facility. Greg parked the limousine just off to the side of the funeral home, put up his feet, and phoned his girlfriend. Mr. Boulangerie was on hand to welcome the Walkers in and showed them to their private room, which had been decorated and prepared for their event. The preparations for Lloyd's burial service were managed by the director at the funeral home and his team, therefore the brochures and itineraries were printed and passed out to guests upon their arrival. Lloyd's body was not yet wheeled into the room, therein they had time to remove their jackets and got relaxed. Marston unexpectedly helped Roslyn to remove her coat, before he removed his, then hung them on the coat racks provided. The hall attendant who assisted them the previous Wednesday, went by the room to say hello to the family. Celine and Lloyd's relatives thanked him for maintaining the order and assured him that his regulative duties would be much lighter that Saturday.

When the door through which they transported the coffin opened, everyone's shoulders shrugged with fright as the mortician wheeled the body in. The room was warm, yet it felt as if a cold stiff breeze had blown through. All at once the ladies began sniffling, shortly before those sniffles turned to full fledged crying. Marston again chose to stay back and allowed everyone else to say their final goodbyes. Tamara and Celine had grown accustomed to Roslyn's extravagant behavior, therefore they walked on either side of her and held her arms. Julien was the first to walk up to the coffin and stood by his father's head, rubbing his hand through his hair. Robin walked up behind her brother and stood beside him, prior to adjusting her father's necktie. As Roslyn approached the casket, those who knew of her antics prepared themselves for whatever drama she had in stored. Contrary to everyone else, Marston had never been at the funeral home while Roslyn was there, thus he had no inkling what was to come. Approximately three feet away from the casket Roslyn began heaving as if she was having difficulty breathing.

"Lord my son! Lord my son," Roslyn shouted in English, before she closed her eyes and began repeating in Portuguese! "I beg of you Lord, please keep him safe in Heaven!"

The instant Roslyn opened her eyes and looked at Lloyd's face, she became lightheaded and fell unconscious. Marston rushed to help Celine and Tamara, who were struggling to hold Roslyn aloft and get her onto a chair. They all got her seated before Robin rushed to fetch her grandmother a cup of water, while Marston sat beside her and held her from falling. Not even a minute later Roslyn came back to her senses and was rather embarrassed to find her head leaning against her ex's shoulder. Robin returned with the cup of water and insisted that she drank it, hence she had no choice but to do as told. To allow their grandfather time to have a private talk with Lloyd, Robin agreed to stay with Roslyn while he went by the casket. With almost twenty-minutes until the beginning of the ceremony, Marston walked to the casket and stood over Lloyd with Julien standing across from him.

"You is really going to miss your daddy, aren't you?"

Julien could barely utter a word, so he nodded his head in agreement. The young lad's eyes were filled with tears as he stood there staring at his father. Marston could tell his son was a great dad due to the affections showered onto him by his children. Even though he financially cared for his children during their upbringings, he knew the bond he had with Lloyd was nothing close to the bond between Julien and his dad. He had walked away from the relationship he had with Roslyn when the children were rather young, but his son used that motivation to become a better all-around man. Both grandfather and grandson stood there staring at Lloyd until the hour for the ceremony arrived.

Minister Shaw who was the assigned preacher, entered the room ten minutes before the start. The minister had not met all the members of the family, so she went around and shook everyone's hand. Donette and Elvis were the first couple to arrive moments later and chose their seats across from the Walker family in the first row. Both families had gotten extremely close throughout the years, thus there were hugs all around between them. Elvis and Donette spoke briefly with Roslyn and offered their condolence for her loss. Over the next few minutes, the guests began pouring into the venue and filling the seats, as the clock ticked closer to the beginning.

Minister Shaw stayed by the entrance welcoming the guests up until three minutes before the program was scheduled to begin. As the time approached, she abandoned the post and left the hall attendant to welcome the late arrivals. The mortician went into the room moments before the ceremony started and closed the casket, then placed a wreath on top of it. Once the mortician departed, a pianist entered the room and went over to the piano close to the alter. Most of the guest were seated by then, after they paid their respects to the family and Lloyd. The pianist began playing hymns from a chart mounted before her, while Minister Shaw made her way to the alter. At the end of the hymn, Minister Shaw who stood with her bible at hand, asked that everyone 'bowed their heads' before she began praying.

The attendants in the audience were from several countries around the world, thus the coloured minister looked out at a multi cultural crowd. Lloyd worked with and befriended people from different nations, such as European, Middle Eastern, Caribbean, and Asians. After observing the nationalities of people who turned out to see the murdered father, Minister Shaw's opening comment was, "Lloyd must have been a remarkable human being by the sight of his friends!" The minister proceeded to preach a wonderful ceremony, followed by another hymn which was sang by everyone while they stood. The three of Lloyd's closest friends and his foreman Mr. Edge added to the eulogy and spoke to great lengths about his character. Each story told brought laughter and tears from those in the audience and highlighted the kind-hearted spirit of their deceased friend. Minister Shaw led with the singing of two additional hymns, before she completed the ceremony with another prayer.

With the ceremonial aspect of the funeral complete, it was then time to transport the body to the graveyard. Lloyd's three best friends, Mr. Edge, Marston, and three other workmates carried the coffin out to the hearse, where the driver rolled it into the transport. Celine and her gang climbed into their limousine and was the first vehicle to follow the hearse. The graveyard was only a few street blocks away, so the convoy formed behind the hearse and collectively drove there. When they reached the graveyard, Julien became the nineth male to help carry his father's coffin, which they brought over to the prepared hole.

Once everyone regathered around Lloyd's gravesite, Minister Shaw again stepped to the front and began the last ceremony with another prayer. Nearly everyone had tears in their eyes knowing they had reached the final leg with Lloyd. They all sang two consecutive hymns before Minister Shaw gave a short speech about going to Heaven and Saving Human's Soul. Following the speech, the minister again sang two Religious' Hymns, before she concluded the ceremony with a prayer. While she spoke the last prayer, the grave's men came in and slowly descended the coffin into the hole. Once they got the coffin levelled on the bottom, they began refilling the hole with the soil they previously removed. Most of the attendants were hugging each other while they shed tears and said their final goodbyes to Lloyd.

With the funeral festivities complete, it was then time for the repas celebration. Julien had already began playing around with the children who attended with their parents, while Robin linked with two teenage girls, who only fidgeted with their phones. Celine ensured that each of the guests had the address to the hall, which was only a few city street blocks up the road. The emotional eulogy speeches extended the time of funeral, so they were already late for the hall. Most of the guests left immediately for the hall, while some lingered by the graveside reminiscing about Lloyd. When Roslyn and the others reached the venue, Marston gave their driver the privilege to eat and drink whatever he desired, before he entered the building. Inside the hall the festivities quickly ramped up, with servers providing drinks and appetizers to the arrivals. The House DJ sounded as if he had played at a few ceremonies in the past, as he easily transformed the mourners to party goers.

The tables were filling up fast, but the handlers for the hall had secured the Walker's head table, which was well decorated with flowers, fruits platters, glasses, wine bottles in tubs of ice, Hors-d'oeuvres, plates, and utensils. Because they were running late the scheduled mealtime was moved forward half an hour, to allow for the other guests to arrive. With liquor and food in abundance, those who were yet to eat that day needed not worry about waiting. There were servers passing every few minutes with different appetizers for the guests to enjoy, until the primary meal was served. Marston called one of the servers and ordered himself a drink of Scotch and a Bailey's Rum Crème for Roslyn. Celine opened one of the wine bottles provided and began sharing it with Tamara and Donette. Robin was still a bit underaged to drink, nevertheless Celine fixed her a glass, before they all toasted to Lloyd.

During their meal Celine told her family members that she had an announcement to make. She had already been crying all day, still fresh drips of tears immediately began flowing from her eyes. Celine looked around the table at her children, their grandparents, their aunty, Donette and her husband, and told them of her decision to leave Nova Scotia. There was not a single negative comment from anyone, in fact her family and friends were elated that she could settle somewhere else peacefully. The already emotional day was made even more so, but it was a joyous occasion, nevertheless. The repas celebration was wonderful, and all their guests danced and had an awesome time. Julien and the other kids ran around until they were fatigued, while Robin and the teenagers complained 'their phones needed charging'! The food was remarkably excellent, and everyone loved the fact they did not have to pay for the liquor all afternoon. Several of the visitors got a bit too intoxicated to drive home and had to make other arrangements.

When they finally left the hall Greg drove Celine and the children home first. It was a very emotional goodbye between Marston and the children, due to him being scheduled to depart for Toronto in two days. They each exchanged contact information and vowed to visit, in order for the kids to keep that bond with their father's family. After they dropped off Celine and the kids and began heading to their second stop, Roslyn changed the directions given to Greg, and instructed him to drop off Tamara instead. Tamara knew better than to argue with her mother, therefore she was taken home while her parents went for a tour of the town.

Chapter 13

Attorney Baren Igby, his personal secretary Carmen Fern, and Celine, sat across the table during their private litigation with the lawyers who defended the CJCH News Station. Across the table were defence Attorney Antonio Calvio a Caucasian, Attorney Will Miser a Colored Man, and Attorney Rachel Olevia who was of Spanish Heritage. The overseer who sat at the head of the table was Judge D. Crowder, a Colored female who was born and raised in the province. Celine was suing the news station for $5.5 million for 'Defamation of Character', which they would have to prove occurred. Judge Crowder was listening and taking notes as Defence Attorney Rachel Olevia argued why she believed the case should be thrown out of court.

"Your Honor, the news business is a complex industry that relies on the truth and honesty of our citizens across this country! Our employer has always been a corporation of transparency and as a result, their reporters try to provide the honest facts behind each of the stories, that made the news cycle that day! However unfortunately, we can never vouch for what our eyewitnesses have to say, so one should not blame the station for other people's misinterpretation of the truth! The unblemished track record of this company proves that they take reporting the facts extremely seriously, which is why I believe this litigation has no merit and should be dismissed!"

"Thank you for your deliberation, Miss Olevia! Your request had been duly noted!" The judge took a few seconds to write down notes. "Your counter Mr. Igby?"

"Your Honor, if your actions result in ah, the degrading, the injury, or the death of anyone, ah, then you are undoubtedly at fault! Miss Devers here and her ah, children have been living through a nightmare because of ah, this news station, yet Miss Olevia would like us to believe that they ah, own no responsibility! Due to the reckless reporting of ah, their news station, Miss Devers has been attacked, harassed, and embarrassed by ah, strangers, for something she was never even ah, charged with by the police! We look forward to proving ah, our case before this hearing. Thank you, Your Honor," said the Frenchman, who struggled with his English!

The judge took a few seconds to jot down some notes before he rendered his decision.

"In light of your arguments, I see no reason why we should dismiss this case; therefore, we will be proceeding six weeks from today, the start of the new year at 10:00 AM on January 11th! We are adjourned until then ladies and gentlemen, happy holidays to you all," Judge Crowder stated before she rose from the seat and began leaving with her notes.

The lawyers bided Judge Crowder a Merry Christmas as she departed from the preliminary hearing. Both legal teams ignored each other as they packed up their documents to exit the Hearing Room. The Defense Team members were already debating the manner with which their case was argued, and who was best suited to take the lead going forward. Attorney Igby, Celine, and Carmen were the last to leave the Hearing Room, after the defense lawyers stormed out enraged because the judge did not side with them. Celine's attorney was quite pleased that the judge chose to hear the case, which she could have easily dismissed on the grounds of Free Press Journalism. Just before her attorney closed his leather bag, Mr. Igby realized he had forgotten to give Celine a newspaper clipping he brought, thus he handed it to her.

Once she read the subheading there was no need for any questions, hence she folded the paper and placed it inside her purse. The subtitle to the leading story read, 'Mall Attacker Slapped With Fine & Community Service'! There was a lengthy story that featured the woman's name and spoke in depth about the incident at the mall, how much she was required to pay for the fine, and how much community service she had to do. The story was definitely one of interest to Celine, but she could patiently wait until she reached home to read the details.

"This is all good news for you Celine," Carmen excitedly stated as she shook their client' shoulder!

"Well, we ah got the hearing date we ask for! So, now I expect that they will go and examine their case, then they might decide, put up fight or they settle with us," Mr. Igby explained!

"What do you believe they will do," Celine enquired?

"You never ah, know with this case! Maybe they ah, see something that, good advantage for them, you never know ah, what will happen," Mr. Igby stated!

"I decided to move back to my hometown before Christmas, to see my mother and other family members down there," Celine declared!

"I think that is ah, good change for you," Mr. Igby agreed!

"Just remind me, the date for the next hearing and I will be here on time," Celine asked?

"You do not ah, have to attend! We have all we ah, need to finish case without, you have come back," Mr. Igby exclaimed!

"Are you sure about that Mr. Igby?"

"If we need any ah, information from you, then ah, we contact you!"

"I have to thank you guys for all your help so far!"

"We still ah, have far to go! Not time we celebrate ah, as yet," the Frenchman declared with a smile, as they shook hands!

Within the next two weeks Celine's apartment went from fully furnished to almost empty. Marston had returned home safely and initiated contact with his grandchildren, therefore they began contacting each other frequently. Celine gave her bedroom set and living room sofas to Roslyn, whose furniture badly needed an upgrade. They donated piles of clothes, shoes, and other items to the Donation Center, which aided people who lived on the streets. Celine gave away their small appliances such as rice cooker, clothes iron, televisions, microwave, and pots to some of the people she had become friends with on their building. Tamara and Donette loved the pictures and decorative statues they had throughout the apartment, so Celine divided them equally and gave them to both ladies.

Two days before Robin and her family were scheduled to depart, Aunty Tamara offered to buy them lunch. Tamara knew that Mary Brown's Chicken was Celine's favorite, therefore she drove them to the restaurant, where they purchased the food and left. Roslyn's apartment was nearby, so Tamara suggested 'they ate there, then said their final goodbyes'. Celine was deeply saddened about leaving Nova Scotia, hence her decision to return home weighed heavily on her mind. She was so deep in thought that she simply nodded her head in agreement, without clearly hearing what Tamara said. Julien and Robin were excited to see their grandmother before they left the city, not knowing when they might again get the chance.

Everyone could tell Celine was depressed by the way with which she lagged behind, as they walked down the hallway to Roslyn's apartment. Tamara and the kids reached the apartment first and vanished inside the dark entrance. When Celine reached the door and entered the apartment, she thought that it was strange there were no lights on. She had been there many times to know where the light switch was, so she searched in the dark and powered on the light.

"Surprise, Happy Birthday," yelled thirteen family friends inside the apartment!

"Oh, my God! You guys nearly gave me a heart attack," Celine screamed as she moved forward into hugs from her children and the people who gathered! "Oh, thank you guys! Thank you so much!"

Roslyn was the third person to hug Celine after Julien and Robin, which surprised Celine despite their recent relationship adjustment. Tamara and Donette walked out from the kitchen holding a cake which had six burning candles around the edge.

"Happy birthday to you! Happy birthday to you! Happy birthday dear Celine/Mommy! Happy birthday to you," everyone began singing as the ladies brought the cake to the birthday celebrator!

"Go ahead make your wish and blow out your candles," Donette exclaimed!

Celine closed her eyes and blew out the candles before she reopened them. The attendants all cheered and individually hugged her before they moved into the days room, where liquor, food, and all the entertainment were taking place. Everyone at the birthday celebration were present at Lloyd's funeral, therefore many of them had to apologise for their intoxicated behaviors. They all enjoyed the cake before the adults pivoted to liquor and made a few toasts to Celine. Following all the recognition the females left and gathered inside the kitchen, while the men began playing Dominos and Poker inside the days room. Julien and the two little kids who came with their parents went into Roslyn's spare room, where they played around and amused themselves. There were no adolescents present, therefore Roslyn used Robin's help to wash and put away the dishes, glasses, and utensils.

"Girl we are taking you out tonight! Your ticket has been bought and we are going to have some fun tonight," Donette declared at which the other ladies began making erotic sounds!

"I don't really have the urge to go anywhere! And I don't want to spoil you guys' night, so I think I should sit this one out," Celine argued!

"No way sis! You have been going through a lot and a night out is exactly what you need to unwind! We are not taking no for an answer, so I'll pick you up at 9:00 O'clock," Tamara stated!

"Ok, but you guys have to at lease tell me where we going," Celine argued?

"That is private information girl! We go party," Donette declared!

"Woo-hoo," the other ladies shouted!

Celine had no idea that when the ladies mentioned taking her out for her birthday, they meant bring her to a sexual experience event such as, 'Girls Gone Wild'. The birthday girl thought they were heading to a club or some private party, until they pulled up at the event. There was already a lineup of females orderly entering the venue, yet strangely no sign of any males participating or stalking like vultures. The group of females had arranged a time to arrive, therefore within minutes they were all present. They gathered in the parking lot then joined the line, yet still Celine had no idea what sort of event they were entering. While they awaited entry, the event began inside with a loud ruckus, as the performers got introduced. There were no advertising signs outside the rented private hall, but as they stepped into the building it became evident what was transpiring.

"Oh my God! No, you guys didn't," Celine quarrelled!

"Yes, we did girl," Donette joked!

The engagement sign read, 'Girls Gone Wild' and featured the photos of three handsome and physically built male strippers. As cold as the weather was outside, some of the females started complaining they needed to cool down, because they were already getting excited. By the time they entered the venue the show had been ongoing for approximately seven minutes, yet there were females rushing to the restroom on a regular basis. Contrary to her counterparts who were heated and eager to enter the hall, Celine lost all her desire to proceed the instant she saw the 'Girls Gone Wild' sign. Nevertheless, as promised she tried to enjoy her birthday and the ambiance, knowing her time with the girls would be their last.

The coat check department was more of a nuisance to some of the ladies, who became frustrated when they had to wait for the others. Inside the hall was quite dark throughout, with a few colored spotlights flashing in different areas. There were indicative markers and lights at the bar, inside the DJ Booth, by the bathrooms, and highlighting the Emergency Exit. The house DJ had the hall buzzing with hype, as the female customers sat around drinking while the main attraction dancers performed. The Chip-N'-Dale Dancers were at different spectrums of the hall, doing sexually tantalizing things to the ladies, who showered them with money. Celine's group found an empty table and sat for a few minutes, before a waitress walked over to take their orders. The decision was already premade to purchase a bottle of hard liquor, therefore Tamara requested a bottle of Courvoisier.

One of the male strippers was servicing the ladies two tables away, by laying on the table while they caressed his shiny and oily muscular body. All of the ladies at the table wore married rings, yet they behaved as if they were single and available. The stripper was completely nude and had his hands inside the unbuckled pants of one female, and his other hand under the skirt of another woman. Both ladies were passionately moaning as they caressed their tormentor, then reached across his body and began kissing each other. Initially Celine and Tamara were the only two women who sat undisturbed by the explicit activities. There was no distracting most of their companions who were hypnotized by the leud actions ongoing several feet away.

When the waitress brought the liquor with the glasses, ice, and other items, Crissy handed her the money she had accumulated for the bill. Tamara opened the bottle of Courvoisier and fixed everyone in their group a shot, then summoned the other ladies for the first toast. The distracted women who were fascinated by the activities ongoing elsewhere, refocused their attention on the group.

"Glasses up high ladies! This is a special happy birthday to my sister-in-law! Many you live to see many more, we all love you," Tamara toasted at which everyone clinked their glasses and drank!

"Wait a minute everybody I have one more toast to make," Crissy stated before she took the bottle of rum and quickly refilled everyone's glass! With the other ladies holding their glasses aloft, Crissy looked at Celine and said, "I know we all share this sentiment, but I wish you success and good health going forward! May the Lord God bless you, and Robin, and Julien, and don't be a stranger, make sure you come back and visit us! But till then, I will make sure that your sister keeps flowers on Lloyd's grave! Here is to you Celine!"

Everyone shouted different cheers before they drank down the shots of liquor. By the time Crissy went around and refilled everyone's glass with the third round, the bottle was creeping close to its end. The hypnotized females went back to viewing the sexual antics, which had changed tables to the one beside theirs. The male stripper was giving each lady at the adjoining table a personal dance, where he would grind on them, and used their hands to caress his genital. If the female client was open to anything and wore a skirt, the dancer would lift them above his head, balanced her on his shoulders, and begin performing oral. Women were running to the bathroom after certain interactions with the strippers left them moist and vibrant.

Once the stripper finished pleasing all the women at the next table, he danced his way over to Celine's group. Donette and three of the women secretly spoke with the male exotic dancer, who then moved directly toward Celine. The dancer approached the mourning mother and started provocatively wining in front of her, before he jumped across her legs and grinded on her while she sat on the chair. The liquor had transformed Tamara from the conservative lesbian she had been all evening, into a liberated party enthusiast. While the dancer grinded on her sister-in-law, Tamara began slapping and grabbing his buttocks. All the women in the group began cheering and applauding, as the dancer tried to use Celine's right hand and rub it over his body. After physically forcing herself to enter the venue, having an exotic dancer fondle her was over the limit, therefore, Celine forcefully eased him off her. The stripper was a professional and knew when clients were only there for the show, therefore despite the agreement he made with Donette he moved to Julie. To avoid ruining the ladies' party, Celine kept smiling and clapped her hands in support of the performance. As she looked around the table her companions were far more into the activities than her, hence Celine drank down her third shot and excused herself. Tamara grabbed Celine's hand as she rose from the chair, but the frustrated mother pretended she was fine and signalled she would return.

"Honey, she probably has to go to the little girl's room and wipe herself up after a dance like that," Crissy commented!

With the rest of her friends having fun, Celine walked over to the bar and bought another bottle of Courvoisier, then tipped the waitress to bring it over to their table. For reasons beyond her understanding, she felt filthy like she needed to rush home and shower immediately. The exotic dancer did not touch any of her private parts, yet she felt as if she had disrespected Lloyd's memory, by having another nude male wine on her. Celine went to the bathroom and used the facility to urinate. While inside the bathroom stall, she used her cell and summoned a taxi to the address. When she emerged from the toilet stall, she washed her hands and walked directly out of the hall. None of her associates realized she had walked out, while they fondled with the stripper and showered him with money. The mourning mother felt as if she did not belong there, so she reclaimed her jacket, got dressed and exited the building. Three minutes after Celine walked outside the taxi pulled up, at which she climbed in and they drove away.

Two days later when Tamara went to pick up Celine, Julien, and Robin for the train station, she was extremely quite for the first few minutes. Robin and Julien knew that their aunty cared deeply for them and thought her silence was due to the hurt she felt by them leaving. To ignore the situation, Robin placed her ear-bugs into her ears and began listening to music. Contrary to Tamara, Celine felt like she should have told her sister-in-law of her intention to leave the Chip-N'-Dale stripper event. With the silence becoming deafening inside the Lexus, she tried to smooth matters over with her sister-in-law before they reached the station.

"I apologize for leaving the show and not telling you the other night, but all of that was way too much too fast for me," Celine stated!

"I apologize to you also sis! You showed me that despite everything mom and I said over these years, you really loved my brother," Tamara responded!

Celine took out the spare train ticket and passed it to Tamara. The gesture brightened up the young lady's face and brought out her pleasant smile.

"I know we have to come and visit Roslyn and the rest of you guys, but you can come by train whenever you ready," Celine exclaimed.

"Oh sis, you are going to make me cry," Tamara declared!

"You don't have to cry Aunty Tamara, I am going to come and look for you," Julien said!

"Thanks Jules!... As for you I wish you had dragged me out of that place before you sent that second bottle over! Girl I got so drunk! They said I was on the table with my fanny in that stripper's face," Tamara whispered loudly!

"You guys went to see strippers," asked Julien who overheard the comment?

"No, no, no, Julien, Aunty Tamara meant to say slippers," Celine intervened!

"But that does not make much sense Mom," Julien argued?

"Julien put your headphones on and mind your own business," fired back Celine!

The young lad did as

nstructed by his mother, who knew the questions would never stop coming. Once Julien placed the headphones over his ears, the female continued their conversation.

"What, how did that happen," Celine asked?

"Too much Courvoisier! Talking about me, you should have seen your girl Donette! She almost got kicked out for trying to rape that second stripper," Tamara declared!

"Ha-ha-ha-ha, you're joking! Did she forget she is a married woman," Celine asked?

"Maybe that was it! But she pinned that guy on the floor and kept telling him, you're going to take this work; and you know how discreet those dancers have to be, so he started calling for security, then they came over and got into it with Donette! Oh, girl you should have seen it! It got crazy in that place," Tamara explained!

Celine laughed until she nearly peed on herself. They continued their chat until they reached the train station, where they parked the vehicle and dismounted. Tamara helped with the many luggage they carried, despite getting rid of the majority of the things they owned. As they walked into the station the tears began flowing among the family members, knowing they were separating from each other. The train was scheduled to depart in twenty minutes, so they said a very emotional farewell to each other, before Celine and the kids checked in. Once they boarded the train it was difficult for Tamara to see them, therefore she walked back to the Lexus with tears in her eyes and a smile on her face.

Chapter 14

The five days and nine hours VIA Rail trip to Winnipeg, Manitoba, was surprisingly quite relaxing on the train. The accommodations purchased by Lloyd, allowed for them to have a room to sleep, and most of the amenities they enjoyed at home. They all had their individual devices to keep them occupied, board games, plus each other's company during those times of boredom. There were many remarkable sights to see across the country, thus they spent a lot of time looking out at the beautiful sceneries. The meals were excellent, and their tickets allowed for them to get smacks and liquor, which was pleasing to everyone. Even though they would have been at their destination in a matter of hours by plane, or a day and a half by car, they knew Lloyd chose the lengthy train ride to spend more time with his family.

By the time they arrived in Winnipeg, Manitoba, they were eager to reach their destination, so Celine chartered a taxi to carry them the duration of their journey. Dominion City, Manitoba, was still 92.3 KM away, and would take an additional hour and thirteen minutes to reach, along the Lord Selkirk Hwy 75 South. After being gone for so long the scenery was a blur to Celine, but once they exited the highway and started driving through town, she distinctively remembered certain places. The town had not undergone any major transformations throughout the years, so aside from a new structure here and there, everything was pretty much the same.

There were still five days left before Christmas when they arrived at Mrs. Shirley Lynn Devers' house. The neighborhood was much older than their residence in Nova Scotia, and most of the houses looked like they needed repairs. Celine's mother's house was one of the few residents on the block, which looked like it had been maintained adequately over the years. The sixty-five-year-old grandmother was inside her living room dressed in workout gear, doing her exercises on a mat. Miss Shirley was mimicking the actions of a workout professional, who she keenly watched on her television. When Robin sounded the doorbell, Miss Shirley could be overheard cursing as if she was upset, she was being disturbed. The taxi had already left, therefore Celine and her children stood on her doorstep with all their luggage. Despite her advanced age, Miss Shirley routinely dyed her grey colored hair, therefore she looked more like Celine rather than their grandmother. Both Julien and Robin were dumbfounded and thought they were looking at their mother's none-existent older sister, when Miss Shirley opened the door and responded.

"Who the hell is disturbing my exercise..." Miss Shirley began before she opened the door and saw Celine and the kids?

"Hello, Mom," Celine declared!

Miss Shirley as commonly known was frozen and stared at Celine, Julien, and Robin for a few seconds with her mouth at awe.

"Celine! This is such a surprise, come in, come in," Miss Shirley said as she hugged Robin and Julien!

"Hi Mom, these are your grandkids, Robin and Julien," Celine introduced the kids before she realized there were pictures of them already framed on the wall.

Miss Shirley noticed the engagement ring on Celine's finger and thought Lloyd and her had gotten engaged. "So, where is Lloyd," she then asked?

Everyone's facial expressions changed instantly from joy to a deflated look. Both Robin and Julien's heads dropped toward the floor, at which the young lad began shedding tears.

"Aaron shot and killed him inside a convenience store a few weeks ago," Celine answered.

"What," Miss Shirley exclaimed as she covered her mouth with her right hand?!

Just rethinking and discussing the incident brought tears to Celine's eyes. Her mother was stunned and had to sit on the chair she stood next to, to avoid fainting. Instead of tears, Miss Shirley's face became hardened with anger, however she pivoted from the sad conversation and chose to discuss those details another time.

"I will pray for them in church on Sunday. More importantly, let me see my grandkids! Just put those winter coats over there and we'll take care of them later," Miss Shirley instructed!

Celine took the kids' jackets and hung them all inside the coat closet, then quickly rearranged their boots. Robin walked over to her grandmother and hugged her, before Julien followed her lead. Instead of bringing the stack of luggage where they should go, their mother walked over and gave Miss Shirley a tight hug with a kiss on the cheek. It was a very emotional moment for them both, after the many years apart, plus the tribulations they went through prior. The house was where Celine grew up, so she knew every aspect of the dwelling. There were three bedrooms, a laundry room, two bathrooms, a dining area, and the kitchen located on the main floor; and two more bedrooms, a bathroom, furnace and hot water tank room, and an open area in the basement. Once they were through hugging, Celine went back to attending to their luggage. Every house throughout the community sat on decent sized lots, with ample space for neighbors to mind their own business.

"You can let Robin stay in your brother Charles' room," Miss Shirley shouted!

"Where is Charles," Celine asked as she dragged two suitcases behind her?

"Oh, Mr. Bigshot now lives in Vancouver," Miss Shirley responded! "Are you guys hungry? Would you like something to drink?"

"Sure grandma," Robin answered!

Julien nodded his head in agreement, thus Miss Shirley stood up and walked into the kitchen with them both.

"You live in this big house by yourself grandma," Julien asked?

"Not really Julien, my other son Coy lives here too, but he is at work!"

"What kind of work does he do?" Julien asked?

"Oh, he has a mechanic shop in town!"

"Where did you get all those pictures of us," Julien asked?

"Your father mailed them to me a while ago."

"Did you...," Julien began before Robin interrupted?

"Jules, enough with the questions already! You have to see with him grandma, he gets carried away with the questions sometimes," Robin stated!

"Ha-ha-ha-ha! It's OK Robin, you guys can ask me anything you desire!"

"See, told you! Did you ever meet my dad," Julien continued?

"No, I was expecting him to bring you guys here to meet me! We spoke a few times over the phone, but I never met him!"

"He was a great dad! We all miss him," Julien said!

"So, what would you guys like to eat? We can make hamburgers, hotdogs, spaghetti, whatever you like?"

"Hamburger with French Fries," Julien asked?

"Coming right up, Julien! And you Robin, what would you like to eat?"

100

"I'll take the same thing too grandma!"

Celine came back from the bedroom and picked up two more luggage and began carrying them to another bedroom. Robin wanted to see more of the house and get some of the family history, which her mother never spoke of before.

"Mom, do you want some help with those bags," Robin enquired?

"Yes honey, grab that last one and follow me!"

Robin got the bag and followed her mother to the room. Miss Shirley had a lot of family pictures in frames at certain areas of the house, therefore as they walked down the hall Robin noticed a picture with her grandmother, an older gentleman, two young boys, and her mom as a little girl.

"Mom, who are the people in this picture? Is that you? I can tell this is grandma, but who are the other people?"

"You are right, that is me! Then that was our father Charles Senior, that is your Uncle Coy and your Uncle Charles Junior!"

"What happened to grandpa?"

"He was in an accident at work one day, where some machine fell on him and crushed him! I never forgot that day. I came home and mom was crying because she had just gotten the news. When she told me I ran to the place where he worked, but one of dad's friend stopped me from getting in! There were so many people angry and shouting, that I ran back home, and things were never the same after that!"

"How old were you when that happened?"

"I was fourteen, and I used that anger to keep getting into trouble after that! Until I ended up in Nova Scotia, with a guy whose mother had kicked him out and sent him to live with his father, because he was getting into too much trouble! His mother thought his dad would discipline him, but the father was a drunk and didn't give a shit! So, before I Knew it, I was hundreds of miles away from home, with a timebomb for a boyfriend, who was just a loser!"

"What kind of a man was granddad?"

A smile slid across Celine's face as she recounted memories of her father. "That man was the greatest! Dad was like a revolutionist and would always talk about his belief, that black folks should exhaust all means of fighting to gain equality, because the white men who he worked with were getting more money than him! When he died lots of people thought it wasn't an accident, but no investigation was ever done. He did everything for his family, worked hard, played with his children, and most importantly, he loved his family! I missed him so much that I searched for that love in the wrong places, until I met your father! Anyways, this is your room and across there is me and Julien, until he kicks me out, then I might have to move to the basement."

By the time Celine and Robin got through putting away their luggage and returned to the kitchen area, Julien was being given the royal treatment. The boy had a slice of Vanilla Pound Cake in a bowl, that was covered with a mountain of Vanilla Ice Cream and a humongous smile on his face. It was already evident that Miss Shirley was going to spoil her grandson, regardless of what anyone thought.

"What were you cooking for dinner Mom," Celine asked?

"Just some vegetables to go with the fish I made for dinner yesterday! I have to watch my figure, you know what I mean Julien," Miss Shirley joked!

Julien raised up his head from the bowl of ice cream for a second to chuckle at the joke, before he dived right back in. Celine walked over to the refrigerator and looked inside.

"Can you drive me to the grocery store mom, so I can pick up a few things? I have to get some cereal and other stuff for breakfast for these two," Celine enquired!

"Of course, I will dear! I'll go freshen up and be back in a few minutes!"

Once Miss Shirley returned from showering and changing her attire, they all dressed for the outdoor temperature and departed for the store. Miss Shirley drove an older model two door Oldsmobile, Cutlas Supreme, which used to belong to her husband. Even though her transport was older than most of the vehicles on the road, her son kept the car in excellent condition. Despite the annoyance of constantly having to readjust the front seats to allow the rear passengers accessibility, the vehicle was quite comfortable and spacious. Contrary to the larger cities, the smaller towns had far less access to food distributors and gas stations, therefore the only place to get groceries for the next thirty miles, was at Calderwood's Country Store Inc, on Waddell Avenue East.

Celine had been driven by Tamara on a few occasions in the past and thought her sister-in-law's foot was rather heavy on the gas. However, her mother drove at a completely opposite pace and was slower than a crawling turtle, which compelled other motorists to honk their horns occasionally, then sped pass her. Regardless of what other drivers did, Miss Shirley maintained her velocity to and from her destination. Before she pulled out of her driveway she would customarily put on her seatbelt, engage the thermostat, and turned on her Gospel Music. There was hardly any snow on the ground, yet she drove at her own pace, thus her Speedometer Needle hardly touched forty miles per hour.

The houses and businesses throughout the town all sat on their individual properties, compared to the larger cities where they were more compact to conserve space. Robin and Julien thought the buildings in Nova Scotia looked more modern than those in town and raved on about the huge malls they would visit. As they drove through the town, Celine began remembering some of the sights from her childhood years. The first recognizable building she saw was her old school, which was located four blocks from the house on Franklin Avenue.

Celine recalled walking along the streets to school with other kids from her area and the antics they would do during those trips. The Roseau Valley School was the only educational center in Dominion City, with the closest facility being Ginew School almost seven kilometers away. The school systems operated differently in the rural areas of Manitoba South, wherein students attended the same facility from kindergarten until high school.

"Hey guys look! That was my old high school slash elementary school," Celine boasted!

"Is that how the schools are down here? Or can I register somewhere else," Robin asked?

"Yep! There is only one school in town. Always has been, and always will be" Celine responded!

"So, you had to go to the same school from my age till Robin age Mom," Julien asked?

"That is how it is here in Dominion City, Honey" Celine responded!

"How about college and university," Robin enquired?

"For those courses, you will have to go to the bigger cities like Winnipeg," Celine stated!

"What do the kids do around here for fun, Grandma," Robin enquired?

"Well, we have an arena for the youths who play hockey, and I guess a few different programs for some other sports, but not very much I believe we should have had more! I think that is the reason why so many young people move away and don't come back," Miss Shirley explained!

"How long have you lived here Grandma," Robin asked?

"Oh, nearly forty years Baby! I met your wonderful grandfather Charles Senior in Vancouver one year; and he said, 'I'm going to take you city girl away to a place where you can feel free and breathe'! Then he brought me to this beautiful town! I've felt free and breathed ever since!"

They reached the Calderwood's Country Store Inc, which like most businesses in Dominion City was the only facility of its kind for miles. Julien and Robin had begun comparing everywhere they saw to the places in Halifax, which had a much greater population and a vibrant city atmosphere. Dominion City was certainly country with its smaller population of one-thousand-three-hundred-and-seventy-five residents. Most of the people knew each other and were relatively polite to their neighbours, aside from a few devious residents. The store was well stocked and had most of the items they needed, so after a walk through the isles they approached the cashier with their packed grocery cart. There were three people ahead of them in line, an elderly man getting his items tallied, and a Caucasian couple standing next to each other behind their cart.

When the female cashier saw Celine's mother with a younger version of herself and the two kids, she immediately stopped calculating the products and walked away from the register.

"Celine Devers, is that you," asked the cashier?

"Yes," Celine exclaimed as she spun around to see who the person was!

"Ah, excuse me! You did not finish with my..." began arguing the old man.

"Shut up and wait Bernie," fired back the cashier!

Once Celine saw who the female was, they ran towards each other and hugged like two lost sisters. Miss Shirley and the kids were surprised to see the reception Celine received, as friends began popping up from all over.

"Karen," Celine shouted as they hugged!

"Oh my gosh, Celine Devers," Karen shouted! "Maxine and Steve look, it's Celine!"

"It's really Celine Devers," Steve exclaimed!

"You have hardly changed since the last time I saw you," Maxine commented!

The male and female who were ahead of them in line joined the hugging party, therefore before long they were all teary eyed and overjoyed.

"Mark, Mauve! You guys come quick, it's Celine from Roseau Valley," Karen shouted!

A female from the produce, fruits, and vegetables section and a male from the butcher department came running from their posts and hugged their classmate like a long lost relative. Celine introduced her children and reintroduced her mother to her old friends, none of whom she had spoken to since she ran away. Each of her ex-schoolmates reacted as if her departure left a void in their lives, and they were excited to have her return. While they stood there reminiscing for the next few minutes, everyone in line were forced to wait until Karen felt like returning to her station. The reunion Celine shared with some of her old classmates gave her a different mindset of Dominion City, which she thought had been abandoned by everyone she knew. They all finally agreed to arrange a date where they would meet up with several of their other schoolmates and enjoy a wonderful evening together.

When Celine and her family members got back home, she unpacked the bags while everyone else went about doing other things. Robin took their Tablets and other devices and began connecting them to the house's Internet WIFI, while Julien played all throughout the upper level of the house with his toys. Contrary to the appetizing meals they received on the train, Celine wanted her children to have a full healthy meal, therefore she began cooking supper. Miss Shirley had a routine of watching certain programs at those hours of the day, so she went into the living room and watched her television. Within minutes the flavourful aromas of herbs and spices began filling the house, as Celine prepared a feast for a king. There was a Maple Honey Ham well seasoned placed into the oven, Curry Chicken with White Rice on the stove, Sweet Potatoes and Yams cooking, Macaroni Salad, Corn Bread baking, a Vegetable Salad, and a freshly prepared Fruit Punch drink. The food aroma began interrupting Miss Shirley, who had to abandon her regularly scheduled programs to check out what her daughter was cooking.

Miss Shirley did not want Celine to think she was watching her to evaluate her cooking talents, so she walked into the kitchen and went to the refrigerator. Celine took notice of her mother, who opened the fridge door and stood there staring inside. It was evident that Miss Shirley did not want anything inside the kitchen, rather than to eavesdrop on her daughter.

"Would you like some of the Fruit Juice I just made mom," Celine asked?

"Well, let me try some? Because I don't see anything else inside here to drink," Miss Shirley argued even though Celine had just stacked a few boxes of juices in there!

Celine poured her mother a glass of her Fruit Punch Juice and passed it to her. Miss Shirley took the glass and smelt the wonderful aroma, then looked over the items cooking on the stove. When Miss Shirley tasted the juice and realized it was absolutely delicious, she began walking back into the living room with a hidden smile on her face.

"I think I am going to need this juice recipe," Miss Shirley demanded as she walked away?

Celine realized that her mother wanted to hold a conversation, but she had become so accustomed to spending most of her days by herself, that she easily abandoned the notion. To make the process easier for her mother, she lowered the fire beneath the pots on the stove and went into the living room, where Miss Shirley sat watching more of Julien playing on the ground, rather than her actual show. The young lad would make all sorts of noises, as he played with his action figures and a few toy vehicles.

"Julien, Grandma is watching TV! Can you please stop all that racket," Celine demanded?

"I'm sorry Grandma," remorsefully said Julien!

"No, no, not at all my Grandson! You keep playing right there, you remind me of your uncles when they were about your age," Miss Shirley insisted!

"So, how have you been Mom? How is your health," Celine asked?

"Well, a little Arthritis here and there, but overall, my doctor thinks I'm in great shape for my age! I exercise at lease five times every week, and make sure I go to church every Sunday, so the Good Lord keeps blessing me," Miss Shirley boasted!

"How are you doing with the bills for the house?"

"We paid off the house with your brothers working a few years ago. So apart from my hydro, water, cell phone bills, and miscellaneous stuff, I pretty much do OK."

"How about the house, does it need any major repairs?"

"No honey, the house is fine! You asking like you won the Lotto or something!"

"I just got some money coming in from Lloyd's insurance; and then I stand a good chance of winning a lawsuit I have ongoing against a news station in Nova Scotia."

"Why are you suing this news station?"

"Because after Aaron killed Lloyd they did an interview with Aaron's girlfriend, who told them all sorts of lies about me! That led to people demonstrating outside our apartment, people being obnoxiously rude out in public, I couldn't take it anymore, so I had to sue the news station for compensation!"

"How much can you get for a lawsuit like that?"

"I don't know, but I'm asking for five million!"

"Five million dollars," Miss Shirley surprisingly exclaimed!

"Grandma, someone just parked in your driveway," Julien stated after looking through a window!

A key sounded in the front door lock before it flew wide open. Celine's younger brother Coy walked in looking around and sniffing the succulent food aroma.

"Where is my big sister," Coy demanded?

Celine stood up and ran into her brother's arms, despite his greasy and filthy overall uniform from work. Robin overheard the excitement and walked out of the bedroom, to find her mother hugging Coy.

"Why didn't you call or visit all these years? I really missed you," Coy stated!

"I missed you too Coy! But, how did you know I was here," Celine asked?

"Sis, nothing happens in this town that I don't know about," Coy stated!

"Get over here kids," Celine yelled! "This is your Uncle Coy!"

Julien ran into Coy's arms like his mother before him, but Robin became rather conservative once she noticed how filthy he looked. Instead of quickly approaching her uncle, Robin displayed a huge smile as she slowly advanced toward him. When she reached approximately four feet away from Coy, she suddenly stopped and unexpectedly stretched out her right fist for a knuckle bump.

"Not that I don't want to get right in there Uncle, but you need to freshen up a bit and change those clothes before we get the hugging thing going," Robin joked!

Coy laughed the loudest of everyone, as he knuckle bumped his niece in return.

"You are just like Celine when she was your age! Nothing dirty could come near her," Coy joked!

"Hurry up and get in the shower Coy, so we can all have supper together," Miss Shirley exclaimed!

Within a half hour the food was ready to be devoured and Coy had transformed his appearance from the greasy mechanic to Mister Devers. Robin was the first to greet her uncle with a warm hug, which Coy graciously accepted with humility. The mechanic was so happy to see his sister after many years apart, that he telephoned their other sibling in Vancouver to gloat. Julien and Robin were able to meet a part of their family they never knew existed, because their mother chose never to mention them. Celine had an awesome homecoming for her first day back, especially after she spoke with her other brother Charles Jr, who promised to visit them during the summer.

Following their phone conversation, the family members sat at the dining table and bowed their heads, while Miss Shirley said a prayer for them all. Coy could not wait to get at the food that he dived right in after they said 'Amen', then repeatedly stated that 'his mother would not prepare such a feast during the week'! They devoured most of the meal, during which Coy took three servings and cleaned every plate. It was indeed a pleasure for Miss Shirley to have her daughter and grandkids under her roof, even though she would not admit the obvious, the look was all over her face. There were still unsolved issues between Celine and her mother to work out; but having her daughter back in their lives was the first step to repairing all ails.

Chapter 15

Dominion City had a small community wherein not much excitement happened daily. Contrary to the larger cities, their Christmas Season went by similar to the rest of the year. There was no dressing up of the town with a decorated tree in the center, neither did they have ornaments nor flowers hanging from light-posts, because they did not have a budget for such displays. Regardless of the town's inability to publicly celebrate the holiday, most residents decorated their homes with extravagant ornaments and lighting. Miss Shirley's front yard was not as decorated as her neighbors, nor did she string up any lights across the house, but she had a Santa carving and Merry Christmas sign in the front window.

Celine moving back to town with her children was the biggest news event in months, thus the locals gossiped about her possible reasons for returning. With all sorts of rumors circulating, news would often get back to Miss Shirley through her girlfriend Lorna, who would always either telephoned or visited to disclose whatever she had learned. There were so many juicy speculations depicting people's assumptions behind Celine's return, that Lorna felt it would be an injustice if she did not deliver them in person to see her friend's reactions. It was 7:27 AM when the news carrier buzzed Miss Shirley's door, but Celine's mother had already been awake for nearly two hours. Since she awakened, Miss Shirley cleansed herself and dressed for the day, prepared a pot of morning coffee, made two Bagel with Cream Cheese sandwiches, then sat down to eat while she read her Bible. Coy emerged from his den moments later and poured himself some coffee inside his thermos, then picked up his sandwich and began eating it. After he gave his mother a kiss on the cheek, the mechanic scampered off to work through the door. Everyone else inside the house was still sound asleep, following an evening where they assembled Miss Shirley's old Christmas Tree and played Monopoly late into the night.

Lorna's buzz of the doorbell awoke Celine, who rolled over in bed and looked at Julien. The resemblance between her son and his father was uncanny, therefore she laid there staring at him while she reminisced on some of the good times she shared with Lloyd. As she stared at Julien she could hear the female visitor's voice, but she had no idea who the person was. Celine thought to climb out of bed and go see who her mother's visitor was, however, she decided to lay there a minute and listened to their conversation. The female visitor had a powerful voice that could be heard quite clearly across the top tier of the house, so Celine did not have to do much to eavesdrop on their conversation.

"I know you enjoying them grandkids, Shirley! All those years you been on those boys telling them they need to produce before you die," Lorna commented as they walked to the kitchen!

"It's surely a big change around this old house I tell you, Lorna! This place was like a graveyard before those two babies got here," Miss Shirley said as she poured Lorna a cup of coffee!

"How is Celine liking it back here so far?"

"Well, she hasn't done much besides going for her walks and helping me fix up this old place! Literally everyday she hooks up with some old friend from school, who got her number and called to see how she has been doing. But its fun having her back home, our relationship is way different now, as you know motherhood changes most people!"

"It sure does! That and time tends to heal all wounds!"

"Amen to that!"

"Shirley, you won't believe some of the things, folks being saying about Celine coming back! I heard that Sister Tinya called, 'Celine a fugitive wanted for killing her boyfriend in Nova Scotia'! According to her big mouth sister Wendy, 'Celine was flat broke and had to crawl to your doorstep begging for food!"

"Say what! Excuse me?"

"Yeah! Them girls down by Cora's Salon have some ongoing bet, where the choices were either Celine is going to rob your money and take off; or live here for free without paying a thing! Someone who was sitting right there when all this happened, told me that almost everybody bet that she was going to rob your money and skip town!"

" Are you serious? The nerve of those people!"

"Good morning," Celine exclaimed as she walked into the kitchen! The instant she gazed upon Lorna, she recalled the face from her early childhood days, so Celine rushed over and gave her mother's dear friend a warm hug.

"Wow, Celine, look at you all grown up! A mother now and you look great!"

"Oh my God! Miss Lorna its wonderful to see you! How have you been," Celina declared?

"I've been keeping well my dear! I just passed through to tell your mother all the disgusting things people have been saying about you behind your back!"

"None of that stuff doesn't bother me at all Miss Lorna! As far as I'm concerned people can say whatever they want," Celine stated as she fixed herself a cup of coffee!

"She sound just like you Shirley! Don't take crap from nobody!"

"You know that's how I raised my children Lorna! I continued after their father died and did my best as a single mother! It was tough for us at times, but God always provided a way!"

"Nice seeing you again Miss Lorna," Celine said as she began exiting the kitchen while she drank the hot beverage!

"It was good seeing you too Celine! I prayed so much over the years for your safe return, that I'm rejoicing in my heart," Lorna responded!

"Mom I'm going to take a shower. But do you think you could bring me to Winnipeg later this morning?"

"No problem, where do you plan on going," Miss Shirley asked?

"Ah, I think we'll go purchase a new car. It's almost time for Robin to start driving anyways; and that boat that you call a car is way too big to teach her with," Celine indicated!

Even though Lorna and Miss Shirley were best friends, Celine could tell that their visitor loved being a broadcaster for the town's gossip, therefore she expected word to get around the community rather quickly. As she walked toward the bedroom, Celine could hear Lorna revealing other comments made by the locals about her. The young mother assembled her son's and her outfit for the day, then awoke Julien as she headed out to the shower. Before she went into the bathroom, Celine peeked into Robin's room and advised her 'to wake up because they would be heading into town'. By the time she finished her shower and exited thirty minutes later, Lorna had gone home, and Miss Shirley was watching television. Once the children showered, got dressed, and ate their breakfast they left for Winnipeg, which was a much larger city than their town.

Before they left town Miss Shirley had to refill her gas tank, therefore they drove to the Co-op Cardlock Service Station on Centennial Drive. Neither Robin nor Julien had ever seen such a unique gas station, which was off the main on a dirt road. There was a small portable office on the property, a single bay workshop and four large tanks that stored the fuel. Contrary to larger gas stations the Co-op Cardlock had one pump, therefore they could only service one vehicle at a time. The service attendant who filled their tank with gasoline, was Julious Simms, a colored seventeen-year-old member of Miss Shirley's church. Julious was the first brown complexion youth Robin saw in town; however, she was dumbstruck by his handsome looks. Miss Shirley looked back through her rear-view mirror at the same time and caught her granddaughter staring at Julious, who was simply doing his job and did not realize he was being watched. The kids were more accustomed to modern service stations, where customers could enter the store and purchase other items, but there was no such facility in Dominion City.

Around town Miss Shirley drove like a hearse during funeral processions, however she immediately transformed to a speedster the instant she entered an inter-provincial highway. Celine and the kids were nervous that the drive to Winnipeg might take them three-hours, but they were pleasantly surprised when they arrived in fifty-eight minutes. During the journey the family member's primary topic was what type of vehicle Celine intended to purchase? When Celine made the announcement 'they were getting a new vehicle', she only did so to silence the town folks, therefore she had no clue where or what to shop for. Julien recalled an interaction he had with his father one day on the street, where Lloyd mentioned that 'he had taken a liking to the Jeep Grand Cherokee 4X4'! With no other preferences mentioned they decided to visit a Chrysler dealer and test drive the Cherokee. Robin located a Jeep dealer's address on her phone and added it to her Google Location Finder, to bring them directly to the dealership. There was a different sense of the Christmas Holiday across Winnipeg, which was well decorated with reefs, ornaments, and lights. Even though the City of Winnipeg was just over an hour away from Dominion City, Miss Shirley disclosed that she had not travelled there in over ten years.

When they walked into the Metro Chrysler Dodge Jeep dealership, most of the salespeople were busy assisting other customers, so they moved about freely looking at the different models of vehicles. Once they came across the Grand Cherokee 4X4, even Miss Shirley was immediately sold by its sleek design and sexy interior. By the time Oneil Carson, a registered car salesman went over to talk with the family, the only question they had for him was, "where were the keys to take a test drive?" Before they could take the Cherokee for a drive the salesman had to fill out several documents and attach a temporary license plate, therefore they were treated to pastries and warm beverages while they waited. As soon as the 4X4 was ready, Oneil brought them outside and showed them some special features on the vehicle, before Celine drove away and tested the performance around the area. The family members were already sold before they drove the 4X4, but the smooth handling and other amenities sealed the deal. They returned to the dealership forty minutes later, at which they made Oneil draw up the contract, before Celine singed and bought her first van.

New vehicle owners would customarily have to pick up their purchases within twenty-four hours, but due to the distance to Dominion City and the business' Christmas closure, they agreed to have the Cherokee ready by 4 PM. That meant the family members had several hours to waste, therefore they decided to do some shopping. Miss Shirley drove them to Cityplace Winnipeg Mall, which was a long distance away from the dealership, yet would allow the kids to get an adequate view of the city. Robin and Julien were fascinated with the size of the mall, which reminded them more of Nova Scotia. There were all types of stores throughout the mall, therefore once they entered the building everyone's head went on a swivel. Celine bought shoes and clothes for everyone, including several church dresses for her mother. Julien received a new Play Station and several new toys, while his sister upgraded her phone and bought some other personal items. They went from store to store until their stomachs grew empty, at which they paused and went for lunch.

When they reached the food court, everybody's head went on a swivel once again.

"I feel like I'll have a hamburger and fried from over there," Julien quickly commanded!

"I think I'd like to have some Thai food," Robin stated!

"Oh, there is my favorite All-Natural restaurant! I'm going over there," Miss Shirley stated!

"OK Mom, since I'm going to get some chicken wings and noodles close to Julien's burger place. Why don't you and Robin go get your stuff over at your restaurants, then we'll meet over there and find a table to sit," Celine exclaimed!

"OK, that's sounds like a plan! Come on Robin, lets go get our food," Miss Shirley stated as they separated!

The food court was packed and busy with holiday shoppers, so it was challenging to get through the crowd. They went to the food stations they individually selected, purchased their meals, and met where they had previously decided. Each of the family members struggled with their bags and food trays, which were difficult to carry at the same time. The female who cleaned the lounge and the trays wiped off a table and signalled them over, therefore they got somewhere to sit and enjoyed their food.

After they finished lunch, they still had two hours to kill before they needed to head back to the dealership. There was a luxury spa inside the mall where clients could get their fingernails done and their feet cleaned etcetera, so Celine treated her mother to a spa treatment. While Miss Shirley laid back and got pampered by a team of professionals, Celine brought their bags to the car to lighten their load. With her mother occupied for a short time, the children and her went to two brand name stores, where they bought lots of decorative Christmas items for the house. Celine knew Miss Shirley would have objected to some of the items they purchased, therefore, she hid them inside the trunk of the car before they returned to the spa.

By the time they returned to the dealership it was 4:20 PM due to the traffic. Their dealer had already completed the necessary paperwork and attached the new License Plate, so their new Cherokee was sparkling clean and ready to go. Having already test driven the 4X4's performance, Celine surprised her mother when she handed her the key to drive her new truck home, while she followed in Miss Shirley's antique boat. Instead of keeping their mother's company, Julien hopped into the rear cabin of the Cherokee, while Robin jumped into the co-pilot's seat. Rather than retrieving her Christian CD from her car, Miss Shirley allowed her granddaughter to select the radio station for them to listen along their journey. Robin started scrolling through the list of FM Stations and got lucky when she found a Hip-Hop station that was playing her jams. They pulled away from the dealership with the Cherokee's occupants bobbing their heads to the loud music, while Celine followed listening to her mother's comforting songs.

Robin and Julien were super excited about spending the holidays with their grandmother, who showed them a different side of herself during their return home. Rather than allowing her grandkids to do their individual thing, Miss Shirley was very interactive with them both wherein, they listened to music, played games, and spoke about family. Both Robin and Julien had many questions they wanted to know about their family history, hence Miss Shirley responded to the best of her knowledge. Miss Shirley was a dark brown complexion female who married a Caucasian male and produced three children with him. Most of her deceased husband's relatives did not approve of her being with him, therefore she knew very little of them even though they lived in Dominion City. Celine's admiration for her father was what led to her choice in men, contrary to her brothers who loved darker toned women. There were a few hysterical and personal stories which Miss Shirley felt necessary to disclose, however the more she told was the hungrier they became for their family's history. They loved hearing the story of how their grandfather and her met and became very saddened they were unable to meet him.

When they reached home Celine placed most of the presents they had bought underneath their Christmas Tree, before she returned outside and began decorating the house. The motivated mother retrieved her father's twenty-foot ladder from the backyard to help her attain the heights she wanted to reach. Miss Shirley had no idea her daughter had purchased the decorative items until she looked outside and saw the transformation occurring. Once the grandmother saw everyone hard at work, she went into the kitchen and began uncharacteristically cooking a large supper. The kids thought the house looked rather dull for Christmas and were happy to help their mother brighten it up with the decorations. The Devers' house went from being the least decorated residence on the street, to one of the most flamboyant Christmas creations in the town. Several locals began either walking or driving by to see the latest developments at Mrs. Devers' residence, after word circulated that Celine was getting a new vehicle. Coy pulled onto the driveway just before they finished with the decorations and was happy to see the transformation.

"I like it, Celine! Reminds me of when dad used to doll this place up for Christmas every year," Coy commented as he reached out and knuckle bumped Robin!

"That is exactly the look I was trying to copy," Celine yelled from halfway up the ladder!

"God damn, this truck looks phat! Word has been going around that you were going to buy some new vehicle," Coy exclaimed!

"No shit! But you approve, Baby Brother! As a mechanic and all," Celine asked?

"Hell yeah! Where the keys at, I want to take her for a spin," Coy stated?

"Julien, go get your Uncle Coy the van key inside on the kitchen table," Celine instructed!

"OK, Mom," Julien declared before he ran into the house.

While Julien went inside Coy retrieved a seat cover from his car to protect Celine's leather seat. A few seconds later Julien raced back through the door and handed his uncle the Cherokee key. The mechanic took the key and pressed the door unlock button; before he instructed his nephew 'to get into the passenger seat'! Julien did not need a second invitation as he ran around to the passenger door and climbed in. The young boy wanted to impress his uncle, therefore he immediately grabbed for his seatbelt and buckled it to prove he understood safety. Coy and his nephew left from their house on Ginn Avenue and drove down the street to Centennial Drive. They turned left on the street and drove to Baskerville Avenue, on which Coy's girlfriend Sandra lived with her two children. When Coy reached Sandra's house he honked the horn several times for her to come out, so he could show-off his sister's new wheels and introduced his nephew.

Julien thought they went to visit one of Coy's male friends until a dark complexion female exited the house, wrapped in her bathrobe to keep warm. It was cold outside, therefore Sandra stood by her door and waited for Coy instead of rushing out to the truck. Coy leapt out of the Cherokee and went to get a hug, but as he drew closer, she untied the rope, and gave him a sneak peek of the goodies. Sandra was naked underneath the bathrobe and caught Coy by surprise, therefore he rushed in and closed her garment before he hugged her. Julien's mouth fell wide open after he caught a view of his uncle's naked girlfriend, whose body was captivating like a work of art. Once Coy explained to Sandra that 'his nephew was inside the 4X4', she felt slightly embarrassed about exposing herself, nevertheless she waved and smiled at him. The moment felt a bit awkward after what he had just seen, still Julien slowly returned the wave and smiled.

After they left from Sandra's residence Coy drove around on several streets before he turned left on Hunter Street, which was one of the main roads that led to Dominion City. The mechanic have used that route many times to test drive vehicles he had repaired, therefore he was quite knowledgeable of its layout. 'Coy had a weird taste in music' thought Julien, when his uncle turned the radio dial to his favorite station, where they played Country Western Music all day long. The FM radio station he listened to was located in Calgary, Canada, which was in many ways similar to cowboy country. Before long Julien found himself bobbing his head and liking the flavor of music, which he had never listened to before. The Cherokee performed quite adequately and was easily managed on the road, so after Coy drove several miles, he concluded his test, and headed back home.

Christmas morning, they awoke to a flurry of snowfall, which was the first major snowstorm of the season. Miss Shirley had already awakened and began her morning rituals, that were somewhat altered due it being Christmas morning. The first appliance Mrs. Devers turned on that morning was her Stereo, which was already programed to the station she wanted to listen. The grandmother bounced her music softly because everyone else was still sound asleep, and she did not wish to disturb them. By the time Celine awoke, Miss Shirley had already prepared breakfast for everyone and was tackling their huge assortment of foods for their evening supper. The table was already prepared with eggs boiled and scrambled, sausages, bacon, ham, greens, biscuits, fried dumplings, bread, waffles, hot chocolate, coffee, orange juice and sliced pineapples. The instant Celine walked into the kitchen that morning she sensed there was a different mood or tempo about her mother, who was dancing about while she prepared the food.

"Good morning, Mom, Merry Christmas!"

"Good morning, Celine, Merry Christmas Honey!"

"Why didn't you wake me up to help you with the Christmas cooking?"

"I figured I would let you guys sleep until you were ready to get up."

Celine washed her hands and started cutting up the vegetables. There was a cake baking in the oven that filled the house with a luscious aroma. Julien came walking from the bedroom, rubbing his eyes a few minutes later. The excitement of the morning quickly transformed him, thus he ran over to look at the snow falling through the window.

"Good morning, Mom and Grandma! Merry Christmas!"

"Morning Julien, Merry Christmas sweetheart!"

"Morning Son, Merry Christmas!"

"Wow, look at the snow falling outside mom!"

"I saw it Julien!"

"When are we going to open the presents mom?"

"Right after breakfast honey!"

Celine began receiving phone calls from well wishers back in Nova Scotia, who wanted to wish her and the kids a Merry Christmas. Donette was the first to call but spent very little time on the phone, because she was on her way to the airport with her husband to pick up his mother. Minutes after they ended their conversation, Tamara and Roslyn phoned to wish them all a Merry Christmas. They both spoke with Celine for a while before she passed the phone to Julien, who conversed with them as he walked toward Robin's room. The young lad shook his sleeping sister and placed the cellular by her ear, then he exited the room quickly. Julien went and used the bathroom, before he retrieved his toys from the night before and began playing. Coy smelt the tantalizing aroma from the kitchen and came wobbling up from the basement to see what was transpiring.

"Merry Christmas everyone! Damn it smells good up in here! We haven't had a Christmas like this since I was a little boy! When are we going to eat?"

"Merry Christmas Litle Brother!"

"Merry Christmas Uncle Coy," Julien shouted from inside the living room!

"Merry Christmas Coy! We'll eat as soon as Robin gets..."

Robin surprisingly walked up behind Coy and hugged her uncle around the waist. "Merry Christmas Grandma, Mom, Jules, and Uncle Coy!"

"Merry Christmas," Julien shouted!

"Merry Christmas Baby," Celine said!

"Merry Christmas Robin! So, can we eat now," Coy demanded?

"Merry Christmas Robin," Miss Shirley stated!

"Yeah, lets eats so that we can open up the presents," Julien stated!

"Wait I have to use the bathroom first," Robin argued!

With everyone awake Miss Shirley walked over to her stereo and turned up the volume. Robin went to the bathroom to use the facility, as did Coy who had gone directly to the kitchen after he awoke. Miss Shirley began dancing around with Julien, who smiled and appeased his grateful grandmother. The telephone rang with Charles Jr. on the other line, calling to wish his entire family a Merry Christmas. After he spoke with his mother for a few minutes, the telephone got passed around to everyone inside the residence for Charles to pass on his Christmas greetings personally. Coy decided to tease his brother and transferred the call to a video feed, so he could show him the spread across the table, plus what was being cooked for supper. To irritate his brother further, Coy went into the living room and showed Charles Jr. their updated Christmas tree along with the pile of presents beneath it. Celine could hear her brother crying over the phone for not being there, so to not let him remain discouraged after they disconnected, she picked up a huge bag and showed him 'that was his present'.

The Devers family members gathered around the meal table and sat, before Mrs. Devers said grace to bless the food, following which they all chose whatever they wanted to eat. The family was missing one other relative to be complete, but even without Charles Jr. it felt great for Miss Shirley to have her daughter and grandchildren at the supper table Christmas morning. Everyone ate their fill and more, before they moved into the living room where the festivities were about to begin. Celine started the gift giving process by presenting Julien with his video game console, which he had been patiently waiting for since they bought it at the store. Robin thought her mother would pass her one of the things they bought at the mall, but Celine surprised her and instead gave her a jewelry box with Lloyd's chain in it. The instant Robin opened the jewelry box and saw the chain she started crying, which dampened her mood for a while.

"Mom, why does she gets dad's chain," Julien commented!

"It's a little too big for you right now honey," Celine responded.

"So is the watch," Julien stated!

"Mind your own business! It's mine, so don't touch it," Robin cried!

Celine kept the gifts moving and went onto her mother, whom she secretly bought gold earrings and a gold watch. Miss Shirley thought she saw everything Celine bought when they were at the mall, therefore she was stunned when she opened the present. The surprised mother broke out in tears at the gesture, knowing she would forever treasure the jewelry. Before Celine proceeded Miss Shirley asked her to exchange the earrings she was wearing, for the ones she just received? While her daughter fulfilled her request, Miss Shirley slid the watch onto her hand and began modelling it for everyone to see. Once Celine finished putting in the earrings, her mother stood up and gave her a huge hug, at which they both started crying.

"Thank you for coming home with my grandbabies and making this the best Christmas we had in years," Miss Shirley exclaimed!

"No problem, mom! I missed you guys so much all these years," Celine answered!

Coy did not think there was any presents for him, so he stood up and walked over to the Christmas tree. Celine had so many gifts underneath the tree that nobody realized Coy had hidden some packages behind the pile. With his mother and sister still hugging like they had no plans to detach, Coy began passing out his gifts to the children. Julien ripped off the wrapping from his gift, to uncover a Mini Drone set which he could fly whenever the weather got better. The young man was so excited that he ran into his uncle's arms and gave him a huge hug. When Robin unwrapped her present and saw a full makeup kit, with thirty shades of color, brushes, eyeliners, and lipsticks, she acted as if she was about to give Coy a knuckle bump, before she stunned him with another hug.

As soon as he got released, the Mechanic picked up his final two presents and gave them to Miss Shirley and Celine. There was an envelope attached to a package that Miss Shirley removed and placed beside her other present. Inside the box was a brand-new cellular phone that his mother badly needed to replace her aging device, which had fallen several times and had a cracked screen. Miss Shirley reached out for her son and gave him a warm hug and whispered, "Thank you" to him. Celine had no idea what to expect when she began ripping off the wrapping, but she saw that Coy had good taste, so she expected a pleasant surprise. As she was about to rip away the revealing wrapping, Celine caught a peek of the picture on the box, and noticed it was a dildo. Instead of allowing her mother or the children to see the sort of present it was, she quickly hid it and shoved it inside a gift bag.

"Merry Christmas," Coy joked!

"Mom, let's see what Uncle Coy gave you," Julien asked?

"It's a little personal honey! My little brother seems to think he is a comedian," Celine stated as she hugged Coy!

Miss Shirley got up and started giving out her gifts to the appropriate persons. She began with Julien who he bought two action figures to play with. The grandmother gave her granddaughter a charm bracelet, which she attached to her left arm immediately. For her son, Miss Shirley passed him a huge shopping bag that was filled with pants, shirts, and underwear. To her daughter Mrs. Devers gave a very personal gift, which was a chain she had always worn with a heart shaped pendant, that had a picture of a little girl Celine with her father inside.

Celine retook the gift sharing after her mother and continued from where she left off. She had bought everyone clothes, shoes, and other apparels; therefore, she began passing out the individual bags. Coy had the least expectations yet walked away with the most gifts, once all the presents were given out. There were several items around the house that Celine remembered from she was a little girl, therefore she surprised her mother by providing their replacements. Although her mother would never admit that some of the things inside her house were ancient, she could only smile when Celine gave her the new stainless steel pot set, a plate set, utensils, cups, glasses, towels, and even a toaster. Before Miss Shirley could open her mouth to defend her belongings, Coy volunteered to empty the utensils' drawer and cupboards, then restacked them with the new items. Even Robin and Julien thought their grandmother's appliances and cutleries were a bit outdated, so they volunteered to help their uncle.

Everyone appreciated everything they received and went about putting their presents away. Coy left after they finished attending to the cupboards and drawers, to drop off a few presents at his girlfriend. The snow was still falling heavily, so Celine worriedly gave him her Cherokee to drive. While Robin went off to contact her friends and family and wished them a Merry Christmas, Miss Shirley and Celine began drinking alcohol while they sat inside the living room reminiscing about Christmases past. There was zero communication with Julien who had new toys to play with and a video console to set up to the television inside their bedroom.

"You remember the way your dad used to carry home those huge Candy

Canes and give them to you kids every Christmas morning? You and your brothers would get so charged off that candy, it was like winding up one those robot toys and watching it go all day long!"

"Eh, Eh! Yes, I remember that! He would always give me the biggest one, got me so hyper one year I climbed on the dresser in my room and jumped off thinking I was Wonder Woman! Busted my head right here! You cursed dad so hard for bringing those Candy Canes home, but he never listened; and did the same thing the following year! That was dad!"

"Yeah, stubborn like a mule! But had a heart made of gold! Very much like your Lloyd! I was really looking forward to meeting him! I was happy when he called me and asked me for your hand in marriage! I thought that was so old fashion and sweet! Then he said he thought that we should reunite the family; and he would carry you all here, for the kids and him to meet me and your brothers!"

Celine was crying just listening to her mother speak of Lloyd's intentions. "Lloyd always reminded me so much of dad! I made a mistake running away from home with Aaron; and paid for it until I met Lloyd! I was pregnant and did not know where to turn, until he offered to help me!"

"So, how did Robin get Lloyd's last name?"

"He and I had started seeing each other; and he wanted her to have his last name. So, when Robin was born, we both went through the procedure together, like we did with Julien."

"Then Aaron is Robin's real father?"

"Yes, he is mom!"

"Does Robin Know?"

"I intend to tell her one of these days, but the time has not been right! We have been at each other's throats for months now, since we came here was the only time, we have spoken civil to each other, without me feeling like I should strangle her!"

"Sounds like you have been experiencing some of the things I went through with you! Were you planning on introducing Robin to Aaron's rest of family here in town?"

"I honestly have not thought that far ahead! That man just killed my fiancé, I hate everything about him right now; and it will take a long time for me to get over what he did!"

"I really don't know too much about them people, except the fact her husband is the manager at our bank! They seem to be real good Christians though, because I see them going to church almost every Sunday! But rumor had it that their son Andrew, was actually Aaron's father's child! She supposedly cheated on her husband who was her boyfriend then, the year when Aaron's father came to town to bury his mother."

"I don't think I will be having anything to do with those people! I still remember the names that fowl mouth woman used to call me!"

"But if Aaron knows she is his child, he just might try to get his mother to meet Robin?"

"I don't think Aaron knows that Robin is his daughter."

"You mean you never told him?"

"No, I didn't see the need when I was with him! I was more thinking about ways to survive and get away from him instead! I already got pregnant for him once, and when I told him he beat my ass into a miscarriage! So, no! I had no intentions to tell him!"

"Then there is really no reason for you to associate yourself and my granddaughter with those people!"

"Cheers to that," Celine agreed as they touched glasses and took a drink!

Miss Shirley's house phone rang, and she looked over at the Caller ID. "Oh, it is my girl Michelle calling to wish me a Merry Christmas! Sorry, honey give us a second please?"

"You have been talking with that lady ever Christmas and birthdays since I was a little girl, and I still have never met her, or have any idea who she is," Celine commented as she got up and walked to the kitchen!

"Go mind your own business! I need to speak with my girl about finding Robin a good job!"

"Then tell her I said thank you in advance," Celine shouted from the kitchen!

Coy returned and unexpectedly brought his girlfriend for supper, nevertheless she was warmly welcomed by his relatives. Julien felt a bit strange having seen Sandra naked, so he behaved shy around her at first. Since the peepshow experience, the young lad had undergone two major accidents, wherein the images he saw gave him wet dreams and caused him to ejaculate and urinate while he slept. Celine was forced to awaken each time and had to change their clothes, washed the bed sheets, and aired out the mattress. As a result, they would have to sleep somewhere else, however Julien never disclosed why he had those accidents. Coy wanted to impress his lady friend and illustrated the great cooks his mother and sister were, knowing they had prepared a feast made for kings.

The Devers' Christmas family dinner was spectacular, wherein they ate various types of dishes, from seafood to vegetarian delights. There was more food across the table than they could eat, yet they still had to contend with a selection of luscious deserts. Watching her daughter and grandkids while they spent time with their uncle and his lady friend, made that Christmas the best Miss

Shirley had experienced in many years. With everyone's stomachs filled, Mrs. Devers turned up the music and switched selections, which enabled them to dance and fully celebrated the evening. The house was filled with smiles and laughter like Christmases of years past, and it was all made possible through the love of family.

Chapter 16

Aaron went to his preliminary hearing where the prosecution team was scheduled to lay out the charges he would be facing. He was being represented by Attorney Gaston Jolli from the Nova Scotia, Public Defender's Office, due to his inability to afford a pricey criminal lawyer. A copy of Aaron's Discovery File was sent to him weeks before he attended court, therefore he knew the list of charges he faced, but not the precise jail time being sought. When he spoke with his lawyer over the phone and asked, 'the approximate sentencing he could receive', Monsieur Gaston told him that 'he could get up to forty years in prison, due to his criminal history'. The Public Defender thought that it would be best if Aaron pled guilty and threw himself at the mercy of the court, to receive the best sentencing outcome.

After killing their beloved relative, Roslyn and Tamara were present inside the courtroom to witness what became of the shooter. While Aaron sat and listened to the proceedings, Prosecutor Beau Duford read out the list of charges and depicted the defendant's entire criminal history to the court. The presiding overseer was Judge P. Harper, whose courtroom was where the accused robbers were arraigned. Even though Aaron sat quietly while the court appointees spoke, he had been through enough deliberations to understand the process. Prosecutor Duford spoke of his lengthy past deeds and the number of criminal charges he was found guilty of, for nearly fifteen minutes, to illustrate the deadly career criminal they were dealing with. Following his dramatic description of the defendant, Aaron was shocked when Monsieur Duford suggested that the judge considered removing him from society permanently, due to his criminal portfolio.

When it became time for Aaron's court appointed defendant to speak, Monsieur Jolli got up from his seat and had very little to say, instead of arguing against everything the prosecutor mentioned. Aaron began getting the sense that the attorneys were gearing up against him, therefore as the proceedings went on, he grew increasingly agitated.

"Your honor, sure my client has made some questionable decisions in the past, but all these incidents don't make Mister Adams a bad person! The prosecution wishes to make my client out to be some sort of a career criminal, that simply is not true! Mister Adams is highly remorseful for what happened and wished it never did, but the court must forgive him for that mistake," Mr. Jolli said before he sat back down!

"What the hell was that," Aaron leaned over and asked?

"Just planting the seed Mr. Adams! We want the judge to believe you are a bit remorseful, but also empathetic at the same time," Attorney Jolli whispered!

"Your deliberations have been taken into the record! What does your client intend to plea, Mister Jolli," Judge Harper enquired?

The defense lawyer leaned toward Aaron and whispered in his ear. "Like we discussed over the phone, it is best we plea guilty and get a plea deal."

"Are you out of your damn mind! Man, I don't want your representation, you fired! I'm not pleading no guilty to that shit! You people think I'm just going to sit back and watch you all conspire against me," Aaron yelled as he stood up and began tossing Mr. Jolli's papers across the room!

The Public Defendant cowardly moved himself away from beside Aaron, who began exhibiting a fleury of rage. The Accused Killer kicked away the chair he sat on and tried overturning the table ahead of him.

"Order in the court! Sit down Mr. Adams, there will be order in my courtroom," Judge Harper yelled while banging his gavel on the bench!

Aaron's boisterous outburst compelled the courtroom officers to rush across and slammed him against the desk. Judge Harper signalled his security officers to remove Aaron from the courtroom, therefore they slapped a pair of handcuffs on his wrists, and walked him from the courtroom, kicking and yelling.

"I hope they lock your ass away forever for killing my brother," Tamara shouted as they shoved Aaron along!

"Judge put he under jail," Roslyn shouted!

"Order inside the courtroom please," Judge Harper repeated!

That afternoon after they transported Aaron back to the correctional facility, he went directly to the phones as soon as he entered the pod. Dismissing his attorney meant that he would have to replace him going forth, therefore the detainee telephoned the only person whom he knew could assist him financially. If the call recipient had not answered, Aaron would have no reason to argue, since he had not dialled that number in over ten years. The person who he was trying to contact was his mother Jacquelin Woolry, whom he last spoke with during his second prison bid. Their estranged relationship had suffered more since Jacquelin sent Aaron to live with his father in Nova Scotia. Because he was never rehabilitated and ended up in prison only a few years later, Aaron hated his mother for sending him there.

Having not contacted his mother in so many years, Aaron felt nervous that the number might have changed, until it actually rang. When the recipient at the other end of the line answered the phone, Aaron was surprised, yet skeptical they would accept the charges. Rather than refusing the operator, the recipient said 'yes' to accepting the call, which brought a smile to the detainee's face. Once the call got connected neither of the communicators spoke for the first few seconds, as if they were both nervous about what to say.

"Thanks for accepting the call, Jacquelin," Aaron then responded!

"I see you are back inside your favorite place to be! What do you want from me now, Aaron," Jacquelin asked?

"Maybe if you were a better mother, I would not be so messed up! Living my life in and out of these damn prisons!"

"Don't try to blame me for the evil that you are Aaron! You did not get that meanness from me! That came from your father; that's why I sent you to live with him so he could deal with that shit! My advice to you son, is seek the Lord before it's too late!"

"Well thanks to your caring mother, these prosecutors want to tag me with mischief, so they can lock me away for the rest of my life!"

"What did you do this time to be in prison Aaron?"

"I didn't do anything! I swear! That's why I want you to cover the cost of a trial lawyer?"

"This is the last time; I ever do anything like this again! The next time you phone me collect from lockup, I will not be accepting those charges, you understand! Give your lawyer my number and I will see to it the bill gets paid!"

"Thank you for the help, Jacquelin!"

"Wait a second! Before you go, your baby brother Andrew has been dying to talk to you?" Jacquelin passed the phone to her other son before she began walking out of the room. "I have no idea why you always want to speak with that demon!"

Jacquelin was a Born-Again-Christian, who had changed her life from a reckless drug addict to the wife of the manager of Dominion City's only bank. When Jacquelin sent Aaron to live with his father, he was seventeen years old and had already become a menace to the town. The young troublemaker was well known to the police, who had detained him numerous times before his last birthday. Aaron's mother had another son at the time who was almost two years old, but she claimed the boys had different fathers. Canada's Welfare System provided them a dwelling and money for food each month, however with a drug problem none of that aide was enough. Instead of using all the Welfare Aide money for food, Jacquelin would squander most of it on drugs, and had to sometimes visit the Food Shelter to feed her children. A few years after she sent Aaron away, Jacquelin conceived another daughter for her new husband, whom she had accredited as Andrew's father.

"Hello, hello Aaron! How have you been doing," Andrew asked?

"Hey Andrew, I'm good Bro! Sorry I haven't been able to give you a call all these years but..."

"I understand Big Brother! It's tough to survive out there in the streets," Andrew interrupted!

"Ha-ha-ha! What you know bout the streets?"

"I'm not well versed like you! But one of these days I plan to move away from Dominion City like you did; and make my own life!"

"Don't be in too much of a rush Little Brother, Dominion City is nicer than most of these places out here!"

"I heard that! I guess that's why some people move back here. Like your old girlfriend, Celine!"

"Oh! So that's where that Little Bitch moved away to! No wonder her number has been cancelled!"

"Yeah, she been back a few weeks now, with her kids."

"That bitch is the reason I'm in this predicament!"

"What do you mean big brother?"

"Don't worry about it, Andrew! I'll take care of it in due time! By the way, what did you want to talk...?"

An operator recording interrupted Aaron and said. "You have five minutes remaining for this call!"

"I just, never spoke with my big brother before, that's it! Mom always said, 'you locked up somewhere', so, I guess, my one question would be, what is it like being in prison?"

"For me I'm a bit more used to it after all these years, but you still miss your people on the outside, and you miss your freedom! I watch guys come in here every day broken down, but they realize they better toughen up quick! But it's like any other place, I guess!"

"Is it dangerous there? I mean, does anybody get hurt?"

"Far worst than that Little Brother. People get killed in here!"

"You don't have to listen to Mom, you can still call anytime. I will make sure to answer the phone!"

"Did Jacquelin have any other kids apart from us?"

"Yes, we have a little sister name Viveen!"

"Viveen huh! Maybe you could send me some family pictures sometimes?"

"We don't take much pictures as a family, but I'll try to send you some!"

"Thanks Andrew! I'll try to stay in touch Bro!"

"Anytime you need anything Brother, just call me," Andrew said before they disconnected the call!

With Aaron removed from B-Pod and among his co-defendants, Nickle and Quest were compelled to make their own decisions regarding their criminal cases. Neither of them had a fairy godmother who would give them the necessary funds to hire better defense representatives, therefore they had to depend on their provided public defendants. Although Nickle was only the driver, 'The Crown' charged him with the same offenses as they did Eddie and Quest. Their most serious charge was the 'Conspiracy To Commit Murder' count, for being Aaron's accomplices throughout the killing, and were caught with him thereafter.

Each of the participants involved in the robbery would eventually contemplate using different strategies to lessen their sentences or regained their freedom. While Eddie chose the most radical approach, Suzie convinced Nickle to take a plea bargain to reduce the number of years being sought by the prosecution. To ensure that Nickle did his best to reduce the number of years being imposed, Suzie brought their son during a visit to the Correctional Facility to remind him of his priorities. Quest decided to heed the advice of some of his jailhouse lawyer companions, who convinced him that if he went to trial, he could have won his freedom, even though none of those inmates ever practiced law. Contrary to his associates, Quest's cellmate tried to discourage him from relying on a public defendant, yet he chose to take his friends' advice. Aaron unknowingly received consent to hire a much more polished trial lawyer, which gave him the best odds of being awarded less prison time.

Detective Laddimer had wrapped up his investigation on the case and filed his report, therefore the court proceedings were ongoing. All four robbers were given separate court dates and physically appeared for their preliminary hearings, except for Eddie whose case was being delayed on account of his recovery. The investigation done by the detective revealed that the crime was not premeditated, thus none of the co-conspirators nor Aaron knew that Lloyd would have been at that location when he was. Contrary to Eddie, neither Quest nor Nickle tried assisting the prosecution team, and chose instead to remain faithful to their friend. The decisions made by Nickle and Quest meant both men stood less of a chance to get their sentences reduced or revoked. The only helpful factor for either accused was the fact it was their first criminal offense, nevertheless the prosecution wanted to sentence them to ten years each for their involvement.

Detective Laddimer kept in contact with Doctor Lue, who provided him with reports on Eddie's progress. The Recovering Detainee had indicated his intention to assist the prosecution against Aaron, whom he blamed for all the misfortunes they had experienced. Eddie's offering meant the government needed a documented statement from him, about all the intricate details of the crime. Several weeks following his operation, Eddie's wounds began healing, but he would need to undergo physiotherapy to regain mobility and control of his limbs. The beating and subsequent injuries he sustained, left him unable to eat, use his hands, or walk upright, therefore he was forced to suck nutriment through a straw for each daily meal. The Recovering Inmate had been taken off the Intravenous Fluids and could get out of the bed, but he still wore a neck brace and had all four limbs stabilized in casts. Each day Eddie spent on his back staring up at the ceiling, left him increasingly bitter towards Aaron. Despite all his bitterness, he refused to personally lay criminal charges against the shooter, for commanding the thugs who nearly crippled him.

On Eddie's preliminary court date his condition did not allow for him to travel, therefore the hospital technicians wheeled him in a wheelchair into a room, where they held a Virtual Court Session. Judge P. Harper and everyone involved in the court proceedings were on a computer screen, while Eddie sat alone inside the closed room. There were no doctors or technicians allowed inside the room with Eddie during the proceedings, so they ensured he was secure before leaving. The defendant sat there unable to speak with his mouth wired shut and incapable to communicate, although the lawyers did not need him to handle the proceedings. Eddie had never personally met the Public Defender, Maurice McAdoo, whom he contacted to argue his case, and in his predicament, he was incapable of objecting to anything.

"Your Honor, the defendant is now present," Attorney McAdow stated!

"What are the latest developments with this case Mister Duford," Judge P. Harper asked?

"Your Honor, the Defendant is being charged with seven counts of armed robbery, which include assault and battery, the most sever of these charges being conspiracy to commit murder! However, prosecution has spoken with the defence council and agree to process this case at a later date, following the defendant's cooperation in other matters," Prosecutor Beau Duford exclaimed!

"Very well, Mister Duford," concurred Judge Harper, who began looking through his appointment calendar for possible court dates! "How about seven months from now, July 13th at 10 AM?"

"That date works for me Your Honor. Plus, that should allow for my client to recover further," Defence Attorney McAdow declared!

"I agree Your Honor," Prosecutor Duford stated!

"Very well gentlemen, we'll reconvene on July 13 at 10 AM! Court adjourned," Judge Harper instructed!

Eddie thought his lawyer would be available after the conference call to explain what was happening with his case, but the monitor went blank after the judge dismissed everyone. A minute later the door opened, at which the technician entered then wheeled him back to his room. Following weeks of recovery where he laid on his back and stared up at the ceiling, Eddie had grown frustrated with the sleeping position. His every waking moment was spent thinking of the beating he had received, moreover, many nights he awoke with cold sweat dripping from the nightmares, wherein he was close to being mauled to death. Despite his predicament Eddie felt safer at the health facility, and wished he never had to return to the main jail, where he was scared what might happen if others uncovered, he was a snitch. Being in the Solitary Confinement Unit was somewhere he might have to get accustomed to staying if he wanted to survive, not knowing who might attack him at any given moment.

Chapter 17

The only two churches in Dominion City were Saint Luke Catholic Church and Dominion City United Church, both of which could be found on Centennial Drive. The worship hall facilities were built seventy yards apart from each other and were on the same side of the road. Saint Luke Catholic was primarily attended by the Caucasians in town, while ninety-six percent of Dominion City United's attendants were coloured, with a four percent Caucasian mix. Pastor Roundtree was Mis Shirley's preacher at Dominion City United Church for nearly thirty years, but Saint Luke Catholic had a new pastor, following the death of its long-time clergyman. The new preacher assigned to the district was forty-nine years old Pastor Keith Hemming, who relocated with his family from New Brunswick, Canada. During the weekdays each church conducted their midweek ceremony on different days, but they both held Sunday services in the morning. To avoid having their members interact, the churches commenced their services at different hours, wherein Pastor Hemming began at 9:00 and Pastor Roundtree started at 10:00. Both preachers performed two hours ceremonies, before they concluded for the day and dismissed their audiences.

The two head preachers had different techniques with which they delivered their sermons. Pastor Hemming had a more conservative style like the pope and was extremely pro the belief of their church. Every social topic that the Catholic Church took a serious stance against, from abortion to same sex marriages were the weekly points of discussion for the pastor. He would always speak with a modest tone and hardly raised his voice, except whenever he sang. Contrary to the Catholic preacher, Pastor Roundtree could be heard halfway down the block. That library type atmosphere inside Saint Luke Catholic was transformed inside the United Church building, where it often sounded like a party in session. There were no limits to the topics covered by Miss Shirley's preacher, who addressed the men as fiercely as he did the women. While the Catholic Church members vacated their facility calm and properly groomed, Pastor Roundtree's adherents materialized as if they had spent all night inside the club partying.

Mrs. Shirley Devers had always offered her children the opportunity to willingly attend church with her. She would normally attend her worship facility twice each week, for Sunday Service and Wednesday Bible Studies. The first time Celine decided to attend with her mother and children was for a Sunday ceremony. There was so much commotion inside the house that morning with everybody getting dressed at once, hair designs getting done, and breakfast devouring, that they reached the facility when Pastor Roundtree was in the middle of his opening prayer. They entered the building and stood by the rear door until the preacher was through before they went in search of their seats. Miss Shirley was accustomed to sitting in the front row, therefore she began walking directly down the isle. Celine was about to follow her mother with the children, until she noticed the number of heads turning to watch Miss Shirley as she went by. Following the numerous observations, each observer turned to their neighbor and whispered something about the proud grandmother.

There was no denying that Miss Shirley looked fabulous in her new dress, low heel leather shoes, makeup, designer handbag, and fancy hairstyle. It was quite easy for Celine to decipher that the audience members were in awe by their reactions, still she felt her mother was being displayed by all the attention. To avoid all the stares and comments, Celine held Julien's hand and pointed out three chairs to Robin, before she darted into the second to last row. The interracial couple who was seated along the isle allowed them by, not knowing that they were related to Mrs. Devers. As Celine snuck pass she overheard the female whispering, "Sister Shirley looking much better since her daughter brought her shopping!" When Miss Shirley reached the front row, she looked back and realized her family members had found seats elsewhere, therefore she sat in her customary seat.

Pastor Roundtree's sermon that morning was about 'being good neighbors to others in the community'. The pastor advised everyone that in order for them to have and continue their peaceful ways of living, each citizen needed to show love and respect to others. To illustrate his point about respect, Preacher Roundtree told a joke that involved Mrs. Devers. From the instant her pastor began telling the joke, Lorna who sat beside Miss Shirley began chuckling, having already heard of the incident.

The preacher man told his audience. "The other day I was in a rush driving down Waddell Avenue, and I came across a short lineup of three cars, driving slowly down the road. I thought that the front car may have had a flat tire, and the driver was trying to get to the garage down the road. Anyways, one car goes around the slower car, then a few seconds later the second car passed the slow car. So, now I drive up because I see it's almost my time to pass, but the first two drivers who passed this older model vehicle, were swearing at the driver and showing her all sorts of hand signs and whatnot! Before I got the chance to pass, I realized my destination was coming up, so I decided to stay behind the slowly moving car. When I got ready to turn into my destination, the same car turned in before me! Now I'm thinking this is not good, her car must have broken down, I'm going to have to do the Good Samaritan thing and I'm already late; the driver stops the car and gets out slowly! When I looked, it was nobody but Sister Shirley!"

The church adherents all broke out in laughter knowing how slowly Mrs. Devers drove. Even Miss Shirley was forced to laugh at herself knowing the preacher-man spoke truth. Once the audience members finally quieted down and stopped laughing Pastor Roundtree continued.

"Now I could have sped up and gone around her and did like the other two drivers did, and in the end, I would have felt ashamed for doing so! Not because I did that to a member of our congregation, or a resident of Dominion City, but especially because I did that to Sister Shirley! Someone who I have great respect for! So, it helps to show respect to our neighbors in this town! Can I get an Amen?"

"Amen," shouted many of the church adherents!

"Preach Pastor preach! Hallelujah," Sister Charmaine shouted!

The preacher man wiped the sweat from his forehead and looked down at his notes laying on the alter. "I say if you are a member of this United Church, you owe it to your brothers and sisters to show them respect! Can I get an Amen?"

"Amen," shouted the audience!

"Your father Jesus Christ and his father never showed you disrespect," the preacher man continued!

"No, he never did," Deacon Blackwood shouted!

"Amen to that my brother! Because if Jesus had disrespected you, then he never would have died for you on that cross! He never would have promised you would go to Heaven if he had disrespected you!"

"Praise the Lord," yelled several adherents!

"Hallelujah," yelled other members!

"Amen," yelled others!

Audience members began rising to their feet, as they applauded and cheered loudly. Pastor Roundtree preached for an hour, before the program transitioned over to hymns, which were sang by their church choir. Robin fell victim to the preacher's hypnotic charisma from the moment she sat, that she failed to re-alize Julious Simms was a member of the choir. By the time the preacher man finished his sermon, several of his congregation members were prancing about, proclaiming they had been struck by the Holy Spirit. Neither Julien nor Robin had ever been to such an eventful church, where the choir's performance had the adherents carrying on as if they were haunted. There were people speaking in Tongues, with their eyeballs rolled back and exhibiting only the sclera. Even the couple seated along the isle were dancing about, while Celine and the kids watched in awe.

131

Celine knew her mother was a faithful adherent of the church after accompanying her a few times when she was a little girl, but she had never seen Miss Shirley under the influence of the Holy Spirit. Pastor Roundtree had Lorna and Miss Shirley among others, prancing about with their hands held high before the choir started singing. Once the hymns of godly praise touched the hypnotized worshipers, people began dancing and parading about as if they were at a party. Sister Shirley and her partner in crime, kicked off their low heel shoes and began dancing about barefooted.

"Now I see why mom's feet are always killing her whenever she gets home from church," Celine whispered to Robin, who giggled at the comment!

Julien tugged on his mother's dress and asked, "Mom are those people, OK?"

"Yes honey, they have the Holy Spirit," Celine responded!

"What is the Holy Spirit," Julien enquired?

"The forces of God Jules," Robin answered!

"Is that true mom?"

"Something like that son!"

"I want to get the Holy Spirit too," Julien stated!

Robin and Celine laughed before the mother responded, "You might be a little too young for that right now Julien."

Once the ceremony ended, Miss Shirley quickly made her way to Celine and the children, to show them off to her church adherents. While everyone mingled before they departed, the grandmother went around with her special guests and introduced them to everyone. The first people who Miss Shirley introduced her daughter and her grandchildren to, was the couple beside whom they sat. The Duncans were the only interracial couple in the church and had been loyal adherents before they married. Eric and Shawna Duncan were stunned to know Miss Shirley's offspring were seated just beside them; and felt rather embarrassed by the comments they had made earlier. Nevertheless, the couple behaved hypocritically and pretended as though they were delighted to make their acquaintance. As the Devers made their way to the front of the church, Miss Shirley introduced her clan to a mother and her three children. The woman's name was Kim Zeel, and she was a teacher at the local school with two daughters Alice and Alison, and a son named Linton. From they walked up to Kim and her children, Julien and Linton asked their mothers if they could meet up another time to hang out and play. Both mothers agreed to make the boys get to know each other, therefore Celine took Kim's cellular number.

The two people who Miss Shirley definitely wanted to introduce her daughter and grandkids to were their preacher and his wife. Pastor Roundtree and Sue Roundtree were extremely delighted that Celine decided to visit with her children and welcomed them back in the future. While everyone else spoke behind

Mrs. Devers' back, the pastor's wife was straightforward with her compliments. "I love the way you have been doing your mother's hair and fixing her up for church! The other ladies are jealous because Sister Shirley looks fabulous! Keep taking good care of your mother, the lord will certainly bless you! It has been a long time since we saw her smile like she has!"

The compliment made Celine came to the realization that not all the church members were charlatans. Despite her first impression, the young mother agreed to revisit with her children, because she genuinely liked the ceremony. Celine had a few friends from school who were also adherents of the church, therefore she felt quite welcomed and at home. While they interacted with the pastor, Karen and Mauve snuck up and borrowed Celine for a few minutes to discuss some private affairs. Robin's mother was occupied with her old school-mates when Miss Shirley brought her and Julien to meet the choir members. When Robin realized she was about to meet the gas attendant, she grew extremely nervous, started perspiring, and developed sweaty palms. Julien was disinterested in meeting the choir and wanted to go play around the hall like Linton and another boy were doing. Rather than allowing her grandson to go make a mockery of their family, by allowing other church adherents to scrutinize the boys' actions, Miss Shirley held onto the young lad and refused to let him go.

There were seven people in the choir, five females and two men. The youngest member of the group was sixteen years old Rebecca Gerbert who sang beautifully. The United Church choir members were discussing their upcoming meeting time for the next rehearsal, when Miss Shirley walked up with her grandkids.

"Wonderful job as always guys! These are my grandkids Robin and Julien, who are here from Nova Scotia," Miss Shirley stated!

"We have heard so much about you guys! Hello, I'm Natalie!"

"Hi, I'm Patricia!"

"Nice to meet you guys, I'm Paula!"

"Hello, I'm Jill!"

"I am Chris!"

"Hello, I'm May!"

"And I am Julious, nice to meet you!"

"Hi," Julien mumbled!

"Hello, this is my little brother Julien, and I am Robin!"

"I think you guys sing beautifully, but it would be an upgrade if you added my granddaughter Robin," Miss Shirley declared!

"Grandma no! Please excuse my grandmother, she doesn't know what she is talking about," Robin said as she dragged the old woman away!

"Robin, but you are a great singer! I've been listening to you singing away inside the bedroom," Miss Shirley argued!

"Let's go grandma! Stop, I'm no singer!"

As they moved away Robin looked back to see if Julious was watching, but the young man was behaving as if he never noticed her.

Karen and Mauve brought Celine to the back of the church, where Christine, Joan, and Shernet awaited them. Celine's old friends had been planning to conduct some sort of a gathering for them to get reacquainted, but it was a challenge trying to find the right date when everyone would be available. After weeks of planning, they finally arranged a date and location, thus they wanted to discuss the arrangements with Celine. When Celine saw Christine and Shernet she remembered them instantly, yet she barely recalled Joan's face. Despite all the years apart, they hugged and greeted each other as if they were long lost sisters.

"Girl we finally decided on a date for the party! Everyone is so excited and can't wait," Karen stated!

"What date did you guys decide," Celine asked?

"Three weeks from today on the Saturday evening," Karen answered!

"How many people finally agreed to come," Celine enquired?

"Pretty much two thirds of the students from Miss Gibbs class, who still live in Dominion City," Shernet answered!

"I also talked with two ladies who think they might remember you, so they will be there also," Christine added!

"Party is on girls," Karen stated!

Over the coming weeks Celine accompanied her mother a few times to church and found herself getting closer to the front with each visit. Julien loved attending with his grandmother and would get up on time each Sunday, showered and dressed by the time she was ready to leave. Wednesday evenings were a different story however, wherein the young lad was impossible to get from around his video console. Miss Shirley already knew how Coy felt about regular devotion, therefore she never antagonized him about attending and left him at home each time she went to communion. In comparison with her uncle, Robin had the same feeling about attending church regularly, until she discovered that the gas pump attendant was an adherent of the congregation. Even though Mrs. Devers once lost her daughter to a young troublemaker from the community, she trusted that as a Methodist the young man who Robin admired was more spiritually grounded.

Unlike her mother Celine became worried she might lose her daughter, when Miss Shirley disclosed what she had suspected. Due to her concerns, whenever Robin began dressing for church, Celine immediately changed whatever plans she had and attended. Having made the regrettable decision to move away from Dominion City, Celine did not want Robin to make the same mistake. To ease her daughter's concerns, Miss Shirley introduced Celine to Julious' mother, who was also an adherent of Dominion City United Church. Celine had not uncovered any evidence that Julious even noticed Robin from they started attending, yet she constantly spied on them both. The notion that Julious came from a decent family was of no concern to her, thus she refused to drop her guard even though their associates never mingled. Robin had become friends with a group of females within her age category and Julious only spent time with his choir mates, nevertheless, Celine had an intuition.

To bring in the New Year, the Dominion City United Church held their annual prayer ceremony for their members. With so much to give thanks for that year, Miss Shirley could hardly wait to get to church that evening. Pastor Geoff Roundtree stood outside the entrance of the church and welcomed all his visitors, who had survived to partake of another celebration. The pastor was happy to see Sister Devers with her daughter and grandkids, who had become regulars at the worshiping center. While Miss Shirley was excited to see her pastor and church relatives, Robin felt tingles every time she saw Julious. Even though they had known each other for a while, Julious acted as if he was unimpressed by the young Nova Scotian beauty and would not even make eye contact with her.

Dominion City children were accustomed to their friends moving away from the town, so they were thrilled to have newcomers into the community. There was a group of three teenage girls who befriended Robin, two of which had darker complexion and the third was slightly lighter than the others. The lighter toned female's name was Marcia Miller, and she was the oldest at sixteen. The two darker toned females were cousins Kim and Erica Bledsoe, both of whom were several months younger than Robin. Each of the young ladies thought Julious was rather cute, yet they all described him as being "weird". When Robin asked why they thought of him as such, none of them provided a direct response, except to say he was! As the newcomer to the group, Robin kept her assumption to herself rather than revealing her thoughts, however, their degrading analysis of Julious made him appeared that more intriguing.

Chapter 18

Andrew Woolrey and his father Thomas Woolrey's favorite activity was firing off rounds of ammunition at the local shooting range in Dominion City. The town with slightly more than two hundred and twenty residents, was twelve miles from the U.S-Canada Border and had a small yet thriving economy. The richest person in town was Michelle Zap, who owned many of the main businesses in Dominion City. Unlike the smaller towns that surrounded Dominion City, the community had a public pool, a museum, a credit union, a general store, a bank, a hockey rink, a shooting club, a gas station, and a curling club. One of the most historic buildings in Dominion City was the All-Saints Anglican Church, however, it was transformed and later became the Franklin Museum. Andrew was twenty years of age and had been shooting since he was ten, therefore he was quite an accurate shot. Thomas Woolrey was the bank manager at the only Royal Bank in town and brought home a decent salary. As a result, their family owned a huge house on a three-and-a-half-acres property, and lived an amazing life filled with regular vacations. The family donated much of their time in the community, wherein they would organize events and parties, as well as fundraisers to help others. Jacquelin Woolrey did not have to work, therefore she volunteered some of her time to cleaning their church six days a week. Both Jacquelin and Thomas had been married for over fifteen years and shared another young daughter named Viveen Woolrey, who was six years old.

Thomas and Andrew's favorite time for target practice was on Saturday evening, when most of the Renegade Shooting Range members were at the club. The father and son pairing were the best among the club's members, who often held marksman competitions to decipher the most accurate. Both Thomas and his son were tattooing their target sheets with kill shots and would compare their results with friends at night's end of their sessions. Thomas had always felt comfortable knowing his son could shoot accurately and would thus be capable of protecting his wife and home if called upon. Unlike her boys, Jacquelin was a devoted Christian who hated guns and the violence they created. Due to her personal stance against weapons, all guns kept inside their home had to be concealed and unable to discharge without unlocking. Her father Frank Kiermyer had been serving multiple life sentences for killing four people in Winnipeg, since she was four years old, so Jacquelin disliked weapons of any sort.

Following their target practice round, Thomas and Andrew exited the range and walked into the customer's lounge, where members drank and socialized. Thomas indicated he would be rushing to the restroom and left Andrew at the bar to order whatever he desired. The female waitress had her back turned as she stacked the fridge with beer; but spun around once she noticed someone had taken a seat by the bar. Andrew was hypnotized by the young fair-skinned waitress' beauty and stared at her initially unable to utter a word.

"Excuse me, can I help you," asked Robin, with her unique Nova Scotian accent?

Once Andrew caught himself, he smiled and pretended he could not hear a word, as he removed an earplug from his left ear. Customers were generally expected to make some sort of commissary demand of a server; however, Andrew thought of many different questions and none of them pertained to her work duties.

"Yes, can I help you," repeated Robin?

"Oh sorry, two Heinekens," Andrew commanded?

Robin walked to the cooler and took out two beers, removed the caps, and brought them over to the customer. There was a Caucasian female on duty when Thomas and Andrew arrived for their shooting session, who was attending to some seated customers. Andrew did not want the other employee to know his intentions, but there was some information he wanted to know about Robin.

"Will that be charged to your account, or will you be paying out of pocket today," Robin questioned?

"My dad will let you know once he gets back from the bathroom," said Andrew!

"Very well, no problem," responded Robin, who was about to return to her previous activity.

"You're new here aren't you," Andrew enquired?

"Yup! My first day on the job," Robin answered.

"Haven't seen you around town before either. You new to the area," Andrew asked?

"Yeah, my family and I just moved here a few weeks ago," Robin stated!

"Where from," Andrew enquired?

"Nova Scotia," Robin exclaimed!

Another male customer went to the opposite end of the bar and raised his index finger summoning the waitress, therefore she excused herself to attend to him. As Robin turned away from Andrew her eyes caught sight of a unique Gold Boxing Glove, hanging from a gold chain around his neck. Andrew sat by the bar and began sipping on the beer, while he pretended as if he was watching the television and kept an eye on the hot fair-skinned barkeep. The tights Robin wore revealed her curvy features; thus, Andrew could not avoid staring at her round derriere. When his stepfather walked up and touched him on the shoulder, Andrew jumped as if someone had snuck up behind him and frightened him.

"Heineken, what are we celebrating," asked Thomas?

"Nothing at all, just felt like having a quick beer," Andrew declared!

"OK, then let us go get a table I got a phone call to make," instructed Thomas!

Robin walked over to collect payment for the refreshments after she attended to the other customer. Thomas withdrew a twenty-dollar bill from his pocket and laid it on the table, then left the bar with his son following. They both walked over to a table and sat down, across from Officer Ray Pedward and Officer Grey Gilmore, who were off duty dressed in regular street clothing. The officers and Thomas acknowledged each other with simple hand gestures, before the peacekeepers went back to their affairs. Andrew placed the carrying cases with their weapons on the floor next to them and adjusted his chair to watch the television directly behind the bar counter. With the bar tender in clear sight, the young man pretended he was watching the program on the screen, as he intently admired the shooting club's newest employee. Thomas stayed on the phone for a few minutes discussing business with a client, before he hung up the call and invested more interest in his son.

"What the hell are you watching on TV," Thomas asked, then turned to see what could have consumed his Andrew's interest?

There was a curling exhibition showing on the television screen and Thomas was quite certain his son hated watching the sport. Hence, after weighing the alternative, Thomas smiled and began heckling Andrew.

"Very exotic, I had no idea you were interested in different flavors," said Thomas?

"What's are you talking about dad," Andrew disclaimed?

"Andrew, we both know you wouldn't be caught dead watching curling at home," added Thomas!

"That's at home dad; and there is nothing else to watch," Andrew argued, as the Caucasian female manager walked by with a bottle of Jack Daniel Whiskey and smiled at him!

"Hi Andrew," enthusiastically greeted Veronica!

The brunet was quite beautiful and behaved as if she was fascinated with the young stud, who simply smiled and nodded at her. Veronica was a very self-absorbed individual who had a routine of looking back at things that appeased her. Expecting to catch Andrew staring at her derriere, Veronica looked back over her right shoulder and caught him instead watching Robin. The Gun Club's new store assistant was oblivious to everything happening while attending to her bar duties. Even though Robin was new to the area, Veronica assumed she might have had a run-in with Andrew prior and sought to further investigate. After replacing the bottle of Jack Daniel on their display shelf, the inquisitive manager moved directly to interrogate their newest employee.

"So, Robin, how do you like the job so far," asked Veronica?

"It's a breeze like you said! I really like working here already," answered Robin!

"That's great! How long did you say you've lived here in town," enquired Veronica?

"A few weeks," responded Robin.

"So, where did you meet Andrew," asked Veronica?

"Andrew who," queered Robin?

"That guy over there with his dad," stated Veronica!

"Sorry, I don't know who he is! Why," declared Robin, after checking to see who Veronica was referring to?

"No reason, I just thought I saw him staring at you! Must have been the TV though," said Veronica who then walked away!

Three men exited the Shooting Gallery Area with their securely encased firearms in one hand and their target paper results in the other. They all walked over to Thomas' table and pulled up an extra chair, so they could all interact at the same spot. Each man felt confident they had made the most accurate shots that weekend and were willing to support their rants with wagers. Officer Gilmore and Officer Pedward finished their beers and signalled Thomas as they made their way to the exit. Veronica went over to the table and collected the other men's orders, before she brought back their beverages and left them to carry on.

"You dummies will be dreaming about getting some get back all week, after I win all your money today," Wayne boasted!

"All that talk from a marksman with a pair of left-hands," Johnny countered!

"Johnny, everybody knows you can't see or shoot straight for shit, not with those soda bottle glasses you wear! So, you shouldn't even be betting money," Steve joked!

"My chart is going to show you degenerates who has two left hands," Wayne disagreed!

"Sorry gentlemen, but I feel like I was on my game today! So, everybody who feels confident make your bets now," Thomas declared as he placed a twenty-dollar bill on the table!

Everyone else withdrew their twenty-dollar bills and placed them beside Thomas' on the table. It was their tradition for the last champion to first present his chart, therefore Andrew stood up and showed them his results. With the bids locked in, everyone else lifted and showed their charts to reveal who they thought won the competition. There was hardly any center circle left for Thomas, Andrew, Wayne, and Steve, whose charts looked rather similar. They had to resort to checking each chart's mechanical readouts of the shooter's accuracy, to determine that Andrew won the competition by one shot over his father. It was the young man's third victory in a row, so the others knew beating him would be a serious challenge, with him getting better each week.

Thomas and Andrew finished their beers and said their goodbyes before they left the shooting range thereafter. There were still a few customers drinking and enjoying the ambiance, but the Shooting Gallery had already closed. Wayne, Steve, and Johnny stayed back and bought two extra rounds of beer, which they drank while they joked among themselves. Johnny had a fetish for young girls, therefore Robin caught his attention as she went about sweeping the floor. Steve noticed his associate keenly watching the new girl and told him whose daughter she was. Contrary to everyone else Johnny did not remember who Celine was, nor did it matter as he continued watching Robin. Veronica noticed him watching her co-worker and knew the sort of person he was, following a few prior entanglements between them.

"Hey Pervert! Quit watching my co-worker," Veronica shouted!

"Whatever bitch," Johnny exclaimed before he chugged his beer, got up, and walked out!

Once the men departed, Veronica walked over to their table, wiped it clean and retrieved the empty bottles, then transferred them to an empty box underneath the bar counter. Johnny waited outside in his Dodge Ram 4X4, smoking cigarettes, drinking liquor, and watching Robin through the glass. The Renegade Shooting Club stayed open for another hour before they closed for the night. Once Veronica turned out the lights to close the store, Johnny started his vehicle and drove away from the parking lot. Veronica saw when Johnny's Ram Truck pulled out, so she decided to give Robin a ride home instead of making her walk. When they arrived at Miss Shirley's house, Veronica waited until her new co-worker entered her residence, before she pulled out from the driveway and drove away.

"Hey grandma," shouted Robin who placed her purse and coat on a chair then walked into the kitchen and poured herself a glass of juice!

"Hi baby, how was your first day on the job," asked Miss Shirley?

"Thanks for getting me that job grandma! I think I'm going to like working at the shooting range, it's relaxing and stress free," Robin answered excitedly!

"Didn't all the loud banging from all that shooting bother you," questioned Miss Shirley?

"We don't hear none a that stuff grandma! It's surprisingly quiet as a library in there," Robin answered, as she sat beside Miss Shirley!

"As long as you feel comfortable working there then I'm happy!"

Robin gave her grandmother a kiss on the cheek, then covered her mouth with her hands and yawned. "I'm going to bed grandma; it's been a long day! I'll see you in the morning."

"Sleep well baby! Good night!"

Chapter 19

Julious' bigger brother's name was Evander Simms, and they had a nine years difference in age between them. Evander was the primary collision repair specialist at Coy's Mechanic & Collision Garage, where they had one other worker named Marshon. They did not have a secretary to assist with the daily running of the shop, therefore Coy handled all the business with their customers. Even though Evander was the person who discussed collision affairs with the customers, Coy was the cashier who collected all payments and paid his employees. Marshon was the mechanic shop's apprentice and his chores involved anything from picking up coffee to assisting Coy or Evander. There was no major auto parts store located in Dominion City, so often times Marshon had to drive to Winnipeg to pick up parts for the shop. The apprentice was Caucasian yet loved listening to loud Rap Music and would always portray as if he was a gangster.

The garage was open six days each week and had been a pilar in the community for over a century. Coy worked for the former owner of the garage since he was fifteen; and got the opportunity to become the boss twelve years later. Being the only mechanics around for eighty-four miles, they serviced vehicles from their community, the surrounding town folks, and tourists passing through. To progress with the newer model vehicles, Coy attended a training course every other year in Ontario, to learn about the newest technologies in his field. The auto repair workers had a terrific working environment, wherein they joked around, listened to music all day, and fixed cars.

Evander lived in his parent's basement and grew up going to church with his mother, before he began rebelling and stopped going altogether. The Tuesday before New Year's Eve he was at work prepping a Chrysler 300 for painting, when a Chevy Corvette pulled onto the property. The beautiful blond female who dismounted rushed into the garage and ran into Marshon, who was on break eating inside the office area.

"Hi, I have a huge emergency that I need fixed right away," Rochelle pled?

"What sort of emergency Miss," Marshon asked?

"I just bumped my husband's car and put a dent in the back bumper?"

"I'm on break, but I'll come out and look at it to see how bad it is!"

"Thank you!"

They both walked out to the yellow Corvette at which Marshon looked at the dent.

"I don't think Evander is going to consider that small dent a priority Miss."

"Is Evander like, the mechanic here?"

"No Miss, he is the body man!"

"Can I speak with him please?"

"No problem! I'll go back and get him for you."

They both returned inside the client's area, where Marshon left her and went into the painting room.

"Hey Evander! There is a woman outside with a small dent in her bumper, who is begging to speak with you about fixing it right now! I already told her that you don't consider dings like that a priority, but she still wants to talk with you."

"Ok, tell her I'll be out there in a minute!"

Marshon returned to the front office and gave Rochelle the response. Evander paused what he was doing and walked into the office, where the female customer was pacing about.

"Yes Ma'am, can I help you," Evander asked?

"I certainly hope you can! I accidentally put a dent in my husband's new Corvette, that he told me not to drive, so I really hope you can fix it or else he is going to kill me," Rochelle stated!

"I am a little busy with a job I have to finish, but maybe if you bring it in the morning!"

"When my husband gets home, he is going to go inside that garage to admire that car until he comes to bed, so I might not live to see tomorrow," Rochelle reasoned!

"You are certainly too beautiful for any man to do without, so I doubt he would want to lose you," Evander argued!

"I wish that was true! But I will pay you if you help me, please," Rochelle asked?

"My boss is going to kill me, but I'll try and get that dent out for you Miss..." Evander enquired?

"I'm Rochelle! Rochelle Pedward!"

"Nice to meet you, Rochelle! I'm Evander!"

It was an extremely cold day across the province with a -27 Degrees Celsius temperature, and a western wind that made it felt closer to -40. The car frame specialist took the Corvette's key and drove the car into a separate bay. There was something weird about the female, who requested to be inside the repair station while Evander fixed the car. The request led the body-man to believe that she had something inside the car she wished to keep secret, nevertheless he agreed. Once inside the garage Evander collected the tools he would need for the job and started working at removing the dent. While he worked Rochelle walked around the garage looking at the tools and other items laying about. Evander was accustomed to the scent of motor oil and gas inside the workplace, but Rochelle's perfume overpowered all the odours.

"Why would you choose to drive a corvette on a day like this in winter?"

"I had an appointment, and my car door was frozen shut. So, I figured I'll just take the husband's new car and be right back, until some old woman backed into me at the hair salon."

Coy walked into the garage and saw Evander attending to the Corvette instead of the Chrysler 300 he should have been painting. The vehicle frame specialist was in the process of attaching a special suction device, that would make repairing the bumper rather easy.

"Evander, what the hell are you doing? Big Roy will be here in about two hours to see the car and you still haven't painted it yet," Coy argued!

"Sorry Coy! This lady came in with a quick emergency, so I'm just pulling out a dent for her," Evander answered!

"Well, you better get it out fast and paint that car before Big Roy gets here," Coy exclaimed before he stormed out!

"Opps! It seems as if I got you in trouble, sorry," Rochelle declared!

"I prefer to be in trouble with my boss, rather than knowing you're in problems with your husband," Evander said!

"You're so sweet! I wish I had a caring man like you," Rochelle responded.

"What! You mean your husband isn't rubbing that sexy body down and easing your stress," Evander exclaimed?

"I wish he was! In fact, he is more interested in this car than he is in me," Rochelle insisted!

"If your husband isn't treating you the way he should, maybe it's time to get a boyfriend who can come through and take care of your needs," Evander offered?

"I don't think that I could do that," Rochelle stated!

"Then take my number while you think about it? If you even need someone to talk to at times, I can be there for you," Evander said!

"Pop," sounded the dent as the body man pulled it out!

"It's all fixed and brand new," Evander reported!

"How much will that cost me," Rochelle asked?

"For me it would be free, but unfortunately, it's not my garage. So, go and ask Coy and I will bring the vehicle out front for you," Evander explained.

"That's no problem, Evander, thank you so much," Rochelle stated before she went in search of Coy!

Coy was in the front office on the phone when the female customer walked in from the back.

"Yes, Mrs. Fields your Subaru is ready for pickup," Coy said then hung up the phone seconds later!

"Oh my God, your employee Evander was a life saver today! If it wasn't for him my husband would have killed me for damaging his new car! How much do I owe you for the job he did," Rochelle declared?

"Just give me a hundred dollars for the service," Coy asked?

Rochelle retrieved the money from her purse and paid the bill, without alerting the insurance company about the incident. To hide all evidence from the transaction, she took the receipt from Coy and tore it into tiny pieces, then tossed them into the garbage. Evander waited by the vehicle door until Rochelle walked out, at which he held it open and allowed her to climb inside. As the body-man turned to walk away Rochelle asked him about the number he promised, although she was hesitant and refused him earlier.

Two days into the New Year on January 2nd, Officer Gilmore, and his associates at the Dakota Ojibway Police Service, in Roseau River, received a nationwide alert from the RCMP Division Headquarters, which requested every law enforcement personnel to remain on the lookout for a U.D.S trailer that contained a stolen shipment of illegal guns. The guns were seized by police over a period of twelve months and were being stored at a warehouse, prior to their scheduled destruction appointment. The officers were not given a specific location, so they were out in search of the U.D.S trailer from the moment they received the information.

On the third day of January, Officer P. Valesquez was heading south along Road 12 North, when he observed something that seemed suspicious. Several meters after he passed over Road 10 North, was a small dirt road that could have easily been missed by commuters. There was a trailer that matched the one in question parked among several trees to camouflage it, and two 4X4 trucks at the tail end of the transporter. When Officer Valesquez went by one of the men saw his cruiser which caused them to panic. Valesquez counted four men when he passed and thought better to engage, in case they began shooting at him. With a humongous territory to police, backup could be well over half an hour away, which would put him at severe risk during a shootout. When Valesquez contacted his dispatcher for support, he learnt that the closest officers to his position were at least twenty-two minutes away, therefore he was advised 'to take caution'.

On the morning of January 3rd at 3:37 AM, Tim Warren who was the driver of the semi used to steal the trailer, drove to that designated location and dropped off his rear load. The men who organized the theft of the trailer in Quebec, were well aware of the nationwide search, so they brought the transporter to that remote location to empty it. The thieves left the trailer for a little over eleven hours while they surveyed it, before they returned to collect the goods at 2:55 PM. The robbers were on the scene for twenty minutes, which was unfortunately the same time Officer Valesquez chose to drive by that route. The weapons thieves were unpacking the trailer when one of them alerted his companions about the cruiser. Although the officer went by without stopping, the arms thieves climbed into a Dodge Ram truck and a Ford F-150 and sped away from the location toward Road 10 North.

When the Dakota Ojibway officer saw both 4X4s depart, he spun around in the middle of the road and drove back to the location. As the lone officer on a crime scene, Officer Valesquez kept in constant radio contact with his dispatcher, whom he advised about which route the thieves used to escape. There were no other vehicles on site, but the officer was unsure if everyone had left, so he exited his cruiser with his weapon at hand and snuck along the side of the trailer. The thieves fled from the scene instantly and left the rear door open, with crates scattered inside the transport and outside on the ground. The correct U.D.S trailer marking had been covered over with a Canadian Farmer's sticker, to conceal it from the authorities. From Officer Valesquez saw some of the abandoned weapons he had no doubt that was the trailer for which they searched. Valesquez was extremely relieved that the robbers had all gone, therefore he gave his dispatcher a description of both vehicles.

Officer Gilmore and Officer Pedward were both at a traffic stop issuing a motorist a hefty speeding ticket, when Officer Valesquez' alert aired. They were southwest of the trailer incident, close to the Letellier and Dominion City exit on Highway 75, and it would have taken them approximately twenty-two minutes to reach the location. Officer Valesquez reported to his dispatcher that both 4X4s separated at Road 10 North, therefore one of the vehicles would be heading towards the responding officers. The approaching officers were driving a Chevy Tahoe and a Chevy Impala, with their flashers engaged to alert motorists of their emergency. Officer Pedward was inside the Tahoe truck leading the charge and kept a look out for any Ford or Dodge trucks, although they were unsure if the thieves had turned off on another route. By then it was nearly 4:30 and the skies were beginning to darken, with the winter nights lasting longer than the days.

As the officers approached Roseau River Reserve, Pedward noticed a black Ford F-150 as it drove towards them, then went by in the opposite lane. There were at least two people inside the Ford and the driver tried to hide his face as they drove pass. Suspecting that it might had been the thieves, Officer Pedward spun the Tahoe around and began pursuing the Ford truck. The driver of the F-150 initially did not want to stop so he led the officers back toward Highway 75. Before the 4X4 occupants reached the highway they pulled to the side and chose to surrender, as the coppers pulled up behind them and took up evasive positions. Officer Valesquez had reported that the thieves appeared to be unpacking the trailer, therefore the officers knew the men were well armed. The Ford truck's license plate was registered to a man who lived in Alberta and had been in trouble with the law in the past.

"Everyone inside the truck! I want you to push your hands through the windows where we can see them clearly," Officer Pedward shouted from his position beside the Tahoe!

The two occupants inside the Ford threw their hands through the window to show their compliance.

"Driver! I want you to open the door from the outside and step out the vehicle with your hands held above your head," Pedward commanded!

The officers made both robbers exited their vehicle, then walked backwards towards them, before they were placed in handcuffs. Neither of the two Caucasian males wanted to get killed, therefore they surrendered peacefully and were taken into custody. Following the arrests, the officers found several crates that contained weapons inside the rear cargo compartment of the Ford. Upon closer inspection the officers learnt that the thieves had weapons without bullets, which may had been the reason they chose to surrender peacefully. Officer Gilmore arranged for a tow truck to transport their prisoners' F-150 to the local pound, after they removed all the weapons and other evidence from the vehicle. By the time Officer Pedward and Officer Gilmore brought the detainees to their lockup facility for processing it was nearly 7:00 PM and their scheduled workday ended at 6:00. The arresting officers still had hours of work to complete, wherein they had to accurately write up the arrest reports, take the detainees' fingerprints, and ensured their rights to contact a public defender were met. To deter his wife from waiting for him to have supper, Officer Pedward telephoned her and advised her that he still had lots of work to complete and would be home in a few hours.

Back at Officer Pedward's residence, Rochelle contacted Evander the moment her husband notified her that he would be home several hours later. The couple had been having marital problems and were encouraged to share an emotional evening once every week to rekindle their romance. Each time they had their romance date, Rochelle either prepared a fantastic meal or they went out to dine. That failed occasion was their second consecutive missed date; hence the female was frustrated after preparing a great meal. Rochelle had spent all day cooking and preparing herself for a pleasure filled evening, therefore she had her hair well done and was dressed in a tantalizing skin-tight red dress, with a split that went up to her thigh. The night she envisioned included her husband pleasing her orally at some point, thus there was no need for an underwear.

They lived in a neighborhood with several other officers and their families, so Rochelle knew that to spend time with Evander she would have to take extra precaution. The night had settled across the province, so it would be much more difficult for her nosy neighbors to see her secret lover. Since her visit to the garage, she had thought constantly about the things Evander mentioned doing to her, thus she craved the experience of his caress. Rochelle felt as though she was living in a sexual prison, with a husband who did not please her intimately, and was through making love before she was even close to an orgasm. Despite her cravings, the married woman knew her husband had a dark temper, nevertheless she was frustrated and could not resist the temptation.

Rochelle instructed Evander where he should park his vehicle, in addition to the path he should take to get to her house. The young vehicle body repair specialist had no idea who the female was, but knew she was married from what she had stated. To ensure that neither he nor his lady friend got into trouble, Evander followed her instructions to the letter, and was at her location within seventeen minutes. The dress that was meant for Rochelle's husband nearly blew her new sideman's mind, once he entered the house and saw her attire. Instead of following his intuition and grabbing hold of the delectably dressed female, Evander decided to gradually make things develop, in case he was being deceived.

"What time are you expecting your husband," Evander enquired?

"Between eleven to midnight," responded Rochelle as she walked ahead.

There were pictures of her and her husband inside the days room, where she brought him to have a drink and got cozy beside the warm fireplace. Rather than bringing Evander into her marriage bed, the cautious wife assembled some pillows and blankets by the fire. Knowing her husband was a suspicious individual, the thought that he might smell her lover's body scent in the sheets, compelled Rochelle to implement another strategy. While Evander got cozy, she poured them a glass of wine, then brought her guest his drink, and sat close to him by the fire. Neither of them suggested a toast, therefore they clanged their glasses together and drank some of the contents.

"That asshole is your husband?"

"Oh, you know Ray?"

"Every person of colour round these parts, know who that racist asshole is!"

"But Ray is not racist."

"If that's what you believe! He has even roughed me up a few times in the past, for selling drugs when I never did!"

"I'm sorry to hear that, but are you here to talk about my husband, or show me some of what you were talking about at the garage," Rochelle asked as she leaned over and kissed Evander?

It was obvious that they were on the clock and the married woman wanted everything that was promised to her before she had to kick Evander out. Contrary to her husband, the autobody specialist had rough hands, which caused her body to tingle with each caress. Rather than taking the lead with the foreplay, Rochelle allowed Evander to seduce her and drifted back onto the pillows. While his lady friend got cozy, Evander began slowly running his fingers down her exposed thigh, before he reached her shoe and removed them both. The young vehicle specialist began massaging and passionately kissing his partner's feet, which sent chills through her entire body. There was no denying that Evander did everything differently from her husband, therefore Rochelle found herself making comparisons of every sexual maneuver. By the time Evander made his way back to her thigh, she was breathing heavily and shivering as if she was experiencing a seizure.

A slight rub over her vagina while he kissed her inner thigh, had Rochelle making all sorts of noises, before the young lover began orally stimulating her. In her eagerness to get at Evander's body, the adulterer began dragging off his sweater to feel the touch of his skin against hers. Thus far the bodywork specialist had managed to outscore her husband in all categories, which had her conspiring how to see him more often. To fully finalize her assessment of Evander's overall performance, Rochelle sat up and halted his antics, before she began removing his pants, while they passionately kissed. It felt excitingly dangerous having another man, made love to her inside the house she shared with her husband, hence that would be a secret she would have to keep. Evander came prepared knowing he would be seeing a married woman, thus he withdrew a condom for safety. Knowing whose wife she was, gave the repair specialist an added incentive to continue the relationship, therefore her pleading for more during coitus was an encouraging sign. By 9:00 PM Rochelle knew she would do whatever possible to prolong their affair, having never had someone made love to her that long.

Even though the question never arose, Evander would have been Rochelle's first sexual contact with a person of colour. The experience enabled the wife to achieve a level of sexual stimulation she never did, without the use of her sexual toys. The heat from the fireplace kept them warm, nevertheless perspiration was dripping from Evander who had been working as if he started a second job. After climaxing multiple times, Rochelle appreciated every minute her new lover spent satisfying her, but as the clock ticked closer to 9:30 he ejaculated. They laid there for several minutes with Rochelle cuddled under her side man's arm, while he struggled to catch his breath. The red dress had been taken off and thrown aside, thus they laid naked in each other's arms.

"So, when am I going to see you again," Rochelle asked?

"Whenever you call me and invite me over!"

"OK, my husband works some weird shifts at times, so stay prepared to come see me!"

"I already can't wait!"

After Evander got dressed and left, Rochelle took all the linen and pillowcases they used and threw them inside the washing machine. While the washing machine did the load, she hand washed and dried the glass that he used, and placed it back inside the cupboard. To ensure that her husband did not find any evidence someone had been there, she cleaned the area thoroughly and turned off the fire. Rochelle went as far as to use a disinfectant spray and cloth to wipe the door handles and remove any fingerprint that remained. Once she had sanitized the areas of concern, she went to her bedroom, put on her nightgown, and went to bed.

When Officer Pedward reached home at 10:37 PM, Rochelle was in bed sound asleep. Both plates with their evening suppers were covered over on the dinner table, and by the looks of Rochelle's meal, she did not consume a bite. He warmed his dinner in the microwave and ate his fill, before he washed the plate and went into his bedroom to go to bed. It had been a long day and the officer only wanted to get a decent night's rest before his morning shift began. The red dress that his wife wore earlier was thrown in the garbage inside the bathroom, so while he brushed his teeth, he noticed the fabric slightly hanging out. Rochelle's inquisitive husband took out the dress, and held it aloft to see the creative design, yet noticed a rip that happened when Evander yanked his wife back onto him. The location of the tear in the dress jolted the officer's curiosity, however because they were having marital problems he excused it as frustration, believing she did so due to her ruined evening. Ray threw the dress back into the garbage and could only shake his head at the thought of how amazing Rochelle must have looked wearing it. Knowing his wife was already mad at him for missing their date night, the officer snuck into bed quietly to avoid waking her.

Chapter 20

Celine brought Robin and Julien to the local school on the first day but had to speak with the principal about their enrollment. Julien already met a few boys at church who he would be sharing classrooms with, so he was quite relaxed and could not wait to begin. Robin on the other hand was extremely nervous, which led to her palms getting sweaty. The secretary inside the main office was very pleasant and welcomed the children to their facility, while they waited for the principal to return. When Principal Mutty walked into the office after she finished attending to the morning attendees, Celine's face dropped with surprise at the realization that her old French teacher was now in charge.

"Principal Mutty that is the mother for the two new students who were registered online during the Christmas break," exclaimed the secretary.

"Thank you," Principal Mutty stated as she walked over to the new students!

"Mrs. Mutty you are the principal here now," Celine asked?

"Hello Celine, it is wonderful seeing you again! And I see you brought Miss Shirley's next generation to attend your old school," Principal Mutty said.

"Kids this was my favorite teacher when I went to school here! Mrs. Mutty this is Robin…"

"And Julien! I have heard so much about you two; and will do my very best to make sure you both enjoy you experiences here at Roseau Valley," Principal Mutty interrupted!

"Principal Mutty the papers are here for signing," the secretary stated after placing several documents on the desk.

"Celine if you don't mind signing these papers for their enrollment," Principal Mutty asked?

"No problem, Mrs. Mutty," Celine answered as she went over and signed the papers!

The Caucasian principal's statement gave Robin a soothing feeling, as if she had someone in her corner. There was nothing further for Celine to do, therefore she left the children in the principal's caring hands. To assign both new students to their classes, the secretary filled out two forms and gave them each a paper to hand to their teachers. Once Celine departed Principal Mutty brought Julien and Robin to their new classrooms but made sure to drop off the little brother first, so Robin knew where to find him. After they left Julien inside his classroom, they went to the other section of the building where the older students attended. The nervousness that Robin had earlier was gone by then, which gave her confidence to step boldly into the class. As instructed, she gave the teacher the paper from the office and was shown an empty seat along the third row.

"Hey Robin! That's my girl Robin from church," Marcia shouted!

To avoid disturbing the class on her first day, Robin only waved to the people who she recognized on her way to her seat. The teacher wanted to introduce her to the entire class yet did not wish to embarrass her, thus he left her sitting while he spoke about her from the information he had received.

"Class I would like for you all to welcome Robin Walker, who is new to our school from Nova Scotia," declared the teacher!

"Hello Robin," everybody shouted!

"Hi everybody," Robin responded!

"Nice to meet you also Robin and welcome, I am Miss Moore! If there is anything you wish to know, kindly raise your hand, or come over to my desk if nobody is there," the teacher exclaimed!

It was a blissfully cold start to the day across Manitoba and the temperature was not slated to get much better. Before Celine exited the school, she buckled up her winter jacket and put on her gloves, to protect herself from the bitter cold. Tamara was aware that Robin and Julien would be starting school that morning, therefore she telephoned just as Celine began walking to her vehicle. The cellular was deep inside Celine's handbag, so she had to search through several items to find it. As soon as she retrieved the phone and saw who the caller was, the relieved mother quickly responded to the call.

"Hi sis, good morning! Did the kids begin school OK?"

"Good morning, Tamara! Yes, they did I just dropped them off! I was so nervous for them until I found out that my old French teacher is the new principal!"

"Wow, so I guess they are in safe hands!"

"Yes, they are! How is mom doing?"

"She sent her love to you and the kids, but she really feels lonely especially after you guys left! I am going to have to move her in one of these days, even though she loves her freedom."

"I know it's hard for her not having Lloyd or the kids around to cheer her up."

"You have no idea! Just last week she asked me if I would consider moving to Manitoba. I told her that my job can not be transferred, and she said nothing after that. I asked her if she wants to move there and still, she said nothing."

"I didn't think us moving away would affect her that bad."

"Listen, I explained to her that you had no choice to leave town with all the madness that you were facing, and she understands that. But she prefers having you guys in town compared to Manitoba, hundreds of miles away!"

Celine had some errands to run around town that morning and her second destination was the grocery store. Tamara had the day off from work and wanted to know how things were going, thus they spoke the duration of the trip. Contrary to freezing Manitoba, the weather was much milder in Nova Scotia, where Tamara was getting ready to prepare lunch. When Celine reached the store and parked her Cherokee there was a Range Rover truck beside hers, but she paid no attention to the vehicle and began retrieving her economical shopping bags from the rear. As she turned to walk to the store with the phone pressed against her ear, Aaron's mother stepped to the Range Rover with her cart filled with groceries.

"I heard you was back living here, and I couldn't wait for the day I ran into you, so I could give you a real piece of my mind! You have always been a slut since you lived here, and you will always be a slut! It's because of you why my boy was the way he was; and you alone is responsible for ruining my son! I told him you was a whore; and you would never stay with him, and I was right! As soon as you got the chance you ran off and shacked up with some other low life, who you ended up ruining his life too, and now you want them to charge my boy! Well, as long as I got money, they ain't sending my son to prison! And if he ends up getting sentenced, you best watch your back missy!"

"It isn't my fault your son is psychotic! With a drug addict mother like you, who wouldn't be," Celine commented as she walked away!

"I'll have you know I'm a born again Christian! But you're still a whore! You're still a whore," Jacquelin yelled!

Celine walked into the store and took a shopping cart to hold the items she wanted to purchase. Tamara was still on the line and overheard the entire conversation, yet was so shocked that she remained silent throughout.

"Who was that Celine? Don't tell me that was Aaron's mother?"

"The one and only!"

"I didn't think you had to deal with that stuff in Dominion City!"

"I really don't, well, unless I run into trash like her!"

Tamara laughed at the comment, while harboring the thoughts of how she truly felt. She respected Celine for the manner with which she dealt with the situation, although she would have preferred if she slapped the menacing mother across the face. Rather than apologizing for her son's actions, Tamara was stunned that Jacquelin would blame Celine for Aaron being a criminal.

"When do you think would be a good time to bring mom down for a visit?"

"Bring her for the summer, so you guys can meet my other brother! We don't have anything like a hotel in town, but there is a bed and breakfast place here that is quite accommodating," Celine exclaimed as she picked up fruits and placed them in the cart!

"We'll work out the exact date, but I'll tell mom to brighten up her spirit."

"OK and send her our love also! I'll call you next week sis, take care of yourself! Love you!"

"Love you too sis! Goodbye!"

Celine finished picking up the groceries they wanted at the house, then moved toward the cashier to pay for her items. There were only a few shoppers inside the store at that early hour of the morning, so the unoccupied cashier passed the time by fondling with her phone. Karen was always happy to see Celine and stopped browsing through the pages of the online retailer she was shopping on, to get her opinion on an item. Before Karen scanned any of the groceries that her friend placed on the counter, she first selected a photo on her phone and showed it to Celine.

"What do you think about this dress? Can you see me in it at the party next weekend," Karen asked?

Celine took the phone from Karen to get a better look at the picture. "I don't think the cup is going to hold your breast that well. Those dresses were made for women with almost no breast!"

"I was thinking that to myself, how about this one," Karen enquired after swiping to the next picture?

"I think this one will fit you better! It's made for bigger size women and the girls won't feel squeezed!"

"I am so happy you came in here this morning! Better yet, I'm happy you didn't have to run into that so called Born Again Christian Jacquelin!"

"Wished I was that lucky! I ran into her the second I pulled into the parking lot!"

"How did that go? That woman wanted to take your head off for years!"

"After her bastard son killed my fiancée, instead of apologizing for him, she tried to blame me for Aaron being who he is!"

"The nerve of that woman! I hope you set her ass straight!"

"Oh, hell I did! I told that bitch the reason her son is psychotic, was because she is psychotic!"

A male customer started a line behind Celine, who was still waiting for Karen to begin scanning her products. The store clerk had no intention of tabulating Celine's grocery until she was good and ready to do so, regardless of how many people waited in line.

"Do you know rumor had it that her son Andrew and Aaron have the same father! She supposedly cheated on her husband when Aaron's father came to visit, then got pregnant after he left, and gave the child to the husband!"

"So there really is another bastard out there who is completely like Aaron?"

"Unfortunately, so honey! Nah, just joking, I heard he is a real quiet young man!"

The male in line began getting impatient and voiced his displeasure. "Excuse me ma'am, but some of us have places to go and things to do! Can you ring up the lady's groceries, so I can get out of here?

"Excuse me sir! But I don't come to your workplace and hassle you for your lousy service, so don't come to mine and try that shit!"

The customer withheld his comments from that moment and waited patiently. Even Celine felt uncomfortable and did not know how to react, having heard her friend made similar outbursts in the past.

"The nerve of some people I tell you! Listen honey, I take breaks when I feel like taking breaks, if I feel like taking a break right now, I take a break, be it two, five, ten minutes, whatever! Ain't nobody going to tell me when to get back to work either, I work when I damn sure feel like it, so don't come up in here like you my boss," Karen argued as she finally began scanning the groceries?

"I might have to run to the mall in the city, to find something to wear to that party myself! That's if I don't find anything inside my closet that fits."

"No need going through any type of hassle getting all dolled up round these folks! Believe me, almost everybody is going to be wearing tee shirts and jeans, I guarantee it!"

"You make it sound like nobody in town have any style," joked Celine!

"Outside of church, what do you see most people wearing," Karen asked?

Celine stopped packing her groceries into her bags and looked back at the customer behind her, then thought to herself. "Come to think about it, you are right! That seems to be all everybody wears around here, except for my brother! He is always in those greasy overalls!"

Karen laughed as she finished scanning the items and handed Celine the bill. "Will you be paying by credit or debit, hon?"

"Make it debit," Celine responded before she tapped her card for the payment.

Karen began scanning the male customer's groceries while Celine finished packing her belongings. Before going back out into the cold, Celine ensured her scarf was tucked tight, jacket closed and zipped to her neck, tuque covered her ears, and gloves fitted on both hands. The aggressive cashier blew her friend a kiss, as she held her Cherokee's key in hand and prepared to leave.

"Say hello to your mom for me; and see you next week, if I don't have to stop by here for something else before then," Celine stated with a giggle!

"OK Celine, talk to you later hon," Karen declared!

Celine left and drove directly home to drop off some meats and dairy products she bought, before she went to her next appointment at the bank. She had managed to fill six bags with groceries, but rather than making two trips to carry the items inside, she grabbed them all and struggled to the door. Miss Shirley heard when the Cherokee pulled onto the driveway and saw her daughter bringing the bags toward the door, so she opened it to assist. To offer further assistance, Miss Shirley took the two bags from Celine's left hand, which appeared to be the lighter load.

While taking the bags Miss Shirley said, "The next time that bitch Jacquelin come at you like that, you best take Karen's advice and slap that bitch into tomorrow!"

"How could you have heard about that already?"

"News travels fast round Dominion City honey! Plus, my girls gotta keep me in the loop!"

"I better cancel my hair appointment, because that's going to be the topic in that saloon all day, and I really don't want to hear about it," Celine argued as she entered the house!

Chapter 21

Julious Simms was an extraordinary artistic colored youth, who was born at the Winnipeg General Hospital and grew up in Dominion City. The young man had an unbelievable music talent, wherein he could play several musical instruments and was the cornerstone of the choir. His primary involvement in the group was creating the rhythms to which the members sang, during which he would play the piano. Chris, the other male choir member sang bass and played the guitar, while May was their best drummer and strongest backup singer. The group performed away from their church a few times, wherein they would sing without their musical instruments. Julious' cohorts in such cases would perform to the beats he provided, but the young musician was always the mastermind behind the music.

Born to a mother of Sudanese descent and a Canadian father, the seventeen-year-old had one other sibling who was seven years his senior. His older brother Evander Simms was his mentor and someone he hoped to be just like. Before his brother went away to college in Ontario several years prior, he promised Julious that he would move back to help take care of him. After Evander completed his academics in electrical engineering, instead of seeking work in the larger cities, he did as he promised. Growing up in such a diverse community with limited cutting-edge medical technology, was indeed difficult for people with physical deficiencies, yet Evander taught Julious to do extraordinary things. Regardless of what the town lacked; their community thrived much better than the surrounding villages throughout the region. Each day one in every four vehicles to pass by Dominion City, statistically stopped for food, gas, or as tourists. The visitors who spent money within the town's limit, helped their economy and local businesses to thrive.

Julious' father's name was Gary Simms, a trucker who worked at a Winnipeg

Industrial Company, for whom he drove their big rig trailers throughout Canada and the U.S. As a trailer tractor operator who travelled across both countries, Gary had a strong view on the state of blackness in both nations and would always share his thoughts with his sons. His mother Evelin was part owner and one of the hair stylists at Cora Salon, where most of the ladies within the community went to get their hair done. That New Year semester should have been Julious' first at his new college away from home, instead Evelin protested him moving away to Ottawa, where he had gotten accepted to attend Algonquin College. The young artistic youth had a fierce love for politics, religion, the environment, and black pride, to which his mother always said, 'he would either become a leader of men or get killed for his beliefs'. Unlike most youths his age who enjoyed playing video games, Julious did not even own a console and instead preferred spending his time, either studying music or black history.

At choir practice one Friday evening, the group was working on a new song that they had trouble perfecting. They would normally end practice by 9:00 PM, then chatted and joked around before they went home for the night. Following all their mishaps they realized it was nearly 10:00 PM and yet they were far from acquiring the right acoustics. With several of team members getting tired they decided to terminate the practice and reconvened from where they ended the next time. Due to the lateness everyone quickly left rather than lingering behind to chat like they customarily did. There was no one else in the building once Julious, May, and Chris got dressed for the weather, so they closed the church doors, said their goodbyes, and went their individual ways. Julious had driven his mother's Toyota Rav-4, therefore he did not require anyone's help getting home.

Over at the Renegade Shooting Club the business held its regular Friday night extravaganza. Thomas and Andrew were there from 7:00 PM that evening and spent two hours unloading clips of bullets inside the shooting range. After their marksmanship trials ended, they returned to the lounge area where they sat down to have a few beers before they went home. The vibe inside the lounge was a bit different from regular nights, wherein they had a DJ playing music with flashing lights like a discotheque. Robin went over to their table and took their orders, following which she left to retrieve the beers. Andrew phoned Jacquelin while they waited for the beverages to arrive, to enquire if she wanted anything from the establishment. Veronica was behind the bar attending to the customers sitting on the stools, but she was also responsible for providing whatever her co-worker requested. As soon as Robin collected the beers at the bar, she returned them to the customers and was paid a twenty-dollar bill by Thomas.

Wherever Robin went across the lounge Andrew watched her keenly, as if he could not take his eyes off her. Thomas had to step away from the noise to hear Jacquelin on the phone, so while walking back to their table he observed his son watching the waitress. There were a few people dancing to the music on a small dancefloor, while DJ D.C played a mixture of tunes from his catalog. As soon as he sat down Thomas signalled Robin over and ordered three Club Sandwiches to go. The chef in the gun club's kitchen made an awesome sandwich, therefore Jacquelin was sure to put her order in. Andrew behaved nervous each time Robin went by their table for service, even though he had mentioned he had no interest in the young biracial beauty. Once the sandwiches were prepared, Thomas and Andrew finished their beers before they left the establishment.

The gentlemen whom they routinely competed against for marksman of the night honors, did not show up that evening. On their way to their vehicle however, Thomas noticed Johnny's Dodge Ram truck parked in the adjacent lot, along the third isle of stationed vehicles. The engine was running, and the headlights were on, so it took some effort to see if the driver was inside the truck. After Thomas moved out into the clearing, he saw Johnny sitting behind the steering wheel, smoking a cigarette, and staring at the shooting lounge. To be courteous Thomas tried waving at their shooting range opponent, who was so focused at whatever he was looking at that he did not even notice him. As soon as they pulled out onto the main street, Thomas addressed his son's actions of which he was not pleased.

"I saw you inside that lounge! You couldn't keep your eyes off that mixed girl if you tried!"

"I wasn't watching anybody dad!"

"So, what do you call what you were doing in there?"

"I was mining my own business!"

"Just make sure you remember what I said! Our bloodline should never mix with others! Your brother made the mistake and where did that get him? But then again, he is not my son!"

Andrew turned his head and started ignoring his father by looking through the window; and did so for the duration of their trip home. Neither of them spoke thereafter, hence Jacquelin sensed there was a problem the instant they walked in. The agitated son went directly to his room and locked the door, while his father took their weapon cases and locked them away safely. When Thomas returned to the main room, instead of disclosing what happened to his wife, he simply collected his sandwich and went to his bedroom.

Back at the shooting range the excitement gradually simmered the closer they got to closing. Once DJ D.C finished playing ten minutes before closing hour and began packing up his equipment, most of the customers left and went home. Robin and Veronica had begun making preparation for closing, while a table with three individuals lingered behind. The customers who remained were friends of Veronica and were waiting for her shift to end, for them to continue their partying elsewhere. There were two males and a female, one of which was Harry Pike, who was Veronica's newest boyfriend, with Suzette and Barry who were also dating. When the chef finished cleaning up his kitchen area, DJ D.C requested a ride home and the cook agreed. Minutes later they left together, as Veronica cleared out the cash register and documented the business' earnings, which she then placed in a safe inside the manager's office.

With Veronica preparing to close shop for the night, Barry went outside to warm up their vehicle. While making his way to his Toyota Corolla, Barry looked around and noticed Johnny's 4X4 parked in the other lot. He had no idea who the man behind the wheel was and could barely see him inside the foggy truck, so he proceeded to his car. When Barry entered his vehicle and started the engine the windshield and other glasses were all covered with frost, so he turned on the defroster and used his glove to wipe away some of it. By the time he finished cleaning the glass and looked where the Dodge Ram had been stationed, the truck had vanished off the premises.

Veronica made sure the business sign lights were turned off and ignited their closed signal. With everything in order inside the lounge, the waitresses began preparing to leave the establishment. Harry and Suzette exited the building before Robin and Veronica, who armed the alarm system and locked the door.

"Robin, do you want a ride home," Veronica asked?

"It's OK, your friends have been waiting for you all night! I'll be fine, see you tomorrow," Robin answered as she placed her Ear-pods into her ears and turned on the music!

"Alright see you tomorrow!"

Veronica climbed into the car with her friends, at which the driver drove away as Robin began walking home. Robin felt safe despite being in a new community that felt like a ghost town by certain hours of the evening. Dominion City was not a place where you would find traffic, unless there was some sort of road work being done. Contrary to Nova Scotia which had streetlights all throughout the city, not every where along the roadways in their small town was properly lit. It was a very cold night, but Robin was dressed for the weather and felt comfortable walking along. As she approached Coulter Street, a vehicle with its high beam headlights barrelling down toward her, forced her to scurry into the pile of snow left by the plow truck along the roadside. There were no constructed sidewalks within the town limits, but motorists were seldomly kind to pedestrians. The frightened female was unsure if the driver noticed her or if they intentionally tried to hit her, so she crossed over to the other side and walked toward the incoming vehicles.

Since that weird incident on the first day of Robin's employment, Veronica drove her home most nights for precautionary reasons. Although they lived in a safe town, Veronica knew there were several undercover perverts in their community, some of whom scared her personally. On those odd occasions where Robin had to walk home, she often felt as if she was being watched. The speeding vehicle spooked her tremendously, therefore she constantly looked around as she walked along. There was a second vehicle coming up behind her and as it drew closer, she heard the brakes being applied. Robin again moved over into the plowed snow and stopped, before she turned around to see who the driver was. Julious pulled up and wound his window down once he noticed it was Robin.

"Hey, can I give, you a ride, home," asked Julious who spoke with different levels and paused in midsentence at times?

"Oh, it's you Julious! Thank you, I would appreciate that," Robin responded.

The young lady walked around to the passenger's door and got into the Rav-4. Inside the Toyota was much warmer than outside, so Robin removed her gloves and placed her hands by the air vent to get them warm. Julious was listening to some sample beats he had created and reached forward to turn off the power, when Robin requested that 'he let it play'?

"That's a unique sound," Robin commented!

"Are you ready, to audition for, church choir? I have a, song I want, to hear you, sing," Julious requested?

"I don't want to embarrass myself, I am really only a bathroom singer, nothing more! But thanks," Robin said!

"Let me be, the judge of, that please? Look inside my, bag and take, a paper out," Julious asked?

The artistic musician made Robin take a music sheet with the song they had been practicing all evening at choir practice. While Robin looked at the words to the song, Julious scrolled through his beats catalog and found the rhythm to accompany the song. With the rhythm playing Julious began humming the words to the melody, which were elegant and beautifully written. Robin found herself singing the song in her head and grasped the words quickly, therefore she requested that he restarted the rhythm?

When Robin started singing the words, "We are all born, In a world of sin, But since I let you in, I've eased my pain, 'Glorious Lord', I sing to thee, In hopes that you will, Forever hear my Plea, Plea, Plea---" Julious became so mesmerized by the silkiness in her voice, that he pulled to the side of the road and stopped the vehicle. The voice and song were a match made in heaven, therefore the young musician requested that 'she performed the tune for the other choir members to judge'? Robin felt shy and lacked the confidence to sing in front of an audience, but she agreed to do it if Julious answered a few questions? To add such a talent to their choir the young man readily agreed, as he checked his mirrors and pulled back onto the roadway.

"Why does the females think that you are..." Robin began then froze?

"What, weird?"

"Yes, weird?"

"Because we might, have the same, skin but that, does not mean, that we are, both black!"

"Wait a minute, say what?"

"If we both, represent different things, culturally I won't, waste my time, with your blackness!"

"Those were pretty interesting perspectives! Why do you feel so deeply about your black culture?"

"Because most of, our people are, illiterate and blinded, by the bling's, of society while, the same people, who enslaved us, years ago are, plotting to annihilate, us next! When you can, rely on illiteracy, to lead and, control generations of, people you exhaust, every strategy at, your disposal to, acquire what you, want!"

"I understand why the females feel the way they do about you now."

"And what do, you think," Julious asked as he pulled onto Shirley's driveway?

"I think you are quite interesting! I like that! Thanks for the drive home, goodnight," Robin stated as she exited the Toyota!

"Goodnight," Julious answered and waited until she entered the house before he drove away!

Chapter 22

E ach day Viveen Woolrey went to school her popularity decreased since the Nova Scotian students began attending Roseau Valley School. As the lone daughter of one of the most prominent families in Dominion City, Viveen was accustomed to being followed by a group of girls and boys wherever she went each day. Since Julien began attending the school, members of her paparazzi group started focusing their interests on learning about the eastern coastline of Canada. Some of the children thought Julien had a fabulous accent and would ask silly questions just to hear him speak. Watching the kids who used to crowd around her, encircle the young newcomer at lunchbreaks angered Viveen, who knew she had to do something to restore her popularity.

One Friday after school Viveen returned home and went to her parents' bedroom to discuss her displeasures with her mother. As she approached, the door was slightly closed, while Jacquelin paced about the room with her phone against her ear. Viveen had no idea who her mother was speaking with, but from the tone of their conversation the person was either some attorney or a government official. The topic of their conversation was another unknown, until Viveen overheard Jacquelin mentioned Aaron's name, at which she snuck closer to the door and eavesdropped. Her mother was getting an update on the trajectory of Aaron's court case, from his talented new trial lawyer, Monsieur Cristophe McGill.

"If my son was never provoked by that witch Celine Devers and her so called boyfriend, he would have never had to shoot him! I know she has been using Aaron since the day he met that tramp! I've watched her manipulate him until she got him to do whatever she wanted! Trust me, she is a devil! But you know how boys are, as soon as they start getting some ass, they lose their damn minds!"

"Well, Mrs. Woolrey we filled the court documents to handle Aaron's trial two weeks ago, and I just received his discovery with the rest of evidence filed in his case so far. I started looking through the files, video evidence, and witness statements and think we have a good chance to get your son free!"

"If you people need me to come up there and testify that Celine has been brainwashing my son since he was a teenager, I will be more than happy to jump on a plane? That tramp thinks she is going to ruin my son's life, then run back to her old province while he gets sent to prison, but she got another thing coming!"

"I don't believe that will be necessary Mrs. Woolrey! But I will keep you up to date on everything throughout the proceedings!"

"Thank you for representing my son, Mr. McGill! I am confident the good lord will give you the tools to get him out of that damn horrible place!"

Once Viveen heard her mother finishing the conversation she slowly moved away from the door. While walking by her brother's bedroom door, the nosy little girl peeped through the cracked opening and saw Andrew staring at a picture of Robin. The picture was taken during one of their shooting practices, following which Thomas and he would have a drink in the member's lounge. Andrew had downloaded the photo onto his computer and was staring at his screen, with his right hand lodged in his shorts masturbating. Viveen obtained a disgust look on her face, as she moved from the door and withdrew her cellphone, which she used to dial her best friend, Marla.

"Hey Viveen, what's up," Marla greeted!?

"You will not believe the gossip I just heard about Julien and his fake family!"

"Don't keep me in suspense, what is it?"

"I heard that their mother used to work for my uncle, as some prostitute or whatever! Then she like ran away and married some other dude, had kids for him and everything, while all the time talking with my uncle on the side!"

"Say what?"

"When my uncle found out what was going on, he killed the guy! So now they had to move from Nova Scotia, because their mother is some sort of a government witness against my uncle."

"That is crazy! They must be in that witness protection program thing!"

"I don't think they expected anybody to find out their business."

"Well, too bad for them, we know everything," Marla emphasised!

"Viveen, come here honey," Jacquelin called from her bedroom?

"Anyways my mom is calling me, so I have to go," Viveen declared!

"OK, later," Marla stated before disconnecting their call!

The first person to whom Marla told the story was her older sister Simone, who was one of Robin's classmates. Although she neglected to mention the story's source, Marla told her sister how Robin and Julien had to flee from Nova Scotia with their mother and were under the protection of Federal Police. Rather than portraying the family as victims, the little girl made it appeared as though her friend's brother was the one being crucified, while Celine and her children got away free. Like every other gossip account revealed in Dominion City, the flawed details travelled at the speed of light among the young Caucasians. Students of colour were the minority at Roseau Valley School, therefore throughout that weekend none of the Walkers' associates heard of the circulating rumor to alert them.

Monday morning when Robin and Julien returned to school, Linton was waiting inside the entrance door for his friend, so they could walk to class together. As they walked down the main hallway with Robin close behind, all the white students began ignoring them, while some whispered among themselves. With most of the children giving them the silent treatment, Viveen, Marla, and several of their reclaimed followers stood by their lockers and laughed at the flustered students. The bias treatment continued until someone yelled, "Snitches", following which several others began adopting the chant. When Robin realized how the other students were reacting towards them, she accompanied her brother and Linton to their classroom, to ensure they reached safely. Students who would normally acknowledge them, were behaving as though they became rivals over the weekend. Though none of the students got physical, their discriminatory behavior was just as provoking, yet Robin was unfazed having learnt how to handle tense situations from her mother in Nova Scotia.

Julien on the other hand was not as tactful and did not understand why the students referred to them as snitches, so he asked Linton 'if he thought they were addressing him'? Linton had no idea who the other students were defaming, thus throughout that experience he was terrified. Once they entered their classroom it became evident who the students had been rebelling against, when Linton's white friends addressed him, but ignored Julien. Mrs. Kirkpatrick their Mathematics teacher began class a few minutes after they took to their seats, therefore everyone began class focused on discussing fractions. Midway through the period Mrs. Kirkpatrick asked them to form groups of four, at which all the Caucasian children rushed to create teams. There was one other student of colour inside their classroom, who was a female named Deborah Tomilson. When the rumors about Robin and Julien's murdered father were circulating, Deborah was not told the details, therefore she had no knowledge of the ongoing conflict. After most of the white children rushed to not get chosen into the group with the new student, the only four persons left were Linton, Julien, Deborah, and Samuel Carleson. By the time the groups were finalized, all the best tables across the classroom had been selected, leaving the one closest to the window. Linton's group had to sit close to the cold window to participate in a quiz that Mrs. Kirkpatrick wanted completed.

Samuel was not content with the outcome and requested a change with someone, but Mrs. Kirkpatrick was not someone who tolerated ignorance. Despite his negligence, Samuel was forced to join the final group or risked being sent to the principal's office. With everyone in place the teacher went around the room and gave each team a paper with several math problems. Mrs. Kirkpatrick promised the winning team a special prize if they finished first with all the correct answers. When their teacher began the clock, Deborah and Julien began dicing through the questions as if they knew the answers. Linton and Samuel were fortunate to find themselves on such a talented team, where none of them had to offer any input into the responses. The other kids expected them to struggle and thereby spend a much longer time beside the cold window, but they surprised everyone by finishing first. After they finished and handed their paper in, they were allowed to leave the class twenty minutes early, so they went to the cafeteria ahead of the upcoming break. To maintain solidarity with the other protesting students, Samuel walked closer to Deborah and Linton in case anyone saw them together. As soon as they got Samuel in private, Linton tried to uncover what was happening with the other students, so he questioned him away from the watchful eyes.

"Why were people ignoring and talking bad about Julien and his sister this morning in the hallway," Linton enquired?

Samuel was a bit hesitant to answer the question and tried looking away.

"Answer the question or I'll never let you copy off my work sheets again in class," Deborah threatened!

"Marla was telling everyone over the weekend how Julien's family was sent here under the witness protection program to hide. And that they were being watched by federal agents," Samuel answered.

"Why is everyone calling my friend a snitch," Linton asked?

"I don't know who started all of this! But word has it that Viveen's brother killed Julien's father after they set him up; and now his mother is working with the Feds to send him to prison!"

Julien was in shock and could not believe what he had heard. After they moved away from Nova Scotia to get away from the madness that surrounded his father's death, the topic ended up right back on their doorstep. The little boy had given thought to what he would have done to the man responsible for killing his father if they ever meet, and he feared going to prison, yet he would have avenged his dad's murder. As much as he had thought of his reaction toward the shooter, he never thought of his interactions regarding the man's family, so he really did not know how to react to the news. Linton tried reasoning with Samuel to determine how Celine's family could be considered snitches, for wanting to put the man who killed their relative behind bars. From Julien heard the words, 'the man who killed his father', nothing else processed through his thoughts, hence his mind lingered from their conversation.

Five minutes after Deborah's group were allowed to leave class early, the second group of students to complete the quiz walked into the cafeteria. The group included the two females who his companions were referring to, Viveen and Marla along with Jake and Annie. The cafeteria employees were busy getting the food ready for lunch, so there were no one supervising the kids. Samuel and his teammates were seating at one of the many benches, when Julien got up and began walking towards Viveen and company.

"What is he doing," Samuel enquired when he noticed Julien moving toward Marla?

"Hey Julien! Where are you going," Linton asked?

Julien ignored his friend's worry some tone and continued walking until he was directly ahead of Viveen and her associates. Jake and Annie knew enough of the situation to remain at the back of the group, in case things got ugly. Miss Belcour who was the cafeteria cashier, was bringing her cash tray to the machine to prepare for their busy lunch period.

"Why were you spreading propaganda that my mother is a snitch," Julien demanded?

Marla felt nervous and tried to react cynical as if she was innocent. "I don't know what you are talking about," she giggled!

"Maybe this will refresh your memory," Julien stated before he slapped her across the face!

"Hey, stop that," Miss Belcour shouted as she placed the tray inside the machine before she moved to intervene!

Marla grabbed for the left side of her jaw and began crying. Everyone was surprised by Julien's reaction, especially Viveen who thought that maybe she was his next victim. Viveen felt the slap as though it was her, therefore she spun in the direction from which they came and tried to escape. When she tried to run, she tripped over Annie's foot, fell awkwardly to the ground, and broke her left hand against a bench. Miss Belcour ran over and grabbed Julien's right hand before she helped Viveen to her feet.

"Why are you putting your hands on little girls? That will not be tolerated in this school! Didn't you parents teach you any manners? Let's go, I am bringing you all to the principal's office," Miss Belcour stated!

Back inside Miss Moore's classroom, Robin experienced all sorts of mockery throughout the period. The young ladies who sat behind her threw balls of paper at her, each time the teacher turned her back to the class. By period's end Robin was beyond frustrated, so much that she planned on telephoning her mother and taking the rest of the day off from school. Miss Moore completed her lessons three minutes before the bell was scheduled to sound for lunch-break, so she allowed the students to talk among themselves, from their designated seats. Simone's seat was directly behind their newest student, whom they had been making jokes about since earlier that morning.

While all the other students chatted among themselves, Robin withdrew her cell phone to send her mother a text message. Simone was speaking with the little girl behind her, but kept taking stabs at Robin's entire family. Although Robin showed no ill effects from the teasing, Miss Moore sensed there was tension among her students.

"Someone said they have almost three families living in Ginew, who are being watched by the same agents that protect Robin's family," Simone said!

"My mom said city people always have to run away to rural areas like Dominion City to save their skin," Brenda commented!

"Well, I guess the life of a prostitute must be tough, but mothers have to do what they must to feed their kids," Simone joked!

Robin had heard enough and stopped writing her text. She stood up and moved to Simone, who was surprised when she reacted.

"Excuse me, Miss Walker please return to your seat," Miss Moore shouted!

Robin ignored the teacher and said to Simone, "What did you just call my mother?"

"I did not say anything," lied Simone.

Robin grabbed her by the hair and pulled her onto the ground, at which Miss Moore rushed over and held onto her. Everyone was on their feet trying to get the best view of the altercation, although it did not last very long. The lunch bell finally sounded, so Miss Moore dismissed the class before she accompanied Robin and Simone to the principal's office. When Robin entered the office the first person she noticed was her brother, who was sitting alone with his head down. It was evident that something had happened, therefore Robin walked over and sat beside him.

"Jules, what are you doing here," Robin whispered?

"I got into a fight with two girls," Julien whispered back.

Viveen was taken to the nurse's office, where she was being evaluated to determine the severity of her injury. Robin looked around the room and saw Marla sitting at the other end of the room. The principal was already speaking with Miss Belcour inside her office, when Miss Moore was allowed in, and joined the conversation.

"Who, that girl," Robin asked?

"Yes! She was one of them."

"But why are you fighting little girls?"

"Because they disrespected mom."

"Oh! I see."

"Why are you here? Did mom call you and tell you to come and check on me?"

"Not exactly! I sort of got into a fight in class with that girl over there."

"But that's Marla's sister," Julien stated!

"Well, she talks too much!"

"So does Marla!"

The brother and sister looked at each other and smiled, as Robin held onto Julien's hand. The principal's office door opened, wherein Miss Moore and Miss Belcour walked out. Neither lady made any eye contact or said anything to the children, as they went by and exited the main office. Each of the children could feel the rising tension inside the office, which was usually abuzz with the secretaries laughing and interacting. Principal Mutty was on the phone pacing about her office and appeared to be having a tough conversation. When she finally hung up the phone, the principal sat at her desk for a few seconds before she began moving toward the door. All the children felt nervous not knowing what to expect, hence Miss Mutty looked out and requested Robin and Julien. Despite the increasing tension Miss Mutty was remarkably calm and polite to her Nova Scotian transfers once they entered her office.

"Are you guys OK," Principal Mutty asked?

"Yes," Robin answered!

"Great! Now, Julien why did you slap Marla," Principal Mutty asked?

"Because she disrespect my mother and my family," Julien said.

"What did she do," Principal Mutty enquired?

"She said my mother is a snitch, and she is working for the government, so we had to move here!"

"Why would she say something as idiotic as that," Principal Mutty said?

"Because Viveen brother killed my father," Julien declared!

Principal Mutty was stunned at the revelation once she uncovered the personal nature of their conflict. The school nurse knocked her door of which she took notice and waved her in. The nurse had a report on Viveen's condition following an extensive evaluation.

"Yes Nurse Christian," Principal Mutty greeted!

"I have completed the examination of Viveen's arm, and it is broken and will

170

need further medical attention," Nurse Christian reported!

"Thank you, nurse," Principal Mutty said at which the nurse left the office!

"How did Viveen manage to break her hand Julien," Principal Mutty asked?

"After I hit Marla, she tried to run away and somehow dropped on the ground," Julien disclosed.

"How about you Robin, what happened today in class between you and Simone," Principal Mutty enquired?

"She called my mother a prostitute," Robin stated with a stern look on her face after hearing her brother's disclosure!

Principal Mutty could see that the young lady was in no mood for any further questions. "I had to notify your mother so she will be here shortly to bring you guys home. Once I get all the facts behind what happened, I will contact your mother regarding disciplinary actions. But thanks for letting me know what happened, it is obviously no coincidence that both of you experienced some sort of bias, but I will get to the bottom of this!"

After the principal showed Robin and Julien out, she motioned Marla and Simone into her office, to get their side of what happened. Nurse Christian had placed Viveen's injured hand into a sling, then brought her back to the office to wait for her mother. As the principal led the sisters into her office, she caught Viveen signalling Marla to remain quiet. Principal Mutty already knew enough about Viveen's personality to speculate that she was the mastermind behind the ordeal, but she needed confirmation on the details. While Viveen waited out in the office, the principal retrieved all the information from the sisters, whose stories coincided with the facts of what had transpired. Midway through Marla's questioning, Jacquelin showed up to pick up her daughter and transport her to the closest hospital, which was the Centre Medico-Social De Salaberry District several miles away. The news that Viveen's hand was broken following an altercation with Celine's son, had her mother blowing steam from the instant she entered the office.

"I want whosoever did this to my daughter charged and locked up in prison right this minute! Or I will personally sue the school board and close this damn place down," Jacquelin threatened!

"Mrs. Woolrey if you could please calm down, the principal is sorting everything out," countered the secretary?

"Do I look like I give a damn? I want the person who injured my daughter lock up right now," Jacquelin continued!

Principal Mutty overheard the quarrelling and asked Marla and Simone to wait until she returned. She then walked out the office and closed the door behind her while she dealt with the intolerable parent.

"Excuse me Mrs. Woolrey, but there is no reason for you to be behaving this way," Principal Mutty exclaimed!

"Listen Principal Mutty, my daughter called me and told me that someone tried to attack her! So, whosoever that person is, I want them locked up for assault," Jacquelin declared!

"OK Mrs. Woolrey enough! Now you can continue if you want all your family business about your oldest son out in the streets! Or you can take your daughter to the hospital and get her the medical treatment that she needs! Matter a fact, keep her home for the rest of the week, because I am suspending her effective immediately," Principal Mutty stated!

Jacquelin knew from the principal mentioned Aaron, that Viveen had done something questionable. Rather than continuing her rampage, the outspoken parent went over and took her daughter's school bag; before they quietly left the office. Celine was walking toward the office when she heard the loud exchange and stopped at the door, therefore as Jacquelin exited, she went right by and kept her head straight. Hearing the gist of the conversation was heartbreaking for Celine, who knew she had to have a serious discussion with her children. Principal Mutty was about to head back into her office when Celine walked in, therefore she paused to talk with the mother.

"I am sorry Celine, but I will have to suspend the kids for the rest of the week for fighting," Principal Mutty said.

"No problem, Miss Mutty, I totally understand. Let's go home guys," Celine calmly said.

Robin and Julien got up from their seats and walked hand in hand ahead of their mother through the office door. When they reached the Pathfinder none of the kids climbed into the front passenger seat, as they would often fight over. Instead, they remained together and sat beside each other supportingly, without uttering a word to their mother. The entire ordeal was difficult for Celine, who wanted her children to adore Dominion City, but found herself contemplating moving again. Celine drove home undecided on what to discuss with her children, yet thought it best to continue withholding certain information, therefore she simply apologized and left them to comfort each other.

It was a very tumultuous week at home with the children, both of whom never wanted to return to Roseau Valley School. Celine tried intimidating them to convince them they had to attend, yet they still declined and would have preferred returning to their old schools. Remarkably even Shirley agreed with her grandchildren and felt the school deserved to offer them an apology for the hurtful incident. Julien slept with Robin instead of his mother and tried avoiding her at all cost throughout the week. Whenever Robin and Celine would argue, Shirley listened and smiled to herself with memories of the old battles between her daughter and her.

Friday afternoon the doorbell sounded, but only Robin and Julien were home at the time. Shirley and Celine had driven to Winnipeg, where they intended to do a little shopping while they got away from the kids. Julien was playing about inside the living room with his toys when his sister attended to the door. Robin was shocked when she opened the door and saw Miss Mutty standing there, along with both their teachers.

"Hello Robin, may we come in," Principal Mutty asked?

"But of course, come on in! I'm sorry my mother and grandmother are not here at the moment, but I could find out what time they will be back," Celine declared?

Julien appeared from the living room and saw the teachers standing by their front door. His teacher waved to him at which he smiled and walked up closer to his sister.

"That won't be necessary Robin! We are here to see both of you to apologize for the incident that happened at school earlier this week! The entire staff apologizes for not taking more steps to prevent what happened, but we will do our best to make sure you guys are comfortable and never discriminated against again! We hope you guys rejoin us this upcoming week, your friends and teachers miss you, and we want you back at Roseau Valley," Principal Mutty begged?

"We are going back to school on Monday," Julien shouted!

"Thank you so much Principal Mutty! You heard Jules, we will be back in school on Monday," Robin said!

Chapter 23

As the date drew closer to Celine's reunion party, she became increasingly nervous having not seen any of those people since she ran away from town as a fifteen-year-old teenager. Rather than getting all dolled up to eventually feel overly dressed, Celine followed Karen's advice and wore a pair of jeans, a casual top, and cowboy boots. To add a little flare to her outfit, she sought out and purchased a brown colored pant, which she wore with a similar color sweater. Everyone was encouraged to arrive for 7:00 PM, therein they could enjoy an evening of music, dancing, and games with friends. The party was being held at Mauve's house, which she inherited after her parents died. When Celine reached the location at 6:30, everything was already prepared including the local musician DJ D.C, who they hired to spin the tunes.

As a past resident who spent most of her years in Nova Scotia, Celine was accustomed to people arriving at functions anywhere from an hour later until whenever. She personally arrived early to help Mauve and Karen with the preparations, and to greet the guests who showed up, however she never expected anyone to be there on time. Mauve, Karen, and Mark were already dressed and ready to party, knowing how prompt their community residents were. To begin the night all four friends enjoyed a shot of rum, while DJ D.C began playing the music. Celine and Karen started dancing with each other in the kitchen, when the doorbell sounded for the first time. By 7:00 o'clock nearly all the invited guests had arrived, which was shocking to Celine who would have arrived late had it not been her event. The last three guests arrived by 7:15, and thereby apologized to the hosts for their tardiness.

Celine was reintroduced to most of her old schoolmates, some of whom she remembered yet failed to recount others. No matter who she spoke with, they had a specific memory of her doing something either at school or in public. Three of the guys admitted they had crushes on her, which was enlightening though she had no interest in any form of companionship. Most of the men in town carried themselves less than desirable, therefore the pickings were slim for those seeking partners. Karen was by her side throughout most of the evening to add context to the faces, some of whom she still did not remember. After her second beer Celine had to use the bathroom, so she went to use the facility which was available. The party had taken off wherein patrons were mingling, drinking, and enjoying the atmosphere. When she exited the bathroom Simone and Marla's mother was standing there waiting, as if she wanted to use the facility.

"You must be Celine," said the woman?

"Yes, I am! And you are?"

"I'm Eve! Marla and Simone's mom from your kids' school!"

Celine recalled the names of the two sisters, therefore took a step back in case the woman had vindictive intentions. If the mother was as upset about the situation like Jacquelin, there was a possibility the party could end earlier than planned. Rather than being ignorant about the situation, Eve surprised Celine and stretched out her for a handshake. To be polite Celine shook the mother's hand even though she still did not know her stance on the issue.

"I am sorry for the problems my kids caused your family! I thought of calling you to apologize but I was afraid you wouldn't take my call," Eve shouted due to the loud music!

"I appreciate the apology! Let go have a beer and talk outside," Celine offered?

They retrieved their jackets and walked into the kitchen where they took two beers from the fridge, then went out the back door onto the porch. While preparing to go outside Celine looked around for Karen, who had gone to her vehicle for something. There were a few people present who were never classmates of Celine but, were either partners of her friends or attended Roseau Valley School when she did. Most of the people present were Caucasians, versus Celine and three other coloured guests.

"I had a long and serious talk with Principal Mutty, and she told me everything she found out after her investigation," Eve said!

"What did she tell you," Celine queered?

"She explained to me that all this was due to jealousy! I am sorry to hear of your loss, but to know that someone would try to use that to gain attention bothers me! I spoke with my daughters to get their side of what happened, and my youngest feels awful that she played any part in all of this," Eve explained.

"It was an unfortunate situation because, my children did not want to go back to that school! I was actually thinking about moving again, but they have since changed their minds! I don't know what got into them," Celine exclaimed!

"You know how kids are, always changing from one thing to the other," Eve stated as she withdrew a Vapor from her purse and took a few tokes.

"I don't get out much, but I don't recall seeing you anywhere round town," Celine said!

"Oh my gosh no! I love this town, but I don't go around those pesky people often, and I don't go to any of their condemning churches neither," Eve argued!

Celine smiled at the comment and said, "So, what do you do for fun in this town?"

"Fun! Honey people crawl to these places to die, not live! You have to hate those big cities and love the peace and serenity of the countryside to live here! And that was exactly what I wanted! My daughters can't wait to leave this boring town. The same way I couldn't wait to get out of those big cities."

"Same here! I could not wait to leave that toxic place after my fiancé died! I finally feel like I can breathe again," Celine said!

Karen walked out onto the porch searching for Celine, with two shots of rum and a Budweiser Beer in her hands. "There you are, I've been looking all over for you!"

"I'll talk to you some other time," Eve said as she walked off and went by Karen without acknowledging her!

"Are you OK? Here, I brought you another shot," Karen said as she passed Celine the shot glass! "That one acts like her shit don't stink! You should see her when she comes to buy groceries!"

Celine shook her head agreeably in response to the question, while pondering over what Eve said about the residents of Dominion City. Both ladies toasted each other then drank their shots with one gulp, after which they drank some of their beer. Three of the male guests walked out onto the porch and began smoking their cigarettes. The men all acknowledged Karen, who had already had a few drinks at that point and was rather flirty. Instead of allowing any of the men to assume she had interest in conversing, Celine smiled and excused herself and returned inside. The night was unseasonably milder than it had been throughout that winter. Every snowstorm had thus far been brutal and most days frigid, so the -3 Degree Celsius weather for them felt more like Spring.

By the time Celine reached inside Eve had already left. It had been a while since she last consumed so much liquor, so the intoxication effect was slowly starting to creep up. Her beer was nearly finished, and the fluids were beginning to run through her, so she went to relieve herself inside the bathroom. Johnny was never a classmate of Celine's, but he attended the school while she did and had driven Venessa to the reunion. Both he and Ronald went to use the facility and realized the door was closed, so they stood waiting for the bathroom to be vacated. While washing her hands in the sink, Celine overheard Johnny outside the door speaking with Ronald.

"I know you don't go to the gun range, but they have a young hot new waitress working there that daddy wouldn't mind putting across his lap and spanking, if you know what I mean," Johnny lamented!

The thought that someone of her age category could develop such ideas for a minor, instantly transformed the mother's mood. Celine shut off the pipe, opened the door, and walked pass Johnny, who had drunk a few beers and wanted to empty his bladder. The enraged female walked into the kitchen and looked around, before she saw a rack of knives on the counter in the corner. The blades of each knife were sharpened, so Celine withdrew the longest stainless-steel cutter and hid it against the side of her leg, as she walked pass the other guests. After living with Lloyd for many years, she knew most men typically left the bathroom door unlatched whenever they urinated. With the knife at hand, Celine pushed pass Ronald and barged into the bathroom, where Johnny was relieving himself over the toilet.

"Hey, hey why the hell are you coming in here," Johnny argued as he backed against the wall when Celine stormed in!?

The unexpected intrusion caused Johnny to urinate all over all over the toilet, the wall, the floor, and himself, while he tried to cover his miniature size penis. Johnny was standing with both his hands rested on his hips and had his jeans unzipped and button unfastened, while he stared up at the roof. The enraged mother charged at him and jammed the blade against his penis, which abruptly stopped the urinary flow. Johnny fearfully threw his hands high in the air and held them pressed against the wall in surrendering.

"You see that little girl you talk about spanking? She is my daughter; and if you ever come near her, I will find you and kill you, you understand me," Celine threatened?

"I was just kidding around," Johnny confessed!

"Do you understand me," Celine shouted?

"Yes ma'am, yes ma'am I do," Johnny exclaimed!

Celine turned around and stormed out the bathroom, leaving those who saw the exchange in awe. As she made her way to the front door, the mother placed the knife on a table and continued through the exit. Mauve tried calling to her, but she ignored the appeals and went out to her vehicle, climbed in, and drove away. After Celine left her engagement, Johnny felt so embarrassed that he fixed himself proper and walked out with his head lowered. Rather than notifying his date that he was leaving, Johnny walked directly through the front door and went to his truck. Once aboard he started the engine and sped away from the party.

When Celine reached home it appeared as if everyone was asleep, so she went to the kitchen and fixed herself a chicken sandwich with lettuce and mayonnaise. While eating at the table she began looking through her social media sites, hoping that none of her cohorts' video recorded the incident and shared it. Although nobody posted a video, Celine expected the incident to become the talk of the town by morning. There were a few text messages of encouragements from her friends, who supported her stance to defend her daughter. Rather than respond to any of the messages, Celine closed her phone after she read them.

Once she finished eating, she went into the bathroom where she brushed her teeth and washed her face for bed. With her daughter being the topic of discussion that ended the night, Celine checked in on Robin as she went by to her room. Robin was sound asleep and was also the only one in her bed, which made her assume that Julien had returned to her room. Her expectation to find Julien in her bed failed, therefore she began looking around the house for the little boy. Having not found him on the main floor, Celine decided to check her brother's room, where he often hung out. As the mother descended into the dark basement, she began hearing a female moaning, therefore she snuck down and looked around the corner that led to Coy's bedroom. The sight of Julien snooping on his uncle through the door opening, while he engaged in coitus with his girlfriend shocked Celine, who walked up and grabbed him by the back of the shirt. To stop her son from screaming and alerting her brother, she threw her other hand over his mouth in anticipation. Julien was so frightened that he nearly had a heart attack, thus his mother dragged him away and brought him upstairs. Celine was so discreet that she removed her son without disturbing Coy and his lady friend, however she realized that she had an issue with Julien that needed addressing.

Chapter 24

Married life had never been better for Officer Pedward, whose wife transformed and was a completely different woman. Whenever he phoned to inform Rochelle that he would be working late, she stopped complaining and requesting what time he would be home? If he forgot to get something she requested from a store, her attitude changed wherein she was much calmer and less argumentative. Whenever Ray came home and wanted his few minutes of intercourse, Rochelle allowed him to please himself without quarreling that 'he failed to make her orgasm'. Knowing how sound her husband slept, she began waiting until he dozed off, at which she climbed out of bed and went elsewhere to sometimes speak with Evander. Breakfast and lunch were always prepared each morning while the officer showered and got ready for duty, before she pleasantly kissed him on his way out the door.

At the commencement of their relationship Rochelle insisted that they be discreet, yet with each passing engagement she wanted more and more of her lover's time. Evander was taping a car's rear lights to paint the body when his cellular rang. The caller on the display showed Side Piece, which was the title he had given Officer Pedward's wife. He took a few seconds to respond to the caller, and only said "OK" before he terminated the call and went back to his duties. Each time she called was for him to go over so they could engage in wild and freaky sex, which got dirtier and more physical with every new encounter. The gentle caresses during their first sexual contact had changed to actual choking and slapping, which intensified their passion and also created marks. Instead of being concerned for her husband seeing the bruises, Rochelle encouraged the physicality from Evander. He had already taken off on extra lunch breaks twice that week and it was only Wednesday, nevertheless Rochelle still kept calling for more.

Coy entered the collision section of the garage a few minutes later to get an update from Evander. The body repair worker had finished prepping the vehicle for paint and was showing Marshon nude pictures of Rochelle and he. The situation was getting extremely serious, yet Evander thought the whole ordeal was funny. With his employees laughing and gyrating Coy went over to see what had them so excited, and was fascinated by the pictures which exposed the romance affair.

"God damn that white bitch sexy," Marshon commented as he grabbed his crotch!

"Holy shit! Is that Pedward's wife," Coy asked?

"The one and only baby," Evander stated!

"God damn she's phat," Coy declared!

"That's exactly what I said boss-man! I might need his phone to take a bathroom break later," Marshon said!

Coy and Evander laughed at the comment.

"Can Miss Lee come and get her car by tomorrow," Coy asked?

"I'll have it painted by this evening, so it will be ready any time tomorrow! By the way boss, I might stretch the lunch a little longer today," Evander stated!

"You know I don't care as long as the work gets done," Coy responded as he walked away.

The collision repair specialist began watching the clock from that point on, as he grew impatient for their lunch break to start. Come midday Evander was the first employee to take a break, as he climbed into his car and drove off site. When he reached Officer Pedward's community, he parked his car two street over and hurried to the house. One of the neighbors across from Officer Pedward was a retired constable named Bart Bateman, who had been experiencing dementia and got confused from time to time. Mr. Bateman had seen Evander pass by on numerous occasions and watched him run to Pedward's house that day.

Rochelle answered the door wearing her robe and dropped it to the ground as Evander walked in. Even though he was filthy from dealing with cars all morning, Rochelle leapt into her lover's arms and began French kissing him. With limited time with which to operate, Evander quickly stripped out of his clothes and took her by the front door. Moments later they moved to the stairs, where they spent some time exploring positions before they took their activities to the bedroom. There were no restrictions to what they did sexually, so Evander ensured that he violated Officer Pedward at every opportunity.

Back at the garage Coy and Marshon had sat down to eat lunch inside the office. Marshon had his ear-bugs inside his ears and bobbed to his music while he ate. Both mechanics brought their personal meals, rather than to leave work

180

in search of. The parts delivery worker from NAPA Auto Supplies walked in with a package at 12:35, which Coy signed for before he left. The garage was considered closed for an hour during lunchtime, but if anyone went by they could still get certain services. At 12:51 Officer Pedward's Chevy Tahoe and Officer Gilmore's cruiser pulled onto the garage property. Coy was in the midst of taking a drink from his Orange Soda in a can, when he observed the cruisers pulling into parking slots. The business owner frightfully spat out the drink from his mouth onto the desk, as both officers exited their vehicles and walked into the garage.

"Hey, how is it going Coy," Officer Pedward greeted as they walked in and looked around!?

"Not bad Officer Pedward! What can I do for you boys today," Coy stated?

"My baby outside needs an oil change and I would like to get the body repair guy to look at a dinger I got on the right side the other day," Officer Pedward explained?

"Well, you can leave it and I'll take care of the oil change. But Evander is out to lunch presently, so when you get back, I'll give you an analysis on the dent repair," Coy said.

"Around 3:00 o'clock should be good," Officer Pedward asked?

"Perfect! See you guys then," Coy declared.

Marshon kept his head buried in his bowl of food and tried to abstain from making eye contact with any of the officers. Officer Gilmore began walking around the office, looking at the plaques and business certificates that hung on the walls. There were pictures of the old owner and Coy, along with customers and famous visitors to the garage.

"This place has been in business for a long time, without you guys we would have to pretty much drive to Winnipeg for car repairs. Keep up the good work fellows," Officer Gilmore commented!

"For sure officers," Marshon mumbled without lifting his head!

Officer Pedward gave Coy the key to his truck and walked out with his associate. Both officers climbed into Officer Gilmore's cruiser, at which they drove away from the garage. Marshon only raised his head when the officers exited the office, as if he was afraid he would have gotten recognized for something. When the officers came onto the property, both mechanics forgot they offered a service and assumed they were there for Evander. As a result, when they walked into the garage neither Marshon nor Coy could breathe freely, fearing they were there to arrest their colleague. Even though they had repaired many cruisers throughout the years, Coy felt as though the officers knew more than they were letting on, and were fishing around for a confession.

Evander returned at 1:18, which was much earlier than he did the other days. Officer Pedward's Tahoe was inside the garage on the vehicle lift getting its oil changed, so he had no idea the coppers had visited. When Evander walked into the garage, Coy and Marshon began looking around the facility through windows and door cracks for undercover officers watching the building. Evander laughed at their silly antics until he realized they were working on his lover's husband's police cruiser. Coy was suspicious of the officers, so he turned up the volume on the radio inside the garage.

"What's going on," Evander asked while getting increasingly nervous?

"I don't trust none of them cops! They came around here snooping for something and used the oil change on the Tahoe as an excuse! But before you start painting, I want you to write up an estimate for the dent on the side of the truck, so I can give it to them when they get back for it," Coy ordered.

"No problem Coy! But were they asking about me," Evander asked?

"Man, I would quit messing with that woman if I were you! Them cops trying to play mind games, then catch a brother slipping," Marshon argued!

"Them dumb ass cops can't catch me slipping! The only thing slipping is this D up in Pedward's wife, you feel me Marshon," Evander boasted as the apprentice and he high fived each other!

A week later Officer Pedward and Rochelle went to a colleague's funeral. Constable Dwayne Steward was a nine-year veteran of the Dakata Ojibway Police Services, who had suffered through a long history of depression and post traumatic stress disorder. Three weeks before his burial date, the officer drove himself home from work after a night where they regulated the scene of a horrific car crash, that involved two families. The scene was covered with debris, along with the bodies of young children who were thrown from their vehicles during the crash. The emotional toll from the accident was too much for the suffering officer, who went home, sat on his couch in the dark, and used his service weapon to shoot himself in the head.

It was a very sad day for Officer Pedward and those who worked with his deceased colleague Dwayne Steward. The funeral was attended by serving members of the force, station commanders, friends, and retired officers from throughout Manitoba and elsewhere. Officer Steward's personal family was also there mourning his loss. Along with his mother, father, aunties, uncles, and several cousins, were his separated wife Judy and their two sons Joey and Benny. One of the retired constables who attended was Officer Bart Bateman, who trained Constable Dwayne Steward when he began working at the station. The church ceremony was very touching, wherein several people whose lives were inspired by Officer Steward spoke on his behalf. Following the church service they transferred the body to the National Graveyard, where only members of the police force and other servicemen were buried.

After they commended Officer Steward's body to the grave, those who attended began mingling and comforting each other. Despite not being in Dwayne's life for several years, Judy and her children received the Canadian Flag that was draped over the casket, and an enormous amount of gratitude for his civil service. There was no repas organized by the family members, so the funeral service was the only means of gathering for friends and loved ones. Rochelle, Judy, and some of the police wives gathered to discuss the rumors that surrounded Steward's death, while their husbands came together to share stories about the deceased officer.

Retired Officer Bateman was there with his female handler, who made sure he stayed on track. Due to his mobility issues the retired officer had to maneuver about in his wheelchair. When Officer Bateman saw Officer Pedward, the regular male visitor to his house came to mind, therefore he began making his way over to his neighbor. To not disturb the group of men conversing, Bateman went a few feet away from them and stopped his wheelchair.

"Pedward, may I have a word," Officer Bateman called out as he waved a hello to the other officers?

Officer Pedward excused himself and went over to his neighbor, who then drove away from his handler through the graveyard.

"How have you been sir? Sorry for not dropping by more often, but you know how tasking the job is," Officer Pedward said!

"No problem! Don't worry about it my dear boy! I have been seeing some weird movements to your house that I feel I must tell you about," Officer Bateman informed!

"What sorts of movements are you referring to sir," Officer Pedward asked?

"I've seen a suspicious dark colored man going into your house several times, while you were at work," Officer Bateman informed!

"Can you describe him," Officer Pedward enquired?

"Sorry, can't really make him out from that far away. The eyes aren't what they used to be," Officer Bateman joked!

"Thank you, Sir, I'll keep an eye out for this visitor you mentioned," Officer Pedward commented before they went their separate way!

The relationship between his wife and he have been going so well that Officer Pedward thought Bateman's dementia must be getting worst. He went back to conversing with his associates and dismissed the idea, for which he knew there must be a reasonable explanation. During their drive home Rochelle began disclosing the information she received about the cause of the separation between Officer Dwayne Steward and his estranged wife. Prior to the funeral everybody only knew what Officer Steward said happened the night he went home, and his wife and kids were gone, but Judy sat the record straight during their conversation.

"Honey, I always told you that guy Dwayne had a problem! Judy told us how he pulled his weapon at her three times, and actually shot at her once! Luckily, he missed, or she would be dead by now! She said for years she asked him to go get help and he refused, then he started cheating on her with that partner he had name Sampson, and when she confronted him about it, he beat the crap out of her! He was getting out of control, he started slapping around the boys for taking up for their mother, so she had to leave!"

"Where did she go," Ray asked?

"She said she was on the internet one day and she saw this site for battered wives, who need to get away from their spouses, so she called and they finally arranged like some underground secret stuff, where she had to be at a place at a specific time, then they brought her somewhere else, then somewhere else, all kinds of crazy shit! But she said they saved her; and for that she won't even name one of the places they brought her, to help whoever might be next!"

"That was a crazy story! Speaking about cheating, I was talking with old boy Officer Bateman who said he saw some guy going to the house a few times," Ray stated!

"I'm surprised that senile old fort remembers anything! You should go ask him if the guy was wearing a brown UPS uniform," Rochelle argued!

"Baby I don't mean anything by it! That fool is losing his mind, do you think I got time to believe a word he said," Ray proclaimed?

"Obviously you do, because you are asking me about it! Just take me home and go sleep in the living room tonight, or better yet, go sleep beside Bateman," Rochelle declared as she began ignoring him!

"Baby I didn't mean anything by it, I was just saying," Ray pled to no avail!

Chapter 25

Thomas did not initially get involved with his wife's handling of Viveen's school situation, until he was made aware of the ordeal. Jacquelin refused to send her daughter back to the school, claiming they were disrespected regardless of what the evidence stated. As the bank manager for the town's only financial institution, Thomas left home early every morning to open the branch's door. By the time he got home in the evenings, Viveen would have already gotten home from school, therefore he had no idea she had not been attending. Following weeks of trying to contact Jacquelin, the school counselor located Thomas' cellular number in Viveen's profile and phoned him to discuss her extended absence.

When Thomas spoke with the counselor he had no idea about the lying incident, nor was he aware his wife had been keeping Viveen away from school. There were no other schools around for nearly a hundred miles, so Viveen had no choice but to return to Roseau Valley School unless they relocated to another district. Thomas was infuriated when he received the call, whereby he learnt his daughter had not attended school over the past two months. Following his conversation with the school counselor, the bank manager decided to take the remainder of the day off and drove home to rectify the situation. Rather than providing Viveen with an alternative study plan while she was at home, Thomas arrived to find the mother and daughter cuddled beneath the blanket on the bed, watching an afternoon soap opera.

When Thomas walked through the door Jacquelin was stunned to see him home at that early hour. Although the guidance counselor advised him of the situation, Thomas was not fully convinced until he confirmed it for himself. As a strong advocate for education, the thought of his daughter idling her life away at home, was unacceptable to Thomas. Contrary to his wife, the bank manager was quite reserved and avoided quarrels rather than indulging them.

"Oh, Honey! What are you doing home already," Jacquelin enquired?

"The school counselor phoned me to ask why Viveen hadn't been at school in two months," Thomas stated.

"Well, she had an issue with some other kid there, so until she was comfortable enough to return, I decided to keep her home," Jacquelin remarked.

"But you cannot keep her secluded because she had an argument or fight with someone Jacquelin! Viveen has to learn how to deal with other people out in the world," Thomas declared.

Viveen felt nervous knowing her father was upset, although he spoke with a calm and relaxed tone. Jacquelin tried desperately to avoid mentioning what the school incident was about and felt relieved that Thomas neglected to enquire about it.

"Sorry Honey, I will make sure I drop her off in the morning, with a note," Jacquelin stated!

"Either you do, or I will carry her myself! Viveen needs her education, Jacquelin," Thomas exclaimed then left the room!

The following morning when Viveen returned to Roseau Valley School, she felt nervous entering the building. As she walked through the hallway with her head lowered, she developed a sense despise, as if everyone were secretly discussing her. The children throughout the hallways were busy mingling with their peers to notice Viveen, who hastily walked to her locker. Marla appeared from nowhere and hugged her from behind, which initially startled her before she saw who the person was. Most of her classmates came over to welcome her back, following which they ushered her into the classroom. Mrs. Kirkpatrick was very happy to see Viveen back in class, having not seen her before the Christmas break.

It was as if all the excitement seized when Julien walked into the classroom, therein everyone became silent and watched to see his reaction. Julien walked to his desk, sat on his chair, then withdrew his lesson book and placed it on top his desk. The youth then placed his backpack on the floor and sat waiting comfortably for the bell to sound, with his focus on the blackboard ahead. At the alert of the bell everyone scattered to find their seats, while Mrs. Kirkpatrick moved to the head of the classroom to begin teaching. Unlike his classmates Julien was not ready to forgive Viveen for the insults, therefore he kept his distance and did not speak to her.

Pastor Hemming asked Andrew to stay behind after church and help with putting away some chairs and tables they had used during the Sunday ceremony. The establishment had a four-wheel hand cart on which they could load the items for transport, therefore the job was quite easy. The pastor's wife was going along the rows of benches collecting the hymn books and bibles left by the congregation. Aside from the three workers everyone else had gone home following the ceremony, that was primarily addressed to the traditional family. Andrew had several questions about what the pastor meant when he said certain things, therefore he asked as they went along.

"Pastor Hemming, why do you consider children born out of wedlock unholy?"

"Well Andrew, like I said during my speech, as long as the man and woman love each other and create that family bond before and after the child gets here, then that child can be saved! Or if that child gets baptised in the Holy Water of our lord and saviour Jesus Christ, they can also be saved!"

"Then Pastor, what did you mean by it is immoral for a woman to have an abortion?"

"Because every developing child deserves a chance at life! No true Christian will ever go to an abortion clinic! Jesus never shun the children! In fact, he said bring them all onto me, so I may give them the food of God! Therefore, it is immoral for any woman to have an abortion legally or illegally!"

"But aren't those women considered murderers Pastor?"

"They should be, even though our society does not judge them as that!"

"Then I suppose, they will never get the chance to go to heaven?"

"Heaven is there for all who seek it my son! No matter what you have done you can be forgiven and allowed back in Heaven! Jesus promised the thief beside him on the cross that, he would be with him in Paradise, so everyone who seeks his word will be allowed to enter!"

"So, Pastor; I have noticed an increased number of mass shootings on TV, especially in the U.S. Do you think any of those shooters will ever be allowed in Heaven?"

"Heaven is there for us all Andrew my son! No matter what you have done, only the Heavenly father shall judge you!"

"Thank you for explaining those to me Pastor Hemming," Andrew stated before he went totally silent through the duration of the task!

Once he finished assisting the pastor, Andrew retrieved his winter apparels and dressed for the cold before he told the couple goodbye and left for home. His Honda Civic was parked on Centennial Drive across the street from the church, so he went out, climbed in, started the engine, and warmed the car for a few minutes. After nearly four minutes of idling the young man placed the vehicle's transmission into drive and drove away. Andrew drove down to O'Brien Avenue and turned left, then continued along that road to the stop sign. As he approached the sign and gradually slowed down, a speeding 4X4 came barrelling down on the opposite side of the street. Instead of halting at the stop sign, the 4X4 ran into the intersection and turned left on McKercher

Street. There was a close encounter between Andrew's Civic and the 4X4, which was narrowly avoided by him pressing the brakes. Even though the occupants aboard the truck were at fault, the driver stuck his hand out the window and gave Andrew the middle finger.

Andrew had taken one of his father's firearms from the lockbox he kept it in and had it sitting inside his glove compartment. The young man intended on going to the shooting range to practice and hopefully see Robin without his nagging father present. The 4X4 conductor's disrespectful gesture after nearly causing the accident grieved Andrew, who reached over and withdrew the Glock 19X, 9mm hand pistol from his glove compartment. Rather than continuing straight home on O'Brien Avenue, the young man angrily turned right onto McKercher Street and began following the 4X4. The numbers on the rear license plate were rusty and impossible to define, so Andrew failed to make out the tag identification, but noted the make was a Ford F-150.

After years of being considered somewhat of a degenerate by many locals throughout town, Andrew decided to become more aggressive as encouraged by Aaron. He followed the F-150 at a distance to the end of town, until it turned off Waddell Avenue onto Barber Street. Behind Barber Street was a stream known as the Main Drain, which flowed water into the Roseau River. Beyond that point was the Dominion City Cemetery, followed by farmlands for many miles. The F-150 turned on Barber Street and drove to the last house on the corner, where the two male occupants exited the truck in a playful mood. Andrew drove up and pulled onto the property, where he climbed out of his car with the weapon at hand. The males were heading into their house when Andrew pulled up and began yelling at them.

"Didn't anybody ever teach you idiots how to drive? You cut me off back there and then had the audacity to give me the middle finger," threatened Andrew expecting the men to begin cowering!?

When the two men saw Andrew standing by his car with the gun by his side, they ignored entering the house and turned back to deal with the menace.

"You sure you not lost boy," Kyler Applewick demanded?

"Obviously you don't know whose property you just trespassed on boy," Russell Applewick stated!

While most of the citizens in town were friendly and neighbourly people, a handful were rather rebellious and lived by their own rules. Kyler and Russell Applewick were two such brothers who lived with their terminally sick mother. The brothers had multiple piercings and tattoos of Nazi swatches that proudly stipulated they were racists. Neither of the brothers got along with their neighbors and they were always disrespectful to the locals, whom they would curse at and make offensive gestures towards. When they began walking toward Andrew and he realized who they were, he tried to retract his brave comment immediately.

"Sorry, I didn't mean it like that, guys! I was just saying, the road is very slippery, and you guys could have slid off the road or something," Andrew reasoned!

None of the brothers took lightly to seeing the weapon being brandished, therefore they continued walking forward. Andrew began sensing that he was in danger, so he began opening the car door to get in.

"Hold on, aren't you the bank manager's kid," Russell asked?

Andrew never felt so happy to hear someone mentioned knowing his father.

"Yes, yes, I am Andrew, Thomas Woolrey's son!"

"Oh, you good people then kid! Sorry for nearly running you off the road! Let's go inside and have a drink to warm up, get to know each other better," Kyler offered?

"Thanks, that sounds great! Just let me turn off the car engine and I'll be right there," Andrew stated!

All three men entered the house, which was filthy with medical supplies and other items thrown about. There was a fierce dog barking from behind the door that led to the basement, which sounded eager to be released. Andrew had heard talks about the Applewick brothers, yet he had never seen or spoken to any of them. The thought to alert his mother crossed his mind just before he entered the house, but he decided to trust his instincts and followed his intuition. Russell walked into one of the bedrooms as soon as they entered the house, while Kyler headed to the kitchen and summoned their guest.

"Calm down Beast, I'll let you out in a minute," Kyler shouted!

As Andrew went by the bedroom wherein Russell disappeared, he looked through the opening and saw his host sitting next to his mother on the bed. Russell had his mother's right hand in his; and spoke to her gently while she laid with her eyes closed. The dog seemed unruly and kept barking while it banged itself against the door to get into the rest of the house. By the time Andrew entered the kitchen Kyler had a pair of Moosehead Beers ready for them to consume.

Before they began drinking Kyler knocked his can of beer against Andrew's and yelled, "White power!"

Russell exited their mother's bedroom and opened the basement door to release the dog. Beast began jumping on his owner, who grabbed the collar around the dog's neck and brought him into the kitchen. As soon as the dog laid eyes on Andrew he began snarling, as if he wanted to attack their guest.

"Hey, stop that," Russell warned at which the dog stopped his aggressiveness and sat back on his hind legs!

Andrew was fund of dogs, but Beast was a massive Pitbull that looked at him as if a command to attack was all he waited to hear. Kyler tossed his brother a can of beer, at which Russell released the dog's collar, opened the bru, and took a huge gulp. The dog was extremely obedient and stood there staring at Andrew, who tried his best to avoid making eye contact with the muscular animal. Both brothers looked at each other cynically then smiled and nodded their heads, at which Kyler moved to the counter and began constructing a cigarette. After he placed some tobacco on a sheet of paper, the young bigot took a glass vile from his pocket, which contained pieces of crystal looking rocks.

"So, do you believe the white man alone should live on this land like your father," Russell questioned?

"What, what do you mean," Andrew puzzlingly asked?

Kyler shattered a piece of the Crystal Meth he took from the vile and sprinkled it across the tobacco content, before he finished rolling the cigarette.

"He means, are you a soldier of God prepared to wipe all these unholy races from the face of this Earth," Kyler demanded as he lit the cigarette and took a huge toke?

Andrew felt the pressure of the moment immediately, as even Beast stood upright on all four paws awaiting the response. While he hesitated to answer, Kyler passed him the cigarette of which he refused. Despite Andrew signalling that he did not smoke, Kyler forced him to take the cigarette, at which point he took a toke. The young Christian began coughing as the smoke filled his lungs, hence the Applewick brothers laughed at him. That was his first time ever smoking Crystal Meth and Andrew began feeling as if his body was lifting off the ground. The sensation was thrilling, therefore he took another toke and thought of how to respond.

"Yes! I am ready to do God's work," Andrew then responded!

"I am now proud to call you my brother of faith," Russell said!

Andrew became so intoxicated that he began hallucinating and seeing strange images, therefore they led him into the living room. Once inside the room the chemically altered young man sat on the sofa and began staring at a hole in the wall, before he fell unconscious. Both Russell and Kyler were equally as high, but they were experienced at how to operate under the influence of the drug. When Andrew regained his senses and looked at his watch, he realized he had spent much of the day with the Applewick brothers, who were sound asleep on the sofas. Beast looked over at him as he rose from the chair, before the animal turned back over, and went to sleep. Rather than disturbing anyone, the drowsy visitor snuck his way to the door and let himself out.

It was 12:49 AM when Andrew walked into his house. All the lights were on and his whole family was still awake concerned for his wellbeing. Everyone was so accustomed to him always being prompt that they thought something foul had happened to him. Jacquelin had tried phoning him several times with no response and had even tried alerting the police department. An officer at the station advised her that he had not been missing long enough to be considered as such, so they were forced to have to wait and see if he came home.

By the time Andrew walked into their dwelling Jacquelin was emotionally drained worrying about his wellbeing, before she changed, and became furious at him for not being responsible. Thomas and Viveen had heard enough of her ramblings, so they went to bed the instant he walked through the door. Even though neither of them knew where the young man had been, they had been listening to Jacquelin fuss for hours, so none of them cared. The young man had never risen his voice above his mother's whenever he addressed her, so he lowered his head in shame and went about his business.

"I have been phoning you for hours; and I know you heard it ringing and probably turned the volume off! If you think you are going to be anything like your brother, you better rethink that thought! We've been worried sick about you, now I have to go and call the pastor and everyone else to let them know you home safe! I even contacted the police to put out a missing report; and might have had them searching around for you if they would get up off their asses! Is that all you're going to do? Don't you have anything to say about where you've been," Jacquelin argued?

Andrew ignored his mother and went into the kitchen, where he took a can soda drink from the fridge, along with a carrot muffin and went to his room. Despite his mother screaming, Andrew went to his room and closed the door, without saying a word in response. Even after he went into his bedroom Andrew could still hear his mother yapping away inside the house, so he put on his headphones and began listening to his music.

Chapter 26

Robin began spending a little more time with Julious, while she learnt the new church song. Julious on the other hand fell in love with her voice and wanted to make her the lead singer on the choir. The more time they spent together was the more Robin's confidence increased, until she sounded melodiously soothing. They both became fond of each other, therein Celine began noticing subtle changes in her daughter's behavior. Instead of the quiet and reserved child she had raised, Robin began singing whensoever she did anything around the house. Miss Shirley smiled behind Celine's back whenever her daughter quarrelled about Julious' influence on Robin, having watched her blossom from her cocoon. Contrary to Celine's fears, her mother thought Julious was a descent and respectable youth who would respect her granddaughter. While her mother remained naive about the situation, Celine began eavesdropping on Robin while she conversed on the phone. Whenever Robin had her girlfriends Kim, Erica and Marcia over, Celine would pretend she was doing something within their space to listened in on their conversations. She of course also had to watch out for Julien, who would spy on Robin's friends while they precariously hung out inside her bedroom.

Two weeks into her practice sessions Julious decided to have the other choir members listen to her performing the song. Every practice they did was held at the church, where the young musician had all the instruments they required to develop the desired sound. Julious and Robin were already at the church fine tunning her approach at certain sections of the song, when the other members arrived. Robin was nervous beyond mention having never sang before an audience, but Julious told her 'To just sing'! The smooth and silky tone that Julious perceived as the new leader of their choir, burst through Robin's vocals as she began singing with her eyes closed.

"We are all born, In a world of sin,

But since I let you in, I've eased my pain,

Glorious Lord, I sing to thee,

In hopes that you will, Forever hear my plea"

When Robin got to this point in the song it was as if they had been practicing all along, as Patricia first joined in and sang, "Plea, Plea!"

Then Chris joined in and sang, "For my family!"

Following which they collectively sang, "I pray to thee!"

"For my friends," May sang!

"I pray to thee," sang everyone!

They all sang the song in its entirety perfectly without practice for the first time. When they finished the song, they all began smiling, high fiving each other, and cheering, while they welcomed Robin into the group. Robin feared the others would reject to her joining the group, so it was a relief having everyone sincerely hugging and congratulating her. Everyone felt they had the song perfected, therefore nobody wanted to practice after such a performance. Chris suggested they all went to a movie theatre and watched the latest romance or comedy film, but the closest location was in Winnipeg. There were two people with vehicles, so they had just enough space for everyone to ride comfortably.

The choir members exited the building and locked up the church, before they separated into two groups once they reached the vehicles. Robin, May, and Natalie all decided to drive with Julious, while the others travelled with Chris. They had yet to choose a specific film that they all agreed on, so they went with the intention to select the movie after they saw the list of what were being played. Rather than climbing into the front seat, Robin allowed May to get into the cabin with Julious. Everyone was quite eager to go to the movie theater, which was not a typical outing that the locals from Dominion City regularly did. Natalie was thirty-three-years-old, and May was twenty-nine, therefore they had very little in common with Julious and Robin. Despite their excitement moments into the trip, all the conversations ended once the females began scrolling through their phones. Once Julious noticed the silence among his passengers, he turned on the radio to his favorite FM station, which was playing quality hit music. While they travelled along the main road to Winnipeg the radio host paused the music, to provide his listeners with a brief news report. Julious reached out his hand to change the radio dial, but May asked him to 'let the announcer speak'?

"In the news today, for the first time in years the Canadian Prime Minister met with U.S President and Mexican President to discuss trade, border security, and other key factors regarding their economies! The Blue Jays are in New York tonight to kick off a three-game weekend versus the Bronx Bombers! And calls for more gun restrictions after a Caucasian man armed with an automatic style rifle, walked into a black supermarket in Connecticut where mothers and children were shopping and opened fire, killing twenty-eight and injuring another nineteen, before he was shot and killed by an armed shopper! That's all we have for you at this time, we'll get back into the music following this commercial break!"

"Oh my gosh that is terrible! Imagine all those people who won't be able to see their loved ones alive again," Natalie commented!

"Sometimes I swear these white people have no hearts! I mean how could anyone in their right mind just sit at home and contemplate killing innocent people," Robin argued?

"That's right our white choir member," May agreed!

"I am not white, OK," Robin rejected!

"Well, your complexion is a lot closer to theirs than mine," May stated!

"So, because my complexion is lighter than yours, I should be considered white," Robin demanded?

"I'm sure white people see you as their own," May continued!

"For your information, white people do not treat me any differently than they do you! In fact, the mere thought that one of my parents is white offends them worst, because that parent mingled with the colored species," Robin angrily responded!

"Oh, I thought all white people were the same," May answered.

To ease the tension Robin refrained from responding to May's last comment and began staring through the window instead. Julious slightly increased the volume on the radio, which was playing a mixture of RNB and HipHop songs. The weather forecast had predicted a cold yet clear evening, with no precipitation detected for the next two days. They had gotten to the latter part of the two coldest winter months, that were January and February. With such a stormy winter, wherein they had experienced a few warm days of rain, the meteorologists predicted the province may sustain massive floodings once the snow began melting.

When they reached the Scotiabank Theater in Winnipeg and parked, Natalie climbed out of the vehicle behind Robin. She had noticed how sensitive the white complexion topic was for Robin, so she walked up close to her and placed her arm around her shoulders. Chris parked his car beside theirs with the second half of the choir, who began exiting while Natalie and Robin walked ahead. May and Julious waited and gathered with the other members, before they all walked off after their group members.

"I hope you aren't contemplating leaving the choir already! Because you sing like an angel! Even though we all competed hard for that lead singer role, you deserve it! So, May might still be a little mad over it, but she will come around," Natalie exclaimed!

"That's OK! I'm not going anywhere," Robin answered.

"Don't mine what May had to say about you being white either, she doesn't understand the concept of color and the lengths some people will go to appear greater than others," Natalie exclaimed!

"I could tell she is totally ignorant to the topic! It seems as if she believes just because a person is as light skinned as white people, they automatically get welcomed into the family," Robin said!

"Huh! That reminds me of those cultures who treat darker skinned people around them with disrespect, while the white racist is looking to lynch them all. I can see you're a young lady with plenty of experience so far! It is hard to teach race and how the world views it," Natalie responded!

"Believe me when I say people with my complexion gets more than our share of hate! Because while most blacks mainly get discriminated by racist white people, I get it from both sides, because the white man hates the black in me, and black man hate the white in me, yet still our blood is red," Robin declared!

They reached the listed movies board and stood there looking at the selections until the rest of their members joined them. Neither of the females had any clue which film to choose, so they quickly made bets on what they thought their companions might do.

"I bet you that we end up choosing different movies," Natalie suggested?

"I think, we all end up watching a sucky movie together," Robin countered?

Despite their age difference Robin felt Natalie was genuine and kind. Once they all gathered and analyzed the available showings, they realized their choices were limited for the films that started at the top of the hour. With only four movies to choose from, some of the choir members began offering their suggestions on which film they best rated. Paula suggested 'it would have been simpler had everyone chose their own movie', however Chris quickly killed that solution. Because they all came in two separate vehicles, the notion of them attending films that ended at different times would not have been logical. Therefore, Robin nudged Natalie on the arm to indicate she had won their private bet. Both females giggled at the gesture, which surprised their colleagues who all spun and looked at them.

"We think the comedy is a good choice," Robin laughingly declared!

"That's the movie we also agree on! So, if everyone is on board, we are getting tickets for the comedy," Chris stated!

They bought their tickets then joined the concessions stand line to acquire popcorn, drinks, and snacks for the movie. By the time they reached inside the theater the final advert was finishing, so they walked up the isle looking for seats. There was an empty row of seats near the back of the hall, where they comfortably sat beside each other as the room went dark. Julious sat between Robin and Jill, but rather than sitting between two women, Chris chose to sit by the isle. The film was quite funny, and everyone enjoyed it despite their preassessment about its quality.

Following the film, the choir members began getting ready to leave the theater. Chris stood up and began putting on his winter jacket, without paying attention to the other attendees who were passing along the isle. He accidentally knocked a woman's hand which was holding her drink, and regrettably spilt the contents all over her. Before Chris could apologize, the woman's boyfriend tried lunging at him, over the female and another associate. The male companion had to subdue the boyfriend, who thought that Chris was attempting to grab the woman's breast.

"Hey, what the hell is wrong with you Goof," the woman yelled?

"You black son-of-a-bitch! Don't you ever put your hands on my woman," barked the boyfriend!

"Calm down man, it was just an accident! I'm sorry," Chris declared!

"You lucky I don't kick your ass for that monkey boy," threatened the boyfriend!

"He said he didn't mean to, it was an accident," Patricia stated!

"Well, next time watch what you doing boy," exclaimed the boyfriend!

"God bless you," Julious said!

"You think I'm being funny? Just wait till I see you niggers outside," argued the boyfriend!

The young Caucasian male extended his middle finger at Julious, who smiled back at him and blew him a kiss. The agitated boyfriend had to get drawn away by his girlfriend and friend, to stop the argument from escalating. It was evident that Chris was at fault, but the manner with which the boyfriend dealt with them was offensive. Chris felt so scared that the young man would follow up on his threat, that he tried to stall leaving the theatre immediately. Rather than going outside into the unknown Chris decided to report the incident to the theater management, so they went outside into the lobby and found an employee. The worker had to attend to the clean up duties before the next airing, so he showed then to the manager's office and summoned her for them to file their complaint. When they told the female manager what occurred, she telephoned the Winnipeg police department which sent over two squad cars.

The incident was filed by the officers who attended to the call, before they searched the area for the young man and his friends. Everyone in Chris' movie party gave an account of what happened and described the three people individuals involved. The officers promised that they would get a detective to investigate more into the incident, wherein he would look over video surveillance footage to get a proper description of the perpetrator. Following the whole incident the officers led them to their vehicles, then drove behind them until they reached the city's limit. As country folks who were unfamiliar with the big city life, many of the Dominion City citizens were terrified and vowed never to return to Winnipeg.

"Oh sweet Jesus, my heart! That guy was so dark and arrogant! I never thought I would ever witness something like that," May astonishingly said!

"Welcome to the real world," Robin remarked!

"Can you imagine if that guy was waiting for us like he said? No man something has to change, these white boys getting out of place! Just take your time and bring us back to our country Julious, please," Natalie exclaimed.

"I honestly have never been so scared in my entire life, especially after hearing about that shooting a few days ago! I will definitely get nightmares after that," May professed!

"Since that white guy shot and killed my father, I wake up at least once a week in a cold sweat! For some reason my brother started sleeping with me; and that has been helping me to get through those nights. But I keep seeing my dad's face, so much that I am starting to hate looking at white people. And I'm half white! Does that mean I should start hurting myself? I don't know," Robin wept as she spoke!

Natalie unbuckled her seatbelt, then slid closer and placed her hand around Robin's shoulder. Everyone inside the vehicle were surprised to hear the revelation, so much that they went totally silent. It was evident that the young teenager had been experiencing some tough times, which she needed help dealing with. Nobody knew exactly what to say to ease Robin's pain, while she wept continuously as if she had never released the hurtful emotions after her father's passing. The notion that she had also entertained the thought of injuring herself was disturbing, thus the ladies knew they needed to inform her guardian. Although nobody sang their unperformed song better than Robin, Natalie thought the words might help to strengthen her, hence she began humming the rhythm.

"We are all born, In a world of sin, But since I let you in, I've eased my pain,

Glorious Lord, I sing to thee, In hopes that you will, Forever hear my Plea,

Plea, Plea, For my family, I pray to thee, For my friends, I pray to thee,

Never leave me, I pray to thee, Till the end, I pray to thee---"

Julious and May joined in immediately to attempt to uplift their choir member, who was overburdened with emotions. Before they reached the third line in the song, Robin turned her tears and sniffles into words and began singing the hymn. With each word she grew ever stronger, until she wiped away the tears and expressed a slight smile.

News of the incident reached the local Suburban Newspaper, which printed the story two days later. Publicity of the incident led the police department to assign a detective to the case, therefore the racist tyrant was tracked down and charged with several offenses. None of the witnesses involved in the incident had any idea what transpired after they filed their report that night, until Detective Minot who worked the case telephoned Chris with an update. After the racist tyrant was taken into custody, a TV reporter from the CBC News Network contacted Chris for an interview, but he refused and chose instead to put the incident behind them.

Chapter 27

Celine received a phone call from Natalie, who was extremely concerned for Robin's safety. Following their movie theater episode, Natalie felt as if Robin might harm herself through guilt, therefore she phoned to inform Celine. When the phone rang the first time Celine was under the warm water taking her shower and was unable to answer the call. The matter was so urgent to Natalie that she phoned back several minutes later while Celine was applying lotion on her body. Although she did not recognize the name or number, the caller had phoned before, so Celine reluctantly answered.

"Hello!"

"Hello good morning, I am on the choir at church! My name is Natalie and I just called to discuss Robin!"

"Yes, is there a problem?"

"Not really, she is great! The thing is we went to the movies the other night and we were verbally assaulted after an accident that involved one of our members."

"Was it Robin?"

"No, no! it was actually Chris, he accidentally hit someone's drink and spilled it, so the guy started shouting all sorts of racial things at us for no reason!"

"Oh no, how did Robin take it?"

"Well, she broke down crying once we got back to the car, and said she doesn't like white people, and thinks about hurting herself because of her feelings."

"I swear she hasn't been herself since some incident at school."

"I know it's none of my business, but Robin told us about her father getting murdered; and it seems to me as if she still carries much of that hurt around as guilt!"

The phone line went silent wherein all Natalie could hear was the faint sounds of someone breathing. After a long pause during which Celine thought of how wrong she was for some of the actions she had taken, she finally responded.

"As a mother, you do what you must to protect your children! Maybe God will judge me differently, but I would do the same things again!"

"Since Robin mentioned what happened I went back and looked through the Nova Scotia Daily Echo Newspaper and, saw the story. I believe you are a very strong woman, and I admire you for putting your children's needs first!"

"Thanks for telling me about Robin, Natalie! I truly appreciate this! Take care!"

Immediately after they terminated the call Celine searched through her phone for Air Canada's business reservation number. She then called the booking agent and purchased three roundtrip tickets to and from Nova Scotia. Celine had observed a slight change in her daughter and wanted to repair whatever problems she was experiencing. Robin and Lloyd had a very close relationship, so Celine failed to analyze how moving the family so far away would affect her. The children were back at school and the trip could not get postponed until March Break, therefore they would have to make a weekend getaway.

Celine discussed what she found out with her mother, who supported the idea of bringing the children back to Nova Scotia. They had started their new lives in Dominion City, however they all had unfinished business back on the East Coast. With her children still grieving over the loss of their father, it was important that Celine gave them the chance to speak with Lloyd and visited his grave whenever they chose. To clear Robin's work schedule that weekend, Celine telephoned her boss and requested the time off for those days. When Robin and Julien returned home from school that afternoon, Celine told them that she had a surprise for them both. The children were eager to find out what the surprise was, but she told them they would have to wait until the weekend. Rather than making Robin and Julien attend school that Friday, Celine woke them up early and had Shirley drive them to James Armstrong Richardson International Airport in Winnipeg. Neither Robin nor Julien knew they were travelling by air until they kept seeing the direction signs for the airport. Before they reached the departure gate Celine disclosed their destination to her children, who became overjoyed and cheered with excitement.

Shirley dropped off the travellers outside the Air Canada departure entrance, where they hugged each other and said their goodbyes. The grandmother indicated that 'she would be waiting for them Sunday evening when their flight returned,' before she climbed back into the Grand Cherokee and departed. Celine and the children spent the next two hours and twenty minutes inside the airport waiting for their flight, before they were finally boarded and allowed to leave Winnipeg. Their flight lasted for four and a half hours and went rather smoothly considering it was the winter season. By the time they landed at Stanfield International Airport in Halifax it was nearly 2:00 PM, so Celine collected their luggage, then went to the Enterprise Car Rental counter to pickup her reserved vehicle. She was so accustomed to driving a higher elevated vehicle, that Celine selected a Jeep Wrangler 4X4 rental to cruise around the city.

They drove directly to the Hampton Inn & Suites on Cromarty Drive, where Celine had arranged for them to stay during their visit. It was a long a tiring flight, so once Celine reached their suite, she decided to take a nap. Robin and Julien had taken an interest in the amenities provided by the hotel, therefore rather than staying inside the room they decided to go enjoy the pool. Because her children had learnt to swim, Celine rested comfortably without worry, knowing they would look after each other. When she rolled over and looked at the time three hours later the children had not yet returned, so Celine climbed out of bed and went to ensure they were OK. Expecting to find Robin and Julien by the pool, Celine was surprised when there were no signs of them there. It was a very kid friendly hotel, thus the children could be anywhere, so Celine went to the games room in search. Everyone who she asked about her children failed to help, thereby she went to the front desk to enquire.

The receptionist at the desk was the only person to calm Celine's nerves, having seen the children passed by the lobby area several times. The woman told Celine that Robin and Julien had come by the desk to enquire about food to eat, therein she sent them to the dining hall. When Celine made the reservations, she requested the meals package knowing how much her children loved to eat. It was dinner time by then and the hall was packed with guests enjoying the ambiance. To locate Julien and Robin, Celine stopped the waitress and asked if she had seen them, hence the lady brought her to their table. The sight of her children brought a pleasant smile to Celine's face, who found them eating Poutine with hamburgers and juice.

"Hi mom," said Julien whose face was smudged with sauce, yet he continued eating!

"Hey guys! You both had me searching all over the hotel for you," Celine argued!

"Well, you told us we could come and get food whenever we wanted," Robin responded!

"Yes, you are right honey, I did! Scoot over so I can sit and eat with you guys," Celine asked?

The waitress came by moments later and took Celine's order. By the time her Spaghetti meal reached the table Julien and Robin had emptied their plates, yet they chose to stay while their mother ate. A few minutes before she finished eating Celine sent the children ahead to bathe and dress, for them to leave and visit family. Before they left the hotel, Robin telephoned Aunty Tamara to enquire about her whereabouts and discovered she was visiting her mother. They drove directly to the children's grandmother's apartment, where neither Tamara nor her mother knew they were visiting. One of the tenants was leaving the building as Celine and her children approached the front door, therefore they were able to gain access without alerting Roslyn. Even though they had been more foes than relatives until Lloyd's death, Celine was just as eager as her children to see his mother and sister.

Julien knocked the door and waited there patiently while Robin and Celine approached. Tamara and Roslyn could be overheard shouting at each other, until she opened the door and saw Julien standing there. When Tamara saw Julien, she was puzzled and thought she was seeing an image, therefore she wiped her eyes and looked again. Rather than waiting on the recognition Julien rushed in and hugged his aunty, who was so happy that she began crying.

"Aunty Tamara," Julien exclaimed!

"Jules, it's really you! Oh, my Lord, it's really you," Tamara yelled!

When Roslyn heard the name Jules, she looked to the front door and saw Tamara hugging a little boy. The grandmother who could barely run, started fast-pace walking toward the door, as Robin and Celine came into view. Julien released his aunty and rushed into his grandma's arms, while Tamara embraced Robin and Celine. Almost everyone had tears in their eyes, with huge smiles on their faces, as if they had not seen each other for years.

"Why you guys back," Roslyn asked, while she hugged Celine and her granddaughter?

"Yeah, did something happened down there," Tamara enquired?

"Come children, take juice on fridge! Grandma do the cake, eat," Roslyn stated!

They walked into the kitchen where Roslyn took plates from the cupboard and forks from a drawer, while Robin retrieved the knife to cut the cake. Julien opened the fridge and retrieved a two-liter bottle of soda, plus five cups for them to drink from. Robin cut five slices of cake and placed each piece on a plate for them to partake of. Everyone sat around the dinner table and happily ate the cake, while they discussed family matters. Rather than isolating Robin's issues, Celine made it appeared as though she was the person who primarily needed to visit Lloyd's grave.

"Everything is fine with us! I just missed Lloyd and wanted to visit his grave and speak with him about some things. Plus, we missed you guys and couldn't wait until summer to see you," Celine stated!

"Me happy," Roslyn exclaimed with a bright glow across her face!

"So, how long are you guys in town for," Tamara asked?

"Just for the weekend." Celine answered.

"I hope you guys are staying with me or Mama," Tamara said?

"I know you guys have small apartments and I didn't want to inconvenience any of you, so we got a hotel suite at the Hampton Inn," Celine explained!

"What inconvenience? Next time make sure you guys stay with us, we are family," Tamara argued!

"Ok, next time we definitely will," Celine responded!

They stayed over by grandma's until it was quite late, before Celine left with the kids and drove back to their hotel. Julien was nearly asleep by the time they left, so once he sat inside the vehicle and they drove away, he was dozing. Robin stayed up until they reached the hotel, because she had a few questions to ask her mother.

"Mom, do you really think that talking to dad at his graveside will make you feel better," Robin asked?

"Honey, I have some things I never got to say to your father before he passed, and I'm going to tell him what's been on my mind! I would like if you and your brother talk to your father and tell him whatever you never got to say to him! And don't worry, if ever you want to come talk with your father, just let me know and we will make the trip," Celine declared!

"Yeah, I wanted to take some pictures beside his grave. Mom, I think this trip was a good idea," Robin said!

"I hope so honey! I really hope it helps us all," Celine stated!

"I would have liked to stay by Aunt Tamara's place, but the hotel is way more fun," Robin joked!

"That's why I chose the hotel, because there is way more stuff to do there, plus they provide food if you guys are hungry," Celine said!

"And you know how much Jules loves his belly," Robin teased!

They both laughed and continued making humorous statements as they drove back to the hotel. By the time they reached the suite Celine's phone was ringing off the hook with calls from her old friends, who heard from Tamara that she was back in town for the weekend. Donette and some of the females tried to entice her to go out to a club for a few drinks, but Celine declined and chose to stay in. Before she climbed into bed Celine took a warm shower, oiled her entire body, then got dressed in her pyjamas. Robin was fast asleep by the time she exited the bathroom; therefore, she adjusted the temperature inside the room to make it more comfortable. Once she got beneath the blanket, she took the remote and began scrolling through the list of movies, before she selected a gladiator film to watch. Despite taking a nap earlier, eighteen minutes into the film Celine dozed off and slept through the night.

The next morning Celine arose with the same nervous feeling she had on the day of the actual funeral. The curtains were still drawn, and the room was incredibly dark, despite the bright sunlight glooming outdoors. Julien was already awake watching cartoons and Robin was on her phone texting with several of her old Nova Scotian friends. Celine said "Good morning" to her children as she crawled out of the bed and went to the bathroom. After she urinated the mother turned on the tap inside the shower, following which she exited the bathroom for a few personal items.

"I need you guys to get your clothes together so you can take a shower once I get out! We need to hurry so we can catch breakfast, then get out on the road early," Celine emphasized before she went back into the bathroom!

Robin prepared her personal items and ran into the bathroom the instant her mother exited. Celine took that as a positive sign to emphasize her daughter's desire in visiting Lloyd's graveside. Julien did not mine showering last, because that gave him more time to relax and watch his cartoon program. Once they were all dressed and ready, they left the suite and went downstairs for breakfast in the dining lounge. The breakfast menu had a wide selection of food, so everyone placed and received their individual orders.

After they finished breakfast, rather than doing anything else they decided to visit Lloyd's grave, which was the reason they were in town. The meteorologist had predicted a frigid -15 Degree Celsius day along the coast in Nova Scotia, yet the temperature felt more like a +11 Degree breezy Spring Day. They went out to their rented Wrangler and drove to the graveyard, where they had laid Lloyd's body to rest a few months earlier. Just returning to the site brought tears to Celine's eyes, thus once she parked the vehicle, she sat with her children for a few minutes to decipher who wanted to go first. Celine planned on leading by example and being the first to speak to Lloyd, but she began shivering and felt weak once they entered the graveyard. As the self-proclaimed 'man of the family', Julien chose to be the first to speak to his father, whom he had gravely missed. With his mother and sister waiting in the vehicle, the little boy walked out to his father's graveside and stood over it. Just watching Julien addressed his father brought tears to Robin's eyes, as she too felt the emotions of their loss.

"Hey Dad, it's me Julien! Mom and Robin are in the car waiting to speak with you too, but they are a little nervous. Mom wants us to each spend time talking to you, about what we have been doing and stuff like that. I miss you dad! I miss you watching cartoons with me and taking me wherever you went! I remember you told me to be the man of the house, if anything ever happened to you, but that's a little hard right now because we are staying with Grandma Shirley and Uncle Coy. We moved to Dominion City, I know you going ask, where is that? But it's the place where mom grew up before she moved here. I'm going to a new school there. My teacher is very nice, and I have some new friends too. Grandma Shirley and Uncle Coy are really fun to live with! I play video games with uncle and sometimes help grandma to bake her delicious cakes! Then she gives me the mixing bowl for me to lick clean! Hmmm, taste so good dad! But mom said we can come and talk with you whenever we want, which is super cool because we all miss you…"

Watching her son chat to his father gradually eased Celine's nervousness, until she became totally relaxed. Robin and Celine thought that Julien would barely get to five minutes before he returned, yet twenty minutes later he was still baffling on. Outside was balmy instead of the predicted bitter cold, thus Julien was unbothered by the weather. By the time he finished Celine felt assured that she had made the right decision bringing them to the gravesite, as it became evident that they had a lot to say to Lloyd. Once Julien concluded and began walking back to the Jeep, Robin jumped out of the vehicle and began walking towards the grave. Celine felt snuffed by her daughter who was hesitant to go before she showed interest, yet she pleasantly smiled to herself.

"Hey Dad, it's your most precious child in the world! I don't know why God had to take you, but that was not a good decision! I guess financially we are OK, but mom tends to hold onto the money a little tighter than you! I finally have my first job at a gun range in our new town, Dominion City which is in Manitoba! I like it so far, the people are nice, and the town is so laid back, it's like nobody does anything there it seems! We have only been there for a few months but so far, I think its going well! We stay with Granda Shirley and Uncle Coy, who is super cool, not into church anymore but still super cool! Oh, and by the way, I won lead singer in grandma's church choir! I guess all those years you were encouraging me to sing, you kind of knew what you were talking about! Mom got this weird idea to come and talk with you, so me and Julien decided to stroll along; and it's been cool so far, we saw Grandma Roslyn and Aunty Tamara! I'm hoping I'll get to see some of my old friends before we leave, but that all depends on what mom has planned for us to do. And guess who was at your funeral? Your dad, he lives in Toronto, and we are supposed to visit him this summer I believe. I think I'll encourage mom to do this trip again more often, so we can come spend more time with you…"

After Julien returned to the Jeep Celine expressed how impressed she was with his maturity. Tamara phoned her seconds later, at which they dived into a conversation while Julien began playing with his toy action figures. Roslyn wanted to see the children again before they left, so they arranged to meet for lunch at Lorenzo Italian Restaurant at 1:00 PM. During their conversation Donette phoned with an ensemble of ladies on a group chat, who all wanted to party with Celine later that night. With all her female friends ganging up against her, Celine was compelled to accept their offer, therefore they agreed to go clubbing at a popular spot. Both conversations exceeded an hour, nevertheless Robin was still rambling on and on to her father. Contrary to the teary eyes that Robin left the vehicle with, once she spun from the grave her face was a glow, as if she had engaged in a self-righteous conversation. Seeing both her children content and happy with the trip was pleasing to Celine, who walked to the grave and disclosed all she had to say to Lloyd.

"Hi Baby! I love you! I miss you! Oh, God, I miss you! As you can see, I am wearing your ring, and yes, I do want to marry you! You know I've always considered us married even though we never legally did so! I'm sure the kids must have mentioned that we moved to Dominion City, where I grew up, after I found those tickets you bought! Only you! Thanks for reuniting us with my mother and brothers! We have kept in contact with Roslyn and Tamara, in fact we are supposed to meet up for lunch this afternoon. I can somehow tell that this trip is going to change the kids, because they have been having a tough time with the transition. There have been a few calls where Robin's biological father have come up, I know you said to never reveal the truth to her, but there are times when I feel she needs to know. Right now, she is starting to hate white people; and this is a world where we all must coexist! I don't know it may be nothing, but she seems to be changing and I can't understand how. You were the person who she told everything, so without you here, it is getting harder to know her. Ah, I miss having you around to take care of the things you were good at handling! Julien is doing a little better, but he went through a phase where he was slapping anyone who talked bad about his father. His teacher phoned me a few times about small incidents, where his temper got the best of him, and he had to be excused from the class to cool off. She understood the pressure he has been under, but he needs to cut that out. My mother and brother sent their love, my mother especially was upset that she did not know about your funeral, or she would have made the trip. But we're here for the weekend to see you. I'm going to go out with the girls later to catch up a little, but apart from that we are back on the plane to Winnipeg tomorrow. Until the day we reunite, I promise to always come and visit your graveside; and if the children wish to do the same, I will carry them to see their father. I love you Lloyd, my husband! Goodbye," Celine exclaimed as she blew kisses!

At the conclusion of Celine's address the temperature immediately dropped and began feeling more like the meteorologist's aforementioned stat. The mourning widow was forced to button up her jacket, cover her ears with her scarf, and put on her gloves as she scampered to her vehicle. When Celine returned to the Wrangler and quickly climbed in, neither Robin nor Julien were paying attention to her to realize she had finished. Julien was in the rear cabin playing with his action figures and cars, while Robin sat in front passenger seat texting with friends. Celine climbed into the conductor seat and sat there for several minutes, with them all staring out at Lloyd's grave. The lonesome feeling of being without their family member began setting in once again, knowing they would be catching a flight to another province in the morning. They drove away with everyone feeling saddened, yet overjoyed, that they had made the trip to see Lloyd.

By the time they reached Lorenzo's they were five minutes late for their reservation. Roslyn and Tamara were already seated and partaking of their first glass of white wine. Lorenzo's was the place where Lloyd would always take his mother and family members for their birthdays and special occasions, so the employees at the restaurant knew them well. Everyone was excited to see Celine and the kids knowing they had moved away following Lloyd's death. The grandmother and aunty arrived eight minutes prior and selected the booth that Lloyd would always choose for his family. The hostess showed Celine and her entourage to the table the instant they arrived; then left and sent the waitress over to take their beverage orders. Despite seeing each other the evening prior, the children and their relatives embraced and kissed before they removed their jackets and sat. Unlike her in-laws, once the waitress arrived Celine ordered herself a double shot of Cognac and two sodas for the kids. It had been a very emotional day thus far, therefore the grieving widow wanted something strong to help settle her nerves.

They were all ready to place their orders when the waitress returned with the beverages. Julien and Robin ordered Lorenzo's famous Spaghetti & Meatball plates, while Roslyn ordered the Fish N' Chips meal, and Tamara and Celine requested their Garden Salad platter. While they waited for the food, Julien told his grandmother about their trip to Lloyd's graveside and described how much he missed having his father around. The gesture from them visiting her Lloyd's grave was truly heartwarming for Roslyn and Tamara, nevertheless, they preferred being abled to see and spend time with the kids. Within twenty-five minutes the waitress brought all the plates to the table, hence they ate and joked and laughed and enjoyed each other's company, with hopes of doing the same rather frequently.

Aside from the well-wishers at the funeral, Lorenzo's entire staff was the only other group of people who sympathetically gathered and gave Lloyd's family their heartfelt condolences. In addition to offering their condolences, management at the restaurant nullified the family's bill and gave them their meals on the house. Celine, Roslyn, and Tamara were moved to tears after the management and staff showed them how special they considered Lloyd, therefore they took pictures and posted it all on their Social Medias. Contrary to the reasons they had to leave Nova Scotia, people throughout the city loved Lloyd and gestures as such showed Robin and Julien how appreciated their father was.

Following their eventful afternoon at Lorenzo's Italian Restaurant, the family members gathered in the reception area to say their final farewells. Tamara had attached herself to the list of party goers later that night, which meant she would be seeing Celine thereafter. While they gathered at the entrance, Julien recalled how cold the meteorologist on the television mentioned it would have been during their time at the cemetery, versus how cold it had gotten since. It was so cold that nobody wanted to get caught outdoors idling, therefore they performed all their affectionate sentiments indoors. Contrary to Celine, Tamara, and the kids, Grandma Roslyn became emotional and cried her way out the restaurant, after she hugged and kissed her grandchildren.

Both parties left and went their separate ways, with Celine and her kids going back to their hotel, while her in-laws went home. On their way back to the hotel, Robin arranged with three of her old girlfriends to come over and swim in the pool. Not having to transport her daughter or son to any of their friends' locations was appeasing to their mother who could relax. By the time they reached the hotel Celine was tired and had to rejuvenate before they went out that night, hence she went and took a nap. Rather than hanging out with his sister and her friends once they arrived, Julien chose to watch movies and played with his toys instead.

When Celine reopened her eyes the clock on the nightstand between both beds was saying 8:34 PM. There was an animation movie playing on the TV, with Robin and Julien comfortable underneath the blanket watching it. As Celine looked through a slight crease in the closed drapes and realized that it had gone dark outside, she remembered that she had not yet eaten. Fearing the kitchen had closed and it would thereby be more difficult to get something to eat, she jumped out of bed and turned on the light.

"Robin, did they already stop serving dinner?"

"Yes mom, but we got you a plate," Robin stated as she pointed to a food container on the table!

"Thank you, guys! I must have been tired because I planned on sleeping for about an hour!"

"You're welcome mom," Julien responded!

Celine got up and walked over to the table, where she uncovered the container and looked at the assortment of foods. She was highly impressed by the selection of items that she picked up the container and placed it inside the microwave. The urge to urinate led Celine to the bathroom, where she used the toilet and washed her hands thereafter. Once she returned to the main suite, the mother programed the microwave timer to a minute and a half, while she prepared the utensil and something to drink. As soon as the food was ready, Celine removed the container from the microwave and placed it on the table. That day had brought her family much joy and redemption, therefore she bowed her head and said a prayer thanking the Lord. Before she took her first bite, Celine smiled to herself and looked at her children with pride, after they compiled the types of food she liked. After dinner the overjoyed mother climbed between her son and daughter on their bed; and watched the remained of the movie with them.

At 10:00 Celine began preparing herself to go out with the girls. She assembled her outfit and shoes, then went into the shower and bathed her skin. Once she emerged from the shower, the mother dried herself off and lotion her body, before she slipped on her bra and underwear. Celine exited the bathroom wrapped in a towel, then sat before her styling mirror to apply her makeup. Julien had fallen asleep by then, while his sister was still awake texting someone on her phone. It took Celine several minutes to finish applying her makeup and transformed the glow on her face, hence once she was done even Robin complimented the excellent job. The skirt suit that she took out to wear made her appear sexy yet businesslike, however she somehow felt overdressed. Robin loved the way her mother looked especially after she slipped on her heels, therefore she took a photo and posted it on her Social Media pages.

It was 11:00 PM when Celine finally left the hotel to meet up with her girls at Club Under-Dome, located on Grafton Street near the old Hide+Seek Nightclub. When Celine arrived some of her female entourages were smoking and getting intoxicated before they even entered the venue. All the ladies agreed to meet up in the parking lot, where they greeted each other and ensured they were all adequately dressed, while they waited for the late arrivals. The girls were happy to see Celine and had her drinking shots of Vodka before they began making their way to the entrance. There were four other women who chose to wear either pants or skirt business suits, which alleviated Celine's fear of feeling overdressed. The club was already jumping when they entered, with a packed dancefloor and party enthusiasts all over the building. While some of the ladies went to the bar to fetch their refreshments, the others went in search of the perfect spot to party. The three ladies who went to the bar bought two bottles of Smirnoff Vodka, with ice and chasers for everyone. They managed to find a table that was already occupied by a couple, who allowed them to rest their liquor beside theirs.

The ladies were out to have fun, get turnt up, and dance the night away. With such a beautiful group of women partying without the oversight of men, it did not take long before the male vultures came scavenging for a feast. The first set of vultures were three Africans from Nigeria, who were standing by the bar when the group walked in. Before the Nigerians moved in to try and claim a prize, they made sure there were no men tangling along. Once that was confirmed, the three friends made their way over behind the ladies, who were dancing and enjoying the ambiance. The African men were direct and did not waste much time, therefore whosoever rejected their summoning was quickly overlooked for the friend, until they had exhausted all their appeals. Neither Celine nor any of her friends paid the Africans any attention and refused their offers for alcohol, so eventually they strolled back from where they came. Contrary to the last time they partied together, the ladies were more behaved and less vulgar, as if they were thots providing sex for all comers.

Moments later four friends changed their location from beside the restroom entrance and moved closer to the group of women. The DJ was playing a segment of Soca Music, which was most of the ladies' favorite Caribbean genre, therefore they were whining and behaving bad. All the ladies kept together in the same area beside the table that held their liquor bottles and other items. Tamara was positioned to the rear beside Celine, who had Donette beside her and Julie dancing in front of them. Celine was bubbling her waistline like a Hawaiian dancer, however, Tamara's waistline was rotating like a Hula hoop specialist. The provocative dances that Tamara was unleashing, caused Celine to smack her derriere in approval. One of the men found Tamara irresistible and bravely moved in to conquer his prey. With Tamara bent forward in the six-thirty position and her hands almost touching the floor, the male admirer moved behind her, grabbed both her waist, and began whining on her plumped ass. Tamara stopped dancing immediately, stepped away from the intrusive male, spun around, and looked defiantly at him.

"Excuse me, what the hell do you think that you are doing," Tamara argued!?

"I'm just trying to dance with you baby! I love the way you move," the man responded!

"Do I look like the type of person who is into men," Tamara asked?

"It seemed as if you were baby," the man answered.

"First of all, I'm not your baby! And secondly, you see me standing here with my girl, so go learn some manners and don't disrespect," Tamara exclaimed!

"Sorry, I didn't know you girls were partners," the man stated before he and his friends walked away!

A pair of older studs were the next victims to try their luck with the pool of women. One of the men who wore glasses noticed Donette from across the room and alerted his friend. They walked across to the ladies' location at which the admirer tried to summon Donette. Rather than wasting time Donette held up her left hand to expose her wedding ring. The man reacted as if he would not accept no for an answer and tried to push pass Tamara and Celine to get at Donette.

"Did you not see that she is happily married," Celine exclaimed?

"Oh, oh, that was a wedding ring she was showing me! It's so dark in here I can hardly see," said the admired who wiped his glasses before he moved on!

Nearly forty different men tried to win a conversation or a phone number from one of the females, yet none were successful. The night was filled with fun and much humor, wherein the ladies drank and partied until management flickered the lights, to indicate the club would be closing momentarily. It was nearly 3:30 AM when the ladies exited the club laughing and joking with each other. After they walked out to the parking lot the ladies shared an emotional farewell with Celine, who was the first to leave due to her early morning flight. Some of the women were too intoxicated and had to leave their vehicles, therefore they summoned taxis to carry them home. By the time Celine reached the hotel, she only had four hours to rescue some sleep and get to the airport to catch their flight home.

When Robin woke her mother three hours later, she had very little time to bathe, pack her belongings, get breakfast, check out of the hotel, and reach the airport in time to return the rental. Julien and Robin had already showered and dressed and had their bags packed to leave. Celine felt as though her body had been through a wreck, so she had to force herself to do everything. To conserve on time rather than showering, Celine simply washed her face and brushed her teeth before she got dressed. Robin had already repacked most of her mother's belongings into her carry-on luggage, therein they were able to vacate the suite in less than ten minutes. With a throbbing headache due to lack of sleep after a night of drinking, the tired mother threw on her sunglasses and requested two pain killers from the receptionist. The female at the front desk offered Celine two Motrin-400 Tablets, which she swallowed with a glass of water. While Celine took care of the check out process, she asked the kids to fetch sandwiches and orange juice from the cafeteria, for them to consume along their way to the airport. Without showering or sitting to eat breakfast saved them valuable time, therefore they reached the airport ten minutes later than the three-hour recommended prearrival time.

Celine drove directly to the rental car agency and returned the Jeep Wrangler, before they made their way to the check-in desk. The Air Canada agent informed them that their domestic flight would be delayed for an additional hour, therefore they had a longer wait time than expected. To avoid having her mother wait unnecessarily, Celine telephoned Shirley and informed her of their flight delay. When they reached the gate, Celine left Robin in charge of everything and went to sleep on a lounge chair. Robin allowed her mother to rest undisturbed until it was time for them to board their flight. Even after an additional three plus hours of sleep, Celine was still tired once they boarded the airplane, hence she slept throughout the entire flight back to Winnipeg. It wasn't until they landed back home that Celine felt more like herself, wherein the headache had subsided, and she could finally remove the sunglasses. Miss Shirley and Coy were there waiting for them when they arrived at James Armstrong Richardson International Airport, then drove them home to Dominion City.

Chapter 28

Officer Grey Gilmore wore a humongous smile that stretched from ear to ear, as he held his three-years-old daughter while Pastor Hemming threw Holy Water across her forehead. His wife Malory was standing beside him, during the Christening Ceremony for their third child, Mary Elezabeth Gilmore. Grey looked dapper in his jacket suit and tie, while Mary was stunningly beautiful in her white gown. The couple had two other children who were seated beside their grandparents in the front row. It was a delightful and bright Saturday afternoon at the Gilmore's private church ceremony, where they only had family and friends in attendance. Most of the officers who Grey worked with were in attendance to support their colleague and his family, during such a special occasion.

Following the ceremony the attendants chatted briefly, while the photographer took pictures of Mary, her family, and their guests. Officer Gilmore went around to everyone present and thanked them for coming, then reminded them about the after function. Grey and his wife had made arrangement to hold a small gathering after the ceremony, where their guests could unwind, smoke, drank, ate, and relaxed before they went home. The couple's Aunty Sadie was back at their house preparing the feast until they arrived, therefore it wasn't incredibly urgent for them to rush back home. Both Malory and Grey's families both got along well, so either side were excited about Mary's Christening. Pastor Hemming was invited to the function thereafter, but he refused due to prior arrangements with his wife.

Grey and Malory Gilmore were the last people to leave the church that afternoon, after they thanked their church pastor wholeheartedly for his blessings. The entire ceremony lasted a little under an hour and was short enough that the troopers on duty who attended, got to watch most of it. Mary was sound asleep inside her car seat by the time her parents finished, so the officer was extremely gentle with her carriage. Both parents exited the church with a pleasant feeling, knowing their daughter had been Christened in the house of the Lord. Malory came from a family of very spiritual Christians; therefore, it was incredibly important to her that her children were Christened.

At the Gilmore's residence the entire street was packed with cars that it was impossible for anyone else to find a parking spot, however the other officers left Grey's driveway available for him to park. The Gilmores drove by several of their guests who were making their way to the house, after they had to find parking distances away. Most of the residents in the community were police officers, either still serving on the force or retired. With winter finally dwindling down it was an enjoyably cool day, so several of the officers were outside the front smoking cigars and conversing. Ray congratulated his good friend Grey by handing him a cigar, as he went pass with the baby car seat.

"I'm going to save this one and smoke it on the day your first child is born," Grey stated as he continued into the house!

Mary was sound asleep until she was brought into the house and heard the screams of other children playing. The house was nearly packed with several women and men inside the family room, some in the kitchen and others inside the dining room area. Grey softly placed the car seat on the floor, and started unbuckling the safety straps, when his daughter slowly opened her eyes. Three children ran by while chasing a fourth, who had stolen a toy and refused to surrender it. The newly Christened little girl pushed herself from the car seat and took after the pack of children, as if she had been awake all along. Malory wanted to preserve the white dress, and thus ran after Mary before she ruined it, but catching the little speedster would prove to be a problem. The humorous chase had Grey laughing, before he placed the car seat inside a closet and went to his bedroom. To feel more comfortable the officer removed his jacket and tie and threw them on the bed, then withdrew his dress shirt that was tucked into his pants and used it to cover the firearm on his hip.

Mary's godmother was Rochelle, due to the close bond between the families. Ray was already godfather to the couple's first two sons, who were born on his birthday two years apart from each other. Rochelle noticed Malory chasing Mary, who was chasing the other kids, therefore she grabbed the little girl as she went by. Rather than kicking and fussing to escape, Mary smiled at Rochelle and hugged her tightly around the neck.

"Hi, my Little Munchkin! How are you," Rochelle stated?

"Hi Aunty Roelle! I'm fine," Mary answered!

"Thank God for you, or I never would have caught her," Malory said as she approached! "Bring her for me? I want to change that dress before she ruins it!"

Rochelle brought Mary along behind her mother, who went to the little girl's bedroom. While Malory selected clothes for Mary to change into, Rochelle sat on the bed holding her goddaughter in her arms. When Malory turned around and saw how loving Rochelle was with Mary, she used her cellular and took a picture of them both. To assist her friend, Rochelle began removing the white dress off her daughter, who kept playing with the curls in her hair.

"Look at you, you're a natural with kids! I can't wait for you and Ray to get your first child together, so I can have you to hang around with more often," Malory commented!

"Huh, I don't know about that happening! Our doctor told Ray months ago that his sperm count is too low right now, and he's not even doing the things he should, to bring the numbers up! Look at them outside, Ray knows he should not be smoking those cigars! Yet, as soon as he gets around the boys, its to hell with whatever the doctor said and light it up! Malory, right now I'm so tired of everything that I don't know," Rochelle lamented!

"That's how stressful marriage can be at times honey. Like they say, you have to trust the process," Malory responded as she passed the clothes!

"Well, screw the process Malory! I feel like I'm getting the shit end of the stick, like I'm needing more than just his five minutes of, Uh, Ah, Uh, and then that's it," Rochelle quarrelled!

"That's why I told you it's better to keep that dildo charged! You better be careful honey; because it sounds like you are being tempted by the Devil to cheat on your husband," Malory conveyed!

"You have no idea! I can't stop thinking of that young stallion's hard..." Rochelle exaggerated while dressing the little girl.

"Rochelle, watch your language, the baby," Malory yelled!

"Oh, Oh, sorry I got a little carried away there," Rochelle stipulated!

Both ladies laughed at the gesture, though Malory could not help but to assume that her girlfriend was contemplating having an affair. Most of the police marriages that ended in divorce had terrible outcomes, so Malory wanted to make sure that Rochelle understood what she might be in stored for. Ray and her husband were great friends, therefore they had spent many nights drinking and conversing about their marriages. Malory had overheard some of those conversations and knew what Rochelle meant to Ray, and the lengths he was willing to go to keep her as his prized wife.

"I've always told you that your husband is that rare lunatic, who would go through a brick wall for you! I have heard that man speak of his love for you, and I know that Officer Ray Pedward would take on an army, if they ever tried to rip you away from him," Malory conveyed!

Rochelle finished putting the clothes on Mary before she responded to her friend. "There you go my Little Munchkin," she said with a kiss, then placed Mary on the floor! After the child raced out to play with her siblings and the other children, Rochelle got up off the bed. "Maybe its that new medication that my doctor has me on. I don't know! But all I know is, I don't give a damn anymore!"

Grey stepped outside to unwind and chat with some of his colleagues before anybody summoned him to do anything. He had been a cigarette smoker for many years, so he brought out a can of beer in one hand and had the lighter and his favorite brand of smoke in the other. There were eight men conversing in the group, most of whom were police officers except for Grant Weska, who was Grey's brother-in-law. Grant was employed by the Town of Dominion City as their road maintenance manager. The officers were telling jokes about traffic stops they had made, where in some instances the victims were seriously injured, yet everyone laughed about the details. Officer Valesquez was entertaining the bunch when Grey walked up and lit his cigarette.

"---so, I guess they were trying to find somewhere to hide the bag of weed inside the car when I walked up. The kid in the front passenger seat must have thought he was Houdini or somebody, because he tried passing the bag around the side to the kid in the back seat, while I moved to the front. But the kid in the back wasn't paying attention, so the bag fell on the floor. Even though I saw the whole play, I made it seemed as if I didn't notice! While talking with the driver I noticed my supporting officers arriving on the scene, so I thought to myself I'm going to outsmart these dumb idiots, and I said to the young man, 'my partners are here with the dogs, that means we are going to make them smell inside this car for any contraband!' The kid who passed the weed got so scared, that he released a loud fort inside the car! Except it didn't sound like that was all he did! The only thing I heard after that was from the kid in the back seat, who was complaining that his friend stunk like a skunk? The kid shitted all over himself, and so desperately wanted to wipe his ass that he just told his boy in the back, to give me the five-pound bag of weed," Officer Valesquez joked!

The group of men broke out with laugher, wherein even Valesquez found humor in his own joke. Officer Ray Pedward felt the need to disclose one of his most private jokes, therefore after the laughter subsided, he began revealing his story.

"You want to talk about shit! Me and Gilmore were working the graveyard one night, and I was way over on Highway 75. Gil was over by the main road down here, in Trapper's Corner waiting on someone to fly by. This old timer from just south of here along the border, drove up to Vusher's Farm and stole four fully grown pigs, stuffed them into his hatchback and was driving back home. That night I was tired as hell and as I sat there listening for my radar alert to go off, all I heard was, 'Hey Pedi, I got a weird one over here by Trapper's Corner!' Anyways, I didn't think much of the alert, I thought it was probably some rich kids from Winnipeg joyriding in their parent's expensive car or something like that! Got over to where he was and saw the hatchback stopped ahead of the squad car, but everything seemed normal. I went to Gilmore's car to hear what he had, and he was just sitting there writing up citations and trying to get in touch with the Animal Care Unit, but all he said was, 'you better take a look for yourself!' I walked up to that car and shined my flashlight in the back and could not believe my eyes! That old timer had four fully grown pigs and his two dogs inside that hatchback, there was shit everywhere, it stunk like a sewer, and he's sitting in the front seat smoking a cigarette, wearing a Santa Clause suit, looking like he was just out late delivering Christmas gifts!"

The group of men again busted into laughter at the humorous sequences. Even Officer Pedward could hardly contain his laughter while telling the joke.

"Needless to say; I was pissed! Because any way I looked at it, I was up to my knees in paperwork and shit! My squad car was stink for days after that," Grey commented!

Everyone laughed at the joke as they imagined what the sight and stench must have been like.

"You should have made Ray bring him in brother," Grant joked teasingly at Ray!

"Oh, hell no Grant! I wasn't bringing that old timer in if he paid me," Ray responded!

"Speaking of old timers! My road crew was patching some potholes around this neighborhood a few weeks ago, and some delivery guy dropped off a package somewhere on your street. The guy passed us and ran back to his delivery car, then a few seconds later, Old Bateman came out of his house hobbling and shouting, 'Stop that guy! Stop that guy!' We thought of going after the delivery guy, but Bateman looked more like he needed the help, because he was fighting to put on his winter jacket, and only had on his undershirt and boxers in minus-twenty-two-degree temperature!"

The group of officers began laughing, which caused Grant to pause mid-story. The account sounded less appeasing to Ray, who began thinking retired Officer Bateman may not be as senile as everybody thought he was. Knowing his colleagues were trained psychological analyzers who had the ability to read body languages, Ray tried to appear undaunted by the story and began laughing loudly even though he was not amused.

"Too bad Bateman had to retire due to memory loss! He was a damn good cop," Officer Gotier shouted!

"Bateman phoned me this morning to apologize for not coming today and wished Mary good luck at her Christening. His memory may come and go, but as a past cop he will always be in detective mode," Grey disclosed.

"Oh, that old man is still fully in detective mode, believe me! He wanted us to move out his way, so he started swinging his cane at us! Thank God he got way slower! But he kept saying, 'I'm going to catch that son of a bitch, one of these days,' as if he knew who the guy was," Grant declared!

Leaving his close friend's daughter's christening early without justification would have raised questions, therefore Ray excused himself and went inside to the bathroom. Whether or not anyone else thought about who the delivery guy was, he became the focal point of Ray's attention. Officer Pedward thought long and hard if there were any clues he had missed while he urinated, following which he washed his hands in the sink. After several minutes of staring into the mirror at himself, his wife knocked the door and startled the officer, who quickly dried his hands and exited. Rochelle had prepared a plate of food for Ray and was walking around searching for him, before she discovered, he was inside the bathroom. Aside from carrying the food in one hand, Rochelle held Mary safely in the other. The moment Ray stepped from the bathroom she handed him the plate, knowing her husband was famished having not eaten since breakfast. The adulterous wife gave him the food with a soft kiss, then walked away with her goddaughter.

Ray could not avoid staring at his wife's derriere as she went back into the kitchen with the little girl fondling with her hair. Due to Rochelle being more affectionate than she had ever been, the officer could not accept the notion that she was cheating. Malory was headed back to the kitchen and took note of their friend's reaction to his wife's generosity.

"Doesn't she look like she would make the perfect mother," Malory exclaimed as she walked pass Ray?

Ray laughed to himself as he rejected going back outside among his subordinates and instead went into the TV room, where several of the older folks were gathered. Most of the elders who comfortably sat in the chairs around the room were related to either Grey or Malory. The television was on with the volume slightly high, still most of the occupants were soundly snoozing. The only alert persons inside the room were two older females, who both sat on a sofa beside each other discussing their girl's club members. There was an unoccupied chair on which Ray sat to eat, as he tried to avoid certain people and passed the time. Despite everything he had heard, the officer was still unconvinced about his wife's guilt and would need concrete evidence rather than speculations. The thought of his wife cheating did not seem possible, especially with their relationship going so well over the past few months. Eventually the evening ended and the Pedwards headed home. Almost everyone who attended lived in the Roseau River Reserve Community, which was the location of the territory's only police department.

Three weeks later most of the snow had melted, except for certain large patches across everyone's yard and elsewhere. Ray typically worked until quite late into the evening and would be away all day once he left home in the mornings. Because his department services covered such a large territory, they attended to calls from over seventy miles away and had to reach the locations as quickly as possible. For his officers to reach endangered victims in an appropriate time, the Police Chief triangulated where each of his constables were positioned each day. The station had been undermanned for years and needed to replace several officers, such as those who were undergoing mental disorders, retired, committed suicide, or the people who quit due to the exhausting workload. With such a smaller staff of officers, committed policemen like Ray were sequestered to work longer hours, which they did at the sacrifice of their families.

One morning Officer Pedward found himself working three kilometers from his Roseau River Reserve Community, along Route 201. The road repair crew was working east of the town on a drainage project that was expected to take two days to complete. The officer was assigned to roadwork duties and served the team of road maintenance specialists as their traffic controller. Although Ray was assigned to direct the traffic, he simply sat inside his cruiser with his flashers on and played around on his phone. There were no separation barriers between the eastern and western lanes, except for the lane marking paint drawn on the road surface. The maintenance crew had two employees at either ends of their construction area, who both communicated with each other on two-way radios, and held aloft signs that directed motorists to either stop or proceed slowly.

The sight of officers usually forced motorists to comply with the directions being issued, therefore city road employees appreciated having the police on certain sites. Evander was speeding along Provincial Route 201 heading to his lover's residence that morning at 11:31. The young manstress' first notification to slow down came when he looked in the distance and saw the red, blue, and white flashing colors of the local police siren. As Evander got closer to the stopped vehicles, he realized that the traffic officer was none other than the cuckold, whose wife he was on route to have sexual relations with. There was a lineup of vehicles caused, due to the eastern flow of traffic being allowed to move through. After a few minutes the lineup of cars heading west were allowed to advance slowly, hence Evander hid his face as he drove by the cruiser. Despite the fear of being seen, the young manstress felt an exhilarating thrill in knowing he was heading to the officer's house to defile his wife in ways he never imagined.

When Evander reached Rochelle's house, she met him at the door as she customarily did, wearing nothing beneath her silk robe. Once she closed the door behind him, the adulterer shoved her manstress against the wall and began passionately kissing. Before Evander could mention seeing Ray along the way, he was being sexually assaulted by the officer's wife. Rochelle knew they only had a limited amount of time before her lover had to return to work, thus she planned on making the best of his visit. Despite not mentioning her husband due to the rush of emotions, Evander constantly thought of the officer being that close to his home. As a result, rather than abandoning his clothes wherever Rochelle removed them, the young manstress cautiously dragged them along.

At 11:55 the road construction supervisor put a halt to the work for their hour-long lunch break. The supervisor had his workers create two smaller lanes for the traffic to continue flowing orderly during their absence. Once everything was in place the supervisor spoke with Officer Pedward and gave him the opportunity to leave for lunch if he chose to. Rather than sticking around the site with most of the employees, Ray decided to drive home and have lunch along with a quickie before he returned. With Rochelle always encouraging him to be more spontaneous, Ray expected to surprise her and left a huge smile on her face that afternoon.

Evander had Rochelle in the frisk position against the refrigerator inside the kitchen, while he pounded her from the rear. Neither of them heard when the officer's cruiser pulled onto the driveway, with Rochelle constantly moaning and groaning. Ray approached the front door and shoved his key into the lock to enter the house. As he turned the lock Evander overheard the sound, therefore he withdrew himself from his lover, grabbed most of his items, and bolted for the back door. Rochelle was so nervous that she walked toward the front door to try and stall Ray, for her manstress to escape unharmed. Just before Ray shoved the door open, his neighbor Nigel who was out jogging called out to him.

"Hey Ray! I hope to see you and Rochelle this weekend at the raffle," Nigel shouted!

"For sure Nigel," Ray answered before he walked into the house!

Rochelle was surprisingly standing directly behind the door adjusting her robe when Ray walked in. His wife had a very astonished look on her face, which she tried to mask.

"Honey! You're home," Rochelle exclaimed!

"Yeah, they got me doing some traffic work out on the two-o-one," Ray stated!

"They need to do that more often, I love it," Rochelle said!

"Why are you only wearing your robe," Ray questioned?

"Well, I was about to try on some clothes and decided to come and get some water to drink," Rochelle answered.

Ray suspiciously walked pass his wife and began looking around the house. He noticed the rear door lock opened and walked over toward it. Safety was one of the officer's primary pet peeves, therefore he always kept the door locks throughout the house. As he looked through the window, he noticed some sort of a shoe print in a small portion of the snow. To obtain a better view Ray stepped out onto the porch, where he first looked to both sides of the house. There was another footprint going around to the left side of the house that could barely be recognized, but the trained officer took note. Rochelle noticed a foot of Evander's sock on the kitchen floor, therefore she quickly walked into the room and kicked it underneath the counter.

"Is there something wrong honey," Rochelle asked?

"Why did you have the back door open," Ray countered?

"Sorry about that honey! I wanted to air out the house a bit while I was down here. I guess I just forgot to close it," Rochelle stated.

Ray was fuming inside at the thought that some man had been touching his wife. Rochelle tried finding ways to distract her husband, who seemed intent on checking his suspicions.

"Did you already eat lunch honey," Rochelle asked?

"No, I came home to eat first," Ray said as he re-entered the house and locked the door.

"OK, then I'll go and get dressed," Rochelle said.

"No! Come here," Ray remarked with a very firm tone!

Rochelle felt intimidated as she slowly began walking towards her husband. She quickly looked at his service weapon and noted that it was still securely tucked in his holster. For some strange reason she felt as though she was making her last walk to the death chamber, after she had been trialed and sentenced. When Rochelle finally reached Ray, she closed her eyes expecting him to possibly slap her across the jaw. Instead of hitting his wife, the officer held her tightly and began forcefully kissing her. Rather than his routine loving and affectionate approach, Ray unbuckled his pant and threw Rochelle against their dinner table. The whole experience felt nothing like her husband's methods, but it was the sort of take-charge attitude that she liked. Although Ray had proven to be a tyrant thus far, his sexual performance had lacked the necessary extension throughout their marriage, thereby Rochelle expected more of the same.

Officer Pedward used the evidence he continually gathered as motivation once they began engaging in coitus. The investigative officer passionately caressed and inspected his wife's body for bruises during their intense meet. Under close inspection Officer Pedward noted several bruises he was not responsible for causing, which added fuel and evidence of her guilt. There was a different mood and vibe to Ray's performance that was entirely pleasing to his wife, who did whatever he requested. Rochelle expected him to ejaculate within his five-minute limit, however he surpassed that time and went well beyond. Twenty-five minutes into their steamy encounter, Rochelle found herself wondering what happened to her husband, who was a different sex animal. Ray had her flipping every which way from furniture to furniture, until they ended up on the sofa inside the living room. When he finally ejaculated fourteen-minutes later, the officer barely had enough time to get back to his post. Ray quickly washed up inside their half bath, then fled from the house, while still buttoning up his shirt and pant zipper. The officer left his wife completely shocked on the sofa, wondering where that lover had been hiding.

Rochelle got off the sofa a few minutes later and picked up her cellular phone to check the messages. It was imperative that she got rid of the abandoned sock, so she went into the kitchen with a pair of scissors, retrieved it, then cut it to shreds. To get rid of the shredded fabric, Rochelle dressed in her winter jacket, placed the remains into a paper bag, brought it outback, and lit the bag on fire inside their backyard fire drum. Once she felt satisfied that there were only ashes, Rochelle went back inside and closed the door. She had Evander's information stored as one of her girlfriend's names, to trick her husband if he ever decided to check her phone. After she looked at his message describing how close they were to getting caught, and advising her to locate the missing sock, rather than responding she placed her phone on the counter and went into the shower.

Chapter 29

Evander's adrenaline was still on overdrive when he got back to the mechanic shop. Coy and Marshon were surprised to hear his vehicle pulling onto the property, knowing he had never returned from his lunch excursion that early. The boss-man and his personal assistant had finished eating and were relaxing inside the office, before they went back to work. The Collision Repair Specialist exited his car and kept looking behind himself, as if he was being pursued. After Evander ran into the shop, he stood to the side of the window peeking out carefully. Both Coy and Marshon began laughing at the manstress, who they thought was acting the fool to attract attention.

"Man stop clowning around! You acting like you being chased by that married woman's husband," Marshon joked!

"I think that he might be following me! I mean, I'm not sure," Evander frightfully commented!

"What the hell do you mean by you think that racist ass cop is after you," Coy demanded as he rose from his seat and went to look out the main door?

"I was inside his house having sex with his wife when he came home unexpectedly! So, I grabbed all my shit and went out the back door," Evander explained!

"God damn it Evander, I warned you about that shit! Them cops aren't nothing to play with! Did he see you," Coy asked?

"I don't think so! I mean, I don't know! It all happened so fast, that all I could think about was getting out of there," Evander stated!

"For your sake partner, I hope he really doesn't know who you were," Marshon commented!

"Do you think that I should let his commanding officer know about what happened," Evander worrisomely asked?

"The first thing you need to do is stay away from that man's wife! Those cops roll as a family, so it's hard to say if that's a good idea," Coy reasoned!

"Don't tell them shit! All these years I've always wondered why black people don't realize that not all white folks are genuine! The same way how y'all have black people who don't represent the struggle, is the same with my race. Not all whites join the call for racial justice and equality, when they know they all should," Marshon declared!

"Yow, I'm not going out like that man! I might have to start carrying protection," Evander proclaimed!

"Just calm down man... Listen, then you'll definitely give him just cause to shoot you down in cold blood whenever he sees you," Coy countered!

"You think if Pedward finds out I'm screwing his wife he won't shoot me, even if I'm unarmed? With all those massacres going on in the states right now, I feel like many white Canadians are dying to get in on the action," Evander argued?

"Well, this isn't the U.S, we have gun laws in Canada," Coy stated!

"Yeah, depending on which party we have in power! But don't you think that black Americans need to arm themselves," Evander argued?

"I'm white and that's the first thing I would advise any black American to do! Especially after seeing the way that cop kneeled on George Floyd's neck, until that man stopped breathing! Brianna Taylor shot inside her own apartment, people shot in the back running away from cops, and the cases go on and on! Now we got all these massacres happening almost every week! How much more is people supposed to take," Marshon declared?

"They can't just arm the whole country, Marshon. But black people are under pressure! So, I stand with people like Grandmaster Jay and the No F-ing Around Coalition! Black folks need to stand up for their rights, like Bob Marley said, or go back to getting lynched like slaves," Coy responded!

"Exactly, you do believe in self-preservation," Evander declared!

"I wish I could tell you different, but in all seriousness it's open season on black men still to this day! Most white folks have the belief they can harm a black person and get away with it, especially the ones in law enforcement. Even though this isn't the nineteen-hundreds, and black people aren't on that type of time, some white people still refuse to change," Coy remarked.

"You dropping facts Bossman! There are far too many hate groups out there that try to recruit guys like me every day! So, they can fill our heads with all sorts of white supremacy crap, just to get us to hate all other skin colors. The white man came to Canada and instead of living with the people already here, he tried to exterminate generations of Indians. If the technology to find dead people underground never existed, indigenous peoples would still be begging for the pope to visit Canada and apologize," Marshon lamented!

"As far as I'm concerned those hate groups are better off splitting up! Listen the white man took the best residential areas across this country for himself, and to deny the same privilege to the black man, they red-lined certain areas! So, no matter how rich we were or how much influence we have, as a colored man, you could never live among those people! Now after they took the black warrior from out of the jungles in Africa, they brought him to countries like these and placed him in the worst ghettos to live. No food, no water, no medicine, then they added drugs, alcohol, and guns for us to kill ourselves! Now after years of watching the African man target his own brothers, those fools who have been shooting at still targets believe they can go to war with the black man? They must be damn crazy, no wonder they only attack soft targets. Because the day they try infiltrating certain neighborhoods, is the day they learn what blackness is," Coy commented!

"Man, even the brown man in certain countries is prejudice against the black man! It's a struggle for us from the womb to the tomb! But all I need to know is how to keep that cop off my ass," Evander declared!

"You heard the boss, stop screwing his wife," Marshon joked!

"Before we start jumping to conclusions, did you see Pedward at any point following you," Coy enquired?

"No, I don't think so! I can't say for certain that I saw him coming after me, but I wasn't taking any chances," Evander argued!

"Listen, they can't arrest you for screwing Officer Pedward's whoring wife! So, we're going to get back to work and deal with whatsoever happens," Coy explained!

Evander thought that Coy's explanation made sense, yet he stood by the window until their lunch break was finished, before he returned to his workstation. Despite being advised to stay away from Rochelle, Evander kept sending her text messages enquiring if she was OK. Instead of responding to any of her manstress' text messages, Rochelle ignored them and left Evander to ponder whether she had been harmed by her husband. Following work that evening, the collision specialist wanted to drive by his mistress' house to check if she was safe, but Coy convinced him otherwise. It wasn't until 7:30 PM before Evander received a return message from Rochelle, who claimed she had been sleeping all afternoon. Contrary to what Coy thought the relationship between Evander and Rochelle had gotten complicated, wherein they had developed loving affections for each other.

When Evander received the text message, he was stacking bullets into the magazine of his Taurus GX4 Micro-Compact 9mm pistol. He had a bigger Walter PPQ-M2 9mm laying on his bed beside him, that was already fully loaded. The Taurus GX4 would provide him easier concealment wherever he went, especially at work where none of his coworkers would know he was armed. The Collision Specialist had several recorded videos of himself engaged in coitus with

Rochelle, which he watched repeatedly on his phone. Julious barged into the room and frightened his brother, who reactively grabbed for the loaded Walter PPQ-M2 and aimed it at him.

"God damn it, Julious! I told you to knock before you rush up in here! See, I could have shot you," Evander warned!

Julious was stunned and initially froze at the sight of his brother pointing the weapon at him. Rather than remaining as he was, the young choir director jumped onto the bed beside his brother. The television was on the surrounding area's national newscast, which was broadcasting the day's events from across their massive territory.

"Why are you, putting bullets in, your guns," Julious asked?

"Just making sure I'm prepared for anything, Little Brother," Evander answered.

"I would like, your advice," Julious requested?

"Sure bro, what's on your mind," Evander questioned?

"I think that, I like this, girl," Julious said.

"What? Who is she? Where the hell did you meet a girl," Evander questioned?

"Not in hell, at church," Julious explained.

Evander laughed at his brother's humor. "OK, so, what's your play? Have you taken her out anywhere?"

"We did go, to the movies, with the other, choir members."

"That's a start. What is her name?"

"Robin."

"What is she like?"

"She is nice! I like talking, to her about, important stuff."

"OK bro, awesome! So, what do you want to know?"

"How do I, know if she, likes me?"

"Does she call you?"

"Yes."

"Does she make time for you? You know like, if she sees you coming does she acknowledge you or stop to say hi?"

"I think so."

"Then bro, just continue being you and if the relationship is meant to happen, then you guys will definitely be together!"

"Thanks Evander," Julious stated as he picked up the Walter PPQ-M2 9mm and aimed it at the mirror!

"You remember what I taught you about handling a weapon?" Evander asked?

"Yes! You said to, always know if, a bullet is, in the chamber. Make sure the, safety is on, or off. Know how many, rounds you have, in the magazine. Hold the gun, sturdy and aim, at your target, then squeeze the, trigger," Julious declared!

"That sounds like everything to me! Always be careful and responsible whenever handling a weapon, understand me," Evander stated!

"I know," Julious calmly said.

Evander finished preparing his Micro-Compact 9mm, then placed the Walter PPQ-M2 9mm inside a box with three other firearms in his closet. The weapon detailer tucked the Taurus GX4 into the night table beside his bed and closed the drawer. Once he put away the guns, Evander laid beside his brother on his bed.

"It would be tough to see you get married and go off to live with your wife somewhere, but I guess I best prepare myself for that, you Romeo," Evander joked!

"Calm down bro, not that fast," Julious responded!

Evander again laughed at his brother's subtle humor, as he threw his left arm across Julious' chest. "Listen bro, if anything should happen to me. I want you to come down here and hide my guns. I don't want the police to find them, so can embarrass mom and make me look like some sort of gun dealer!"

"Nothing is going, to happen to, you, bro," Julious remarked!

"Just promise me you will do what I asked," Evander exclaimed!

"No problem Evander," Julious answered!

Their mother Evelin arrived home after a long day at work and could be heard alerting them once she stepped inside. Evelin called out to Julious for help with bring in some items she had inside her vehicle. Evander would normally leave his brother to handle such matters, but instead he accompanied Julious out to help. As he went by his mother Evander paused and unexpectedly gave her a warm hug with a kiss on the cheek. It had been years since her son expressed such raw emotions, therefore he caught his mother shockingly off guard. The hair stylist graciously accepted the hug and returned the affection, which was a rare treat from him.

Julious did not require any help with the four bags of groceries that Evelin left in her vehicle. However, when he brought them in and placed them on the table, Evander helped to unpack the bags and stacked away the items in the cupboard. Evelin looked suspiciously at Evander as she walked out and went to her bedroom to relax. The mother felt as though something was strange about her eldest son, yet rather than asking she neglected to snoop.

At 9:00 PM that evening, Evander was laying on his bed watching a movie, when he received a lengthy text message from Rochelle. The manstress was accustomed to receiving explicit messages from his mistress, who often sent him pictures of her in the nude. From he started reading the message Evander developed an uncomfortable sense there was a problem. As he dived into the message, he initially thought that Rochelle was seeking some sort of temporary separation, until he realized she was ending their relationship altogether. When he finished reading the message Evander was heartbroken, therefore he withdrew the Taurus GX4 9mm from the drawer and sat staring at it. The shame and hurt felt unbearable at that moment, thus he placed the weapon to the side of his head; yet could not succumb to pulling the trigger.

The more Evander thought of their passionate lovemaking and the number of times his mistress had whispered the words, 'I love you' in his ears, was the more he felt that Ray had to be involved. Every type of scenario ran through his thoughts, as he fought to come to terms with being dumped. If Rochelle was to dismiss him as she so chose, Evander wanted the world to know what happened between them both. With anger as his driving motivation, the repair specialist signed onto a porn website, which allowed sex tape developers to upload and sell their movies. While on the webpage, Evander selected the raunchiest sex video between Rochelle and himself, then uploaded the contents.

Chapter 30

It was a gloomy day across the Province of Manitoba with a mixture of rain and snow fall ongoing. The national meteorologist had forecasted a miserable day for areas like Dominion City, Roseau River Reserve, plus the entire southern section of Winnipeg. The Northern Territory of the province was expected to experience hail and ice pellet type weather. The temperature had changed over the past two weeks, but winter had not yet fully released its grip on North America. Motorists who were travelling through Alberta, Saskatchewan, and Manitoba were advised to take extreme caution due to unpredictable weather.

It had been six days since Russell and Kyler Applewick lost their mother, who fought a valiant battle against cancer. Their family had some of the least liked residents throughout the town, hence there were only eight people present at her funeral. Aside from the Applewick brothers, there were Andrew, Preacher Man Hemming, and an older couple who looked more like farmers. The old woman wore a dress that was covered with flowers, stockings, ankle high boots, a wool trench jacket, and a wide-brim western hat. Her male companion also wore a western hat, along with blue jeans, a long sleeve denim shirt, suspenders, and cowboy boots. The last two men present were the grounds keepers, who waited inside their Toyota 4X4 truck for the proceedings to conclude, so they could move in and cover the casket.

Pastor Hemming had no idea who the Applewick family were before the funeral, and only agreed to perform the eulogy as a favor for Andrew. During the ceremony Kyler and Russell were disrespectful throughout, by either smoking cigarettes or taking sips from a 750 ml bottle of Fortress Rum they carried. Andrew was the only person who paid attention to the pastor, while the old man and woman spoke softly to each other about their private affairs. As the preacher approached the end of his commendation, he signalled the grounds keepers over for them to begin the casket's descent. The two men walked over and commenced the final phase, while the preacher and Andrew sang two consecutive hymns. Pastor Hemming had never presided over such a funeral that was poorly attended and felt like he was burying the witch of Dominion City. None of the other attendants participated in any junction of the funeral, as if they were atheists who had never been to church. Following his final prayer, Paster Hemming went about the grounds and shook the hands of those in attendance, before he departed and went directly to his church to pray.

The grieving attendants stood there and watched the helpers refilled the grave with the soil that was previously removed. Andrew tried to appear decent while Pastor Hemming was present, but once he left all hell broke loose. The self proclaimed new white nationalist began drinking and smoking with his peers, who were intoxicated despite the early hour. After the grounds keepers finished their task, the couple turned to the brothers and gave them their blessings. Andrew had no idea who the man and woman were until he overheard his partners addressed them before they left.

"Take good care Aunty Mavis and Uncle Henry," Russell stated!

"Yeah, we love you both! Thanks for coming, mom would have appreciated it," Kyler remarked!

When the three men finally left the cemetery nearly an hour later, Andrew had to drive them home because Kyler and Russell were too intoxicated. It was only 1:21 in the afternoon and even Andrew was slightly under the effects, though significantly lesser than his companions. Russell wanted cigarettes at the store, so Andrew had to drive there before he brought them home. As they drove down Waddell Avenue they came upon Shirley in her antique automobile. The mixture of rain and snow made visibility a little poor, yet the young driver was speeding along. Andrew was becoming a regular smoker, therefore he reached for a cigarette from the pack on the armrest and lit it ablaze. At the speed with which they were travelling, once he raised his head to refocus on the road, he realized they were strikingly close to rear-ending Shirley's automobile. The young driver narrowly missed the collision and reactively swerved their vehicle onto the adjacent lane and around Shirley. Although he would have been at fault, the transitioning Arian wound his window down and thrust his arm through to extend his middle finger at Shirley.

"They need to take away that old bag's license," Andrew commented!

When they reached the grocery store, Andrew left the brothers in the car and walked in and bought the cigarettes with a case of beer. They then drove back down Waddell Avenue to their house, where they drank and smoked for the remainder of the afternoon. The brothers were vividly emotional about losing their mother and sobbed multiple times at the sight of her pictures. While they were visibly disturbed, the death of their mother managed to embolden their resolve to inflict harm against peoples of different cultures, faith, and skin tone.

The Applewick brothers continued giving Andrew cigarettes laced with methamphetamine to smoke for more than a week, before he learnt of the included addictive substance. By the time the devoted Christian learned he had been smoking the illegal drug, he was fully addicted and had become an expert at constructing their joints. Andrew grew dependent on the drug, wherein he either contribute to their daily acquisition or paid for the entire purchase. With each passing week he spent less time at home and attended church fewer, while he increased the amount of time he spent at the Applewick's residence. During his visits the brothers would show him all sorts of rhetoric videos, with racist and Neo-Nazi leaders who spoke candidly about exterminating other races.

On his way home from the Applewick's residence, Andrew tuned into a satellite radio station that Russell implied he listened to. The station was an underground broadcast and aired people with conspiracy theories and weird beliefs, in addition to Atheists and racist commentators. The host at that hour was talking about white man's privileges, and his beliefs that they should be able to take whatever they wanted due of their superiority. Everything that the host mentioned appeased Andrew, who pulled onto his driveway, yet stayed in his car listening until the program had ended.

"Back on our slave plantation whenever my granddaddy felt the urge to buss a nut, he didn't have to go through all the yellow tape we have to go through nowadays! He didn't have to wait until he went back home from the fields to get that loving from grandma! Hell no, he would just pick whichsoever one a them slave whores he wanted; and took her wheresoever he pleased! Your property was your property, and you could do whatsoever you chose with your property, whensoever you chose to! We got these political leaders nowadays in this country, who are messing with our rights to own slaves! No man should have the right to tell another man how he should live his life! So, if I decide to keep slaves that should be my decision! If I decide to carry arms, that should be my right and my decision! It was written in the god damn constitution of our country, that all men have the rights to bare arms! This country belongs to the white man; and no matter how them politicians try to do; this land will always belong to the white man! Until next time, this is the Real Patriot signing off! Reminding you that white power reigns," the host exclaimed before he went silent, and music began playing!

It was 12:47 AM when Andrew finally staggered into his house. The only illuminated light throughout the whole house was inside the living room, where Jacquelin was half asleep in front the television. The clack of the door lock unlatching awoke the concerned mother, who was the only person worried about Andrew's wellbeing. Thomas and Viveen were sound asleep and had given up on concerning themselves with his coming or going. When Andrew walked into the house Jacquelin sat up and went to confront him, before he disappeared into his bedroom.

"Do you know what time it is Andrew," Jacquelin asked?

"Mom, I'm not a child! I can come home at whatever time I please," Andrew responded!

"Oh no! Not in my house you don't! By the way, where are you coming from at this hour? I've heard rumors that you're hanging around those Applewick boys," Jacquelin argued!

"It's nobody's business who I hang around with mom," Andrew declared as he looked inside the fridge for something to eat!

"Well, since you have so much time on your hands, you need to go and find a job," Jacquelin stated!

"And where in Dominion City am I going to find a job," Andrew remarked while preparing himself something to eat?

"Are you even looking to find a job? And if there are no jobs here, then I guess you will just have to travel to Winnipeg," Jacquelin said!

"Enough with the job already! I'm not working in Winnipeg, OK," Andrew countered!

"Then you are going to have to find somewhere else to live if you refuse to work, because nothing in life comes free," Jacquelin responded!

"God damn it mom, just leave me alone, will you," Andrew stated as he walked off to his room with a plate of food and a cup filled with milk.

Jacquelin was furious with her son's lackadaisical responses as if he cared less about what she thought. She stormed into her bedroom where Thomas was sound asleep and began ranting about Andrew's behavior. Thomas tried putting a pillow over his head to avoid listening to her whining, considering he had to get up early for work.

"Thomas Woolrey, I want you to get out of bed and go talk to that son of yours! Because if he thinks he is going to constantly keep coming in here at these hours without having a job, he is seriously mistaken! He looks like he has been getting high off something; and smells like he has been in some smelly whorehouse! Stop acting like you can't hear me; and get up go talk to that boy before I'm forced to sin in the eyes of my Lord," Jacquelin cursed!

"Jacquelin it's too late for all this right now! I have work in the morning, I got to get some sleep," Thomas stated!

"Well, if you can tolerate the disrespect then I can't! I refuse to be disrespected in my own house, so it's either he finds a job; or he has to find somewhere else to live," Jacquelin quarreled!

"Andrew is not some kid Jacquelin! He can pretty much do whatever he wants in the eyes of the law," Thomas said.

"Not in the eyes of this law he's not! Obviously, whosoever he has been hanging around with is a terrible influence on him! Every night he now comes home well into the morning, then sleeps until the next evening and does it all over again," Jacquelin declared!

"I'm sure it is only some faze he's going through. For Christ's sakes the kid doesn't have much friends as it is! He'll be back to himself in no time! Just go to bed and relax! I have to get some sleep, goodnight," Thomas remarked!

"Make sure you speak with him tomorrow about coming home at a decent hour," Jacquelin insisted! She then turned off the light and sat on the edge of the bed, until she crawled beneath the sheet and went to sleep.

Chapter 31

When Celine brought her children to Nova Scotia to visit Lloyd's grave for the weekend, Miss Shirley refrained from mentioning the trip to her girlfriends, who would have informed the entire town. Despite all her attempts, word still got out about the trip, and thus opened a floodgate of conspiracies theories by the gossipers across Dominion City. The most far-fetched theory came from Joan, who suggested that Celine had returned to Nova Scotia permanently with her children, due to the hardships she encountered. Most of the town folks believed that Celine either had to testify against her husband's murderers or prepared their legal strategy for the upcoming trial. Viveen's school incident primarily unveiled the story to the community, which was unaware of Aaron's legal troubles in Nova Scotia. Jacquelin acknowledged her son's legal troubles to a few friends after Viveen's suspension, in addition to disclosing that it was her who monetarily secured his defense team. Even though Aaron was being charged for first degree murder, his mother insisted that 'he was innocent and would be vindicated of the crime'! Rather than accepting that her son was possibly guilty due to his lengthy criminal history, his mother accepted his side of the story and supported him wholeheartedly. To further strengthen her belief that Aaron would get released, Jacquelin went by their church each day and prayed for the Lord to grant her one wish. In trying to prove that she knew all the details of the case, Jacquelin debunked one of the gossiper's assumptions, that Celine went to testify against Aaron.

Coy's girlfriend Sandra heard of the rumors and told him, thus he translated what he heard to Celine and the rest of his family. Miss Shirley, Celine, and the kids shared a huge laugh over the assumptions they heard, considering many were outlandish and illustrated how sinical the residents were. Instead of remaining home each day, Celine wanted to do something to generate an income and remained busy. With her brother being a business owner, she wanted to also own her own business, however she was unsure which industry might be favorable in such a small town. To derive at a decision Celine drove around town and visited a few businesses. One of the first things she noticed was the lack of places for female friends to meet and chat. Despite the healthy living of many locals, a large population of them were overweight. The town also had a lack of places where one could acquire specific beverages, such as a cup of mocha or a glass of wine. There were no exercise gyms or coffee shops in town because Dominion City residents considered themselves as country folks, rather than actual city dwellers. Most people in the community would rather everything remained as they were, yet Celine decided to become a trailblazer and accumulated a business license for the first fitness, wine, and coffee shop.

There used to be a roller-skating rink in town that closed their doors several years prior. Since they went out of business nobody took over the building or tried opening another franchise. Most business renters wanted a much smaller facility from which to operate, therefore Celine was able to acquire the building from the bank for a great price. To silence their critics, Celine bought the building to show them she was permanently back in town and planned on incorporating a successful business. When word got around that she had purchased the building, people suggested that she had wasted her money and would have been better off opening a store elsewhere. Nobody had any idea what sort of business she planned on opening, yet there were all sorts of discouraging remarks made.

Over the next few weeks Celine hired Steve and his team of renovation specialist to remodel the interior and exterior of the building. The inside was split into two businesses under the same roof and provided an atmosphere unlike anywhere else in Dominion City. The larger section of the space was designed for all the equipment necessary to manage a gym, while the smaller area was conformed for the wine and warm beverage drinkers. Many residents passed by the location daily and wondered what sort of business was being constructed, as Celine remained tight-lipped about her plans. The advertisement company in Brandon, Manitoba from which she bought her business sign, brought the materials to install four days before she was scheduled to open. The business sign was the first clue anybody had of the sort of enterprise being built, which was the first of its kind for the town and surrounding areas. Most residents who drove by the location from that point scoffed at the concept, with the belief that the business would close within three to six months.

At the grand opening of 'A Cup of Exercise' there was only fifteen ladies from Dominion City and the surrounding areas. The biggest guest of them all was Mayor Elise Bathurst, the first female elected overseer of the territory. Over the last number of years, the town have lost several businesses, so Mayor Bathurst was elated there was a new enterprise opening. There were a few males in attendance such as Coy and Marshon, who went by to take a tour of the facility, which had a range of fitness machines. Most of the females were Celine's friends and family members, who attended to take full advantage of the free temporary membership promotion and sample some of the wines. The business concept initially did not seem like something the locals would support, until the visitors discovered the type of exercise classes being offered, in addition to the items on the lounge's menu. The concept of exercise with everything else the gym offered impressed the guests, knowing they could come by to simply sit and read a book over a cup of their favorite brew.

For the first four days thereafter, Celine did not get a single new customer, even though her establishment was the new talk of the town. The mayor and many of her friends took advantage of the opening day free six months membership special she gave away, to keep exercise enthusiasts inside the gym. Celine had begun her own personal fitness regiment, but the facility had no personal trainers available. In such a small town it didn't take very much for anyone to feel discouraged, especially with the number of people unwilling to support the gym. On the fifth day when Celine expected much of the same, three large sized Caucasian women walked into her gym seeking memberships. Dee, Kerry, and Helyn were well beyond the four hundred pounds weight; moreover, they were thrilled there was a gym built in the territory that they could attend.

"Hello, welcome to A Cup of Exercise," Celine greeted!

"Hi, we would like to enquire about your membership," Dee asked?

"Sure, no problem," Celine responded as she reached for three pamphlets from a rack and gave them to the visitors!

The visiting ladies took the pamphlets and opened them to the first page, where three separate packages were highlighted. Each package was more expensive than the other and lasted for a significant longer period. The other pages discussed the rules of the gym, their members' code of conduct, and the locker situation while you were at the facility exercising.

"Are you girls from here in town," Celine enquired?

"No, we came all the way from Ginew, in Roseau River Reserve! We been meaning to come by since we heard about this place a few days ago," Dee responded before she got together with her friends and discussed the packages!

Following a short debate between the visitors Helyn said, "I believe we will go with the three-year membership."

"Thank you for selecting our longest membership package! Here is a form you will each have to fill out and just give them back to me once you have finished," Celine instructed!

The business slowly and remarkably grew despite the early criticisms. Dominion City was home to several overweight residents, who were advised by their doctors to exercise and lose weight, yet they all procrastinated when the gym opened. Once news broke of the three out-of-towners becoming members at 'A Cup of Exercise', those hesitant people quickly sign up. Celine went from nervous times to having to employ her mother on a parttime basis, with added resources provided by Robin and Julien whenever they were available. Within the next two months the new business boss had to hire another employee, to help with the ever-rising workload. The gym became such a popular location, that even Coy and his employees became members who exercised regularly among other things.

Dominion City United Church was over capacitated with adherents, that some in attendance had to stand at the back. Miss Shirley ensured that she invited everybody she knew to attend on that occasion, to listen to her granddaughter's choir debut. Even Celine invited her friends who normally abstained from attending churches, nevertheless many of them made the effort to support her daughter. The day was made extra special when Coy brought Marshon and Evander with him, to cheer on his little niece and the choir. None of his co-workers had ever met Robin, therefore the proud uncle immediately pointed her out to them. Evander instantly thought about his brother's secret crush that was revealed to him in confidence, therefore he refrained from mentioning it. The choir was scheduled to perform their new hymn, which they had been working on for several weeks.

Nobody could recall their church ever being that packed with a mixture of adherents and first-time visitors. Pastor Roundtree had a glow on his face that expressed his true thoughts, as he looked out at the large crowd inside their hall. The pastor was delivering one of his best sermons ever, which he hoped would captivate most of the first-time visitors to return. Although the preacher-man had his audience captivated, he understood that the mass was there to listen to their new choir leader, therefore he had to quickly wrap up his speech.

"--- truly righteous people only seek knowledge about the one who created them! They have heard the stories about his son Jesus Christ who died for our sins, yet it is the Lord who we all crave knowledge about! The wicked have tried to disclaim his greatness, by saying that man came from monkeys, when the Lord created everything on Earth! From humans to the animals, to the birds, to the fishes of the ocean, the fruits and vegetation from plants and trees, all for us to survive and look after. Yet, look at all we have lost, the dinosaurs, millions of animals extinct, millions of birds, plants, and all for the greed of humans, who can't replace any of those things, but mankind have found ways to destroy them. This planet is millions of years old, yet we have some preachers and slick talkers who haven't lived for one hundred years, trying to convince others that the creator doesn't exist! If any man could be glorified as God, they would do anything to take that throne! This is why we have different continents, with different climates, and challenges, or some man would seek to rule it all, because it is the greed of mankind to rule instead of worship! But the truly righteous only seeks to praise the one who has created us all. Therefore, on your spiritual journey do not allow any priest or slick talker to dim your thirst to worship God, because he is deserving of our praise! Can I get a Hallelujah?"

"Hallelujah," shouted several attendees who began applauding at the conclusion of the preacher's speech! Pastor Roundtree used his handkerchief to wipe away the sweat that had developed, as he packed up his bible and the papers he brought to the alter. Some of the adherents had stood to applaud his brilliant speech, which was very well delivered. Robin never envisioned so many people attending, therefore she became so nervous that she felt her hands shaking. With the pastor about to introduce them, she felt lightheaded as if she was about to faint, until she looked at Julious, who signalled her to relax and breathe.

"Thank you, thank you... thank you! At this point in our program, we have reached the primary reason some of you are here today, which is to listen the new sound of our choir! So, without any further delays, may I present to you the D.C United Choir, with their newest leading singer, Miss Robin Walker," Pastor Roundtree introduced!

Celine who was seated beside her mother, Julien, and others in the front row, leapt to her feet and began applauding and cheering. Nearly everyone else who were seated jumped to their feet and followed the proud mother, who could barely wait to hear Robin sing. Coy and his companions began barking and cheering, which increased Robin's confidence and brought a smile to her face. Julious began playing the chorus, while he waved the baton, he used to conduct his choir members. Rather than sitting, those who were standing remained as they were, as those seated rose to their feet.

"We are all born, In a world of sin,

But since I let you in, I've eased my pain,

Glorious Lord, I sing to thee,

In hopes that you will, Forever hear my plea, plea, plea,

For my family, I sing to thee,

For my friends, I sing to thee..."

The entire audience was rocking to the hymn as if they were at a live concert. By the time Robin came around to the second chorus, everyone inside the hall were singing along as if they knew the words. Pastor Roundtree had a much larger grin on his face at that point, as he sat on the stage dancing in his chair. Miss Shirley began crying seconds into the song and infected Celine, who stood beside her mother weeping with their hearts filled with joy. Julien stood beside his guardians with his mouth wide open for most of the hymn, having never heard his sister sing that divinely. At the end of the song, there had never been a greater round of applause given in the Dominion City United Church, wherein everyone clapped, whistled, and shouted for nearly five minutes, before they slowly simmered down. Uncle Coy was chanting his niece's name throughout, while Evander and Marshon joined their boss.

The entire choir felt proud of the job they did and deserved the recognition they received. Most of the first-time attendants vowed to return at that point, after they were treated to such ravishing music. Julious felt elated for Robin, who finally saw the potential her Artistic friend and choir leader saw in her. Despite the praises and the glamour, Robin looked out into the crowd and felt saddened that her father was not there to watch her perform. She wiped away a single tear from her right eye, as she imagined Lloyd among those in attendance. After the ceremony ended everybody created a line to individually congratulate the performers before they departed. With such a boost in confidence the choir members began discussing competing in competitions that they had competed in the past. Pastor Roundtree delivered a very moving speech that would generally have him circled by his audience members after church, yet the only intrigue everyone showed was toward Robin.

Following all the recognition Julious found himself in a headlock by his brother, who was extremely proud of him. Evander had Marshon with him to discuss ways that Julious could profit off the musical beats he created. As the eldest sibling, Evander knew of his brother's challenges and talent, and wanted that creativity to pay him handsomely, rather than him wasting all his skills doing free things for the church. Knowing Julious only went to a few places in town, Evander thought that the female he mentioned might be an adherent, so from he entered the building that Sunday morning he began looking around to decipher who she might be. Just from watching Julious' interactions with Robin, Evander could tell she was the person his brother was referring to, before he even asked. When Julious finally admitted that Robin was the female he had been admiring, his brother smiled at the idea that Coy, and he could become relatives. To persuade Julious to consider some of the self promotional tactics Marshon explained to him, Evander suggested that 'for him to eventually look after Robin and his family, he needed to get serious about making money'!

Once their conversation ended Julious excused himself to visit the bathroom. As he approached the restrooms, Robin exited the female's bathroom ahead of him. Their new choir leader was still floating on air after all the amazing comments she received, that she gave Julious a huge, unexpected hug. They were about to release each other from the embrace when Julious turned his head to say something to Robin, while she was doing the same. Both their lips met accidentally, yet neither of them quickly pulled away as if it were their intention. When they finally unhanded each other, the moment felt special yet awkward, therefore they pleasantly smiled and went their separate ways. Julious went into the bathroom with a humongous smile on his face, while Robin rejoined her family members with a similar grin.

Chapter 32

Officer Pedward pulled over a BMW 550i that was travelling at a hundred-and-fifty-nine miles-per-hour in a ninety zone. Ray had been having a tough time after he uncovered his wife's adulterous secret, therefore with each passing day he grew more and more unstable. For a person who often did things by the book, Ray began doing things out of character like drinking on the job, therefore he kept a bottle of vodka inside his personal bag. After the officer finished advising his dispatcher of 'his location, the make and model of the detained vehicle, and the number of visible passengers,' he then exited his cruiser and walked up to the car. Should the interaction between the passengers and Officer Pedward got ugly, the lawman all knew how far away their reinforcement were, and how long it would take for them to arrive. Officer Gilmore who was closest to Ray was eighteen minutes away, but he had also made a traffic stop and was issuing fines. The first thing Officer Pedward observed as he approached the driver side window, was that the couple were of mixed races. The female passenger was a young and beautiful Caucasian madden, who had unique portrait like facial feature and long flowing blond hair. Her male companion was of the Native Indigenous Culture, therefore the officer's mood immediately changed. The woman sat staring directly through the windshield, as if she was being abducted or did not wish to make eye contact with the officer.

"Are you aware of the speed you were travelling," Officer Pedward demanded?

"I think around one fifty," the driver answered!

"I clocked you at a hundred-and-fifty-nine in a ninety zone," Officer Pedward warned!

"I'm sorry officer, I just wanted to show my girlfriend here how fast this car was," responded the driver!

"License and registration, please," Officer Pedward requested?

"I really don't think I was going that fast," mumbled the driver as he withdrew his license from his wallet.

"At the unsafe speed which you were travelling on a public roadway, it is my discretion whether I seize your vehicle! So, I would be extremely careful what I say from now on," Officer Pedward argued.

The young man reached across into the glove compartment and began checking for the vehicle's registration paper. Ray looked at the female and thought something was odd with her mannerism, as she abstained from looking in his direction. The driver final found the document he searched for and handed it to the officer with his license.

"Where were you heading tonight Mister ah, Louie Albus," Officer Pedward asked after he looked at the name?

"Like I said, I was just out having a joy ride with my girlfriend," Louie answered.

"Sit tight and I will be back in a few minutes," Officer Pedward instructed!

Ray walked back to his cruiser and started writing the ticket, when he noticed the BMW's occupants making hand gestures at each other. It was obvious that they were arguing about the traffic stop and something else, which intrigued the officer to uncover. The more Ray watched their interaction was the angrier he became about being deceived, therefore he ripped up the ticket, powered off his bodycam recorder, and stormed out of the cruiser. He walked back to the driver's window and loudly tapped on it, which startled the unaware conductor who quickly wound down the glass.

"I don't feel as if you were being truthful to me earlier. So, I will be seizing the vehicle due to the excessive speed you were doing of one-hundred-and-fifty-nine, in a ninety zone," Ray warned!

"But I thought you were only going to give me a ticket? Oh, my lord my dad is going to kill me for this! Is there something I could do," Louie begged?

"Do you have any firearms or drugs inside the car," Ray questioned?

The female for the first time turned and looked at Officer Pedward with a worried look in her eyes. She then looked at her male counterpart and said, "You better tell him, before he finds it!"

"Before I find what," Ray asked?

"Tell him Louie," said the female!

"I borrowed one of my father's guns; and gave Nadine to hide it," Louie responded.

Ray pulled his service weapon and held it by his side. "Where is the firearm, Nadine?"

"I have it underneath my sweater," Nadine responded.

"Mr. Albus, I want you to place both your hands on the steering wheel, and if you remove them for any reason, I will shoot you! You understand me," Ray ordered before he made his way to the passenger side?!

"Yes, officer," Louie cried.

"As for you, I want you to put your left hand on the dashboard, then slowly use your right hand to lift up your sweater, so I can see the weapon! If you do anything else than what I told you, you will get shot," Ray instructed!

"Yes Sir," Nadine frightfully responded.

Nadine slowly did as instruct until the weapon was visible to the officer. Once Ray saw the gun he made the female placed both her hands on the dashboard, before he opened the door and retrieved it. With the weapon secured, the officer holstered his service firearm, then checked if the confiscated handgun was loaded. The BMW's occupants were carrying a Springfield Hellcat Pro, Semi-automatic 9mm, with a 3.7" barrel, and held fifteen rounds in the magazine and one in the chamber.

"Are you a killer Mister Albus," Ray demanded?

"No, officer sir," Louie answered!

"Then, why you taking your father's gun? You a gang member," Ray questioned?

"No sir," Louie responded quickly!

"Get your ass out of that damn car now," Ray instructed the driver as he stomped his way around to his door!

Had Officer Pedward done his homework before he overreacted, he would have uncovered that his male detainee was the youngest son of Chief Nathaniel Albus, from the Manitoba, Banting Cree Nation. The female inside the BMW began getting scared something terrible was about to happen, as she watched the raging mad officer marched around the front of the car to her companion's door, while continually aiming the gun at them. Louie was barely through the car door when Ray grabbed him and threw him to the ground. Nadine was terrified for their lives at that point, so she made sure she kept her hands on the dashboard to avoid further enraging the officer. They were out in the middle of nowhere, miles away from the closest town, where there were no witnesses to vouch for what might happen to them. Ray grabbed Louie by the shirt collar and dragged him off into the dark behind the BMW, where Nadine could not see a thing. All she heard was Louie yelling each time the officer presumably struck him, as if he were torturing him for information.

"Do you know what guns do to people out here Mr. Albus," Ray demanded before he slapped Louie across the back of the head with his hand?

"Aw! They kill people," Louie said!

"So, why are you trying to show off carrying a gun," Ray questioned with a slap?

"I wasn't thinking, I'm sorry sir," Louie declared!

"Mr. Albus you are lucky tonight I'm in a good mood, or else you would have lost your car," Ray threatened then slapped him again in the back of the head.

"Aw, thank you officer," Louie cried!

"Instead, you're lucky I'm only taking this gun," the officer stated then slapped him again.

"Ahh, yes sir," Louie concurred!

"Might have lost that pretty little girlfriend of yours," threatened Ray followed by a slap!

"Ahh, I promise I'll never be that stupid again sir," Louie pled!

"And you could have lost your life," Ray argued then delivered a slap!

"Ahh, I've learnt my lesson! I swear," Louie exclaimed!

"You're going to get your ass up! Get in that vehicle and drive slowly back to wherever you came from! And if I ever hear of, or see you back around these parts, I guarantee you, nobody will ever find your body," Ray threatened before he slapped the young man one final time!

Louie was so terrified for his life that he scraped himself off the ground and painfully made his way to the car door, then slowly slid into the driver's seat. Officer Pedward stepped to the driver's door and tossed the license and car registration onto Louie's lap. Nadine still had both her hands on the dashboard to illustrate her continuous corporation. The officer had seized the Hellcat Pro 9mm handgun without issuing any citation or court date, but Louie and Nadine were just happy to be leaving with their lives at that point. The Cree Indian Chief's son drove away at a modest speed to avoid being further harassed by the officer, who thrashed and humiliated him.

Ray's work shift was long and eventless except for that one traffic stop where he got to release some of his built-up frustrations. That winter season was long and brutally cold, but Canadians hoping for an early spring were disappointed when the groundhog emerged from its borrow and saw its shadow. Tradition-ally the groundhog meant the country would not be rid of winter for another six weeks, therefore those who believed such superstitions buckled up for the extended season. The southern portion of Manitoba did not experience a snow-storm for almost two weeks, yet they received patches of scattered snowfall almost every day. On the night in question the Canadian Weather Services predicted two to three inches of snow overnight, which was to begin falling after midnight. When Ray departed from the station at 10:18 PM, the snow was just beginning to trickle down, however it gradually got heavier and heavier.

Ray thought the loss of his beautiful wife would ruin his image, therefore before she left him, he decided to kill her first. Earlier that morning while on patrol, he visited a small hardware store in East St. Paul, Manitoba, where he bought several items. The emotionally distort officer had a recyclable bag on the passenger seat, that contained plastic gloves, a pack of garbage bags, bleach, pinesol, duct tape, and a hacksaw. Officer Pedward planned to kill his wife and cut her body into transferable pieces, so he could easily get rid of her. While driving Ray withdrew his bottle of vodka to take a drink, but unfortunately there was only a sip left. The developing snowstorm angered him greatly, knowing that his vindictive plans would have to wait until another day.

When Officer Pedward returned home, he tossed all his work equipment on the sofa and went to fix himself a drink. He took the handgun he confiscated from the young man earlier and shoved it into his pocket. There was a plate of food covered over on the table, with a glass of juice beside it. Over the past few days, he had lost his appetite, so he picked up the plate and placed it into the refrigerator. Rochelle was always sound asleep whenever he reached home, thus he walked into their bedroom and stood over her on the bed. It was evident that she had been drinking by the unfinished glass of wine seated on the night table. Ray withdrew the Springfield Hellcat Pro and aimed it at his sleeping beauty, who had no idea he was standing there.

With his eyes fixated on the woman he loved; her cellular notification icon brightened up her phone screen and distracted him. It was not typically his style to snoop through his wife's affairs, but with their relationship on the brink of collapse, there were no boundaries. Ray inquisitively looked over at the phone to see who the messenger was, at which he noted that the sender was Rochelle's sister. From the officer read the first line of the message he knew that it was not coming from her sister, due to the emotional content within. The message read, "Baby please don't do this to me. I need you in my life. I'm going crazy without you. I can't stop thinking of the passionate and wild..." To read the rest of the message Ray needed to unlock his wife's I-phone. Rochelle had gotten intoxicated before she passed out on their bed, therefore she had no idea what her husband was doing. The officer knew his wife was a sound sleeper, hence he could do pretty much anything he wanted, and it would not disturb or awaken her. To get as much information as possible about her partner, Ray pointed Rochelle's I-phone at her face to capture her features, at which the device opened and was activated.

Once he got the phone unlocked, the officer went into the days room and closed the bedroom door, before he relocated the message. The remainder of the message read, "sex we used to have. Please reconsider, I know that worthless husband of yours can't satisfy you. Call me baby I'm going crazy. I love you," with several love emojis following. He forwarded some of the pictures and videos to his personal phone, which clearly showed his wife and her manstress entangled inside his house. The filthy sex recordings enraged the officer to the extent that he picked up the stolen 9mm and stormed into the bedroom to kill his wife. Just before he pulled the trigger, Ray thought of something he needed to do before he cancelled Rochelle, therefore he walked back into the days room and went back on her phone.

To repay his wife's manstress, the officer wrote Evander a text message which stated, "Hi baby I miss you too. Sorry for not calling you but my stupid husband was watching me. I can't take living with him anymore, so I am leaving town tonight before he comes home. I want to see you before I go, because I will not be going back to Ray. Maybe you could come away with me, if you still love me? If you want to see me, meet me at 1:00 tonight off Route 246, by the Red River Bridge heading into St. Jean Baptiste."

Evander was home watching a movie inside his bedroom with Julious and quickly reached for his phone. Their father was home from work for a few days, therefore their parents were locked inside their bedroom. When the text message notification sounded the car collision expert knew exactly who the texter was. The appeasing thought lit up Evander's face like a Christmas tree, even before he read the message. After he read the text, Evander leapt off the bed and began dancing around the room. Julious was steadily falling asleep until his brother's overreaction to the message caused him to awaken.

"I told those idiots at the garage that my baby can't get enough of me! You see that message, she just texted me begging me to run away with her," Evander boasted as he retrieved a travelling bag from his closet and began packing some of his clothes inside!

"What are you, doing that for," Julious asked?

"Remember when I said that one day, I might have to move away from Dominion City. Well today is that day, little brother! I can't tell mom or dad, so you will have to spring the news on them tomorrow after I'm gone," Evander said while responding to Rochelle's text!

"Are you sure, that is smart, thing to do," Julious asked?

"I know you are worried about me, but I'll be fine! Listen, you get whatever you want from my room, but whenever I get back here, make sure my Janet Jackson photo is right there on that wall," Evander exclaimed!

"OK, big brother I, love you," Julious stated before they hugged each other for the last time!

"I have to get out of here if I'm going to get up to Red River by 1:00! The car is yours whenever you guys get it back, and I love you too bro," Evander declared before he rushed off!

There was a much easier direction to St. Jean Baptiste from Dominion City that brought motorists along Provincial Route-201 to Interstate-75. The route along which the text message asked Evander to meet, was far more dangerous whenever they had bad weather. While street cleaning crews were quicker to clear the snow from busier roadways such as PR-201 and I-75, they left back streets such as Provincial Route 246 for last. Rather than becoming suspicious about the location, Evander thought Rochelle was trying to avoid getting seen by any of her husband's comrades. As a result, he blindly drove himself into the officer's trap.

Following the confirmation response, Ray wiped the messages between Evander and he from Rochelle's phone, then carefully returned the device. He had already purchased the items he needed to cover himself during his wife's killing, so he went down to their basement and retrieved a bag. Inside the bag was a brand-new pair of construction boots, a pack of shoe's sole covering, and a black overall, which he got dressed in. To prevent his shoes from leaving any marks on the floor, Ray used two of the shoe's sole covering and placed them underneath his boots. Knowing his wife may not roll out of bed until late morning, the officer took her car key and left with her vehicle. When he reached the location, the officer pulled off to the side of the road and turned on his emergency flashers. Warnings of severe snowstorms usually deterred motorists from travelling, therefore PR-246 was baren at that hour. After ten minutes of waiting Ray began wondering if Evander was still coming, considering it was then 1:04. As the clock struck 1:05 the officer looked into his rear-view mirror and saw a vehicle's low beams approaching.

The tires on Evander's car were slightly worn, which affected its speed, maneuverability, braking, and stability. In his haste to reach the location before Rochelle departed, he narrowly slid off the snowy roads several times. The car's performance in wintery weather was his reason for being late, moreover he could have ill afforded to release the steering wheel to text or call. When Evander tried to stop his vehicle along the side of the roadway that had black ice surfaces beneath the snow, the car slid on the ice and slightly bumped into Rochelle's bumper. The contact shook Rochelle's car and created a small dent, but the lone occupant could be seen collecting his belongings, following which he exited and started moving toward his transport. Evander wanted to put some of his belongings inside the trunk and banged the compartment door for the driver to open. The officer looked up ahead then checked the rear-view mirror for oncoming motorists, before he opened the trunk compartment and exited the car with the confiscated weapon. There was no time for Evander to escape or react once Ray walked up on him and began pulling the trigger. Even after he had dispersed of all the bullets from the gun, Officer Pedward was still hatefully pressing the trigger.

The snow was falling heavy and thick at that point, so it was difficult to see very far in the distance. It took the officer a while to regain his senses and realize that his wife's manstress was dead. He then looked up and down the road and noted there were no vehicles coming, so he threw the bags into the trunk and began searching through Evander's front pockets. The vehicle frame repair specialist had a coil of money in his left front pocket and his wallet in his right pocket. Officer Pedward stole everything from his victim's front pockets, to give the impression it was a robbery gone bad. Evander's cellular was inside his left rear pocket when he fell backwards, yet the officer neglected to search him thoroughly. Ray picked up Evander's keys from beside the body, then grabbed his legs, and pulled him down to the river.

To make it difficult for the body to be seen by motorists and others, Ray stayed close to the bridge. Most of the water was still frozen, but there were sections of the ice that had melted over the past week. Officer Pedward shoved the body onto the thin ice by the banking and left it there, hoping that once the ice melted the corpse would wash away and not get found. He rushed back to his car and turned off the engine, closed the door, and climbed into Evander's vehicle. A Freight Line trailer drove pass before he pulled onto the roadway, so Ray waited until the trailer disappeared visually before he took off. The heavy snow would help to cover much of the evidence, however it would also hamper his efforts to quickly vacate the scene. The drive across the bridge into St. Jean Baptiste seemed like an eternity from the crime scene, which was not visible due to the darkness and the snowfall. The officer would have preferred to bring Evander's car much further away from the corpse than he did, but the weather had dictated his every move.

Under a mile away from the scene, Ray abandoned the vehicle after he entered the small town and turned right onto Railway Street. There was a lineup of parked cars along the right side of the road, which had a few houses further along. To avoid getting seen, the officer left the car behind an old stationed, Pontiac Sunfire, then hurried back from where he came. The drive across the bridge into town took him nearly four minutes due to the compiling snow, moreover it took another nineteen minutes to run back to his wife's car. The snow had already risen three inches thick and was increasing rapidly, so it was difficult to quickly maneuver his way through. Before he entered the car, Ray removed the overall and boots and threw them into a bag, which he placed on the passenger floor. The clothing he selected to wear was not warm enough for outdoors, therein once he got back he was freezing, yet he still had to clean off the snow, defrost the windows, and warm up the interior before he fled the scene.

Chapter 33

Coy reached the mechanic shop twenty-six minutes before the business was scheduled to open. It was customary to start a pot of freshly brewed coffee for the employees and customers, so the owner filled their machine with water, added a pack of Blue Mountain Peak, and turned on the coffee maker. The main office was filthy, hence he used a cloth and wiped off the desk and other areas, then took the broom and swept the floor, before he disposed of the garbage. With the office cleaned, the boss sat at the desk and orderly assembled his business receipts from the day before. Marshon arrived eight minutes before the shop opened with his loud music that could be heard at a distance. Evander was always either the first or second person at the shop, so Coy found that rather odd. At 8:00 O'clock when the business opened and Evander had not arrived or called, Coy grabbed his cellular to phone him, then realized that his body-man had sent him a message.

While heading to meet up with his expected lover, Evander recorded and sent a message to his boss and friend. Coy knew how committed Evander was to manage the collision repair department, therefore he felt as though something was wrong and placed the recording on speaker.

"Hey boss-man it's me! I told you guys my baby would come crying back for this loving! Anyways, look I'm sorry man, I thank you for everything, but she is leaving her husband and wants me to run away with her! I love her man, and I know if I called you, you would have probably talked me out of going! So, I'm doing this for love my friend! I wish you guys the best! I already miss the shop man; but tell Marshon I'll give him a call when I find out what we doing. One love to you guys and, I'll be in touch! Peace!"

"Oh, shit that's dope! My man really knows his woman! I can't believe she ran away with him," Marshon stated!

"I can't believe it either. Marshon actually stole that cop's wife," Coy declared!

"I hope that ignorant cop doesn't know he worked here! You know what I mean," Marshon joked?

"I think I'll try to call him later. I won't feel right about this until I hear his voice and know he is safe," Coy argued!

"I'm sure he is great right now! He has that woman to himself all the time, what could be better than that," Marshon said?

"In his case you're right! Oh shit, I need to find a new body man," Coy suggested!

"Give me a shot boss-man? I've watched and helped Evander all these years, I know I can do the work," Marshon asked.

"Marshon, you know how I get about quality work on people's cars," Coy argued?

"I know boss-man, I wouldn't be mentioning it if I wasn't sure," Marshon related!

"Well, if you think you can handle it, go finish the van Evander was doing and we'll see if you have the job! But now we're going to need someone to replace you, to do the stuff you did," Coy declared.

Officer Pedward drove Rochelle's car onto the property and parked outside the main hanger door. Dressed in his regular street clothes, it took Coy and Marshon a few seconds before they realized who he was. Ray walked into the garage where both occupants were just discussing his wife and her manstress, therefore the mechanics were frightened beyond mention. Neither of them knew what Ray wanted, so watching him approach them felt like death getting closer. Coy had never been asthmatic, yet he could barely breathe fearing that the officer was there to seek answers regarding his wife's whereabouts. Marshon thought of trying to run away, but he knew how vicious Officer Pedward could be and thus stood beside his boss.

"Morning to you fellows! Coy my wife put a little dent in her back bumper, I was hoping you could pull it out for me," Officer Pedward asked?

"Oh, Officer Pedward, you fooled me there for a bit! I don't see you out of uniform often. Sure, we can help you with that, just let me go take a look," Coy responded!

Marshon decided to stay close to Coy at all cost, but neither of them wanted to walk ahead of the officer. The mechanics' hearts were pounding loudly with fear that the officer was there to execute them both. Ray walked them to the back of the car where he showed them the dent in the bumper and stood by while Coy inspected it closely.

"This little dent won't be a problem, it's not even going to affect your insurance rate when you claim it," Coy explained.

"Oh, no, I don't want to involve the insurance company," Officer Pedward quickly responded!

"That's no problem, however you wish to pay cash or credit is all up to you," Coy explained.

"Cash! I brought enough cash to handle it," Officer Pedward said.

"Whatever your preference Officer Pedward! Marshon, you want to go and bring that suction device," Coy asked?

"I'm going to need you to come and take out the new one, the other one broke yesterday," Marshon calmly asked?

Coy understood exactly what his employee meant and knew Marshon did not want to be alone while the officer was present. "Yeah, I forgot it broke yesterday! Officer Pedward if you don't mind waiting in the office for a few minutes, possibly have a cup of coffee, we'll get this fixed right away for you," Coy remarked?

"No problem Coy! Thanks for taking care of this for me," Officer Pedward responded as he withdrew his cellular and walked off into the office!

Marshon and Coy went into the collision repair section for the device to fix the minor dent. Neither of them knew what to make of the situation, which was weird to say the least. Although they were still terrified for their lives, they were unsure what to believe and had more questions than answers. The mechanics remained silent until reach inside the collision bay, from which it was impossible to hear people speaking.

"There is something weird about this! Why is this guy acting like his wife didn't just leave him," Coy softly said?

"I think he is trying to play us! We should just get out of here through the back door and run for our lives," Marshon suggested!

"And where the hell are we going to run to? Listen, put your phone on record and hide it somewhere inside the garage, in case anything happens," Coy instructed!

"OK! We need to get rid of this guy, he is seriously freaking me out," Marshon declared before they gathered the device and exited the collision section.

Regardless of what the officer portrayed, Coy felt assure that he was hiding something. They carefully exited the station and pinpointed where the officer was located, before they walked toward his vehicle. Coy made Marshon keep watch on Officer Pedward, while he knelt on the ground and used the suction device to yank the sunken bumper back into place. There was a slight dent on the trunk door, which Coy noticed when he rubbed his hand across the car frame to check the smoothness. Officer Pedward was on his phone speaking with his dear friend Officer Gilmore, when Coy sent Marshon inside the driver's compartment to open the trunk. When Ray saw Marshon climbed into the driver's seat, he went running from the garage waving his hands like a madman.

"Stop, stop! Don't open the trunk, I have some top-secret police files in there," Officer Pedward ran out shouting!

Marshon had already unlatched the trunk, but before it swung open and revealed Evander's belongings inside, Coy abided and closed it. Ray walked around to the repaired section and shook his head pleasingly, in lieu of the fact that the mechanic did not see inside the trunk. The officer switched the conversation to the business aspect, therefore they returned into the main office, where Marshon continued to remain close to his boss. Coy wrote up the bill and handed it to the officer, who withdrew a coil of cash and paid the sum. Both mechanics were overjoyed when Officer Pedward finally left the garage, although he left them wanting answers.

"What the hell was that boss man? Did you see the look in his eyes like he wasn't really there," Marshon stated?

"I need to check my boxers to see if I shitted on myself! I swear that man was going to kill us," Coy exclaimed!

Coy withdrew his cell phone and called Evander directly for the responses he sought, wherein the ringer sounded three times before the call went to voice mail. Contrary to the none-response the boss was not worried, thus he wrote a text message asking Evander 'to contact him' and sent it instead. Due to Evander's unexpected departure, Coy could imagine the sorrow unveiling inside his house, so he phoned Mrs. Simms to offer his condolence. Evander's mother only responded to the call because she recognized who the caller was. Mrs. Simms knew her son loved working with Coy; yet felt saddened that he abandoned his duties at the shop. It was evident that she had been crying just by the way she responded, nevertheless she sniffled all throughout their conversation.

"Good morning Mrs. Simms, how are you guys holding up," Coy said?

"Oh Coy, I can't believe Evander would do something like this! To run away with some woman who nobody in your family has ever met! Why would he turn his back on everybody like that," Mrs. Simms cried?

"I guess he was in love Mrs. Simms! His lady friend had to move away, and he did not want to lose her," Coy explained.

"Yes, I understand that! But this is where his whole life has been, you don't just pick up and go somewhere else overnight," Mrs. Simms argued!

"We just hope he is successful wherever he goes," Coy stated!

"You have been very good to this family, and I thank you for contacting me this morning Coy. I might have been a little selfish, expecting my boys to stay home forever, but I guess I better get used to the idea they could find wives and move on. It's kind of hard to swallow, but their dad and I did pretty much the same thing," Mrs. Simms remarked.

"No problem Mrs. Simms, the garage will slowly survive without Evander! Just take care of yourself; and before you go, may I have a word with Julious? Thank you, and goodbye," Coy declared!

Evelin passed the phone to Julious, who walked away with the device into his bedroom.

"Hello," Julious then answered!

"Hey what's up Julious, this is Coy, Evander's boss," Coy stated!

"Yeah, I know it, is you," Julious responded!

"Tell me something, did you see your brother before he left last night," Coy enquired?

"Yes, we were watching, a movie," Julious said.

"Did he tell you anything, like where he was going to meet his girlfriend or where they would be staying," Coy enquired?

"Evander told me, he was going, to meet his, lady friend at, Red River Bridge," Julious said.

"Did he say anything else before he left," coy asked?

"He said that, when you guys, find his car, I can have, it," Julious answered!

"Thanks for that Julious! I'll come by and see you sometimes, and you can come to the garage and hang out anytime," Coy declared!

"That would be, cool," Julious said before they disconnected!

Chapter 34

When Louie returned home following the incident with Officer Pedward, he felt utterly humiliated yet did not wish to inform his father about what happened. The female with whom he was with took note of his displeasure while they journeyed back home, during which Louie remained silent throughout. The fun loving and pleasant male companion she had been spending her evening with, changed after their interaction with Officer Pedward. Nadine did not want Louie to allow the incident to define anything about him, therefore she suggested that he spoke with someone to determine if the officer broke any laws. Louie advised Nadine that 'he had no intention to discuss the matter any further and would prefer if she never mentioned it to anyone'. Regardless of how Louie felt about the situation Nadine thought he would be wasting a humongous opportunity to raise awareness to some of the injustices his people experience.

After Louie brought Nadine home, she could not stop thinking about how close they both were to being killed. Those degrading stares which Officer Pedward gave her were looks she would not easily forget, as if he did not consent to them being together. The officer obviously had some sort of bias against mixed couples that was triggered once he walked up and saw who the occupants were. Unlike Louie Nadine could not simply react as if the incident never occurred, hence she located his father's contact information on his Social Media Webpage and phoned the Cree Chief directly. It was nearly 12:40 AM when Louie's father heard his phone ringing and was hesitant to respond.

"Hello!"

"Hello, Chief Albus, excuse me for calling you so late! My name is Nadine, and I am a friend of your son Louie!"

"Yes, I remember Louie mentioning you! Did something happen? Is Louie, OK?"

"No, Louie is fine, he should be back home any minute now! But something did happen while we were out for a drive earlier!"

"What is it? It seems like it was bothering you enough for you to call me to discuss it, so don't be afraid you can tell me."

"Louie wanted us to forget about this, but I don't believe it is right for any officer of the law to hit someone unprovoked!"

"Why don't you try telling me the whole story from where this all started?"

"Well, Louie wanted to show me how fast the car was; so, I guess he was speeding a bit. Some Officer Pedward came from nowhere with his bright siren lights and pulled us over! Louie had taken one of your guns to give me a shooting lesson out in the country, so when the officer stopped us, he passed the gun to me for me to hide! The officer walked up to Louie's side of the car and saw who the driver was, then he started cursing at us for no reason! We were out in the middle of nowhere, with no witness to tell what happened, so I got scared that cop was going to kill us; and told him that I had the gun... Anyways, he had me put my hands on the dashboard, then walked around and took away the gun. I thought that once we gave that officer the weapon our situation would change, but the next thing I knew he was dragging Louie from the car and pulling him to the back! I could hear Officer Pedward hitting Louie each time he did, although I could hardly see the physical action, because I was warned not to move my hands off the dashboard!" Nadine began telling her story quite saddened, but by this point she was driven to tears.

The Cree Indian Chief was cringing his teeth with anger at every word spoken. "Was Louie bleeding when he returned into the car?"

"No, I did not notice any signs of blood! But Louie was so angry that he didn't say a word for the trip back, except to tell me not to discuss it with anyone; before he dropped me home!"

"Did this Officer Pedward give the gun back to Louie?"

"Not to my knowledge! I believe he kept it without even issuing Louie a ticket."

"You are telling me that this officer did all this without giving you guys a ticket?"

"I'm afraid he did sir!"

"I must thank you for bringing this news to my attention Miss Nadine! My son is very headstrong and thinks only of himself at times, but there are some issues that require managing not only for you, but for those before you who never had voices, your family, and your community! Have a goodnight!"

Once Chief Albus finished speaking with Nadine, the vivid thoughts of the cruelty they underwent enraged him further. The officer's actions were against the department's Code of Conduct; thus, it was imperative that the chief ensured such violations never reoccurred. Before he appropriately addressed the discriminative police behavior, he needed confirmation that everything he heard was indeed factual events. There was only one person from which he could acquire the confirmation he required, so he waited for his son to return home. The instant Louie stepped into the house Nathaniel could tell something had happened by the dejected look on his son's face. As chief of the Banting Cree Nation, it was his duty to ascertain if his people were being fairly treated by the lawmen hired to protect them, therefore he telephoned his attorney to act.

While Louie went to bed and slept that night, Nathaniel was restless and could not wait until morning. To teach his son the importance of legally contending with law enforcement institutions that have violated his rights, Chief Albus brought Louie with him during his errands the following day. Louie felt terrified that something might happen to his father and he, when Chief Albus parked his General Motors, Hummer-H4, in a visitor's parking slot at the Dakota Ojibway Police Station. They had filed assault and theft charges against Officer Pedward at the High Commission Court in Winnipeg, then went to make a formal complaint at the Ray's primary headquarter. Chief Albus was a peaceful and traditional Indian who knew the rights of natives, therefore he arranged with his legal council Judith Swan, to accompany them.

The Police Chief was a man who Chief Albus had bumped heads with several times over the treatment of his people, at the hands of the department's officers. Chief Albus wanted to speak with the chief directly, to voice his displeasure at the events that surrounded his son's detainment. Once they entered the precinct, Nathaniel spoke with the officer at the desk regarding placing a complaint against the officer in question. Rather than speaking with whomsoever operated their complaint division, Chief Albus requested an audience with Police Chief Hardly McIntyre. The Desk Officer took the chief's name and asked them to wait a few minutes while he summoned his boss. Seven minutes later Police Chief Hardly McIntyre walked out and greeted them.

"Chief Albus, it's always good to see you! I'm sorry for the delay but I was in a meeting," Chief McIntyre stated as they shook hands!

"No problem at all Chief McIntyre! This is my attorney Judith Swan, I'm sure you recall! And my youngest son Louie," Chief Albus responded!

After Police Chief McIntyre shook everybody's hands, he looked at the Indian chief and said, "Let's take this conversation somewhere more private, shall we!"

They walked to a consultation room where they all sat around a table with the police chief across from his visitors. The front desk officer had informed the chief as to why they were there, so McIntyre withdrew a recorder device and placed it on the table.

"Chief McIntyre, you know I hold no ill-will against your family at home, or those who serve under you here. But one of your officers have dishonored my son, which is the reason we are here today! I will let my son tell you in his own words, what happened to him just last night while out with his lady friend,"

Chief Albus said!

Louie was nervous and feared some sort of reprisal from the local officers, who always placed their comrades ahead of others. The young man could neither look at his father nor the police chief, therefore he looked at the female attorney who confidently gave him a nod to proceed.

"Well, Sir, like my dad said, I was out driving around trying to impress a female friend of mine. I don't recall how much more than the speeding limit I was doing, but we got pulled over by an Officer Pedward. When the officer stopped us, I remembered that I brought my dad's 9mm along to teach Nadine how to shoot, so I gave her the gun to hide underneath her shirt. I tried apologizing to the officer for speeding, but the only things he wanted were my driver's license and the car insurance information. After I provided all the information the officer wanted, he went back to his cruiser for maybe one or two minutes. From Officer Pedward came back to the car he started traumatizing us, so much that Nadine got scared and confessed to having the gun. The officer was already mad at us, yet it was as if he became more furious! He barked at me to get out of the car and started walking toward me with the gun pointed at us! When I tried getting out the car and almost slipped, he pulled me off to the side away from his cruiser's headlights; and started slapping me in the back of the head, each time he made a statement! I thought he was going to kill us," Louie explained before he broke down crying!

Chief Albus rubbed his son's back to encourage him to continue telling his story, as Judith passed him a piece of tissue to wipe away his tears.

"What happened after all that Louie," Chief McIntyre asked?

"It's OK son, be strong! Your mother would have been proud of you," Chief Albus stated!

"I don't know what finally made him release me, but I crawled back to the car and got inside. Officer Pedward threw the identification documents I gave him on my lap; and told us to have a good night. So, I drove Nadine home, stopped up the street from her place, and cried, because my hands kept trembling," Louie said!

"What of the firearm, did Officer Pedward returned it or provided you with any formal documents," Chief McIntyre asked?

"No Sir! He never gave me a ticket for speeding or for dad's gun," Louie responded!

"What type of firearm was it," Police Chief McIntyre questioned?

"Here is the receipt for that gun! It was a Springfield Hellcat Pro, Semi-Automatic 9mm," Chief Albus responded as he slid the bill across the table.

Police Chief McIntyre used his cellular phone and took a picture of the receipt.

"Is there anything further you remembered about the incident Louie," Chief McIntyre asked?

"No Sir," Louie responded!

"I must commend you for bringing this matter to my attention; and I assure you that I will look into this further and discipline Officer Pedward if indeed these accusations are correct," Chief McIntyre exclaimed!

"With all due respect Chief McIntyre, Officer Pedward is a known repeat offender of aggression against native peoples across this province; with numerous complaints made against him! So, why do you still employ this officer," Chief Albus stated?

"Chief Albus we are already short staffed and undermanned, so we can barely afford to lose any of our officers right now," Chief McIntyre responded!

"Apparently your excuse for not firing officers like this is not good enough Chief! This police department being undermanned or short staffed is no reason for the ill-treatment or the poor policing your officers provide," Attorney Judith Swan exclaimed?

"Well, Miss Swan we cover a large territory and do not have the manpower to get to some of these emergency calls on time, so yes, we are very much undermanned! My officers work long strenuous hours and are under a lot of stress to perform," Chief McIntyre revealed!

"Chief McIntyre we are not talking about the performance of your officers, but rather their racist attitudes against native Indians," Attorney Judith Swan argued!

"There must be some underlying reason why Officer Pedward did this, so we will go over his bodycam footage to get a better idea of what happened, before I get back to you on this," Police Chief McIntyre declared!

"Whatever his reasons were for doing this to my son, that officer could have killed my boy! Because of this, we will be taking him to court to get back my gun, and especially to have him removed from being a lawman in this territory," Chief Albus declared!

Following their meeting Police Chief McIntyre returned to his office where he had his secretary try to arrange a meeting with Officer Pedward. His secretary uncovered that Ray had stayed home that day, therefore they had to reschedule for another time. Despite the emotional outburst from Chief Albus and his son, McIntyre did not feel as if his officer broke any policies except regarding the taking of the firearm. The next day when Ray returned to work, he was notified to meet with Chief McIntyre, whom he went to see during his lunch break. Both men had been friends and co-workers for many years, therefore the chief was more sympathetic to Ray's mischief.

"Hey Chief, what's going on?"

"Nothing much Ray! Guess who came to see me about you yesterday," Chief McIntyre said as they shook hands?

"Who?"

"Your old friend Cree Chief Albus! It seems as if you pulled over his boy the other night and took a 9mm from him! What the hell were you thinking? We just busted a weapons' heist a short while ago, why didn't you take a gun then," McIntyre stated as he walked over to his bar and fixed two glasses of Scotch?

"Oh, that kid? It didn't even cross my mind that he was Albus' son!"

"Well, the chief ain't too happy about the way you treated his son! So, you might need to find a good lawyer because they plan on taking you to court, to get that gun back; and possibly get you kicked off the force," Chief McIntyre said as they knocked glasses and drank the liquor.

"Thanks for the heads up Chief! I'll make sure to get that lawyer," Ray stated as he went to finish the rest of his lunch break!

Chapter 35

When Rochelle opened her eyes at 10:47 AM the day after Ray killed Evander, her murdering husband was sitting on his side of the bed staring at her. He looked like he had not slept all night and smelt like he had been using gasoline fluid. The blank stare he gave Rochelle made her feel as though he was looking right into her soul, as he intensely watched her without blinking. Although she felt intimidated, she tried to appear at eased, in order to change Ray's attitude.

"Oh, honey, good morning! I thought you were at work! I'm happy you decided to stay home, but Malory asked me to head out today with her for a few hours, so I'll be gone for a little while," Rochelle stated as she slipped out of bed and grabbed her cell phone on her way to the bathroom!

Ray sat on the bed like an emotionless robot watching his wife, who frightfully went into the bathroom, removed her underwear, and sat on the toilet seat to urinate. Rochelle dialled Malory's number and the phone rang five times before the call went to voice mail. Instead of leaving a message, Rochelle dialled the number again, hoping that her girlfriend responded the second time. When Malory did not answer the second call, Rochelle began fretting she would have to spend the entire day with her unpredictable husband.

"Come on Malory, save me please! Answer the phone please," Rochelle mumbled to herself knowing that Officer Gilmore's wife was the only person Ray would allow her to be around!

Hoping her third attempt might be the charm, Rochelle pressed redial and held the phone to her ear, as it rang five times then went to the answering machine. After she finished on the toilet, she felt nervous going back out into the bedroom, so she opened the tap and got undressed. As soon as the water temperature was to her liking, Rochelle went into the shower and began bathing. The sound of the shower protruded her from hearing anything inside the other room, therefore her nervous tension raised tremendously. After a lengthy shower during which she pondered over what she could do that day to stay away from Ray, Rochelle exited the bath and began drying herself with a towel. The body lotion she used was in the cupboard underneath the sink, so she bent over and retrieved it. When Rochelle stood back upright, Ray was standing directly behind her with the Springfield Hellcat 9mm at hand.

"Oh, honey, you startled me," Rochelle responded as she grabbed her chest!

Ray was behaving like a man possessed; hence he grabbed his wife by the front of her neck and wrapped his other hand with the weapon around her waist. Rather than the gentle kisses he normally administered, Ray began biting and licking her shoulders and neck area. Rochelle tried to surrender herself to him, but it was difficult with him squeezing her neck as if he wanted to strangle her. All at once the officer stopped, then shoved her forward onto the countertop; before he unbuckled his pants. The nervous female wondered if her husband was readying to assassinate her, when her cell phone rang and indicated it was Malory.

"Oh honey, look its Malory calling me back," Rochelle stated before she answered the call!

As quickly as the sexual sensation started was as quickly as it ended; when Ray refastened his pant's button and walked away from his wife. Rochelle's heartrate was racing with fear, believing her husband was about to execute her. There was something different about Ray and without him talking or showing any emotions, it was impossible to know what his issues were. The officer walked back into their bedroom and laid in bed, then turned on the television and switched the channel to the area's newscast. The scared wife applied her body lotion as she softly spoke with their family friend.

"You have to come and get me!? I need to get out of this house right now or I'm afraid that Ray is going to kill me," Rochelle pled once her husband left!

"OK girl, let me get these kids in the van and I'm on my way," Malory stated knowing the importance of such a call!

"There is something totally different about him today, Mal," Rochelle stated!

"Like what," Malory enquired?

"His eyes, its like he's not completely there," Rochelle whispered!

"Come here little girl, we have to go save Aunty Rochelle," Malory said as she grabbed hold of her daughter and began putting her shoes on. She knew she couldn't waste any time with an armed psychotic officer, therefore her children had to wear whatever they were dressed in.

"Stay on the phone please? I'm literally shaking right now! Ray refuses to put down his gun," Rochelle whispered as she slowly walked from the bathroom!

"Where is he right now," Malory asked?

"Bedroom," Rochelle whispered!

"Apologize for leaving and tell him something sexually freaky you're going to do to him once you get back home," Malory instructed.

"Honey I'm sorry Malory is taking me away from you today, but when I get back home, I'm going to lick you from your head to your toes," Rochelle teased yet Ray's focus on the television never wavered!

"That's good, try to get his mind focused on something else! I'm going to phone Grey on the other line and have him call Ray to chat with him for a bit. Maybe he can find out what's been bothering him," Malory said.

Rochelle walked over to her dresser with the towel draped around her. To illustrate what Ray would be missing should he exterminate her, Rochelle removed and threw the towel onto the bed, then bent forward to select underwear from her drawer. Instead of immediately choosing a pair of bra and panty, the curvy female loitered in the position for a short while. With such an irresistible wife the officer could barely keep his eyes on the television, thus within seconds Ray was staring at her delectable frame. Once Rochelle sensed her husband`s eyes on her, she selected his favorite pair of pink underwear, and slowly slid them on. There were no further dangers or threats with Evander out of the way, therefore Ray's attitude slowly began softening.

"What time is Malory bringing you back home," Ray surprisingly asked?

"Oh, Ray! What time are you bringing me back home Mal," Rochelle stated?

Malory was on the other phone line speaking with her husband Grey, who had installed a speed trap to catch excessive speeders. Officer Gilmore was stationed off South Highway-75 by North 11 Road, which was several miles north of the Letellier and Dominion City exit. Once Malory explained the situation to her husband, he instantly agreed to phone his dear friend and assist him in any way possible.

"Malory said sometimes this evening, honey! You might have to make supper or eat leftovers though," Rochelle lied with her friend on the other line!

Malory returned to their conversation seconds later and said, "I just spoke with Grey, and he is about to phone Ray and see what's going on with him! And I'm putting the kids in the van as we speak, so I'll be outside in four minutes!"

"OK Mal, see you in a sec," Rochelle declared!

With her husband in an unpredictable mood, Rochelle dressed herself conservatively in a pair of jeans with a sweater. Ray's cellular rang with Officer Gilmore and two other officers on the line, who called to invite him out for beer and a few games of pool. The interests by his peers seemed to brighten Officer Pedward's mood, as he agreed to meet up later that night with the boys. Rochelle took advantage of that brief moment and kissed Ray goodbye, before his personality switched to someone unpleasant. She walked out into the days room where she first noticed a fire burning inside a huge metal drum, that they kept in the backyard. They would occasionally use the drum to burn wood fires during chilly climates, whenever they had guests over. Aside from the burning drum everything else seemed in place, so Rochelle put on her shoes and jacket and waited by the door.

For her personal security Malory pulled up on the street and honked her horn, to ensure she did not put herself or her children in danger. Rochelle noticed that her vehicle had been moved as she ran out to get away from her husband, who stood in the window watching her leave. As soon as the van drove away Ray moved away from the window and went to the basement. The officer retrieved one of Evander's bags from behind the furnace, in which he already had a pair of scissors, that he had been using to cut up the clothing within. Ray searched through the items for Evander's cell phone and became irate that he could not find the device. He finished cutting up the clothes and threw the remains into a paper bag for compost, then carefully brought the bag upstairs. The flammable fluid he used to ignite the items was outside by the patio door, so he brought it along to burn the remainder of Evander's belongings. Officer Pedward looked around and ensured he was not being watched before he started emptying the compost bag's contents into the burning fire.

As wives of police officers Malory and Rochelle knew to recognize dangerous situations and got away from certain conflicts before it was too late. They were friends of families that have gone through terrible acts of violence due to officers' mental collapse, therefore it was their duty to help each other during times of crisis. With matters tense between Ray and Rochelle, Malory did not think it wise to simply return to her house and hanged out for the day. There was always that chance that Ray might stalk her; and possibly go psychotic if he uncovered that they were still in the community, so they drove to Grant Park Shopping Centre in Winnipeg and spent the day. During the journey, both ladies constantly checked their side mirrors to ensure they were not being followed by Ray.

Later that night at 8:30 the officers met up at Kiko's Bar & Lounge, located in Roseau River Reserve. The bar was a favorite hangout spot for cops and locals alike, primarily because the male owner was a former member of the Canadian Armed Forces. There was a pool table in the back, and the facility offered Karaoke every night, for whosoever chose to sing. They also had an old Jukebox that was filled with rock and classical tunes, which many of the customers played quite often. Kiko's sold some of the best chicken wings around for miles and was owned and operated by Kory and his wife Kimora. Other officers wanted to help and support Ray throughout his depressive times therefore, Officer Gilmore was accompanied by four other officers. None of the officers had gotten any excessive time off and were burnt out due to the employee shortage, therefore they all deserved such an evening to unwind.

When Ray drove into the parking lot his friends were all smoking cigars beside Officer Valesquez', GMC Sierra 4X4 truck. The officers' favorite method of decompressing was to smoke cigars as a unit, so as Ray joined the group, he was immediately given a Gurkha Black Dragon. There was an underlined message in giving the officer a cigar that cost over eleven-hundred dollars and Ray fully understood what his peers meant. The officers fist bumped each other, then stayed outside for another few minutes, smoking and criticizing hockey players and other athletes. Although they collectively believed that they should discuss their mental problems, those talks were expected to be had with one's psychologist, who was the professional being paid to listen such problems. All the officers experienced the same tragedies regularly, yet there was a stigma placed around those who could not cope. Officer Pedward knew of the harsh judgement given to those who suffered through mental breakdowns, so to avoid having his peers believed he was weak, he desperately tried appearing more relaxed.

It was not a very busy night at Kiko's Bar & Lounge, as most of their regulars chose to stay home because of the unplowed roads. The winter season had exceeded its usual termination point, so the salt rations that was collected by the territory had run low. The plows out on the street were merely shoving the snow to the side of the roadways, instead of plowing it into dump trucks for it to be taken to the dump. The small amount of salt that was left at the depot had to be used on the main highways such as I-75, which meant there was no salt left to thaw the residential streets. The officers ordered a round of Tequilla shots and drank those down, before they got beers from the waiter, then moved to the pool table that was unoccupied.

Malory telephoned her husband at 10:38 PM to get his verdict on Ray's mental stability. Grey was so enthralled in his other friends that he failed to properly assess Ray, who was being interactive and his regular self around the guys. Her husband did not see through the mirage that his friend so dearly fought to project, while all the time fearing that they might uncover his dark new secret. The casual responses Grey provided Malory did not calm Rochelle's nerves, as she listened in on the call. Rather than returning home to the fear she felt, she decided to stay by the Gilmore's for the night and give Ray some time to calm down. Rochelle sent her husband a text message, thereafter, stating that 'she had gotten intoxicated with Malory and would not make it home until morning'. None of the guys knew that Ray was having marital problems, but they thought that the pressures of job might be getting to him. Some of the officers had work the following morning, so they played until 11:00 before they called it a night and left the bar.

The jukebox music and the small crowd were so deafening that Officer Pedward failed to hear the notification sound, which stipulated he had received a text. When they left the bar the group of officers joked among themselves as they walked to their vehicles. Grey was not drunk even though they had individually consumed four rounds of beer and two shots of Tequilla, nevertheless, he took a tumble along the slippery driveway. Everyone who saw the tumble laughed at Officer Gilmore, who stepped on a sheet of black ice, did a slight twirl, then went down awkwardly. Despite being the closest person to Grey when he fell, Ray had gotten distracted by his wife's message and refrained from offering help. Contrary to Officer Gilmore the liquor had Ray feeling slightly woozy, hence when he looked up from the phone, he thought his peers were laughing at him rather than at his friend. The disheartening text message reinfused the officer's rage, therein he walked right pass his friend on the ground. Ray refrained from saying anything further to his co-workers, climbed into his vehicle, and drove away.

When Officer Pedward reached home, he felt sick to his stomach due to the liquor, so he went into the bathroom, opened the toilet, and vomited. He had not eaten a proper meal all day, so he went into the kitchen and made himself two peanut butter and grape jelly sandwiches. While eating the sandwiches, Ray looked through the back window at the drum, in which he had burnt most of Evander's belongings. The flames had gone out by then, still the officer wondered if all the evidence had been destroyed. He turned on the outdoor light and went out onto the porch to get a better look at the drum, with all the burnt-out material inside. An arrogant smirk slid across Ray's face, as he reminisced about shooting Evander. A short while later he returned inside and retired to his bedroom, where he removed most of his clothes and crawled beneath the blanket wearing his boxer shorts and tee-shirt. Before he went to sleep, Ray reached into his night table drawer and removed Evander's wallet, which he kept as his personal trophy. The officer thoroughly looked at each piece of identification before he returned them exactly where they were stored.

Ray wanted Rochelle to remain at home and away from the public's viewing, while his wife wanted to spend less time than she normally would around him. Rochelle felt relaxed in their residence whenever Ray was away at work, however her nerves felt unsettled every time they spent extended amounts of time together. There was something different about her husband that scared her, nevertheless all she hoped was that it was not because he had found out about her extramarital affair with Evander. Whenever they engaged in coitus, Rochelle participated fearing what might happen if she refused, furthermore she had deep concerns about what to expect during the procedure. Due to Ray's more aggressive sexual techniques wherein he began choking, biting, slapping, and punching his wife during intimacy, she had no idea if his madness would one day lead to her murder.

To stop his wife from visiting Dominion City, the officer began taking care of the chores which required that she travelled to the town. There were far more essential businesses in Dominion City than there were in Roseau River Reserve, therefore many locals visited their neighboring town quite often. When Malory heard of Celine's new fitness center, she discussed becoming a member with her husband before, she asked Rochelle to accompany her in becoming members. After Ray did everything possible to prevent his wife from going into Dominion City, he came home days later to discover that Malory and she intended to join the gym. At the disclosure of their plans, Ray tried to avoid appearing as though he was against Rochelle's fitness idea; yet was more concerned that someone might recognize her.

Malory's mother was staying by her house for a few days, therefore she had more freedom to do things without bring her children along. The following morning both ladies travelled to Dominion City, where they met Celine and got a tour around the facility. There were only a handful of people working out, hence Celine was able to spend a little more time with them. Both Rochelle and Malory loved the business concept, especially the lounge area where one could relax and enjoy a good book. They filled in the registration forms, paid the fees, received their personal entry codes to the building, and became active members of the gym, but instead of beginning their training they chose to start the next day. Rochelle and Malory were excited about their newest venture, thus they drove to the Cityplace Winnipeg Mall, where they bought several exercise outfits, water bottles, and sneakers. Once they acquired their workout gear the ladies had lunch then drove back home, eager to begin exercising and getting into shape.

The scandalous gossip that involved Evander and Officer Pedward's wife was not beknow to everyone in Dominion City, primarily because the married couple resided out of town. While nearly everyone knew who Officer Pedward was, not very many people knew of his wife, whom he had always kept private. The next morning the new gym members arrived at 7:47 to begin their fitness quest. There was a handful of people already there working out, so the ladies put away their personal items inside two lockers, then went to the stationary bicycles. Following a lengthy ride to warm up, they moved to a stair machine to continue working out their legs, then transferred over onto the treadmills. Once they busted a proper sweat, they moved to the weight area to work on their upper bodies. Neither of them was powerhouse lifters, so they worked with the lite weight machines for several minutes. Both ladies exercised until they were completely exhausted before they decided to call it quits for the day.

Miss Shirley managed the lounge area which was typically less busy than the gym. Unlike Celine who had transformed her life into being an exercise junkie and was at the gym by 5:30 each morning, her mother still preferred going through her daily routine and would arrive by 9:15. Whenever Miss Shirley arrived, she would begin a pot of her favorite coffee, before she opened the door for business. The aroma from the coffee could easily be smelt by those inside the gym, who would begin flocking toward the lounge for a cup. Rochelle and Malory were about to finish their weight curl reps when that coffee aroma crossed their noses. Immediately after they finished exercising, they went into the lounge where they ordered two cups of coffee for the road. While preparing the orders Miss Shirley looked curiously at Rochelle, whom she thought resembled the adulteress who supposedly ran away with her son's employee.

On their way to their vehicle Rochelle and Malory walked pass Sandra, who was polite enough to wish the ladies 'a good morning'. Sandra was heading to the gym for her daily workout session and appeared to be in a rush, despite it only being 9:33. Her workout partner who was a dear friend had already been waiting for nearly ten minutes, so she scurried to get inside the building. Coy's girlfriend was stunned when she saw Rochelle, whose beauty was unmistakable and unique. Although she had heard the rumours, she thought that maybe the facts had changed since, therefore she proceeded into the gym.

Chapter 36

fficer Horace Hibert was at home in front of his laptop watching pornography. There was no one else at home except him, yet he had the door locked tight to obstruct anyone seeking entry. His wife Jane kept pictures of their family all throughout the house, thus the center table was stacked with pictures in frames. The laptop was on the table beside the pictures of his family, nevertheless Horace kept scrolling through movie covers of porn next to them. He clicked on a newly uploaded video and began watching the contents, where a male predator bust into a female's house. The lady who lived inside the residence ran into her bedroom screaming, while the predator chased her with his camera focused on her. From Officer Hibert saw how delectable the female actress looked, he unbuttoned his pant, then reached into a drawer and withdrew a tube of lubricant oil. The officer quickly lowered his pant and boxer shorts before he squeezed some lubricant into the center of his palm, then moisturized both hands. The female in the video was wearing a florescent colored lingerie which left very little to the imagination, therefore if revealed her sensuous shape and round derriere. The male in the video had yet to reveal himself, but his female co-star, had Officer Hibert slowly masturbating while she slid onto the bed and began fondling herself.

The camera only caught side angles of the beautiful maiden for the first few minutes, while she played with her breasts and vagina. The female actress was so sensual that the officer felt hypnotized by her slightest movement, hence he closed his eyes and envisioned she was there with him. By the time the male actor slipped into the video Horace had already ejaculated yet was fascinated to watch the rest of the video. Once the dark complexion male started approaching the woman Officer Hibert got a better view of her face. When he saw the female was Officer Pedward's prized wife, he paused the video and enlarged the screen to make sure he was not seeing things. As one of the persons who had always admired Rochelle, rather than deleting the video or making his colleague aware, Horace played the entire short film, then rewound it and watched it several times. After he masturbated several times to the scenes and tagged the video as a favorite, Horace forwarded the link to five of his closest friends on the police force.

When Officer Z. Rayman received the message, he was at his desk at work filing some reports. The note attached to the video said, 'Pedward's Hot Wife' hence the officer paused his work and took a quick peek at the video. Seconds into the video Officer Rayman had to stop the airing once he noted how sexual the content was. Many of the officers had crushes on Rochelle and daydreamed about spending some time with her, so it was a thrill for them to see her naked. While on duty the officers were not allowed to be loitering on their phones, so Officer Rayman had to wait until he had finished work before he could watch the entire video.

Officer Dru Ivy was parked along Highway 75 engaged in a speed trap, with his radar detecting all the southbound traffic. Dru had been waiting patiently for nearly forty minutes, yet every vehicle that went by was travelling below the speed limit. His partner Officer Dean Sutton was nearly four kilometers away ahead of him; but would be there to back him up within minutes if he needed assistance. The roadway looked clear without a vehicle in sight, when the officer's phone began notifying him that he had a text message from Officer Hibert. The attached note sparked more interest by the officer, who pressed on the message to view the contents. From Dru began playing the video he was frozen, thus he temporarily stopped paying attention to the radar alerts. A Mercedes Benz 400 AMG and a BMW-M4 sped by at more than twenty kilometers above the limit, nevertheless Officer Ivy chose to ignore them, radioed Officer Sutton, and continued watching the video.

"We have a Mercedes Benz and a BMW heading towards you Dean, radared at one-fifty-eight! But I'm unable to pursue at the moment, just received some stunning news from Horace," Officer Ivy reported!

The surprising twist on the video was who Rochelle was with, as it was not her expected husband. Officer Ivy immediately phoned his colleague Officer Hibert for the details behind the video, and to uncover if the couple was or would be going though divorce proceedings.

"Hello," Officer Hibert responded!

"Holy shit that was Rochelle with some other black guy! Was Pedward the person recording it? How the hell did you get that video," Officer Ivy asked?

"Ha-ha-ha-ha! Slow down man! Hold on the line, I have Dean calling me now also," Officer Hibert stated!

Officer Dean Sutton was also stationed along the side of the roadway with his radar detection system enabled. The officers knew that it was a number of drivers tendency to increase their speeds once they have passed an officer, therefore with two cruisers separated they stood a better chance of catching the speedsters. The Mercedes Benz and the BMW were travelling so fast that by the time Dean heard Dru's comment and pressed on the message to watch a bit of the video, his detection system started beeping. The Mercedes and the BMW had increased their speeds and were travelling at nearly thirty kilometers above the limit. To indicate his intention to commit a traffic stop, Dean ignited his red, white, and blue flashers, then gazed at the phone screen. The sight of Rochelle wearing a lingerie made the officer's eyeballs nearly popped from their sockets, thus he deactivated the sirens and his intention to chase. Both speedsters noticed the ignited flashers and completely slowed their pace, fearing the officer was about to give chase. Being one of Rochelle's greatest admirers protruded Officer Sutton from giving pursuit, therefore he continued watching the video and allowed the drivers to proceed. For clarification regarding a number of things like his partner, the officer immediately telephoned the source from which the video came.

"Hello," Officer Hibert immediately answered!

"I need to know everything you know of the situation," Officer Sutton asked?

"Hold on Sutton, I have Ivy on the other line! Let me link us up on a three way call before you start getting into it," Officer Hibert said before he proceeded to connect the callers.

Officer Sal Sallis was on the scene of a car accident over on Hunter Street just south of Roseau River Reserve. There was a red Cadillac CTS being driven by an older couple and a Ford Ranger with a plumber aboard involved in the accident, of which there were no injuries. Both vehicles were heading north when they came upon a construction area where the work crew were repaving the roadway. As they crept slowly along at twenty kilometers per hour the plumber took his eyes off the road when he reached into the glove compartment for a pack of cigarettes. The vehicles ahead were instructed to stop yet the plumber failed to recognize the yielding traffic and struck the Cadillac. An ambulance was called for precautionary reasons and was on route, but Officer Sallis was the first emergency responder on the scene. Neither of the vehicles were severely damaged to the extent that they needed a tow truck, so while the officer wrote up the traffic violation for the plumber, he made everyone wait in their vehicles. Officer Sallis found a bit of time to watch the video for the first time, while writing up the accident report and the ticket inside his cruiser.

The ambulance arrived on the scene with the paramedics who were unsure who to attend to. Rather than walking over to the medical team and instructing them to first check on the older couple, Officer Sallis simply wound his window down and pointed at the Cadillac. Sal was too fascinated by the porno to leave unnecessarily without watching the complete film, so everything else got temporarily placed on pause. The video was thirty-six minutes in length, therefore when Sal finished viewing and looked through his windshield, the ambulance had departed, and both the old man and the plumber were outside their vehicles having a conversation. Officer Sallis picked up the ticket and brought it out the plumber, who was irate along with the old man that he took so long. As the only officer on the scene, Sal apologized and blamed the long wait on his faulty computer, then sent the drivers on their way. A smile slid across the officer's face as he thought of returning to watch the video again, but while walking back to his cruiser he received a dispatch alert about a fire just east of his location. In case anyone needed help, Officer Sallis ran to his cruiser, climbed in, and sped away.

'Pedward's Hot Wife' was all the notification Officer Wilkes needed to see to quickly click onto the forwarded information. Officer Elan Wilkes was one of the 'young rookies' as referred to by the veterans, despite being a member of the force for nearly three years. He and the rest of his close associates were members of the same graduation class, therefore they interacted more often with each other, rather than with the older officers. There were very little attributes that the young rookies admired about their older colleagues, but one thing they all found irresistible was Officer Pedward's wife. Officer Wilkes was scheduled for work during the late shift that evening, while Officer Hibert was also placed on the same shift. After he rewatched the video several times, Elan forwarded it to Officer Lovette and two of his male cousins.

When Officer Lovette received the video and finished viewing its contents, he forwarded it to Sergeant Hank Ross who was at his desk at the station. Rather than putting an end to the despicable trend, Sergeant Ross forwarded the video to Officer Valesquez who found the film extremely offensive. The video was shared with two other officers by Sergeant Ross, neither of whom were mentioned in the complaint. As a friend and colleague to Officer Pedward, Officer Valesquez brought the matter directly to Chief Hardly McIntyre, who had no options but to intervene. Because the matter was an internal affair, the chief had several options with which to resolve the issue. With their staffing shortage a major concern, Chief McIntyre could ill afford to lose all the officers involved in the complaint at once, therefore he was somewhat lenient with his disciplining.

The officers involved should have each received a lengthy suspension, during which they had to take some sort of sensitivity training before they were reinstated back onto the force. Instead of punishing the violators who had disobeyed the department's policy, Police Chief McIntyre called Officer Pedward into his office first, to get him up to speed on what had been happening. Nobody had mentioned the porn video to Ray at that point, thus he had no idea of the ongoing internal riff around the station. The veterans on the force were in a silent dispute versus the rookies, who had violated their colleague's rights. The Police Chief could not have his officers erupt in a grand brawl over the video, so he had to gain control of the situation before tempers flared.

"Chief, you wish to see me," Officer Pedward declared once he entered the office?

"Ray what I have to tell you isn't easy for me, as you know we go way back, so I have a lot of respect for you and Rochelle! But, I guess it's best I just showed you what I'm talking about," Chief McIntyre stated before he passed Ray his cellular with the video playing!

Officer Pedward took the phone and looked at the screen for about three seconds, then stopped the video and passed the device back to the chief.

"That video had been shared by several officers before it was brought to my attention. I assure you that this is an internal matter; and I will deal with those involved personally! I will allow you to take a few days away if you wish. I know this is a sensitive time for your family; but if you and Rochelle need any form of counselling, I will make sure that the department covers the total bill," Chief McIntyre exclaimed!

Ray's head dropped to the ground with shame as he imagined what his colleagues must think of his marriage. "I think I'm going to need a few days," Officer Pedward responded.

"Take as much time as you need Ray! This territory needs you as a lawman, so take whatever time you need before you come back," Chief McIntyre said!

Everyone throughout the building tried to avoid making eye contact with Officer Pedward as he made his way from the station. Chief McIntyre sat back on his chair after Ray left with concerns of what might happen. It was a very explosive situation and with Officer Pedward being in a fragile state, he could easily lose his mental faculties and terminate his wife. While the chief was somewhat concerned for his wife's health, Ray was more worried about what could transpire if they found Evander's body. The news was out that Rachelle had been having an affair, thus the officer felt enraged and pounded on the steering wheel several times once he entered his cruiser. To avoid being seen Ray started up the engine and began driving out of the parking lot. As he drove through the access gate and turned onto the main street, he saw Coy, Julious, Gary, and Evelin entering the precinct.

Officer Pedward realized that he would have to get rid of everything that belonged to Evander, which he had kept as trophies. He rushed home to clean house in case he received a surprise visit from Internal Affairs, to search the residence for evidence. Rochelle was always either out with Malory or reading a book at her new gym's lounge, so Ray did not expect to find her there. When Ray entered his house, the place was extremely quiet, thereby he thought his wife was away somewhere. Despite the silence Officer Pedward was shocked to see Rochelle asleep in bed, hence he softly walked over to his night table. The drawer squeaked as it slid open and frightened his wife, who grabbed for her chest fearing Ray was a burglar.

"Oh, honey you nearly gave me a heart attack! What are you doing home already," Rochelle exclaimed?

"The chief believes that I should take a few days off to clear my mind," Ray responded!

"What is he talking about, you're fine aren't you," Rochelle argued?

Ray kept quiet and used his cell phone to log onto the porn website on which Evander uploaded the video. Following a short scroll through the list of videos he found the one with his wife and her manstress, thus he pressed play and threw the phone onto the bed beside her. Once Ray recouped the wallet he went into the room for, he walked out and left his stunned wife watching the video on the bed. At first Rochelle had no clue that she was the female in the video, until the camera clearly caught her face.

"Oh my God! I'm sorry Ray! I didn't mean to do it! Could you please forgive me, I'm sorry," Rochelle pled?

Officer Pedward had other concerns, hence he walked out and headed down to the basement, where he retrieved some other items that belonged to Evander. Ray picked up a bottle that contained the fuel he needed, then returned upstairs and went directly into the backyard. Rochelle was scared beyond belief and wondered what her husband was doing in the basement. To avoid being surprised again she snuck from the bedroom and moved close to the window, where she began watching her husband empty Evander's wallet. The officer was tossing individual pieces of Evander's identification into the fire, which stunned Rochelle who recognized the wallet and other items. The only conclusion Rochelle could imagine was that Ray had murdered her ex-lover, therefore she ran back into the bedroom and grabbed her purse to leave. When she emerged from the room and began walking to the front door, her husband who had returned inside called to her.

"And where do you think you are off to," Officer Pedward demanded?

"Oh, Honey! I thought you wanted me to give you some space! So, I was going to," Rochelle stated!

"Go where? To see your side man, Evander," Ray asked?

"Please forgive me Ray? I made a mistake, I'm sorry," Rochelle pled as she turned around and saw Ray holding a 9mm handgun!

"I'm going to use your car. I'll be back in a little while, I have something to take care of," Ray declared as he walked pass his trembling wife and went through the front door.

Ray intentionally left his cell phone at home to avoid being tracked to his destination. He headed west along Route 201 pass Letellier and continued out to St. Joseph. With things unraveling around him the most important piece of evidence in his possession was the murder weapon, therefore he had to find a way to get rid of it. There was no way he could burn the weapon and destroy it inside his drum, as he had done with most of Evander's belongings. The ground was still frozen hard so digging a hole to bury the handgun was difficult; and with the rivers and lakes still partly frozen, he could not simply dispose of it in any deep waters. After driving around for more than an hour searching for the ideal place to hide the stolen Springfield Hellcat Pro, the officer drove into St. Joseph, Manitoba. The small farming community did not have much to offer, but Ray was getting desperate at this point. Route 426 provided the only intersection the community had, but the trail went along dirt roads which were treacherous during the winter seasons.

Ray made a right onto the route and traveled northbound for several miles alongside farming lands, before he came across a death tribute to someone killed at that location. Whoever made the tribute piled several huge stones onto each other and used them to display the person's picture. As he went by the tribute, Ray noticed a drainage pipe that was constructed beneath the roadway to allow water to flow. He pulled to the side of the dirt road that was seldom used and placed on his four-way flashers. After checking his mirrors to ensure there were nobody coming, Ray exited the car with the weapon wrapped in a bag. The officer walked through the snow to get to the base of the drainpipe, where he hid the handgun inside the pipe. Officer Pedward was not totally comfortable about his choice to conceal the weapon, but he had no choice but to live with it.

The police chief was inside his office nearly two hours following Ray's departure, when his secretary advised him that the officers, he requested were present. Chief McIntyre got up from his seat and walked to the front of his desk, just as all the officers involved in the Rachelle porn saga began entering his office. All eight officers who violated the department's code of conduct walked in and formed a single line, then stood at attention in front the chief.

"You asked to speak with us, Sir," Sergeant Ross exclaimed!?

"Each of you gentlemen have not only violated Officer Pedward's family, but you have also violated this department and its policies! I expect each and everyone of you to apologize to Officer Pedward, who had to take time away from work because of this bullshit! Now each of you will be suspended for two days, starting tomorrow, Ross, Hibert, Ivy, and Sallis will serve their suspension, and once they return the rest of you can serve your punishment! If this department did not need your services out in the public, I would have suspended each of you for at least a month! You're all dismissed! Get out of my office!"

Chapter 37

Julious, Gary, and Evelin Simms became increasingly worried about Evander with each passing day; thus, they went to the station to file a report. Their first attempt at trying to notify their local police department of Evander's disappearance, ended with an officer explaining that "In order for an adult to be considered missing, a period of two to three days must expire." Following the forty-eight-hour expiration time needed, a different officers notified them that "Evander moved away voluntarily, so there was little they could do about the situation." Instead of taking the family's missing persons report, that officer wanted them to return home and wait several additional days for Evander to call.

Over the first seven days of Evander's disappearance his family members visited the Dakota Ojibway Police Station three times. Each of Evander's relatives knew there was something wrong, yet they could not get any assistance from law enforcement. Neither Evelin nor Gary had returned to work since their son went missing, and they had no intentions of doing so until they uncovered what happened to him. Most of the officers knew of the adulterous relationship Evander had with their colleague Officer Pedward's wife, therefore they were in no haste to help locate him. Every day the Simms family visited the police station they departed with Evelin in tears, due to the lack of help from the people assigned to assist.

The night after Sandra saw Rochelle at the gym, her mother ended up in the hospital, when she fell and injured herself. With her mother's health the most important issue at the time, it slipped Sandra's mind to mention seeing Officer Pedward's wife. Her mother was kept overnight in the hospital for precautionary reasons, but the doctors had already stipulated that she would be just fine. Knowing her mother would recover without anything major other than a broken arm and fractured ribs, lifted a weight of worries from Sandra's shoulders, thus she recalled that she had something of importance to tell Coy. When she called her boyfriend with the news, it was so late that she thought he would not respond having to work in the morning, yet he picked up before the call went to voice mail.

"Hello, hello! Is your mother OK," Coy asked?

"Yes, she is doing much better, the doctors believe she is well enough to go home tomorrow. But you would never guess who I saw at the gym this morning," Sandra stated?

"That is good news about your mom. Tell her I said hello," Coy said!

"Stop playing around! Guess who I saw," Sandra exclaimed?

"I give up babes, you just woke me up, so I have no clue," Coy responded.

"That woman who your mechanic supposedly ran off with," Sandra declared!

"What mechanic," Coy asked as his eyes widened?

"Evander, your collision specialist guy," Sandra lamented!

Coy woke fully from his tired state and sat up in bed. "You are telling me that you saw Officer Ray Pedward's wife at my sister's gym?"

"Yes, she is now a member I believe! I thought your body man returned for his old job, but with mom and everything I got all tied up and forgot to ask you," Sandra said.

"Thanks for that piece of information babes! But we still can't find Evander. I even phoned him again earlier tonight and still nothing," Coy declared!

"Well, we've all been praying for him. And we still hope he comes home safe," Sandra said.

"According to his mother they have been getting nothing but the run around from the officers at the station, so I think I'm going with them tomorrow," Coy stated!

"Well honey, be careful and don't go doing anything crazy that might get you locked up," Sandra instructed!

"Alright babes I hear you! I love you and have a good night," Coy said.

"I love you too Honey! Good night," Sandra stated!

Coy looked over at the clock and saw that it was 1:51 in the middle of the night, nevertheless he dialed Mrs. Simms phone number. Evander's mother had told him, "She did not sleep at nights and would not until she found out what happened to her son," thus he thought there was a chance she might answer. The phone hardly rang in Coy's ear when Evelin responded, as if she was right beside the device.

"Hello, hello," Evelin immediately responded believing Coy had some news of her son!

"Hello Mrs. Simms, I apologize for calling your house so late! But I just spoke with my girlfriend, and she told me that she saw the woman who Evander was to run away with, in town. I believe yesterday," Coy said.

"What! Did she ask her where is my son," Evelin asked?

"No! Sorry she did not. She said she was too surprised to see her there, so I guess she didn't know what to say," Coy explained!

"That is fine. I thank her for letting us know this," Evelin said!

"What did Coy, tell you mom," Julious touched Evelin and asked?

"As you heard, Julious can not sleep either! Coy said his girlfriend saw that policeman's wife at the new gym in town yesterday," Evelin stated!

"Then where is, my brother," Julious lamented?

"Mrs. Simms, if you don't mind, I would like to accompany you guys to the police station tomorrow," Coy asked?

"Certainly Coy! Gary, Julious, and I would be delighted if you came along! Hopefully this time we can get those cops to start looking for Evander," Evelin remarked!

"One way or the other, they are going to open that case! I'll see you guys in the morning Mrs. Simms; and tell Julious I said goodnight, please," Coy stated!

"Thanks, Coy! We'll see you in the morning. Let's say around 9:30 at the police station," Evelin said before they disconnected.

Julious got up from beside his mother and went into his room, where he grabbed his laptop off the desk and jumped onto his bed. Although Evander's cellular phone died, Julious went on the Internet and triangulated the area around which the phone was last detected. The last signal pole his brother's cellular connected with was just outside of the town of St. Jean Baptiste, thus Julious believed that Evander was somewhere within that vicinity. Each time they had gone to the police station to report Evander missing, Julious had informed them where his brother said he was to meet up with his lady friend, yet nobody chose to listen to him.

Chief Nathaniel Albus had already begun applying pressure on the District Attorney Office to investigate and prosecute Officer Pedward for violating the oath he took to protect and serve. Officer Pedward had done so many illegal things and gotten away with them throughout his career, that he expected his police chief to always have his back. The following morning at 8:18, three black Chryslers pulled up in front the Dakota Ojibway Police Station. Seven special agents from the Internal Affairs Bureau exited the vehicles and entered the station. The team of agents was led by Special Agents Jacques Latour and Alain Gorbon, who were the senior agents in the group. Agent Gorbon had a signed search warrant that specifically stipulated what the agents were after. When they entered the building and walked to the desk, Agent Gorbon showed Officer Wilkes the warrant and insisted that 'he opened the door immediately'! Officer Wilkes did as instruct, then quickly dialed Chief McIntyre at home and informed him of the developments. The police chief had not yet gotten ready to head into the office, nevertheless he instantly removed his pajamas, then threw on his uniform without showering. Within nine minutes of receiving the call, Chief McIntyre was inside his vehicle heading to the police station.

The Internal Affairs agents stormed into the building like gangbusters and made everyone stopped whatever they were doing. For them to do their jobs without interference, the agents made all the office workers exit the building until they were finished collecting their evidence. None of the station officers knew what the agents were after, therefore they speculated among themselves once they were relieved of their duties. The only officer inside the building who was left at his post was the front desk operator, who had to assist all visitors who came in. The team of agents were there to review and collect all the work files and body camera recordings, from Officer Ray Pedward's policing history.

Coy arrived at the police station at 9:18, parked in one of the assigned spaces, and waited patiently inside the car until the Simms family members arrived at 9:27. Once Evander's family members arrived, they all greeted each other then walked into the station. Officer Elan Wilkes was temporarily reassigned to desk duties and had been in a terrible mood following the reassignment. There was a lady ahead of the Simms's entourage, who was signing several documents for the release of her under-aged son. As they waited behind the woman, a side door came open and her son walked out. The woman finished signing the documents and walked out of the station with her son, without uttering a single word to the officer. Once the woman left Officer Wilkes signaled Coy and Evander's family members up to the desk. Despite all that was happening behind the scenes, none of the visitors had any idea of the ongoing disruption.

"Yes, how can I help you," Officer Wilkes stated?

"We are here to file a missing person report," Gary explained.

"OK! Who do you know is missing," Officer Wilkes asked while he retrieved the proper document?

"My son Evander Simms," Gary responded!

That name belonged to the male porn actor who was in the video with Rochelle Pedward, and was also the reason he had been reassigned, so Officer Wilkes paused before he started filling in the form. When Gary saw that the officer paused once he heard the name, he became concerned that they might receive the same treatment they had gotten thus far.

"Is there a problem officer," Gary asked?

"Not at all! What did you say that name was again," Officer Wilkes repeated?

"Evander Simms," Gary repeated!

"And how long has Evander been missing," Officer Wilkes questioned?

"It has been seven days now," Gary responded!

"Listen Sir, this is obviously a sensitive topic for some of the officers here, but I'm going to send out someone for you to talk with," Officer Wilkes warned!

"Thank you, Officer Wilkes," Gary said before they moved off to the side and waited.

Several minutes later the same side door swung open, and Officer Grey Gilmore showed them in. From Coy saw Officer Gilmore he began thinking that Officer Wilkes was a snake for pretending he was trying to help them. Coy knew that Officer Gilmore and Officer Pedward often worked together, so there was no way he would be partial to helping them find Evander. Grey showed them to a private room which had a table and six chairs inside, but only one entrance.

"If you guys don't mind waiting in here a little while, someone will be along shortly to take your statements," Officer Gilmore explained.

"Thank you, officer," Gary answered as they sat around the table!

Coy thought the police officers were up to something, therefore he remained extremely curious to see who came to collect the evidence. He began thinking of Sandra's warning to avoid getting into trouble and thus arrested, however there was no way he could just sit back and accept the injustice. Four minutes after Officer Gilmore left them alone, three elegantly dressed males walked in and closed the door behind them.

"Good morning, everyone! I am Detective Folier, and this is Special Agent Jacques Latour of the Internal Affairs Bureau, and his partner Agent Alain Gorbon! They were here today on some other business; but heard of your complaint and wished to sit in while I took your statements," said the French accent, Detective Folier.

"My son has been missing now for an entire week; and none of these police officers even care to help me find my boy! It is no secret that he was having an affair with one of these officer's wife, which may be why none of them wish to help find him. Right now, I don't care what state they find my Evander in, as long as they bring his body home," Evelin declared while her tears began flowing!

"This is tough on my family because we know that something is wrong with Evander! He was never the type of kid who stayed away from his family! So, wheresoever he went he would always come back home! Trust me, if we had the manpower to find him, we would be out there right now searching for him! But we need help man," Gary argued as he held his wife's hand.

"Do you know who this officer is," Detective Folier asked?

"Ray Pedward," Coy responded?

"And you are," Detective Folier enquired?

"Coy Devers! Their son Evander used to work for me, so I heard all this from him personally," Coy stated!

"You heard from Evander that he was sleeping with Officer Pedward's wife," Detective Folier asked?

"Yes! Almost every afternoon whenever she called him to come over, he would gloat about it! He even used to show us pictures and videos of them having sex," Coy answered!

"Did Evander ever mentioned her name," Detective Folier asked?

"Rochelle, I believe! Or something pretty close to that," Coy remarked.

"Which of you saw Evander last," Detective Folier asked?

"I did," Julious answered.

"Did he mention where he was heading," Detective Folier enquired?

"He said he, was going to, meet his girlfriend, at Red River," Julious answered.

The detective wrote down everything he heard thus far. "Did Evander tell you where he was heading?"

"No! He said he, would call when, he got to, wherever he was, going to stay," Julious answered!

"Did he tell you anything else," Detective Folier enquired?

"Yes! He said that, I can have, his car," Julious said!

"Was that supposed to mean, he planned on leaving you the car in Red River," Detective Folier questioned?

"I believe so," Julious responded!

"So, how do we know Evander isn't just laying low somewhere? Maybe he just got tired of Dominion City and wanted a new start somewhere fresh," Detective Folier declared!

"My son always responded to my phone calls! And if he was too busy, he would call me right back! Don't chastise me detective, my son is missing! Now we need help to find him," Evelin exclaimed!

"Evander also left me a message the night he went away, to say he was moving to be with Officer Pedward's wife; and apologized for leaving the shop. If Evander said he was moving away to be with his lover and she is still here in town, then my question to you officers is, where is he," Coy reasoned as he showed the investigators the message on his phone?

"We will make sure to find your son Mrs. Simms! Thank you all for coming back here again, to try and get help," Agent Latour stated!

"Here is my business card. If anything changes in Evander's status please phone me immediately, or if you think of anything else that will help us solve this case," Detective Folier said.

"Thank you," Gary said!

Detective Folier slid the Simms family a business card with his information across the table. Julious picked up the card and shoved it into his pocket. Within three hours of them leaving the police station, an officer located Evander's car on the road in St. Jean Baptiste where Ray left it. The vehicle was towed to an inspection station in Winnipeg, where the agents planned on checking it thoroughly for evidence. Once the police found the vehicle with no sign of Evander, those who were skeptical about his disappearance became more convinced. The agents immediately put out a nation-wide search alert to anyone who may have seem Evander or knew of his whereabouts.

The next day Detective Folier went to the Pedward's house to speak with Rochelle. The detective knew that Ray had returned to work after he took a few days off to clear his head, therefore his timing was ideal to avoid notifying his primary suspect. It was 10:22 AM when the detective rang the doorbell, then showed his badge as identification to the suspicious homeowner. Rochelle had never met the detective; hence she was understandably hesitant to open her door to the stranger.

"Yes, how may I help you," Rochelle asked from behind the door?

"Morning ma'am, I'm Detective Folier from the Dakota Ojibway Police Department; and I'm here to have a word with you about Evander Simms," Detective Folier stated while showing his badge?

The detective heard the deadbolt lock unlatched before the door slowly swung open. Rochelle stood by the door and held it open for the investigator to enter. Detective Folier stepped in and stood by the door, holding a note pad and pen in hand.

"Thanks for speaking with me this morning," Detective Folier commenced!

"What would you like to know detective? Whether or not I gave Evander consent to film that video? I've heard how the rest of you officers at the station have been laughing at Ray since you all watched that video! But we were having problem and I cheated on him a few times, that was it! I stopped sleeping with Evander a long time now, so if you are here to degrade my husband, please don't waste my time," Rochelle argued!?

"I'm only here to ask you if you have any idea where Evander may have gone? He has been missing for more than a week now, so we're desperately trying to find him," Detective Folier declared.

Rochelle frightfully covered her mouth with her right hand. "What do you mean he is missing?"

"There have been reports made that he supposedly moved away to live with you," Detective Folier said.

"No! That's crazy! I stopped seeing him when I thought that Ray was about to find out about us," Rochelle explained!

"When was the last time you spoke to Evander," Detective Folier asked?

"I'm not sure, maybe a month! I mean he has text me a few times begging for us to get back together, but I haven't responded to any of his messages," Rochelle answered.

"Could I see some of those messages? Maybe Evander said where he would be in one of them," Detective Folier asked?

"I'm sorry! I got scared my husband might see them one day and deleted them a few days ago! Only to find out that Evander had uploaded a porn video of us on some sleazy website," Rochelle exclaimed!

"I assume that was the same video you were talking about earlier," Detective Folier questioned?

"Yes, it was," Rochelle stated!

"Why did you think Evander posted that video," Detective Folier asked?

"He was probably hurt; because he wanted to be with me," Rochelle began, "Oh my god, you don't think that Ray had anything to do with Evander's disappearance?"

"Right now, we're just trying to find Evander! So, thank you for answering my questions," Detective Folier exclaimed before he exited the residence.

Two additional days passed without any developments in the case. On the morning of the third day, Detective Folier received a phone call from Julious. The timing and place for the call was slightly unusual, because the detective was driving into work early in the morning.

"Hello," Detective Folier responded!

"Hello Detective Folier, this is Julious, Evander's brother," Julious said!

"Good morning, Julious, did something happen regarding Evander," Detective Folier asked?

"I tracked Evander's, phone to the, bridge that cross, into St. Jean, Baptiste," Julious stated.

"What? I thought they said his phone's battery was dead," Detective Folier!

"I still tracked, it there," Julious said.

"That just might be helpful in finding your brother. Thanks Julious, I'll have a few officers head out there with me later to search around," Detective Folier responded.

Later that morning Detective Folier and two marked cruisers pulled up on the east side of the Red River Bridge, while two other cruisers pulled up on the west side. From the officer along the east end of the bridge exited their vehicles, they immediately smelt the foul stench in the air. Much of the snow that fell during their last snowstorm had melted, which enabled one of the officers to notice the blood along the side of the roadway. The detective and the other officers were notified of the finding; hence they followed their noses and the blood trail to Evander's body. The corpse was inches from falling off the ice and could have gotten covered by another snowstorm, thus the officers had to work quickly to safely recover it. With the body out of the river, Detective Folier's work was just beginning, therefore he gathered all the officers together and gave them all assignments. Folier wanted two of the officers to block off the crime scene and four officers to search around the area and collect clues, while he inspected the corpse. Before the news leaked by chance, the detective assigned Officer Lovette to drive to the Simms's family residence and informed them about the finding. Officer Lovette was also instructed to arrange for the parents to travel to the morgue and identify the body, which was found without any identification. Although the police could somewhat distinguish that the victim was Evander Simms, his body still had to be legally identified.

Just before the team of officers went into action, three large black van and four vehicles pulled up just alongside their cruisers. The vehicles' doors began popping open and a host of well-dressed federal agents exited. The occupants who exited the large vans were all properly covered in white overall suits, and other protective equipment like a forensic team. The Dakota Ojibwe officers had never seen any such convoy, therefore several of them felt nervous and placed their hands on their weapons. Two of the agents walked over and showed Detective Folier and his team of officers their badges, along with a signed document that stipulated, 'The crime scene had been reassigned'!

"Wait a minute! Who the hell are you guys? This is my crime scene, we found the body," Detective Folier argued!

"Detective, you, and your men are no longer required here! If you need any further information, you can contact Chief McIntyre and he'll fill you in," Agent Legot declared!

Detective Folier took the paper and read a few lines as his companions began slowly moving toward their vehicles.

"This is bullshit! We found the body, so it should be our case," Detective Folier implied!

"It doesn't seem as if the government trust your department to investigate itself, Detective," Agent Wu implied!

"Thank you, officers, and kindly watch where you step when leaving, we wouldn't like to tarnish any of the evidence left behind by the perpetrator," Agent Legot suggested as he waved the forensic technicians over!

None of the Dakota Ojibwe officers were pleased about surrendering their crime scene, but they had no choice in the matter. According to the orders in writing on the document, none of the officers were supposed to discuss the finding with their peers or anyone else. They were all sworn to secrecy to protect the integrity of the case, knowing that an officer from their precinct may have been involved.

While their forensic technicians went to work, the agents thought to inform the victim's relatives about his discovery, hence Agent Wu drove to the Simms's residence. When Agent Wu reached the house and buzzed the door, Gary responded expecting some friends to pass by. The sight of the agent immediately erased the father's pleasant smile, therefore he turned and looked over his shoulder to locate his wife. Evelin was only a few feet behind her husband and could clearly hear the agent, who was choked up to deliver the news. Mrs. Simms dropped to her knees as Agent Wu began apologizing for having to report 'the death of their son'. Julious stepped from his room at that instant and caught sight of his mother tumbling to the floor, therefore he immediately rushed to her aide. Gary also rushed to help Evelin off the floor, but the distressed mother refused to budge. With his mother bawling unbearably, it was difficult for her youngest son to grasp what was happening, until he saw the disheartened Agent Wu at the door. Rather than lifting his mother off the floor, Julious fell to his knees beside her and hugged her tenderly, while they both cried. Although the family expected to receive disturbing news with Evander missing for so long, the disclosure of his death was gut-wrenching and had the entire household in tears.

It was important to Evelin that they placed a wreath and created a memorable tribute at the place where her son's soul was taken, so they had the agent describe where the body was found. The next day all three family members went to the flower shop and bought a wreath that could survive all four seasons and brought it to the location by the bridge. They placed the wreath with pictures of Evander attached to it, as a permanent tribute to their son. Evelin said a prayer then sang Amazing Grace, while Gary and Julious wept for their relative, whose life was taken much too soon.

Chapter 38

Andrew was locked inside his bedroom which he had completely remodeled once he began hanging with the Applewick brothers. He had painted the entire room black and stopped maintaining the clean environment his relatives had grown accustomed to. There were clothes and trash tossed all over the floor, yet none of that bothered the disturbed Christian. Despite his new arian stance wherein he was anti blacks, natives, and all none-white races, the curtains inside his room were also black. Some of the posters on his walls included target practicing circles, which he often aimed at with his handgun while he imagined people from other ethnicities. The only person who Andrew regularly made time for was his brother Aaron, whom he self-appointed as his personal mentor. They initially began a ritual to converse once per week, but that quickly changed to two conversations, before Aaron was calling nearly every day. Jacquelin would not have dared intervened, knowing the brothers were reuniting after all those years apart. Both brothers had been on the phone since Aaron exited his cell, and they would quite often spend his entire break talking.

"I see that ex-girlfriend of yours Celine, driving through the town as if she the mayor or some shit! Her high tech gym that she opened had folks saying it would close real soon, yet still they the same people signing up to become members," Andrew stated!

"That's how them old ass country people are Brother! Just wait around then jump on the bandwagon," Aaron said!

"You right about that Aaron," Andrew remarked!

"Don't ever forget what I said! Make sure you don't trust those backstabbers," Aaron instructed!

"I won't forget nothing you said Aaron! Matter a fact, I'm about to do something big, that will make you real proud of me," Andrew boasted!

"That's my little brother! Don't worry about where you end up, whatever institution they have you, we'll try and get you transferred," Aaron declared!

"Man, it's cool having you as my big brother! You're nothing like mom and dad, always on my case over everything," Andrew exclaimed!

The voice operator interrupted the conversation and said, "You have five minutes remaining for this call."

"Hey Little Brother, there is something I have to do before lock down, so I'll catch up with you tomorrow," Aaron said!

"Same time Brother! I'll be right here waiting for your call," Andrew responded!

Following their talk Andrew got off his bed and threw his handgun, lighter, cigarettes, cellular, and some other items into his backpack. He then exited his room with the bag over his shoulder, closed the door behind himself, and went into the kitchen. Jacquelin was sitting at the dining table working on her laptop, when the young man walked to the fridge and began looking inside.

"Pastor Hemming is concerned about you! He wants you to phone him sometimes if you ever feel like you need someone to talk with," Jacquelin said.

"I don't need the pastor's advice," Andrew decreed!

"I'll have you know that man cares about you; and you will not disrespect my pastor! As long as you continue on the way you are going, you will end up in prison like your brother Aaron," Jacquelin said!

"Right now, that sounds like the better option than being here," Andrew implied as he grabbed a banana and a bottle of water!

"And what if the police kill you Andrew," Jacquelin reasoned?

"White cops don't kill white men mom! Don't you watch the news," Andrew remarked before he went through the door?

The young man drove to his friends' house, where Russell and Kyler had two females over. The front door was always unlocked, so Andrew simply walked in unannounced. There were several unopened envelopes with past due bills on a table close to the entrance, which caught Andrew's attention as he closed the door. When Andrew entered the house, the four occupants were inside the living room sitting on the sofas intoxicated, with the television on the weather network. The brother's female guests whom they picked up at the shooting range lounge, were two of Andrew's most despised admirers in Dominion City. Russell was passed out with one of the ladies laying on his lap on the long sofa, while Kyler and the other female sat on the smaller chair. Even Beast their dog who had been around the smoking was too stoned to get off his cot, therefore the animal only turned its head and looked at Andrew, then laid right back down. From the looks of things Andrew could tell they had been partying all night, due to the unfinished cans of sodas, beer cans, cigarette packs, half bottle of Vodka, and drug paraphernalia scattered across the table.

"Andrew! That's our friend Andrew," Kyler yelled as he entered!

"Oh, I know him! That's Alter Boy, from my old church! He's tamed as a lamb," the large sized females said!

Andrew grabbed a beer as he walked by everyone and went to the far end of the room, where he sat in the corner then retrieved his personal stash from his backpack. The female who stated that 'she knew him' kept watching him as he fixed himself something to smoke. To attract Andrew's attention the female started kissing Kyler's ear and neck, despite him being so intoxicated he could hardly participate. Venise Taylor was someone who Andrew remembered quite well, as a person who would torment him at bible school before her family stopped attending church. Rather than giving her the satisfaction that he cared to watch, Andrew reached into his bag and withdrew his sunglasses and placed them on his face. He then took out his Bluetooth headphones, covered his ears, and began playing music from his cellular. The crystal meth laced joint he rolled was ready to be smoked, therefore he sparked it ablaze and began smoking, while he bobbed his head to his music. When Venise realized she was not the entertainment Andrew sought, she stopped fondling with Kyler who had fallen asleep.

Andrew smoked until he passed out in the corner, but everyone else were asleep by then. The instant Russell reopened his eyes, he reached for his beer on the side table and took a drink. As he looked around the room, he remembered partying with his brother and the two females, yet he could not recall Andrew being there. The female sleeping with her head on his lap was drooling all over his leg, so he shook her and woke her. Kyler, Venise, and Andrew were still sound asleep, so Russell got up while holding onto his lady-friend's hand, then led her into his bedroom. Beast opened his eyes, lifted his head, and watched as his master brought the female into his room, before the dog rested his head back on his cot.

Behind the closed door both Russell and Veronica began kissing the instant they entered the bedroom. It went quiet inside the room for several minutes as if they had gone to bed. Russell could not wait to get his visitor out of her clothes; therefore, he started undressing her before he removed his clothing. Veronica shared similar sentiments, thus she quickly unbuckled his pant and started sliding them off.

"I don't normally cheat on my boyfriend, but he is out of town for a few days," Veronica grumbled as she pressed Russell against the door!

"Then I guess I'll be locking you down for the next few days," Russell responded!

"I just love your take charge bad boy attitude," Veronica expressed as they locked lips again!

The sexually aggressive female began dragging off her partner's tee-shirt as she sucked all over his neck. To not hinder Veronica's progress, Russell assisted her by removing his tee-shirt himself, as she continued to his chest area. The temptation to devour her lover was overwhelming, yet Veronica did not wish to give the impression she was some sleazy thot, so she stopped licking him above his navel. While she electrified every nerve throughout his anatomy, Russell closed his eyes and had a tantalizing dream she would perform fellatio, until she withdrew a condom from her pocket and handed it to him. Veronica sensually walked away and out of the remainder of her clothes, as she slowly moved to the bed. Russell ripped open the packet and did as instruct before he kicked off his pants hanging at the base of his foot; and followed the tempting waitress. The deafening silence immediately disappeared, as they engaged in coitus and began making menacing sounds. Their sexual exuberance continued for a while and grew increasingly louder as they progressed, thus the noise levels eventually awoke Kyler. To drown out the intimacy sounds coming from his brother's bedroom, Kyler turned on the stereo and began playing his favorite heavy metal music.

It was well into the evening by then, after they all slept through most of the day. The loud music awoke Venise who got up and went directly to the bathroom. Contrary to everyone else Andrew could not hear the music with his headphones already activated, therefore he continued sleeping comfortably. Kyler was automatically coupled with Venise when Russell approached Veronica and piqued her interest, however he had no real interest in being with her. When Venise awoke and overheard her girlfriend with Russell inside the bedroom, she thought Kyler might be in the mood for sex also, yet he refrained from entering the bathroom even after she left the door opened. Nearly ten minutes went by with Venise wishing Kyler would join her, before she exited the bathroom and returned to the living room.

While Venise was inside the bathroom, Kyler led Beast to the back door for the animal to go outside and relieved himself. The dog was super excited to spend time outdoors that he ran around the backyard enjoying every second of freedom. Moments after the animal finished relieving himself, Kyler summoned him then went back inside and closed the door. The Weather Forecast Service had issued a warning about a torrential snowstorm that was to begin around 11:00 PM, thus the winds were gradually intensifying in strength. When they re-entered the house Venise was inside the kitchen looking through the refrigerator for something to prepare. The brothers did not have very much food items to construct a meal, but she found an opened pack of hot-dogs which had seven singles left. There were a few slices of bread inside a bag on the counter, which had an expiration date that had passed two days prior. Regardless of the expired warning, Venise threw each slice into the oven for them to toast.

By the time Russell's bedroom door swung open and the two sex maniacs emerged, Venise and Kyler were devouring their portion of the hot-dogs. Veronica went directly to the bathroom, while Russell sat back on the sofa and lit himself a cigarette. Venise and Kyler had managed to leave three hot-dogs, which was a struggle considering they could have eaten them all. The odd pair were laughing and more social following a respectful conversation, wherein Kyler admitted "He was not physically attracted to bigger body ladies."

Veronica emerged from the bathroom when she heard her favorite song began playing. She danced her way over to the platter of hotdogs and grabbed herself one, which she ate while she moved around. Russell had constructed a joint to get them all high, which he lit ablaze and took a few tokes before he passed it to Veronica. The snow was beginning to fall lightly outside, yet the heat was just increasing inside the Applewick's house. Kyler and Russell were accustomed to relaxing once they had gotten intoxicated, but their lady friends were party enthusiasts whenever they got high. Venise and Veronica began dancing around the room barefoot, doing all sorts of idiotic things as they enjoyed themselves.

Andrew had his head tilted backward against the wall with his mouth wide opened, as he comfortably slept in the corner. His bothersome snoring was loud and annoyed the playful females, who were laughing and partying among themselves. Veronica found a plain sheet of white paper and began ripping off and crumbling small pieces, which she tried to toss into Andrew's mouth. Venise joined in on the fun and made it a worthwhile competition; until Veronica accurately threw a piece into the sleeper's mouth.

"Tut, tut, tut," Andrew reacted by spitting the paper out of his mouth, then adjusted his head, closed his mouth, and went back to sleep!

The females burst out with laughter, then went back to dancing and parading, yet were not done messing with the sleeping visitor. Neither Russell nor Kyler cared anything about what their lady friends were doing to Andrew, hence they paid them no attention.

"Everybody round town thinks he is still a virgin, but he's probably gay," Venise said softly.

"Well, I wouldn't mind picking his cherry," Veronica stated!

"I think you have devirginized enough of Dominion City's men," Venise declared!

"There are always new victims, my dear Venise! But I don't think he is a virgin," Veronica remarked!

"He wouldn't know what to do with a vagina if he woke up and it was right in his face," Venise responded!

"Girl you better stop, he might be a killer like Beast over there," Veronica joked!

"You think I'm playing? I'll show you," Venise declared as she danced over to Andrew and pulled down her legging and underwear, then stuck her derriere in his face!

Andrew awoke and was disgusted by the act; therefore, he shoved the female away and wiped his face with his hands. Everyone inside the room burst out with laughter as Andrew got up and grabbed his belongings and headed for the door.

"Hey Andrew, Buddy calm down! I'm sure they were only messing around with you man," Kyler explained!

"Ah, let him get out of here! He's just ruining our party any ways," Veronica declared!

"I told you he was a virgin," Venise joked as they continued laughing!

The enraged and embarrassed young man stormed through the door and out into the developing blizzard. His vehicle was not yet covered with snow, nevertheless Andrew still had to wipe the windshield clear to see. The vision of everyone laughing at him was the only thought that replayed through his mind constantly, as he started up the engine and drove away. Andrew felt as though he was too sober to return home and deal with his family members, so he drove to the cemetery where he could smoke and get intoxicated peacefully. The snow was getting heavier by the minute and started forming lumps of ice at the far corners of his windshield. There was nobody walking the streets and the town appeared barren, as the weather made it incredibly difficult to get around. With much of the smaller roads throughout Dominion City unpaved, any wrong turn would have spelt disaster, therefore he had to drive slower. When Andrew reached the cemetery, the narrow roadway made it difficult to navigate, hence it was even harder to turn the vehicle around.

There was a cautious fear in Andrew to do certain tasks such as driving through snow, that disappeared whenever he got intoxicated. To reach that level of arrogance, he stopped the vehicle in the middle of the road and began preparing his laced joint. "I'll show them! I'll make them all see who I am! They want to clown me! I'll show them all," Andrew said to himself as he lit the joint and inhaled. The compiling snow would need to get physically removed to lessen the burden on his windshield wipers, which began struggling to clean the glass. While parked by the side of the cemetery the troubled young man looked over at the graves and envisioned a small group of people encircling his casket. The effects of the drug slowly rendered Andrew incoherent, whereas he began dozing off to sleep. Just before he fell into that deep state of consciousness, his cellular rang and displayed Jacquelin's face on the screen, thus he watched it ring without responding. Whether Andrew responded or not his mother was determined to deliver her message, therefore several seconds later he received a text message stating, 'there was to be a severe snowstorm'. The shock from the message clouded Andrew's thoughts, therefore he neglected to exit the vehicle and cleaned the windshield.

Robin left work later than she normally would because she had to clean up the establishment by herself. Veronica was scheduled to work alongside her, but she called in sick at the last minute. It had been a tough two weeks filled with 'Nine-Night' functions and a 'Celebration of Life' event for Evander Simms, who was violently killed by his adulterous woman's husband. The entire family felt destroyed by the loss and received many kind sentiments from some within the community. There were those who felt differently about Evander's demise and thought he deserved what happened to him for sleeping with a married woman. Julious thought of her as his close confidant and would speak to no one else about his feelings, so she made sure she was there for him in every way. The funeral was scheduled for that coming Saturday, which was expected to be the toughest day yet for the Simms family.

Celine told Robin 'To phone her if she wanted a drive home after work' but sighting the late hour her daughter decided against waking her. The walk home from the gun range was one that Robin had made several times without serious worry, therefore she buckled up for the cold and started walking. If she had to run from someone Robin felt confident her native made boots would provide her with good grip on snow and ice, while her winter jacket provided the warmth and an extended hood. The winds were howling and slashed flakes of snow in her eyes, which made it hard to see very far ahead. To see where she was going, Robin had to walk with her head slightly lowered while she shielded her face with her hand. Even though there were no vehicles going up and down the street, the gun range employee stayed to the side of the road for adequate safety.

Andrew was coming along the roadway having gotten intoxicated and thus braver behind the steering wheel. Despite the limited visibility he was cruising along in the middle of Waddell Avenue, when he drove pass Robin headed in the opposite direction. With no one around the intoxicated bigot thought he would never get a better chance, so he tapped the brake pedal, lifted the emergency handbrake, and spun the steering wheel, which forced the car into a hundred and eighty degrees turn. The menacing bigot drove back toward the unsuspecting female, who also had trouble battling the brutal winds. The snowfall had already began blocking his headlights, yet he turned them off to avoid being noticed approaching. As the vehicle got close enough to Robin, Andrew sped up then lifted the handbrake and spun the steering in the opposite direction. The vehicle swerved and bumped Robin into the deep snow along the sidewalk, before it came to a stop. The attacker leapt from the car and ran over to the injured pedestrian, who was trying to raise herself out the snow. The falling snow made recognizing the approaching attacker difficult, thus he ran over and stumped her in the face. With his victim unconscious, Andrew dragged her back to his car and placed her on the back seat. After he looked up and down the street to make sure no one was coming, Andrew jumped into the driver's seat and drove away.

The only place Andrew thought of that offered the privacy he sought was back at the cemetery. Therefore, he drove back to the location and parked with the engine running, to keep the car's interior warm. The degrading comments told to him by Veronica and Venise kept replaying in his mind, therefore he felt a lack of sympathy for women. Robin was still unconscious and had no idea where she was, hence, her abductor climbed over onto the rear seat and partly undressed her. Andrew believed he was satisfying his personal desires and avenging his brother simultaneously, when he began raping Celine's daughter. The young rape victim blinked her eyes a few times during the process and saw shades of the pendant on his chain, as it swung while he violated her. Within six minutes the rapist ejaculated inside his victim, then fixed his clothes and pulled her from his vehicle. Robin's clothes were barely on, and she looked like she was near death, when Andrew abandoned her and left her laying in the snowstorm.

Several minutes after she got abandoned Robin regained consciousness and quickly brushed away the piling snow, before she buttoned up her frosty clothing. The raped victim was shivering after her abductor left her exposed to mother nature in -28 Degree Celsius temperature. Her purse was nowhere to be found with her cellphone inside, therefore she could not alert the authorities or called her mother for help. Robin had no choice but to begin walking, thus she slowly began dragging her legs through the mounting snow. To determine which direction she should take, she used the graveyard as her compass and walked to the northeastern section. When she reached the edge of the cemetery and saw there was a T-intersection, she realized she was on the right path, therefore she turned left and headed back into town.

Robin had to walk all the way back down Waddell Avenue until she reached the location from which she got abducted. As she approached the location, she began hearing her cellular ringing somewhere along the roadside. Quite a bit of snow had fallen since she was kidnapped, therefore her purse had gotten covered and could not be seen. Despite feeling frozen and numb in many areas, Robin had to sacrifice stepping into the deep snow and tracked the ringing directly to her purse's location. The phone had stopped ringing by the time Robin cleared away the snow to retrieve the purse, but according to her display she had missed sixty-eight calls from her mother, Coy, and Julious combined. Robin's battery indicator was showing that it needed to get charged immediately with only 3% power remaining. A period of one hour and forty-three minutes had also elapsed, of which she remembered very little except the fact, she was raped.

The phone sounded again with her mother on the line, but as she responded she found that she could not utter a single word. Her mother was elated that someone answered the phone, although she felt scared that it might not have been her daughter.

"Robin, baby are you OK," Celine asked?

The words were difficult to muster, but the pain from being personally violated caused her tears to erupt. Celine could hear her daughter crying and knew for certain it was Robin, although she was uncertain what dangers she was in.

"Robin, where are you," Celine questioned?

"Some man just raped me," Robin declared!

"Baby, where are you," Celine asked?

"On Waddell Avenue," Robin cried.

"I'm on my way," Celine declared as she left Coy to watch Julien and brought her mother along.

They found Robin on Waddell Avenue and immediately drove her to the police station. The thundering snow extended the seven minutes journey, which took them an additional thirty-two minutes at the slow speed they had to travel. Both Miss Shirley and Celine tried desperately to console the distort teenager, who felt as though her entire world had been stolen. When they reached the police station, Officer Molly Burley was placed in charge of the case rather than a male officer. The stump and other hits Robin received to her face had caused bruises, therefore the officer obtained a camera and took photographs for evidence. Officer Molly sat down with all three ladies, but first had to ensure Robin was comfortable disclosing all the details with her mother and grandmother present. Celine had already concluded who the culprit was and was not shy to reveal the incident that occurred at her welcoming party.

When Officer Molly heard that the culprit had ejaculated inside Robin, she was excited by the news and immediately called in a paramedic team to examine the victim. The technicians collected hair and sperm samples from Robin, who broke down emotionally and could not stop crying. Her condition could have worsened had it went untreated, thus the technicians wanted to admit her at the hospital. Miss Shirley thought of a solution to help her granddaughter regained her sanity, and thereby telephoned Julious for them to converse. From Robin heard the young man's voice she stopped crying, and gradually calmed down, thus they were abled to bring her home rather than have her admitted.

Chapter 39

Officer Pedward brought home a carton box with an adorable Yorkshire Terrier puppy inside, as a present for his wife. He had been waiting for the breeder's animals to produce another litter for months, thereby once the puppy was born, two weeks later he received the call to pick up the dog. The officer had recognized that Rochelle needed some sort of hobby after her cheating venture, therefore he went out and found a suitable companion that would keep her occupied. Despite not mentioning, Ray hated the fact that Rochelle had begun spending more time with Malory, thus he wanted to infringe on the amount of time they shared. Contrary to whatever was said about his wife, the officer loved her very much and was willing to overlook the scandalous affair she had. Ray also had to accept the fact that many people were going to watch the porn video of her, which was forever uploaded to the Internet.

When Officer Pedward walked in with the puppy inside the box, Rochelle was sitting inside their living room painting her toenails. The television was on the female's beauty shopping channel, which she watched occasionally. There was a bottle of white wine on the floor next to her that she had been drinking. Ray entered with the box and placed it on the floor while he removed his jacket and boots. The puppy sensed that she was indoors from the outside cold and thus started barking. The Yorky's little bark startled Rochelle, who had not paid her husband any attention when he originally entered.

"What is that," Rochelle enquired?

Ray hung up his jacket and brought the box over to Rochelle, who seemed super excited to see what was inside. The officer placed the box on the center-table and slowly opened it, before he lifted out the small puppy. When Rochelle saw the small animal emerged from the box, her face lit up like a Christmas Tree. Officer Pedward saw the immediate love connection once the dog's eyes met Rochelle's, therefore she grabbed the animal from his grasp and began hugging it like a little child.

"Oh, Honey it is beautiful," Rochelle declared as she gave him a huge kiss!

"It is a female dog Baby. I thought that you would like her," Ray responded!

"Are you crazy? She is so adorable! I love her! What should I call her," Rochelle said?

"I don't know, whatever name you like I guess," Ray answered.

"Oh, I'm going to have to think about that," Rochelle responded!

"Well, you have all the time in the world to figure that out. I'm going to get my uniform ready for tomorrow," Ray exclaimed.

Following the questioning by Detective Folier, Rochelle was left feeling conflicted about what to believe. No matter how she tried to convince herself otherwise, if something had happened to Evander, she felt as though Ray would have been involved. Regardless of the unknown, the Yorky pup was something she appreciated getting, therefore she took a picture of the animal with her cellular and text it to Malory. Once the message was sent, she dialed her friend's number to boast about her new companion.

"Hey girl, meet my new puppy! I still have to decide on a name to call her, but say hello puppy," Rochelle excitedly stated!

"Is that what Ray brought you? She is totally adorable Rochelle," Malory asked?

"Yes, I am in love," Rochelle answered!

"Hold on honey, let me go somewhere that no one can hear us," Malory exclaimed as she went into her bathroom and closed the door.

"What's going on? Sounds like you have some hot news to mention," Rochelle said!

"Listen, Grey showed me that porn video with you and that guy they found in the Red River the other day! Because of the video Grey wants me to end our friendship! He thinks that doesn't look appropriate for a Christian woman, and his kids to be going around with a porn star," Malory explained!

"I'm sorry Malory! I should have told you, but I," Rochelle started!

"I'm not sure how much I'll be able to talk to you after today, because Grey said we could possibly be charged with perjury, if I told you certain things about what's been happening at the precinct! According to Grey everybody has been keeping hush-hush about the body, since some federal agents went in and took over the whole investigation," Malory whispered!

"Why did they do that," Rochelle asked?

"Because they believe your husband... Oh shit, Grey just came home I gotta go," Malory whispered before the line went dead!

The story was a local discussion mainly talked about by the usual chatterboxes around the area and was only written about by a community newspaper in Winnipeg, until 'Pete The Scandalous' mentioned it on his web channel. The slowly building story went from country gossip to intriguing the interest of Canadians across the country. Almost overnight the quiet towns of Dominion City and Roseau River Reserve, became the epicenter of Canada, wherein they had news reporters and strangers who made the journey to support their causes. There were still no arrests made in the case, despite the numerous accusations by people who believed they knew who the shooter was. Celine and many other business owners looked through their store windows and were surprised to see crowds forming with people carrying signs, while they shouted all sorts of anti-racism, anti-black, and anti-police sentiments.

News reporters who traveled to the region to cover the story, went to Celine's Gym and other businesses to get some of the local's take on everything that had occurred. Rather than appearing on camera, Celine made the reporter speak with Miss Shirley and a few of her other customers, while she hid in the background. When the crowds originally began forming with visitors who came off buses and different types of transports, there were no police presence in the area, therefore the store owners became scared for their businesses. Several minutes later however, local officers and RCMP personnel arrived on scene and began monitoring the crowd, yet they kept their distance.

The crowds that gathered mainly at the Dakota Ojibwe Police Precinct in Roseau River Reserve and Dominion City had peaceful demonstrations. However, many locals wanted to know why the police were not in place to deal with the crowds before they gathered in both towns. For such huge, coordinated demonstrations to take place, activist group leaders would normally contact law enforcement departments and made them aware prior to the events. When the RCMP investigated to uncover who organized both demonstrations, they learnt that people from across the country heard of the case and decided on their own to travel to the towns. Almost everyone who was ask why the chose to make the trip said, "They wanted to see justice done for the Simms family."

The Federal Forensic Team that combed through the crime scene, recovered all the bullet casings and Evander's cell phone. The team felt they would locate the information they needed to effectively make an arrest if they were abled to get the cell phone working. When Officer Pedward shot Evander, he fell backward onto his derriere and cracked the device. With water damage one of the pertinent issues with the phone, the agents were unsure if they would get any information to advance their case. The repair process was time consuming, moreover the agents had to send the device to a specialist in Quebec, thus they would have to wait a few weeks for the result.

Due to the condition of the cellular, none of the agents felt confident they would be abled to scavenge anything from it, so they began checking into other means of solving the murder. The shell casings gave them a huge confidence booster they were on track to get their prime suspect, yet it was all circumstantial evidence without the weapon. The bullet casings proved that Evander was killed with a Springfield Hellcat Pro, which was the same type of handgun stolen by Officer Pedward. The agents knew the Prosecution Office would never consider prosecuting an officer of the law on pure speculation, therefore they obtained a search warrant to look through Officer Pedward's house. So far, they had recovered Evander's car, yet there were no signs of his clothes and other items, hence the agents had a list of things to search for.

The agents wanted to question their leading suspect and get his testimony on file; moreover, they also wanted to thoroughly search his house without alerting him. The pathologist and his forensic team had determined the date on which Evander was killed, therefore they wanted to know what Ray did after he finished working that night. To arrange an appointment Agent Legot telephoned Officer Pedward and asked him to swing by their Winnipeg office the following morning at 10:00. Ray had expected to get questioned with all the hoopla surrounding Evander's murder, therefore he agreed to meet with the agents. It was almost a week since Evander's body had been found, thus Officer Pedward knew that if the investigators had a solid case against him, he would have already been behind bars. Ray knew the agents would be trying to get him to confess, so he arranged a surprise for them.

With his life and career on the line, Ray walked confidently and brash into the meeting the next day with his new lawyer Angelo D'amus, who was an excellent criminal attorney. Ray understood what his police chief meant when he warned him to get an adequate lawyer, so he showed the agents that he would not be railroaded. Once they all shook hands, the officer and his attorney sat across from Agent Legot and Agent Wu, who dived into the questioning. The agents had a camera mounted on a tripod in a corner of the room to record Ray's reactions and emotions while he responded to the questions. They also had a tape recorder on the table in front of them, that was collecting the audio from the meeting.

Before they went into anything serious, Agent Wu slid a copy of their warrant that was underway at that very moment. Defense Attorney D'amus was not amused by the agents' trickery, but Ray only scuffed at the paper and paid it no mind. Officer Pedward was a veteran on the force, so he predicted the questions in advance and had a direct response whenever he was allowed to answer. Agent Wu and Agent Legot thought they would have gotten to pressure Officer Pedward into a mistake, but Attorney Angelo D'amus objected to most of their questions and would explain why his client did not have to answer. Rather than helping the agents' case, Ray left the meeting feeling as though they had frustrated the agents into reconsidering their entire approach.

Rochelle was getting ready to head out to the gym when the agents showed up to search the house for evidence. There were ten agents involved in the search team, all of whom arrived in two passenger vans, which they parked on the street. The lead agent went to the door and rang the bell to gain entry. When Rochelle responded to the door and saw all the agents outside, she was somewhat surprised yet not totally shocked. Agent Dufferin introduced himself and handed the female owner the warrant to search the house. Instead of arguing the inevitable, Rochelle allowed them to enter while she grabbed her gym bag and her dog and went outside. While the agents searched through her home, the female owner tossed her bag into her car and took her dog for a walk down the street. Without Malory to call and discuss what was happening, the officer's wife felt more alone than ever. All her intuitions told her that her beautiful life was about to change, as she feared her husband was the person who killed Evander.

The agents who went into the Pedward's house gave the entire interior a thorough search. They found nothing of interest inside; but emptied the burnt contents from the drum in the backyard into plastic bags. Their entire search lasted forty-two minutes, after they left no rugs unturned and departed with very little evidence. Rochelle watched them leave from inside the warmth of her car with her dog, before she went and looked inside. The place was a mess with her cushions thrown on the floor, her furniture rearranged, closets left filthy, and kitchen items across the counter. Rather than taking one step into the filth, Rochelle locked the door, went into her vehicle, and drove away. As she drove down the street, she dialed her husband's number. Ray was still being interrogated and did not respond to the call, therefore she left him a message 'to clean the house whenever he reached home!'

After the Internal Affairs agents left the Dakota Ojibwe Precinct with the evidence they went to collect, they brought the material back to their headquarters for evaluation. The bureau's investigation into the incident involving Louie Albus, revealed some startling information. The scope of the agents' investigation was very specific, however while looking into that matter they learned about the management of the precinct and its disciplinary structure. When Agents Latour and Gorbon among others watched the view cam from Officer Pedward's cruiser; and saw the manner with which he intentionally dragged Louie Albus off camera to assault him, they were appalled. While Ray should have gotten fired from the force for issuing threats and assault, his commander Police Chief McIntyre kept him on active duty. The Internal Affairs agents realized they could not trust the Dakota Ojibwe officers to investigate themselves with Evander's murder, therefore they notified the Canadian Federal Agency and got them involved.

Agent Jacques Latour and Agent Alain Gorbon were expected to provide a final report on their investigation to their supervisors. Chief Nathaniel Albus who filed the original complaint was a very prominent person, hence his legal lawsuit against the province was guaranteed to become national news. With all the bad publicity the government had endured regarding native affairs over the years, having an officer assault an Indian chief's son, then confiscated his handgun without issuing any seizure documents, sat an awful precedent. The Internal Affairs agents were at the station on a day when lots of activities were ongoing, therefore they learnt of the officers' refusal to take a missing persons report, Evander Simms's murder, and other crucial affairs. Both men stipulated that the biggest issue at the precinct was leadership, then pointed to the length of suspensions given to the officers involved in Officer Pedward's wife scandal.

The Winnipeg Tribune was the first news station to print the story about the internal dysfunction happening at the Dakota Ojibwe Police Precinct. According to the editor, he received the story from a credited source, then went into stating factual evidence about Rochelle Pedward's affair and the internal scandal it caused. The news station sighted that Police Chief McIntyre ran a racist and loose department, wherein officers committed multiple violations and were hardly punished for them. There were leaked documents from the police station's archives, which showed the amount of time given to officers over the years for various violations. The news story came out during a very sensitive time at the precinct, wherein the entire workforce was split on the Pedward scandal.

When the news broke about Chief McIntyre's incapability to manage a respectable organization, two of his biggest supporters throughout the years immediately voiced their disapproval of his handling of the precinct. Mayor Bathurst said in a report that, "She believes Police Chief McIntyre had failed the community he was hired to serve, and as a result should resign his post!" The mayor also said that "The suspension times awarded by the police chief were an insult to the people who those officers offended, time and time again!" The M.P for the area, Fiz Valso, shared his thoughts through his social media account wherein he wrote, "Police Chief McIntyre should step down from his post immediately, for encouraging a work atmosphere that was not conducive for the town of Roseau River Reserve and the surrounding areas!"

Chief McIntyre received all sorts of disappointing messages from people of all walks of life. There were messages from relatives, friends, haters, politicians, and foreigners, who all felt the need to make their opinions known. Majority of the comments were against his bad handling of the precinct, which many people had complained about for years. Police Chief McIntyre would have preferred to keep his job, but with the massive drop in his approval ratings and the lack of support, he was pressured from the department and therefore resigned.

Five days after the police chief resigned, the phone specialist who the federal agents sent Evander's cellular to in Quebec, repaired the device and mailed it back to them. The agents were all sitting around the office disappointed they knew who Evander's killer was; yet could not arrest him without proper evidence. They had searched everywhere for the 9mm Ray used to kill his victim, yet they had no luck at finding it thus far. None of them had spoken to the repair specialist since they sent off the phone, therefore they were elated when the specially mailed package arrived with the phone. The only thing they needed to do was power on the device before they were abled to look through its contents. Everybody kept their fingers crossed when Agent Wu began checking the messages and came across the discussions between Evander and Rochelle. Evander was so fascinated with Rochelle that he saved every message they shared; therefore, the agents were able to view all the conversations that led up to the murder. In addition to the text messages were the sex videos and naked pictures of Rochelle, which were more than enough to make any husband crazy.

The New Interim Police Chief, Tod Humez, had placed Officer Pedward under suspension until the Evander Simms matter had been resolved. As a result, the officer was home preparing to barbecue and sizzle up some stakes for the wife and himself. Their little Yorky overheard something outside and began barking continuously, but the loud music drowned out her tiny bark. Outside the house were agents circling the exterior, to block off all access points and ensured their assigned target did not find a way to escape. Ray had just seasoned up the stakes and was about to carry them outback for the barbecue when their doorbell rang. Rochelle went to respond to the door; but bent down to pick up her annoying dog before she opened the lock.

"Federal Agents madam, we're here to take Officer Ray Pedward into custody," Agent Legot stated as he showed Rochelle the warrant and stood by the door!

Ray turned and saw Rochelle looking back at him with a concerned stare. The agents did not wish to storm the residence and get into a shootout with the officer, so they stood by the entrance with Rochelle. The officer's service pistol was on the counter approximately three yards away from him. When Officer Pedward turned back around and looked through the patio door, there were three armed agents aiming their weapons at him. It was a possibility that the agents found something to advance their case, however Ray thought it was highly unlikely, so he placed the plate on the counter and slowly raised his hands. Once the agents realized Ray was surrendering, they slowly moved in and placed him in handcuffs. The sight of her law enforcement husband in handcuffs brought tears to Rochelle's eyes, however the agents allowed Ray to give her one final kiss as he went by. Agent Wu read the officer his rights while they walked him out of the house and into an awaiting cruiser. Within fifteen seconds after they escorted Ray through the door, all the agents and their vehicles were gone. Rochelle was left standing there hugging her dog with an astonished look on her face, before she angrily slammed the door shut.

Chapter 40

Robin felt as though she was trapped between four walls without an exit. She found herself crying all the time and felt depressed as if she was no longer valuable. There was no going to school, work, or even church, in fact her entire world stopped turning and all she wanted to do was crawled into a hole and died. The young and talented female, who only few weeks prior felt as though she was on top of the world, found herself contemplating suicide. Two days after the rape incident, Robin went into the bathroom to take a shower. After she removed all her clothes she stood before the mirror staring at herself for a while, then decided to wash her face, and opened the Medicine Chest to get her personal soap. Celine left a razor that she used to shave her legs on the second shelf, which Robin picked up and looked at, before she started breaking away the plastic covering. When she finally broke away the plastic wrapping to expose the razorblade, she looked at her wrist and thought to cut her vein; but paused and looked at herself in the mirror. Her eyes drifted to the chain around her neck, then all she could see in the mirror was Lloyd's face staring at her. It was as if she had fallen into a trance and only awoke when Lloyd yelled, "No", at which she tossed the razorblade into the trash can.

Whenever Celine returned home from work, she went directly into Robin's room and checked on her. That evening after she looked in on her daughter who was asleep, she was seated on the toilet when she observed the broken razor inside the garbage can. Celine picked up the razorblade and thought to herself, then covered her mouth in fright as she imagined her daughter harming herself with it. Although she recalled seeing Robin breathing as she slept, as soon as she got off the toilet, flushed it, and washed her hands, the mother rushed back into her teenager's room. To ensure Robin was not injured, Celine turned on the light, removed the blanket, and physically checked her.

The fear Celine felt knowing Robin could have injured herself, compelled her to collect all the sharp blades from the bathroom and all throughout the remainder of the house. Due to concerns for her child's safety, Celine only left the butter knives for everyone's usage. The concerned mother knew she would have never forgiven herself if her child harmed herself, therefore she brought all the sharp blades in a pillowcase outside to her vehicle. Celine wanted to lock the blades inside her father's old shed, in the back yard, but the seventeen inches of snow they received during the storm made accessing it difficult. After she confiscated all the blades Celine went back inside and went to her mother's room, to inform her of what she assumed and did as a result.

There were no outreach programs for such mentally challenged individuals in Dominion City, so Robin had no professional assistance to help her get through the emotional roller-coaster. Whenever her guardians tried discussing what happened to show Robin it was OK to talk about, she went into a quiet mode and would storm off into the bathroom. Celine and Miss Shirley knew as women that she needed the emotional support, therefore they tried being there for her, but it was evident that she needed someone else to speak with. Rather than being too proud to ask for help, Celine swallowed her pride and telephoned the only person who Robin seemed interested in speaking with. Julious had been there for her daughter unconditionally even without having any idea what she had been through. The Simms family were experiencing their own personal trauma, but it was important that they supported each other. What happened to Robin was not something the family wanted everyone to know, yet Celine felt they needed to tell Julious and thus contacted him and told him.

Robin's rapist had not only taken her self-esteem, but she felt vulnerable as though she had to hide from the world. The family had asked the police not to release their information for privacy reasons, therefore they expected their wishes to be respected during their tough times. Due to the victim's age the media could only report certain things about the case, nevertheless reporters were eager to get her story. The pressure the family was under trying to get Robin back to herself was immense, hence everyone was on edge. Although Robin would prefer to suffer in silence and insisted that Miss Shirley and her mother went about their daily routines, her grandmother chose to remain at home with her regardless of what she requested. Celine was at work by the front desk several days later when she received a phone call from a private number.

"Hello," Celine responded!

"Is this Celine Devers, mother to Robin Walker," a French accent female asked?

"Yes, I am," Celine said!

"Madam, I am telephoning you today because we would like to interview your daughter..." the female continued?
"Where the hell did you get my number? Listen bitch, leave my damn daughter alone and don't you ever call back my phone," Celine yelled before she hung up the call!

Everyone inside the gym heard Celine and began looking if she was OK. With everyone staring at her, the gym owner calmly exited the building and walked out to her vehicle. Celine knew her reaction was unprofessional, but they had been so overwhelmed with Robin's problems that she lost it momentarily. The irritated mother went into her van and began crying due to her situation, not knowing if her daughter would experience a complete mental breakdown and thus had to get admitted to a psychiatric ward. With so many visiting protesters already on edge over the Evander Simms murder, the family wanted to avoid creating another demonstration event.

Julien still had to attend school without his bigger sister, but he was more settled and had way more friends, so he managed on his own. Robin gradually went into isolation from being raped and did not wish to speak to any of her friends. As a result, she refrained from answering any of their calls and muted her phone, so as not to be disturbed. The first few days of Robin's absence went basic enough for Julien, but once a week went by with church services included, all her friends began wondering if she was OK. Students who Julien never met began stopping him randomly across the school compound to enquire about his sister. To encourage Robin and assured her that people were concerned and cared for her, Julien made sure he transferred every message he received for her. Kim and Erica who were also members of Robin's church, went as far as to ask Miss Shirley about her granddaughter, who was said to be under the weather.

Robin's assault gave Celine a different outlook on the safe community she grew up in. It was evident that times and some of the people in town had changed, therefore she had to change with the changes. There were days when she would allow the kids to either walk to or from school by themselves, but those days for her were over. Dominion City was a town where the children were always safe, but Robin's incident and the fact that the culprit was still at large changed Celine. Julien had friends he could have walked with, who lived relatively close to his house, yet his mother preferred picking him up in the afternoons. With a business to manage and time of the essence, Celine brought Julien back to the gym, until she finished working then they went home together.

When Coy learnt that Johnny was the suspected perpetrator, he drove to his mechanic shop early the morning and searched through his pile of receipts for an invoice with the accused name. Once Coy found the receipt, he looked around the shop and picked up a three-foot piece of metal pipe, before he jumped back into his vehicle and drove to the address on the paper. The light of a new day was barely across the skies, yet Coy pulled onto Johnny's parent's driveway and ran up to the door.

"Boom, boom, boom," sounded the door as Coy banged on it with the pipe iron! "Boom, boom, boom!"

"Johnny, Johnny! Get out here you damn rapist," Coy yelled!

"Who is that? Johnny is not here! I'm calling the police, so you better leave," the scared old man inside said!

"Johnny! I'm going to kill you for touching my niece you son-of-a-bitch," Coy shouted as he banged the pipe iron against the door!

"I told you that Johnny is not here! Please go away? The phone is ringing with the police," the old man yelled!

The loud exchange was alerting other neighbors, therefore Coy ran back to his vehicle, jumped in, and drove away. As an uncle living in the house where his niece had been raped, it was heartbreaking for Coy to watch her deteriorate from the lively teenager she was. He drove back to his garage and parked his car inside an open bay, then closed the hanger door to hide it in case someone caught the make and color. It was never Coy's intention to scare Johnny's parents, however he thought the old man's son was cowardly hiding inside the house. The pressure that Celine and Miss Shirley were experiencing had gotten to him, still he regret frightening the old man who could have gotten a heart attack.

While investigators waited for the results from Robin's rape examinations, they named Johnny Webber as 'a person of interest'. The case was given to Detective Folier who immediately went and spoke with Officer Burney, who had interviewed the victim. The details of the case were still quite fresh to Officer Burney, who was deeply sympathetic toward Robin. The female officer desperately wanted them to arrest the perpetrator, thus she told the detective all she learnt from the family. Detective Folier tried to authenticate the information they received from Celine, who testified that 'she assaulted Johnny at a party for indecent remarks she overheard him making about Robin'. To justify what Celine said the detective spoke with Karen at the grocery store, as well as Mauve and Mark who were also present at the party. All three friends testified to the same chain of events, during which they stated, "Celine overheard Johnny from inside the bathroom, before she exited and warned him about her daughter." When Detective Folier spoke with Veronica at the shooting range, she confirmed that Johnny had been watching their new employee. Veronica told the detective that, "They were concerned about Johnny stalking them, but he was a member of the club, so he had all rights to be on the premises."

As person who was already known to the department for watching young girls, Detective Folier had no option than to name Johnny Webber as someone they needed to speak with. To get Johnny into the station for questioning, Detective Folier searched for his criminal file and located his personal information. The evidence the officers had to effectively arrest the rapist was being analyzed to determine the correct culprit, therefore the officers had to wait a few weeks for the results. Until they received the results, they could not get a warrant to bring in their primary suspect, so the detective called the number listed on Johnny's past arrest report. The phone number was no longer in service, so Detective Folier coupled with Officer Burney to visit the address on file. Both officers drove together in Officer Burney's cruiser to Johnny's parent's house. When they knocked the door, it took almost three minutes for the old man to respond, but they could here him inside saying he was on his way.

"Good day sir, I'm Detective Folier and this is Officer Burney," Detective Folier introduced!

"Oh! More police officers, what can I do for you both," Mr. Webber said?

"More police officers! Were there other officers here already today," Detective Folier asked?

"Yes, earlier this morning some crazy guy was banging off my door, yelling for my son! When I told him my son wasn't here and I was calling the police, he finally stopped and ran away! Look here, I even showed the other officers who came by, where that lunatic was banging on my door," Mr. Webber answered!

"We are sorry to hear about your experience this morning Mr. Webber, but your son wouldn't happen to be home, would he," Officer Burney asked?

"What has he done now," Mr. Webber enquired?

"Nothing for sure sir, we just wanted to ask him a few questions about an incident that happened," Officer Burney said.

"No! Sorry you guys came all this way, but Johnny has been away at work since the beginning of the month," Mr. Webber stated!

"Do you know where your son work sir," Detective Folier asked?

"Junior works for some construction company in Winnipeg. I can't seem to remember the name right now, but they send that boy across the province to work at different places sometimes," Mr. Webber declared.

"Do you have any idea when he would be back," Officer Burney asked?

"Sorry officer, but I have no idea," the old man said.

"Thank you for your help, Mr. Webber," Detective Folier exclaimed before they began walking away!

"Oh, Detective Folier, the name of that construction company was Sydney Construction," Mr. Webber recalled!

"Thank you again for that information sir," Detective Folier remarked!

The officers located the business information for Sydney Construction Company in South Winnipeg and telephoned the head office to enquire about Johnny whereabouts. The female who responded to the call transferred them to her manager, who had the information about all their employees. It took the manager a few minutes to contact the site foreman and retrieved the information, at which he told the officers that Johnny had not been at work for the past three days. Detective Folier found their suspected rapist sudden disappearance strange, so he asked the manager where was Johnny scheduled to work, and the location they housed him while he was there?

Sydney Construction had a new condominium housing project in East St. Paul, which was several kilometers north-east of Winnipeg. To get more information on Johnny's whereabouts, the officers drove to East St. Paul, and found the residence on Glenlivet Way where the employee temporarily stayed. When the officers reached the location and spoke with two of Johnny's roommates, they learnt that he had left to visit a friend one evening and had not returned. All of Johnny's belongings were left at the residence, which led the officers to believe something was wrong.

Officer Burney felt disappointed they were unable to find Johnny for questioning. The female officer thought that Johnny's disappearance maybe due to his guilt, therefore he went on the run to avoid getting caught. There was something weird about Johnny's disappearance that did not sit well with Detective Folier, who sat in the cruiser quietly thinking about everything they had learnt. The idea that Johnny went away to work yet went missing, had the detective wondering if someone else had found the old man's son. Maybe Johnny had perished for messing with the wrong person's daughter, there were too many unknowns to his disappearance, therefore Detective Folier went on their on-board computer to check their police database. Seconds after the detective inserted Johnny's name and pressed enter, the man for whom they searched appeared as a RCMP detainee.

Rather than driving back to Roseau River Reserve without accomplishing their mission, the officers drove to the RCMP station on Dominion Street in Winnipeg. Detective Folier and Officer Burney knew several of the officers and commanders employed at the location, therefore they had a chance to speak with Johnny without a signed consent form from their superiors. When they entered the facility Detective Folier asked the desk officer to speak with his commander, to whom they could explain their current situation. A Lieutenant Mackridge went out and spoke with the officers, who explained the entire scenario that led to them being there. Ironically Johnny was being held on similar charges, after he approached a fourteen-year-old local girl and made advancements toward her. The suspected rapist was arrested when he went to meet up with the under-aged girl, whom he telephoned and made a date to spend time with. To get clearance for the interview Lieutenant Mackridge brought the matter to Chief Dufort, who approved the detective's request without bias.

The Dakota Ojibwe Precinct officers were led into an interrogation room, where they sat and waited for Johnny to get transferred into. After ten minutes of waiting an officer led Johnny into the room and removed his handcuffs for them to sit and chat. Officer Burney had an extremely serious look on her face, from being in the child molester's presence. Johnny sat down across from the officers, thinking they were there due to his latest charge.

"How are you doing, man? I'm Detective Folier and this is Officer Burney from the Dakota Ojibwe Police Department," Detective Folier said.

"What the hell y'all doing all the way up here," Johnny argued?

"We are investigating the Robin Walker's case! I'm sure you remember her.

The little girl you raped during our last snowstorm," Officer Burney barked out!

"Man, I ain't raped nobody," Johnny declared!

"Where were you on that night of the snowstorm," Detective Folier asked?

"I was back at the place I stayed, plus I even have witnesses," Johnny said!

"All your so-called witnesses aren't going to save you when those tests results come back," Officer Burney threatened!

"You are currently being charged for messing with minors. Why should anyone believe that you did not rape this other little girl," Detective Folier asked?

"All I know is I never raped anybody in Dominion City," Johnny insisted!

"We never mentioned anything about where this crime took place," Detective Folier stated!

"Well, where else could it have been? I mean that's where that girl Robin lives," Johnny clarified.

"Why didn't you inform your boss about what happened to you," Detective Folier asked?

"And what's the sense of that? If that damn judge had sent me home when I went to court, they would have never found out about this," Johnny declared!

The officers were through questioning Johnny, therefore they got up and signaled the officer to open the door. Once the officer opened the door, the visitors exited the room and left Johnny yelling, "I did not rape no under-aged girl! You heard me detective! I did not rape no under-aged girl!"

Chapter 41

I t was a tough three weeks for the Simms family from the moment they discovered Evander's body. The family had to visit the coroner department at Morris General Hospital, where Evander's body was taken following its discovery. Evelin could not conjure up the strength to go to the morgue and identify her son, therefore Julious and his father did the honors. When they reached the hospital, Gary checked the information board for the department they wanted. Getting to the morgue was slightly challenging, as they had to walk to a secondary elevator, rode a car to the basement, then walked through a maze of corridors. The temperature inside the hospital gave Julious the chills, but when they stepped inside the morgue, he felt as though someone had thrown him inside the frozen waters of Roseau River. Julious had always known his father to be an iron man, whom he had never seen shed a tear. However, when the pathologist brought them beside the body and lifted the sheet off Evander's face, Mr. Simms broke down crying like a child. The sight of his son's lifeless body became unbearable for Gary; hence he squeezed Julious' shoulder while he hugged him.

"Is this your son Mr. Simms," the pathologist asked?

When Julious saw that his father was having a difficult time speaking, he looked at the doctor and said, "That is my, brother!"

The doctor thought that seeing Evander's face was too much for his siblings and started covering him. "No, no, no, wait! I need to see how my son died," Gary requested?

"Well, Mr. Simms your son was shot sixteen times," the pathologist answered.

"Can we see it," Gary asked?

"No problem, sir, if you insist," the pathologist responded as he lowered the sheet!

Julious' eyes were filled with water, mainly from watching his father's twist of emotions. When the doctor lowered the sheet and he saw how dismembered his brother's body was, the young man's tears began flowing freely. Gary stood over his son's corpse staring at him for several minutes, as if he was coming to terms with what happened. After he was done looking at Evander, Gary covered his son with the sheet himself. There were some documents prepared for Gary to sign, which stipulated that they had positively identified the body. Having completed the requirements for which they went to the hospital, Gary and Julious then left and went home.

Evelin awaited their findings with mixed emotions, therefore as much as she wished it was not Evander, she wanted it to be him. Gary and Julious returned with the news she dreaded hearing, yet the disturbing reality was more of a relief. Knowing that Evander was deceased gave them the opportunity to prepare a funeral, rather than the emotional turmoil they had experienced with him missing. Evander's murder had sparked a criminal investigation; therefore, his body was not released to his family for burial for nearly three weeks. The corpse was scheduled for an autopsy sometime during the first two weeks of recovery, due to a staff shortage at the hospital. Until the body was cleared by police, the family purchased the burial lot, Evander's casket, and a suit for him to get buried in. Nearly everything was prepared for the funeral, nevertheless, they still had to wait until the body got released.

News of Officer Pedward's arrest came as a surprise to the Simms family, who like most people throughout the territory believed the officer was guilty. It was impossible for the agents to notify the family before they made the arrest, therefore they found out once the story exploded across the airwaves. Pedward's arrest occurred at a time when neither Evelin nor Gary felt assured, they would ever receive any justice for their son's murder. The officer's incarceration gave the mourning parents hope their son won't die in vain, regardless of the reason he was killed.

When Agent Legot contacted Gary Simms two and a half weeks after Julious and he identified the body, the agent wanted to inform them that they could proceed with Evander's funeral. Once the family received the clearance, Evander's funeral got scheduled within days of the actual event. Gary was very appreciative for the call from Agent Legot, yet he also had to thank the agent for putting Officer Pedward behind bars. The first person they contacted once the body got released was Pastor Roundtree, who was to perform the burial service. With everything already prearranged, it was just a matter of letting those involved know the date of the proceedings, therefore Evander's funeral was to take place in four days.

Evelin wanted to have a small and private ceremony, with only Evander's dearest friends and several of her church adherents. Whenever Evander's body was released to them, his parents planned on having his viewing before the actual funeral service. People throughout the community had different views of the case, so the family only wanted enough privacy to bury their relative without some grand spectacle. To get an estimated count of those who were attending,

Evelin asked Julious to contact Robin and asked if she would be coming with the rest of her family? Julious had tried to get Robin out of her house several times since the assault, but she was still uncomfortable being around people. Although Julious did not want her to feel pressured, he thought there would only be a few people if she accepted, hence he phoned to ask her.

"Hello," Robin responded after the phone rang several times!

"Hey! How are you, feeling today," Julious remarked?

"I was just dozing off and the phone woke me up," Robin said!

"I'm sorry for, disturbing you! I could call, you back later," Julious stated!

"No, it's OK! I can't sleep comfortable anyways. Chances are I'll wake up sweating from a nightmare. What's been going on with the choir," Robin said?

"They have no, more life in, the music. We all miss, having you there," Julius answered.

"Tell them all I said hello! I wish I was well enough to come back to church, but I..." Robin started!

"I am going, to tell you, something I never, told anyone before. When I was, around fourteen I, was in a, dark place in, my life so, I wanted to, commit suicide. I felt like, I was holding, all my family, members back from, doing what they, wanted to do. So I thought, it would be, better if I, was not around!"

Robin could hear Julious sniffling and crying as he revealed something that was difficult for him to talk about. The Artistic young man caught her attention when he mentioned the word suicide, which was something she had been grappling with.

"I was at, home alone one, day searching for, a pliers when, I found a, piece of rope, in my father's, tool cupboard. I took the, rope and made, a noose and, was going to, put it around, my neck but, then I thought, what when my, mother finds me, strung up like, that! I could not, go through with, it after that! Since that happened, every time I, think about suicide, I think about, my mother's love, for me," Julious said!

Robin found herself crying at the end of Julious' story. She was at that dark place Julious spoke of being but had no idea how to pull herself from the abyss. Listening to Julious talk about surviving such a depressive state, allowed her to realize that people have gotten pass the emotional unbalance she was experiencing. The tone of her artistic friend's voice also encouraged her to discuss whatever bothered her, regardless of how difficult that was.

"I was... Ah! Raped by someone on my way home from work," Robin began, as she started choking up. "He knocked me down with his car, and when I was trying to get up, he hit me across my face! I must have blocked out, because when I woke up, I was out by the cemetery, with half of my clothes off!"

"I am sorry, to hear that, happened to you! Even though you, are very beauti-ful, no man should, rape a woman! I guess that, is why you, don't want to, leave your house," Julious remarked.

"I'm scared to go anywhere, even the bathroom," Robin joked!

"Well we are, going to have, to get you, out of that, afraid mode! I want you, to come to, my brother's funeral, with the rest, of your family," Julious exclaimed?

Robin paused and could be heard breathing yet said nothing for a few sec-onds, "OK! I'm going to come!"

Many out of towners still cared about the injustice done to Evander, hence once word broke that Officer Pedward had been taken into custody, they gath-ered at the Dakota Ojibwe Police Precinct in Roseau River Reserve and protest-ed. At the height of their protest, nearly seven thousand people were present and swarmed the police precinct, and thus made it difficult for officers to get in and out of their headquarters.

At Evander's viewing early that Saturday morning, a crowd of people began arriving some two hours before the proceedings was set to commence. When Pastor Roundtree and his wife arrived nearly an hour later to open the church doors, they were surprised to see the lineup of viewers that stretched from the church door, all the way down the street. The pastor telephoned Evelin and asked her if she had changed the list of attendants from private to public? It was hectic inside the Simms house that morning with everyone getting ready to head out to the funeral, so Evelin was confused by the pastor's question. Pastor Roundtree further explained that 'there were already hundreds of people wait-ing in line for the viewing', which came as a total shock to Evelin.

Winter had finally broken its strangle hold on the Manitoba climate, therefore the outdoor temperature was balmy. The cool air in the early morning was easi-ly subdued with a light jacket or a sweater, so everybody was modestly comfort-able. The Simms family members arrived a short time after that conversation to find the line had been extended, from the point where Pastor Roundtree said it ended. From Evelin reached and saw the number of viewers lined up to see her son, she began crying and smudged her makeup even before the festivities began. As the family members went by perfect strangers, everyone they passed greeted them with well wishing and condolences. The hearse carrying the cas-ket arrived a few minutes after the Simms family parked and began walking up to the church. When Gary saw the hearse pulling up he abandoned his wife and son to assist the operator. Julious accompanied his mother into the church amid multitudes of greetings for which she was grateful, as a mother who lost her son horrifically.

Evander's casket was taken from the hearse and brought into the church, where Pastor Roundtree blessed it and said a prayer to begin the viewing. The family members were the first persons allowed time to spend with the deceased. Both Gary and Evelin stood by their son's casket, crying, and speaking to him as if he was just resting. Julious crept in during his parent's time with Evander, and stood there staring at his brother, whom he can't believe was gone. After they spent several more minutes saying their goodbyes, the family members moved on and allowed the viewers to begin paying their tributes. The scheduled time for the viewing was 9:00 AM until 10:00 AM, due to the small number of visitors that were expected. From Pastor Roundtree saw the large crowd he pulled Evelin and Gary aside and informed them that 'there was no way the viewing would last for only an hour with that amount of people waiting'. The special guests who were on the list had not yet began arriving, still they had to commence the proceedings for the viewers to see Evander.

Julious grew concerned for Robin's mental health from the moment he saw the long line of people already at the church. He quickly contacted her cell phone while escorting his mother into the building, but she was inside the shower and did not hear the ringing. Pastor Roundtree wanted several added seats in case some of the viewers decided to stay for his sermon, so he gave Gary that project to manage. Gary wanted help rearranging some of the seats, in addition to bringing some extra chairs from a back room, so Julious got quite busy after he made the call. When Robin returned his call a few minutes later, he was busy holding some chairs with his father, and could not get to the phone inside his pocket. Robin sent him a text message several minutes later stating that 'they would be leaving their home quite soon', to make him aware her family was on route. By the time Julious got finished helping add the extra chairs and read the message, he assumed the Devers family were on their way to the church. The only person who Julious thought could prevent a possible meltdown by Robin was Celine, therefore he dialed her number.

"Hello," Celine responded!

"Hi, Mrs. Walker, this is Julious! I am sorry! My mother expected, to have a, small ceremony for, my brother's funeral, but all these, people showed up, before we got, here! It maybe a, good idea not, to bring Robin," Julious exclaimed!

Celine and the rest of the family members were elated that Robin chose to attend the funeral and got out the house. Although they were ecstatic about her brave decision, Celine could not afford to make one event destroy her daughter forever. They were two blocks away from the church, so before they arrived and the mounting pressure caused Robin to suffer a nervous breakdown, Celine pulled the Cherokee to the side of the road. Coy sat alongside her sister in the front cabin, while their mother and Robin sat in the center seats, and Julien occupied the rear seat. Once she brought the vehicle to a stop, Celine spun around and faced her daughter while she addressed her.

"Robin, Julious is on the phone, and he said, 'tons of people showed up unexpectedly at the church', so the funeral might not be as private as they planned for it to be. We really don't want to pressure you into feeling you have to go, so if you want to head back home, I'll turn right back around," Celine stated!

Robin looked down at her hands and pounded her left fist into her right palm. She began imaging the times she saw Evander and how pleasant his smiles always were. There was no doubt that Julious loved his bigger brother, therefore she had to attend to support her dear friend.

"It's OK mom, you can keep going," Robin then declared.

"Ah, Julious, does that mean we have to join the line," Celine then questioned?

"No, Mrs. Walker! You guys can, come right inside, the church," Julious said.

"OK, we'll be there in a few minutes," Celine added!

The invited guests began arriving and were all surprised to see the lineup of people, therefore Evelin began receiving multiple calls. To avoid disturbing the viewing, Evelin had to turn off her phone volume and rushed to the back of the church to speak with each caller. Everyone who phoned had the same concern, therein they wanted to enquire 'if they needed to join the long line'?

The lineup of viewers slowly went by the coffin showing their respects until the last couple at 11:50 AM. The ceremony was planned as a private event, nevertheless each viewer felt they needed to show their support for Evander and thus attended. Most of those who went to the viewing left once they saw Evander, but several of the viewers stuck around for the ceremony. The honored guests did not get their chance to view Evander's body until the lineup of viewers had ended. Many of Dominion City United adherents who knew Evander, recalled when he used to attend church regularly with his mother. Even though the murdered young man was no longer a regular, the members still considered him as one of their own. Celine and Julien didn't know Evander as well as most, but they accompanied Miss Shirley and Robin who could hardly stop crying. Marshon and Coy spent the second longest time beside the casket speaking to their co-worker for the very last time. The two mechanics took Evander's murder the toughest, thus they cried so hard that they had to console each other to get through the viewing. It was indeed a day of sorrow for most of those who attended the funeral, as all across the church hall were the sounds of sniffles.

There was only a small amount of Evander's service programs printed, on account of the number of guests who were invited. Those who showed up unannounced to pay their respects were not given any of the service programs, yet some of them participated in singing the hymns. Pastor Roundtree stepped to a microphone that was placed beside the casket and began addressing the crowd. The hall was packed with mourners who all gathered to say goodbye to a talented man, who was gunned down for loving another man's wife.

"I would like to thank all of you for attending Mr. Evander Simms funeral service! I'm sure his parents, Evelin, and Gary, and even his brother Julious, appreciate you also for taking the time to help mourn their sibling! This morning, we have a eulogy for Evander being done by his aunt, Mavis Shuttlefield, we have a song being done by Kim and Erica Bledsoe, as well as a bible reading by Sister Lorna Tiller. To begin we would like to open with a hymn, so if we could get everyone to please rise? For those who have schedules, if you would like to turn to the first page, we will be singing Amazing Grace," Pastor Roundtree exclaimed!

The music began playing and nearly the entire church joined in the singing. Following the song, Pastor Roundtree stepped back to the microphone and said, "If you could all please remain standing, I would ask that you bend your heads with me in prayer, so as we may invited the lord into our holy midst," the preacher-man began? "Heavenly Father, we come together today to lay to rest Mr. Evander Winthorp Simms! During this time of serious tension, we pray for calm sweet Jesus, we pray that everyone involved avoid all conflict, and are abled to return home safely my God! Merciful Father, we ask that you be with his parents at this time Lord! We ask that you strengthen them and surround them with your angels, Hallelujah! They have been so worried about their son, that they have been away from the spiritual family, Sweet Jesus! May you bring them back into the fold, so we may pray for them, and glorify them with compassion, Oh God! We also asked that you take Evander into your bosom and keep him safe dear lord! We know without your blessings, we have no life Almighty God! So, for those in attendance, we ask that you bless their homes and their families, oh lord? Amen!"

"Amen," repeated the crowd!

The pastor invited up Evander's aunty Mavis Shuttlefield, who gave a stunning eulogy that lasted eighteen minutes. Pastor Roundtree then invited up Sister Lorna, who went up and read from the Bible Book of 1st Kings. At the conclusion of Lorna's reading, Pastor Roundtree invited up the singing sisters, who performed and had the entire audience rocking. Following all the performances it was time for the main event, therein the preacher-man stepped forth and delivered his most powerful speech ever. The pastor spoke of respect, trust, compassion, faith, and love, with such intrigue that he had most of those in attendance crying. After his lengthy speech the preacher had his audience sing the second song on the schedule, which was How Great Thou Art, before he said a final prayer and concluded.

Following the ceremony, the viewers began leaving while the invited guests got to view Evander for the final time. Robin's friends who watched her walk in with her family could not wait for the ceremony to end for them to maul her. There were so many people around Robin expressing 'how much they missed her' that Julious never got a chance to get anywhere close to her. Instead, their eyes met several times as they looked around for each other and would smile whenever they made contact. Julien stood protectively beside his sister throughout her dealings with her friends, rather than going off to hang with his associates. Evelin and others began reminding the invited guests, where the repas was scheduled to take place, whenever they left the cemetery. Once the family and friends got their last looks at Evander, the handler closed the casket and wheeled it out to the hearse. Evander's private funeral became a huge spectacle that not only interested the viewers who attended, but when the family exited the church, they realized a news reporter was on scene to capture the event.

When everyone was ready to leave the church, the hearse drove away first, followed by Gary Simms and his family. Pastor Roundtree and his wife were inside the third vehicle, with everyone else trailing behind. They drove to the graveyard a short distance away, where only those invited were allowed by the graveside. Even though there were only invited guests inside the cemetery, there were still several out-of-towners who stood outside the walls watching the proceeding unfold. Pastor Roundtree again took charge and began the burial proceeding with the third song on the schedule, which was Morning Has Broken. The funeral had exceeded the time frame it was scheduled into, therefore the preacher had to hasten his final thoughts. The lengthy time in church also meant his adherents would need nutrition, thus the pastor added another prayer, before he led them into the final song on page four, which was The Lord is my Shepherd.

Evelin had made arrangements with two of her church adherents to cater the food, therefore everything was prepared and waiting for the mourners to arrive. The caterers had brought the food over to the Shooting Range, which she rented from the owner for the repas. Julious had not had a chance to hug and speak with Robin, therefore he went to the lounge expecting to consume all her time. Robin started feeling a little lightheaded when they were at the church, but she attributed it to over anxiety and brushed it off. When they reached the graveyard, she stood beside her mother and Coy for several minutes before she accompanied Julien back to the vehicle and stayed there. Julien started complaining he was hungry, so when they reached the lounge Celine quickly brought them food. They were all seated at a table with some of Miss Shirley's friends, when Robin took a bite from the Barbecue Chicken on her plate. Almost instantly she jumped up, holding her hands over her mouth, and ran towards the bathroom. Celine went after her to see what was wrong and entered the restroom to find Robin vomiting in the toilet. The concerned mother immediately developed flashbacks, wherein she recalled the circumstances that led to her discovering she was pregnant with Robin.

"Oh my God! You are pregnant," Celine exclaimed just by looking at her daughter!

Robin looked back at her mother as if she was crazy, then continued puking. Celine recalled getting sick after some strange woman revealed to her that she was pregnant, so to avoid her suspicions and the numerous questions, she decided to take her daughter home. Julious' entourage was parking in the parking lot when he noticed Celine ushering Robin away from the venue and into their Cherokee, as if she was her daughter's private security. Before they could park and give him the chance to say hello, Celine sped from the parking lot as if they had an emergency. Julious felt disappointed he would not get to spend some time with Robin, for whom he had developed strong feelings.

Chapter 42

Kyler pulled up at the gas station and was the third in line behind two vehicles, which both had out of the province license plates. It had been raining for most of the day, which was typical for the Spring Season. The plate on the Mazda ahead of him said, Newfoundland & Labrador and there were two people inside the car. It took Kyler a little while longer to make out the front camper's license plate number, which identified the vehicle as an American tourist from Texas. Before taking a drink from the bottle of Vodka between his legs, the male customer looked around to ensure nobody was watching. Julious was the gas attendant servicing the customers up ahead, therefore Kyler expressed a devious smirk.

The raincoat that Julious wore kept him quite dry from the showers and allowed their customers to remain inside the vehicles. Each time the Applewick brothers went to the gas station and got served by Julious, they mimicked and teased him with racial slurs. From Julious saw the brother's vehicle his mood changed, knowing they were troublemakers who always picked on him. Evander was forced to threaten the Applewicks to leave his brother alone, but without him around the gas attendant feared he would experience increased pressure. As Kyler waited for Julious to finish filling up a camper, he noticed there was a brown couple from India inside the Mazda. The couple from Newfoundland & Labrador was headed south toward the U.S Border, but Kyler mistook them for protesters and began honking his horn.

The couple inside their vehicle began looking back through their rear-view glass, wonder what the problem was. Kyler lit himself a cigarette and began puffing on it, while he pressed the horn every five seconds. Bruce who owned the gas bar looked out through a window from the attached convenience shop and saw the make of the vehicle honking its horn. The rain was coming down heavily and the last thing he wanted to do was leave his dry and cozy spot, but that was a situation that could have escalated easily.

"God damn it, here we go again," Bruce stated to himself as he grabbed his cellular phone, threw on his raincoat, and walked out to Kyler!

Julious finished refilling the camper's gas tank and collected a debit card payment. The Caucasian couple inside their camper from Texas was happy to pull away from the service station, fearing the agitating customer might have gotten violent. The Mazda driver quickly pulled up to the attendant, but only opened his window a small fraction.

"How may I, help you," Julious asked?

"Yes, could you fill up the gas tank," the male driver asked?

"No problem just, open the lid, for me please," Julious asked?

Bruce walked up to Kyler who had his music loud and his window rolled up shut. Although Kyler saw him coming, he held his head straight and tried avoiding the business owner. To get the troublemaker to stop honking the horn every few seconds, Bruce knocked on the window to get his attention. Rather than lowering the window immediately Kyler acted as if the button could not work, then signalled that he could do nothing about the problem. After Bruce motioned him to open the window several times, Kyler finally rolled the window down and spoke to the owner.

"I'm sorry, but my button wasn't working," Kyler lied!

"Can you stop honking the horn please," Bruce asked?

"Why don't you stop serving all those blacks and different nations of people who come here," Kyler shouted?

"Sir, if you don't like our policy, you are free to find another gas provider somewhere else," Bruce argued!

"You only say that because you know there is no other station anywhere near here," Kyler exclaimed!

"If you keep blowing your horn and disturbing my customers, you might find yourself having to drive to the closest gas bar next time," Bruce warned!

"I don't think you would want to see your business go up in flames," Kyler remarked?

"Was that a threat," Bruce asked?

"Of course not! I'm just saying that you know how these old places go up in smoke sometimes. Nobody wants that to happen," Kyler declared!

"Get your gas and move on Applewick! One of these days, you boys will get what you got coming," Bruce stated as he walked back to the shop!

By the time Kyler refocused on the Mazda, the vehicle was pulling away from the pump having been served. Another customer had driven onto the property and stopped behind Kyler; thus, the driver honked his horn when he realized the vehicle ahead of him was not moving. After hounding the Indians inside the Mazda, both Bruce and Julious found it hilarious that the same treatment was given to Kyler. When the bigot finally pulled up to the pump, he was so irate that he only requested the $20 gas he wanted. To avoid giving the troublemaker any ammo to begin insulting him, Julious remained quiet throughout the transaction and only did his job. For payment he stepped to the vehicle door and could smell the liquor coming from Kyler, who purposely dropped the money on the ground. When the agitator finally drove away angry, Julious felt as though he had gained a victory, but he expected a very fierce reprisal.

The thirst for revenge ate at Kyler as he drove down Waddle Avenue. He looked over at the passenger side footrest area, where he had a can of white spray paint. What he had to do seemed clear as daylight, yet he would have to wait until it got dark to implement his idea. The seasonal change also brought change to when outdoors got dark, compared to winter when it was night by 4:30 PM. To get his revenge, Kyler drove to Andrew's church and parked behind the building. As he went into ninja mode by pulling his hoodie over his head to hide his identity, then maneuvering his way across to the D.C United Church, Kyler failed to realize that he was being surveyed from he pulled onto the Catholic's property. Once he snuck his way over to the church, Kyler took the spray paint and wrote 'Niggers' across one of the side walls. After spray painting his graffiti, the hateful bigot ran back to his vehicle, climbed inside, and finished his bottle of Vodka. Kyler felt so proud of his actions that he tossed the bottle out onto the asphalt, so it shattered as he drove away.

The main cleaner for D.C United Church arrived at 8:25 the next morning, to begin doing some work on the grounds. Mr. Biggz had some flowers to plant and some grass seeds to sprinkle across the church lawn, so he pulled up and began unloading his supplies. When he went around to the side wall Mr. Biggz was appalled at what he saw, therefore he quickly telephoned Pastor Roundtree and informed him. The Dakota Ojibwe Police Station was contacted, and Officer Grey Gilmore responded to the alert. Officer Gilmore was on location for nearly eight minutes before Detective Folier arrived to begin an investigation. After the detective spoke with the emotional Mr. Biggz and a very angry Pastor Roundtree, he surveyed the scene, and began walking around to see if there were any surveillance devices about.

When Detective Folier reached the Catholic Church down the street, the first thing he noticed was the surveillance cameras mounted on the building. At the time when Kyler chose to cause his hate crime, the darkness that sat in helped to conceal the cameras, which recorded his every move. Detective Folier walked around to the parking lot and saw the broken bottle of Vodka on the ground, therefore he put on a pair of latex gloves, and placed the broken pieces of bottle into a plastic bag for evidence. To get the recordings from the church cameras, Detective Folier contacted the Catholic Church handlers and requested someone came by to assist him. Pastor Hemming was at the church within ten minutes and allowed the detective to look at their overnight recordings.

The D.C United Church handlers contacted the local news station, which sent a reporter to capture the story. For an area that had been plagued with such violence over the past few weeks, people were surprised that racist events kept occurring. Regardless of who the reporter spoke to, they believed their town was not racist, although they sighted that a few residents with such views may be sprinkled in the midst. When asked what percentage of the population they thought was racist, nobody could pinpoint an exact number. There was way more optimism toward where the country was going on the topic of race due to social media, rather than where they had been. Canadians on a whole felt pride that as a country they were better than the U.S with race relations.

It was 5:41 AM when a team of eleven officers from the Dakota Ojibwe Police Station executed a warrant for the arrest of Kyler Applewick. The two brothers were strung out on the sofas inside their living room, when the door got stumped in by the arresting officers.

"Police, police, put your hands up," yelled the first officer through the door!

Beast jumped up and fiercely growled as he charged at the officers, who were forced to open fire at the animal. Three bullets struck the dog as it charged and stopped him in his tracks, thus Beast fell dead at the base of the TV stand. Neither of the brothers heard any of the officers' alerts, but the loud gunshots awakened them instantly. The Applewick brothers had fallen unconscious under the influence of the methamphetamine they were smoking; therefore, they were lackadaisical in reacting to the police raid. Russell opened his eyes and saw his dog laying dead on the floor; thus, he callously jumped off the sofa and rushed the officers.

"Ahhh," Russell yelled as he attacked!

"We have a warrant! Get your ass on the floor," yelled another officer through the door!

Even though the brothers opened their eyes once they heard the loud blasts, they were still quite discombobulated and unsure of what was transpiring. When the lead officer shot the dog, he froze for a milli-second with his service firearm pointed at the animal, to ensure that it was dead. Russell surprised the officer when he lifted him off the floor and slammed him on his back. The traumatized dog owner formed his right fist to strike the lawman for his pet. One of the officer's comrades used his Tazer Gun and shocked Russell on the side of his neck, which sent him crashing to the floor. The retaliating dog lover fell to the ground and began shaking while the officer continued administering the electric shocks. Kyler slowly opened his eyes and saw mirages of armed men, as two officers rushed towards him. Before the sought-after vandalizer could sit up on the short sofa, the officers grabbed him, and tossed him onto the floor on his stomach. The arresting officers aggressively placed both brothers in handcuffs and led them out the house into individual cars, that transported them to the station. The house was searched while officers waited for Animal Control, thereby three illegal weapons were found and seized.

The brothers were brought to court the following afternoon on separate charges and appeared before Provisional Judge Herbert Horn. Kyler was charged with Hate Crime, Vandalism, Weapons Violation, and Resisting Arrest after he shrugged multiple times when the officers tried to handcuff him. While being detained at the local jail, he contacted the Public Defender's Office and arranged for a lawyer to defend him when he got to court. The Public Defender's Office had one team of well qualified attorneys managing their criminal cases for the Southern Territory of Manitoba, and that team was led by an Asian female attorney. When Kyler got led into the courtroom and saw his attorney, he began throwing a temper tantrum as he walked to the bench. The judge was speaking with his court clerk and failed to see the accused.

"Your Honor, could I request a white lawyer," Kyler asked?

"Excuse me Mr. Applewick," Judge Horn asked?

"Sir, I would feel better represented, if a white lawyer handled my case," Kyler declared!

"Well Mr. Applewick we do not have another lawyer to take your case, so unless you wish to get out of lockup today, Miss Choo is all that is available to you," Judge Horn instruct!

Kyler looked at the Asian lawyer and her Caucasian assistant and said, "OK, judge!"

The proceedings began with a very insulted public defender, who remained professional throughout her presentation, nevertheless. The most serious charge that Kyler faced was the Hate Crime, which if convicted would have imprisoned him for a few years. The judge looked over Kyler's criminal history and saw that he had not been in trouble over the past three years, therefore he ordered the bigot released with a court date to appear for trial.

Russel was charged with Aiding and Abetting, Assaulting an Officer, Weapons Violation, and Resisting Arrest. From Judge Horn saw the last name Applewick and looked over the charges, he knew the type of personality to expect before Russel entered the courtroom. The judge watched as the court officer led a handcuffed Russell Applewick into his courtroom. Unlike his brother Kyler, Russell was heated from the moment he entered the courtroom, therefore he walked in with his head lowered and kept grumbling to himself. When he reached the bench and held up his head and saw the Asian attorney, the accused turned to the judge and said, "Your Honor, them police officers killed my dog! They shot my dog, man!"

"Please control yourself Mr. Applewick? I am sorry to hear of your dog," Judge Horn instruct!

Russell was aware that his brother had gotten bail with the Asian attorney's excellence, therefore he bit his lip about her representation and allowed them to proceed. The two brothers had been in trouble with the law many times, but when their mother got terribly sick a few years prior, they stopped going to jail for petty crimes. As a result, Russell had not been locked up for more than five years, therefore after his review of the accused criminal history, Judge Horn also released the other brother with a similar court date to address his charges.

Chapter 43

When Celine confirmed that Robin was pregnant, they had a serious discussion about what her daughter wanted to do. The thought alone of carrying a child for someone who assaulted and raped her was repulsive, hence Robin wanted whatever was inside of her out. Miss Shirley and Celine agreed with her one hundred percent; therefore, they made her an appointment at an abortion clinic in Winnipeg. As a woman Celine understood how tough such a decision was, hence, she brought her to her appointment at Doctor Rustiq's private clinic on Kenaston Boulevard. Robin felt nervous going to such a place, so she wore a track suit with a hoodie to cover her head. The mother and daughter had been through a lot, but regardless of their rocky relationship Celine was always by her side for support.

Doctor Rustiq's Clinic was on the third floor of an office building, toward the rear of the structure. Robin and Celine arrived ten minutes before their scheduled appointment and waited inside the patient's lounge after they finished filling out the questionnaire. When the time came for Robin to enter the operation room, she was incredibly nervous. Dr. Rustiq customarily went out and invited his clients back with him, therefore he eased her fears by assuring her that everything would be fine. The procedure was successful, and Robin left the clinic feeling encouraged that her life would not be ruined, by proceeding with such an emotional toll.

Dr. Rustiq's clinic was an attack forum for anti-abortion groups, that would revel in seeing the clinic closed its doors. While they were inside at Robin's appointment, eight women and three men who claimed they were pro-life supporters, arrived outside the building's entrance and began demonstrating. The protesters were all members of St. Barnabas Catholic Church, located on the west side of Winnipeg. The eleven demonstrators were walking in a circle holding up plaques, which read various statements pertaining to their anti-abortion stance. Neither Celine nor Robin could see the demonstrators from inside the building, therefore they were surprised when they exited and saw the group walking in circles.

"Oh, Sweet Jesus we must be cursed," Celine stated when she saw the demonstrators!

"Are you kidding me mom? And they couldn't protest anywhere else in town than here," Robin exclaimed as she quickly dragged her hoodie over her head?

"Just hold your head down and take your time," Celine stated, as they walked across to the van!

Robin was in a bit of pain after the procedure, so she walked very gingerly while she held onto her mother's hand. Contrary to her daughter Celine could care less what anyone thought of her, therefore hiding her identity did not appease her. When Robin thought matters could not get any worst due to the demonstrators, they saw a cameraman recording the demonstration from the sidewalk. There was no reporter interviewing the protesters, so Celine thought the cameraman was some unemployed freelancer. It was evident that Robin had just completed an abortion by her movements, thus the protesters began yapping all sorts of anti-abortion, pro-life statements.

"Why would a young woman like you want to throw away something beautiful that God gave you," one woman shouted?

"You are a murderer," another woman yelled!

"Abortion kills lives! That was someone you just threw away," a man shouted!

"God made us to produce children, not abort them," another woman shouted!

 Celine helped Robin into their vehicle and walked around to the driver's door. She made sure to pass where the demonstrators could see her clearly and extended her left middle finger at them. The cameraman caught the entire exchange as Celine climbed into her Cherokee, started the engine, and placed the gear shifter into drive. Some of the statements made by the demonstrators emotionally hurt Robin, who began crying and tucked her head close to her knees to avoid being seen. When Celine saw her daughter crying, she thought to pull out of the parking space and run them all over, but instead she turned toward the other exit and left the premises.

➤ ➤ ➤

Thomas had a business conference for the bank in Vancouver, BC, that he went to once each year. Jacquelin wanted to get away from Dominion City for a while, so he agreed to carry her and Viveen along for his five-day trip. Andrew would always accompany them wherever they went, but when his father asked if he wanted to tag along, he declined. On the morning before they left to catch their flight in Winnipeg, Jacquelin encouraged Thomas to try asking Andrew

320

once again to come with them, yet he adamantly declined.

Four days after the cameraman caught the video footage at the abortion clinic, the television program he recorded the piece for, aired it on national TV. After the United States changed their abortion laws, many Canadians wanted similar laws passed in their country. When the program 'Our Entire Canada' aired their piece on abortion, Andrew was at home alone playing his heavy metal music loud. He had the house to himself for several days, so the place resembled a pig's pen. There were dirty plates, glasses, and drug paraphernalia across the living room table and sofa. The television inside his bedroom was on, but he paid it very little attention as he danced around with a pair of Glock 17 in both hands.

"Pow, pow, pow, pow, pow....," Andrew kept saying as he imagined shooting people!

Andrew aimed one of the guns at the television set, when he saw a black male in an advertisement, then pretended he shot the actor. Immediately after that ad ended the station began airing their story on abortion. With a general election upcoming in two years many analyses predicted that abortion remaining legal across Canada would be a major topic on the ballad. As Andrew was about to turn away from the television, he caught sight of Celine extending her middle finger at the protesters. The last footage the cameraman caught of Celine, was while she sped by with her passenger holding their head down.

"What the hell have they done? What, what, what the hell were they doing there? You are supposed to be Christian people, the bible says true Christians must not go to such places as abortion clinics! Don't tell me she did! I mean she must have been pregnant for them to go there! Of course, she was pregnant, she is supposed to be the mother for my children! And you were supposed to be my mother-in-law, you bitch! How dare you get rid of our child! Someone has to pay for this," Andrew said to himself as he stared at Robin's picture!

A wave of emotions overtook Andrew, who picked up his cellular, and dialed Pastor Hemming's phone number with tears rolling down his face! The phone rang as if the call would go unanswered, then at the last alert someone responded, "Hello, Pastor Hemming hear!"

"Forgive me Father, because I've sinned," Andrew pled as he sobbed?

"In whose eyes have you sinned my child," Pastor Hemming asked?

"In the eyes of humans, Father," Andrew cried!

"Never fear what humans may think of you my son, for it is in the eyes of the Lord alone that you should seek favor," Pastor Hemming said!

"Father Hemming, is it not written that a woman must obey her man, as her master," Andrew enquired?

"Yes, my child, a married woman should make her husband the king of their castle," Pastor Hemming stated!

"But didn't the bible warn Christians against committing abortion," Andrew questioned?

"That is correct my son, the bible teaches us that every life is precious! So, for anyone who violates the laws of God, they will feel his wrath," Pastor Hemming warned!

"What should I do about these voices in my head; and the evil thoughts that I have been having Father," Andrew asked?

"What sort of evil thoughts my child? Tell me of them," Pastor Hemming questioned?

"Evil thoughts to hurt people, Father Hemming," Andrew implied!

"And who specifically would you like to hurt my son," Pastor Hemming enquired?

"Those who were not born of true white blood! The Muslims, the blacks, the natives, I hate them all," Andrew stated!

"But you are forgetting that Jesus taught us to love each other, my son! What of all the great things that he did for mankind," the pastor declared?

"Even Jesus had limits to his love Father Hemming! When he went into the temple and saw all those false merchants, he hated them for ruining his father's house, and kicked them all out! I think you have shown me what I must do, Father! I need to take action like Jesus did," Andrew implied.

"Listen to me my son, I would like you to come back to church this Sunday, so that we can start working on strengthening your love for others," Pastor Hemming exclaimed?

"It's too late for me Father Hemming! I already made a date for tomorrow. I just want you to pray for my soul," Andrew asked before he disconnected the call?

Andrew went down to Thomas' weapon's storage and opened it. There were rifles and handguns displayed on the wall and boxes of ammunition on a lower shelf. The troubled young man grabbed an AR-15 Assault Rifle, an AK-47 Assault Rifle, and a StG-44 Assault Rifle, along with a box of ammunition for each weapon. After he brought those weapons upstairs, Andrew returned and selected a Glock 17 Blowback, with three extra magazines and another box of 9mm bullets. When he returned to his bedroom with the items, he began loading bullets into all the magazines and readied them for use. Once all the weapons were loaded, he grabbed the AR-15 Assault Rifle and began practicing preparing himself. Andrew moved through the house aiming the rifle at nearly everything, to assimilate his moving through a building. After he went around the house he ended back in his room, where he posed and admired himself holding the guns in the mirror. The confidence Andrew felt with the weapons in hand, led to him taking several pictures of himself, some of which he uploaded to his Social Medial page with the caption, 'Sleeper Cell'.

It had been several days since he last visited the Applewick brothers, so he packed up all his weapons and extra ammunition and went through his front door. Andrew drove to the brother's house, where they had just buried their dog Beast earlier that day and were mourning the animal. Most of Andrew's days away from his friends were spent locked inside his bedroom away from everyone else, so he had no knowledge of their arrest. The first indication Andrew got that something awful transpired at his friends' house, was when he saw the front door lock busted. To gain entry he simply pushed the door open and stepped inside, where the brothers were smoking and drinking like usual. When Beast neither ran to him nor growled, was his second clue that something awful had transpired.

"What the heck happened around here," Andrew asked?

"The cops paid us a visit. Came here with a warrant for my arrest, for spray painting all over them nigger's church," Kyler stated!

"So, where is Beast? The cops have him impounded or something," Andrew asked while looking around?

"Them bastard cops killed my dog man," Russell declared!

"They did what," Andrew demanded as he walked over and sat beside Kyler?

"Yeah man, just buried Beast this morning," Kyler said as he finished rolling a joint!

"I'm sorry to hear about Beast guys! He was a soldier of a dog," Andrew remarked!

The meth laced joint got sparked and they all began getting intoxicated. There were beer and liquor available, so Andrew opened a can of brew and held it high.

"To Beast, the best dog I ever knew," Andrew toasted!

The two brothers raised their glasses and saluted that toast. Andrew felt poised to make a statement and wanted to know if any or both brothers would accompany him. He already had the weapons prepared to do work and only needed the manpower to handle the hardware. They had been friends for several months and Andrew joined their hate group primarily due to their tutelage, therefore he wanted to know if they were about the violence they had been projecting.

"So, what happened during the police raid," Andrew enquired?

"Dude it was crazy man! Them cops kicked the door in! Stupid idiots, they could have just turned the door handle, it was open already! After they came in,

Beast rushed them to tear them apart; but then, that cop shot him a few times! Man by the time I opened my eyes, I saw Rus holding one of them officers on the floor about to whoop his ass, until his partner started tazing the hell out of my brother! I was getting up to go help when two a them officers jumped me and slammed me on the floor! Locked us up for a while, but we passed court and got bail. So now we got court dates and all that crap to look forward to," Kyler explained!

"I think we should avenge Beast," Andrew stated!

"What," Russell asked?

"I think we should get revenge for beast," Andrew continued!

"And what do you propose we do to get revenge against the police for killing my dog," Russell asked?

"We commit a mass killing, like our true white patriot brothers in America," Andrew remarked!

"And that's your solution? Kill a bunch of cops to get killed by cops eventually," Russell countered!

"Yes, that was my plan! It's better than you sitting around here doing nothing but talking about stuff you'll never do! At least we'll die famous," Andrew argued!

"And what have you ever done, Andrew? Besides raped little teenage black girls! Oh yes, I figured you was the one who kidnapped that mixed girl that night, when no one else but you was out in those snowy conditions! So, don't come around here pretending as if you're all about white power, and you hate all other cultures, when you are raping little black girls! No matter how white she might appear, if any part of her past was mixed with anything but white, then she ain't a hundred percent Caucasian," Russell declared!

Kyler began laughing at the statement. "You joking! Say it ain't so Andrew? Oh, my lord, it's true! I can see it on your face! So, you would prefer turning down big girl Venise, who was more than willing to give you some, to go rape some black teenage girl? Man, you must be sick in your head bro!"

"I don't need no backup! You guys may laugh at me now, but you will be telling your kids and grandkids about my greatness," Andrew stated as he slowly got up as if he was about to leave!

Russell and Kyler were amused by his silly comment and began laughing at him. Andrew knew that the brothers must have been unarmed once the officers raided their house. He expected the officers to have removed every pistol the brothers illegally owned and laid charges against them, therefore he withdrew his Glock 9mm and callously shot Kyler three times.

"Andrew, Andrew, please, I was only playing around brother! Don't shoot me man, please," Russell begged as he held up both hands?

"I was willing to let you both live, to tell people my story. But they'll hear about me anyways," Andrew said before he opened fire and shot Russell four times!

It was no secret that the Applewick brothers were hated by their neighbors, as well as most of the town's residents. Aside from it being nearly impossible to hear gunshots because of the distance between houses, Andrew knew the brothers' neighbors stayed out their business. With his friends laying dead on both sofas, he sat back down beside Kyler and slid the ashtray over with the joint. Before he partook of the joint, he picked up his drink and held it high and said, "This is to you my brothers" then drank it!

When Andrew awoke the next morning, he sat forward on the sofa and stared blankly at the wall, as he contemplated what he had to do while he smoked the remainder of the joint. After he finished smoking, he walked into the bathroom and urinated in the toilet. The voices inside his head kept reminding him that 'he was disrespected so he must get revenge', therefore he flushed once done and stepped to the sink, where he washed his hands then washed his face. As he stared at himself in the mirror, he began talking to himself to encourage himself. He walked out into the days room where he stopped and looked at his deceased friends, then grabbed his belongings and checked the time. The clock on his cellular showed 10:23, which was the perfect time for him to strike. Andrew knew the police would be looking for him, but before they killed him or had him in custody, he wanted to make his statement.

With all the activity that surrounded Evander's discovery, several weeks passed with which Evelin and Julious missed attending church. Following the funeral during which Pastor Roundtree welcomed them back to the congregation, Gary decided to accompany his wife to church to gain some blessings. Julious was still extremely disappointed and heartbroken; therefore, he chose to stay home by himself.

Robin was saddened after her abortion clinic experience; however, Celine advised her that 'nobody but her had the right to decide what was good for her body', thus she gradually felt encouraged by her decision. Each day since brought out a more pleasant side of Robin, who was spending less time inside her home and was becoming more interactive. Although she was still not ready to return to school, church, and the remainder of her activities, the signs of her recovery were promising. Miss Shirley, Celine, and Julien had however decided to attend church that morning, to worship inside their house of the Lord.

Andrew drove by his church and slowed down out front to admire the building before he proceeded on his way. When he pulled up in front the United Church building, he was prepared to accomplish his mission, therefore he jumped out and tucked two 9mm handguns into his pant waist, then grabbed the AK-47 Rifle. With all the recent activities throughout the territory, police presence in and around Dominion City and Roseau River Reserve had been increased. Officer Valesquez was slowly cruising around the town that morning, ensuring that the peace was upkept. As the officer came around the corner onto Centennial Drive, he saw Andrew walking from his car to the church entrance holding the assault rifle.

"Dispatch I have identified an armed man holding a rifle, who is entering the United Church building on Centennial Drive," Officer Valesquez reported as he threw on his flashers and drove to the entrance.

From Andrew entered the church he began opening firing at everyone with darker complexion. The entire church erupted in screams, as adherents tried either hiding or racing for the emergency exit. Officer Valesquez pulled up outside and stood behind his car door, pointing his weapon at the building as he waited for backup. There were adherents pouring out the far end of the building, racing to get as far away as possible. The officer began calling to some of the escapees and made them run behind his cruiser for protection. Back inside the church the sound of ongoing fire continued, while Andrew kept shooting at the church adherents. As he made his way down the church isle the shooter killed Eric Duncan, then locked his sight onto Shawna Duncan.

"Oh shit, I'm sorry! You might want to get your head down," Andrew said to the Caucasian female before he continued the massacre!

Shawna was frightened beyond belief, but when she realized that the shooter had spared her because of her race, she began looking around hysterically. Old man Garrett who walked with a cane was killed in the isle ahead of them, therefore she picked up his cane and walked up behind the shooter. The loud assault rifle blasts prevented Andrew from hearing Shawna approached from behind, therefore she snuck up and clobbered him over the head. The pictures of her dead husband sent Shawna into shock; therefore, she kept hitting Andrew until a female adherent stopped her. Officer Valesquez refused to enter the church until his backup arrived, hence even after the shots stopped firing, he remained in position behind his cruiser's door. By the time Valesquez' backup officers arrived nine minutes later, the massacre had ended, and the shooter was laying unconscious on the church floor.

The officers entered the building to find the hall littered with bodies. Andrew was being subdued even though he was unconscious, and all his weapons had been confiscated. There was nothing but the sounds of weeping, as some members tried to help those who were still alive. The officers began taking control of the situation and started bringing out the adherents who hid from the gunman. Ambulances and other officers began arriving on the scene and racing into the building, while family members began searching for their loved ones. News crews from different stations began arriving and recording the events, which was guaranteed to set off another wave of demonstrations.

"Celine, Julien! Has anybody seen my daughter and my grandson," Miss Shirley asked?

There were others inquiring about their loved ones and piecing together who they thought had been killed. According to the deacon's estimation, he thought that the gunman shot and killed at least twenty-eight people, but that number had not been confirmed. The D.C United Church did not have a large congregation, therefore such a loss in members could prove catastrophic for their survival. Shawna had been escorted from the building and stood watching as ambulance technicians began bringing out some of the injured. Miss Shirley walked up to her and hugged her, after hearing mumbles that 'she saved the day yet lost her husband'.

"I am sorry to hear about Eric my dear! May God grant you the strength to get through this," Miss Shirley said!

"Oh, Sister Shirley I'm so sorry! All these loved ones lost," Shawna cried more profusely!

"It's OK, my dear! We'll be here for you! I'll get Celine to donate to help with Eric's burial," Miss Shirley said!

"Nobody told you," Shawna asked?

"Told me what," Miss Shirley questioned?

"The gunman shot Celine; and I believe I saw him shoot Julien also," Shawna revealed!

Miss Shirley's entire body went numb, and the grandmother crumbled to the ground. Pastor Roundtree and other church adherents raced to her aide, as she became lightheaded from all the excitement. It took several minutes before Miss Shirley slowly regained her senses, yet regrettably all she did was shed tears. When the police led the shooter from the building, Pastor Roundtree was not entirely surprised to hear profanity being hurled at him for the bloody massacre he created. While Miss Shirley sat on the ground in a daze, a paramedic inside the church performed CPR on her grandson, who was found barely alive.

When Andrew broke into the church and started shooting, Celine and Julien were seated in the fourth row of seat from the back. They started running to the corner isle, but the panic caused everyone to begin tumbling over each other. As Andrew got closer to them, Celine tried shielding her son with her body, when a bullet ripped through her and struck Julien in the right side of his chest. When Celine fell on top of Julien, he banged his head on the floor and passed out, so it was difficult for anyone to see him. It wasn't until one of the officers who went around checking vital signs, noticed that Celine was on top of him, before they realized that he was faintly breathing. The officer started CPR before a paramedic took over and revived Julien, yet he was still in critical condition. Julien was wheeled out on a gurney wearing an oxygen mask while attached to an I.V; when Deacon Blackwood saw him and began calling out to Miss Shirley.

"Sister Shirley, Sister Shirley, Sister Shirley it's your grandson! They're getting ready to take him to the hospital," Deacon Blackwood shouted!

Miss Shirley awoke from her daze and sprung to her feet, as she began racing over toward the ambulances. She could see the little boy on the gurney and recognized his clothing, therefore she alerted the technician that 'he was her grandchild'. The paramedic technician welcomed the grandmother to ride with them and help support Julien, who could have passed at any second. As they wheeled Julien into the ambulance his vital signs detection machine began beeping, therefore while the door closed all anyone saw was the paramedic working hard at preserving the little boy's life.

Chapter 44

It was a beautiful Sunday morning across Downtown Vancouver, the sun was out blasting the turf while the Woolrey family partook of breakfast downstairs at their Courtyard Marriott Hotel. Thomas did not have any conference business scheduled, therefore the family planned on spending the day doing a little shopping and enjoy the city. The restaurant was elegantly designed with families scattered all over enjoying their meals. There were a few television sets attached to the walls, which either featured the National News or Sports Center. Viveen was dealing with a stack of pancakes, Jacquelin had a bowl of cereal, and Thomas had eggs, toasts, sausage, and beans on his plate. They had been in Vancouver for four days, so the two servants inside the restaurant knew of them. Although the televisions were on there was no volume, hence Thomas neglected watching while he ate.

The waitress was walking around with a fresh pot of coffee for any of her customers who needed a refill. As she went by each table she would ask, "How was the meal" then chatted with whosoever struck up a conversation. When she reached the Woolrey table, everyone nodded that the food was spectacular as they continued eating. Thomas requested a refill as the news channel began airing the recent developments in Dominion City.

"That would just ruin my entire day Mr. Woolrey! If someone with my last name did something as terrible as that," the waitress commented!

Thomas, Jacquelin, and Viveen slowly lifted their heads from their plates and watched the National News coverage. When they looked at the television their mouths fell wide open with 'Awe', as they watched an officer lead Andrew from Dominion City United Church in handcuffs. The caption beneath the video read, 'Twenty-three dead and four critically injured in Dominion City church shooting'.

While being led to the police cruiser Andrew saw there were news crews filming him, therefore he shouted, "White power!"

"Can we have the check please," Thomas asked?

"Why sure you may sir! I'll be right back," the waitress answered as she walked on!

As soon as the waitress returned they paid their bill, then went back up to their suite and packed their belongings, while they purchased flight tickets over the phone. The family members then returned to the front desk and checked out of the hotel before they caught a taxi to the airport. Their flight back to Winnipeg was in four hours, nevertheless Vancouver had lost all its lust and all they wanted to do was get back home as soon as possible. When they landed back in Winnipeg the family retrieved their vehicle from the airport parking lot and drove directly home. As the turned onto their street, Thomas began driving by news station cube vans that led to the end of his driveway.

"What the hell is going on around here," Thomas wondered?

They pulled onto their driveway and began exiting their vehicle with their carry-on luggage. As soon as they stepped from the car, there was a gang of reporters and cameramen rushing to heckle them about Andrew. Thomas held Viveen and Jacquelin to protect his family, as they made their way to the front door under a slew of questions.

"Could you tell us if you are also members of the KKK Party," a female reporter shouted?

"What kind of Catholics are you if you're son is a bigot towards other races," another reporter asked?

"Mrs. Woolrey why would your son go on such a murderous tirade, then claim to be associated with the White Nationalist Party," another female reporter questioned?

"Listen, my son is no murderer! Someone from that church must have provoked him into doing what me did! But Andrew is a good respectable God-fearing young man," Jacquelin stated!

"As the bank manager here in town, would your colored customers feel comfortable knowing you were a racist, Mr. Woolrey," a male reporter asked?

"I'm no racist; and all my clients know that," Thomas fired back as they reach the door and went inside!

~~ ~~ ~~

Dominion City was such a small town that the relatives of deceased residents, stood a greater chance of finding out about their loved ones from gossipers, before law enforcement officials actually delivered the news. Within two minutes of the shooting the incident became the talk across town and only minutes later was the biggest trending topic across Canadian social media. Chris and the remainder of the choir were some of the first persons to exit the church, because they sat closest to the emergency exit. The adherents who valued sitting in the front rows were the first to flee from the building. Despite his love for his church members, Pastor Roundtree was one of the first escapees through the exit, when the sounds of gunfire erupted.

Chris telephoned his choir leader, who was already heartbroken over losing his brother Evander. Evelin left Julious in charge of cooking the rice and peas for supper, after she woke up earlier and prepared a pot of Oxtail and some Steamed Fish. The only thing that kept Julious' mind off his brother was creating musical beats, therefore he was inside his room working on his computer and other instruments. When Andrew answered Chris' call, all he heard was crying on the other end of the line, so he had no idea what to do but listened.

"Hello Chris, what's wrong," Julious kept repeating?

After nearly thirty seconds of sobbing Chris responded, "He, he killed my mother and..."

"Who? Who killed your, mother," Julious asked?

"Not only my mother! But he killed both your parents," Chris informed!

It felt like time froze for Julious, who could not process what he just heard. He could hear the crying and arguments in the background through Chris' phone, yet the news did not seem realistic. Julious walked from his room and stood in the days room staring at the front door, reminiscing on watching his parents leave through the door that morning. Chris informing Julious that his parents would never be walking back through those doors did not sit well with him, thereby he hung up his phone. When Chris or anyone else tried to contact Julious thereafter, he ignored their calls and simply watched the phone ring. Contrary to everyone else, Pastor Roundtree felt somewhat responsible for Gary and Evelin's deaths, primarily because he asked them to come back to church.

At 1:04 PM Officer Rayman went by the house to inform Julious of his parents' murders. Julious only opened the door because he knew the officers would keep coming back, until they informed the family about Gary and Evelin. Since he received the news of his parents, Julious had cried constantly and thus opened the door with tears flowing from his eyes.

"Good afternoon! Would you be related to Gary and Evelin Simms," Officer Rayman asked even though he could tell that the young man had gotten the news?

"Yes, they are my, parents," Julious fought back tears to answer!

"Sir I'm sorry to inform you that your parents were killed earlier, while they attended church," Officer Rayman exclaimed!

"What happened to, the gunman," Julious enquired?

"Ah, he was taken into custody by the officers on scene," Officer Rayman answered.

"Thank you officer," Julious stated then started closing the door!

"Wait, wait a second! Listen, I understand that this is a tough time for you, but here is a number for some people if you just need someone to talk to," Officer Rayman said as he passed Julious a personal help pamphlet.

Julious took the pamphlet and looked at it as he closed the door.

The technician was busy working on Julien and Miss Shirley did not wish to distract him, so she slid toward the driver's cabin and spoke with the man up front. The team of paramedics were together inside the church recovering their patient, therefore she thought he would know something about Celine.

"Excuse me, I'm the boy's grandmother. May I ask you a question," Miss Shirley asked?

"Yes madam, go right ahead," the driver stated.

"The lady who was right beside my grandson, was my daughter! Any news of her status," Miss Shirley questioned?

"I am sorry madam, but the lady who was holding your grandson, had already passed away," the driver responded.

"Give me strength Sweet Jesus," Miss Shirley declared as she held up her right fist? "Thank you for that information. Now if you don't mind going a little faster?"

Hearing confirmation from the paramedic was difficult for Miss Shirley, but that was something she had to know. Immediately her thoughts shifted to Robin who she knew was suicidal, therefore she retracted her cellular from her purse to contact Coy. The grandmother had tears constantly flowing from her eyes, though she had to be strong for Julien. The paramedic was still trying his hardest to keep Julien breathing and get him to the hospital, thus he encouraged Miss Shirley to continue speaking for the injured boy to hear her voice.

Coy was still in bed dozing after a late night at Sandra's house, where they got quite intimate. When the phone rang and he responded, Coy expected his mother to ask him to take something from the freezer for supper? Miss Shirley had been through a lot that morning, having to run from a building with frantic people trying to get out. With the gunman randomly killing everyone in sight, had any escapees fallen while they raced from the church, that person would have gotten trampled.

"Yes Mom," Coy responded!

"Good morning son! Huh! We had a shooting at the church a short while ago," Miss Shirley began.

"What," Coy exclaimed!

"Some gunman ran inside the building and just started shooting everyone for no reason! Your sister and your nephew were close to the back and the guy... shot them," Miss Shirley began crying!

"He did what," Coy emphatically demanded?

"Please Lord give me the strength? Listen Coy! The gunman killed Celine, but Julien is barely alive and heading to the hospital right now! I want you to break the news to Robin, but Coy, you have to watch her to make sure she doesn't do anything crazy," Miss Shirley explained!

Coy was so hurt by the news that he was crying and needed a minute to say a prayer for Julien before he could move. "Lord God, I know that I don't come to you often to ask for much, but I am here now to ask that you help save my nephew's life? Losing my sister will be tough to overcome, but Lord please don't take Julien too?"

Following his short prayer Coy walked out his room and went upstairs to find Robin putting on her shoes by the front door.

"What are you doing," Coy asked?

"What are you doing," Robin questioned with tears running down her face? "I'm sure you've heard what happened! I'm going to the hospital to help support my little brother!"

"Oh! And mom wanted me to worry about you! Wait for me, let me go put some clothes on and grab my wallet," Coy declared?

"Did you hear that Evander's parents were killed," Robin cried?

"You can't be serious," Coy remarked! "I promised Evander I would take care of his brother if anything ever happened him. Do me a favor, contact Julious and let him know to pack some stuff and we will come by to pick him up soon?"

"OK, Uncle," Robin said as she telephoned her dear friend!

When she phoned Julious, he had already received the notification about his parents and was ignoring the calls without even screening the callers. After she phoned him back twice, they had their own family business to look after, therefore she sent him a text message as they went through the door. There were a few possibilities where Julious could be and time was of the essence, thus Coy vowed 'to locate him after they left the hospital'. As they sped to Morris General Hospital, Coy felt confident Robin would be OK after watching her conduct herself, following the toughest loss she would ever experience. They both had teary eyes and felt deep sorrow knowing Celine was gone, but Julien was their primary concern.

"Julien is going to make it, he is going to be OK," Coy lamented as he held onto his niece's hand!

"I have no doubt about that uncle! I just want us to get there to let him know that I'm there," Robin stated!

Although Miss Shirley sounded very calm over the phone when she spoke to Coy, she was a nervous wreck barely holding it together at the hospital. The grandmother was sitting alone in a small waiting room crying, staring at both her hands that had been soiled with her grandson's blood. Coy and Robin rushed in and embraced her as they sat on either side of her, thus she revealed everything that she had learnt about Julien's status. Seeing Robin back to her usual self was an encouraging sight to Miss Shirley, who knew that her granddaughter could have easily plunged into the darkest parts of her mind.

Three members of the Smith's family arrived and went to the desk to enquire about their injured relative, who was also in surgery. Once the nurse revealed all she knew about their relative, they retreated to the waiting room, where both families tried to console each other. They all formed a circle and held each other's hands, while Miss Shirley said a prayer for both of their injured relatives. There were only two of the four injured adherents sent to the Morris General Hospital, hence the other two members were sent to Altona Community Memorial Health Centre. To provide the critically injured adherents with the best chance to survive, they were sent to separate hospitals where they could all receive immediate treatment.

Julien was in surgery and was expected to be inside the operating room for several more hours, so the family members hunkered down for the long wait. Coy hated seeing the blood on his mother's hands, therefore he had Robin bring her into the lady's room to wash it away. While Miss Shirley and Robin where inside the rest room, he contacted his girlfriend and informed her of what had been happening. When Robin and Miss Shirley emerged from the bathroom, the grandmother went by the nurse's station and asked for a few sheets of plain paper and a pen. Once they returned to the waiting area, Robin sat beside her grandmother who began writing a letter.

Three hours and twenty minutes later a female doctor came out of one of the operating rooms and began calling for members of the Smith family. When the family members gathered for the update, they learnt that their relative would survive, however she would be a multiple amputee. The doctor revealed that the patient lost both her legs and would need to undergo further surgeries to address other problems. There were lots of sobbing and sorrow after the news, but once they considered what the Devers family was still experiencing, all those emotions eventually changed to gratitude.

It would be another hour and fifteen minutes before Chief Surgeon Dr. Neil Bradwick came out with an update on their efforts to save Julien's life. Dr. Bradwick emphasised that they had managed to stabilize Julien, but he was still in a critical condition state. The doctor explained that in protecting her son, Celine unintentionally fell on top of Julien, which caused him to hit his head against the concrete floor. Julien suffered a cracked skull due to the impact, which landed him in a coma and left his overall recovery in question. The only thing everyone wanted to know was if they would be abled to see him, but the doctor recommended that they allowed him to rest after the long surgery and returned the following morning. Grandma Shirley told Doctor Bradwick that 'she would be spending the night keeping her grandson's company no matter what', therefore the doctor allowed her to stay inside the room with Julien. Robin would have also loved to stay, but she was more grateful that the doctors saved her brother's life. While in the Intensive Care Unit, Miss Shirley checked her cell phone for the information she required, then asked Julien's nurse for an envelope. The staff nurse felt so emotionally affected by what happened to Julien, that she offered to mail the letter for Miss Shirley along with her work department's personal mail.

Before leaving the hospital with Robin, Coy dialed Julious' cell number. Julious was not an alcohol drinker, yet he had opened a bottle of the special liquor his father stored inside a cabinet. Evander had always had high praise for Coy, therefore Julious always tried to show him respect. Despite his ignoring phone calls all day, the artistic young man responded to Coy's call once he saw the identification on the display.

"Hey Coy, how you doing," responded an intoxicated Julious!?

"Hi Julious, listen I want you to pack some clothes in a bag. I'm leaving the hospital with Robin right now, so we will be coming by to pick you up and bring you to our house for a while, until we figure some stuff out. OK," Coy explained!

"No problem Coy, see you soon," Julious stated!

When Coy and Robin reached the Simms's residence they parked in the driveway and walked to the front door. It was 3:23 AM and the streets of Dominion City were once again quiet after the hectic Sunday. Robin was tired after the few hours at the hospital, but she felt more positive that her little brother would pull through. Julious staggered to the front door dragging a suitcase that had fragments of clothing touching the ground as he walked. The intoxicated young man planned on carrying the bottle of Goslings, Black Rum, which he held in the other hand with another bag. Coy knew Julious was artistic, but he never saw him on a consistent basis to determine that he was intoxicated. At the door Julious paused, released the suitcase, then began tapping all his pockets as if he was searching for something.

"What are you looking for, your house keys," Coy asked?

"Yes, my house key," Julious stated!

"You have it right in your hand," Coy responded!

"Oh," Julious said!

"Are you drunk," Robin questioned as she began laughing at her wobbly friend?

"This is one day he has the right to do whatever he wishes! Let me help you with that buddy," Coy stated as he grabbed the bottle from Julious and helped carry the suitcase!

Julious had ignored everyone since he received the news about his parents, so he had no idea who else had gotten killed or injured. The intoxicated young man could be heard sniffling and sighing in the back seat, as they drove along the deserted streets.

"Why were you, guys at the, hospital," Julious asked?

"That gunman was about to kill my mother and Jules, and mommy tried shielding him from the bullets. But Jules is alive thank God! That killer killed my mommy," Robin cried!

When they reached home Coy went to place Julious' suitcase inside his sister's room. As he opened the door and looked inside, he immediately began crying, once he realized he would never have his sister at home again. Robin walked up and hugged her uncle, hence they consoled each other and wept. Despite his personal hurt, Julious felt the pain that Coy, and Robin were experiencing, so he walked up and hugged them both. They consoled each other for a few minutes, before they retreated to the kitchen where Coy took out three glasses and poured liquor into each.

"Here you go Robin, your first drink! These people are forcing you to become a woman before you really should! Raise your glasses! To Mister and Misses Simms, Celine, and everybody else killed yesterday, salute," Coy toasted!

After that drink Coy refilled everyone's glass, then walked away into the living room with the bottle. He turned on the television and sat down on the sofa, as he threw back two more shot of rum. Rather than going to their bedrooms, Julious and Robin entered the living room also and made themselves comfortable on the other sofas. The first channel Coy went to was talking about the church shooting, so he switched to another channel that also had the same coverage. Coy was frustrated hearing about the shooting and wanted to watch something different, so he switched to a third channel that was showing the video of Andrew being led from the church. Robin took a sip off the liquor and looked up at the television, wherein she felt as though a sudden jolt of electrical charge shocked her brain.

"That is the asshole who raped me," Robin exclaimed!

Following the massacre patrons from the community and beyond began dropping off flowers and other sentimental items on the church's lawn that created a makeshift memorial. People from around the community were left stunned by the latest event, which advertised their town in a very negative light. That evening at sunset, people who denounced the violence and racism that have been plaguing the territory for months, held a candlelight vigil to remember the lives of the twenty-four church members killed. One of the survivors who was taken to the Altona Community Memorial Health Centre, was pronounced dead when he reached the hospital, therefore the original number of deceased had increased.

The candlelight vigil began with most of the people who had been at the church since the shooting. Pastor Roundtree who had remained with many other led the mourners, as they silently prayed and reminisced on all the lives lost earlier that day. Never in the town's history had there ever been such an appalling act, therefore even Mayor Bathurst showed up to show support. The community had no idea how many people would attend the vigil, but once it started people just kept coming. It became a very emotional event, wherein people were crying and comforting each other as they tried to understand the senseless killings. Activists who were seeking to hold a rally to demonstrate against the ongoing racism, began passing out flyers and information. Most of those present vowed to show up and expressed their voices against an issue that they felt strongly towards.

Chapter 45

With the spotlight shining on Andrew, he felt as though he was the man of the century and thus became rather brash and obnoxious. Instead of heeding the advice of the arresting officer who told him, he had the right to remain silent, Andrew chose to gloat about his murderous accomplishments. Due to his willingness to offer information, investigators brought him from his cell late that night and sat him inside an interrogation room. The proud killer told the investigators during questioning about his dead friends' bodies inside their house and boasted about executing them. After officer impounded his vehicle and thoroughly searched it, they confiscated the weapons left inside and asked Andrew about them. To avoid appearing as though he could not accept rejection, Andrew refrained from mentioning that he asked Russell and Kyler to help him, and instead told the investigators that he intended on striking other targets.

When police officers went to the Applewick family home early the Monday morning, they found Russell and Kyler as described by the killer. A forensic team had to be sent to the Applewick's house to collect evidence, photographed the bodies, and documented the surroundings. There were bullet casings collected at the scene that were fired from one of the 9mm handguns taken from the accused. The two additional bodies gave investigators just cause to prolong the indictment against Andrew, therefore he could not pass court as expected on that Monday.

When the reporters who were sent to cover the shooting learnt of additional victims, they sprinted to the location to capture the story. The neighbors who lived closest to the family did not like the brothers and were not afraid to admit it. Even though none of them heard the fatal shots fired, they claimed they would not have alerted the authorities had they heard it. The reporters tried to uncover the link between Andrew and the Applewick brothers and discovered that they were the ones who converted him. They had only been friends for the past few months, yet the brothers were very influential in getting him to stop attending church regularly. Each reporter tried to uncover why Andrew would assassinate men whom he admired, still none of them could find the logic behind the shootings.

Detective Folier and Officer Burney were disappointed when the results of the semen and pubic hair tests did not reveal Johnny Webber as Robin's rapist. Since they received the report, they had been trying to cross-reference the results with all the DNA samples they had on file; but had been unlucky to find a match thus far. Because Andrew had never been arrested and inserted into the police database system, the computer could not locate the ideal match, therefore the officers felt as though Robin's rapist could possibly get away. Officer Burney and Detective Folier were about to move on from the case until they received some ground-breaking evidence, when Robin called the detective's cell phone. Folier thought that the rapist was possibly a first-time offender, therefore catching him would be incredibly difficult.

"Good morning, this is Detective Folier!"

"Morning Detective Folier, this is Robin Walker!"

"Hi Robin! How is it going?"

"The reason for my call is to let you know that I now remember who raped me!"

"You do?"

"Yes! It was Andrew Woolrey!"

"What makes you so sure it was him?"

"Because I remember opening my eyes and seeing the boxing glove on his chain."

"Thanks for contacting me with this information Robin! I will get on that right away," Detective Folier said as the line went dead!

"Who was that," Officer Burney asked?

"That was Robin Walker. She said that she was raped by Andrew Woolrey," Detective Folier exclaimed!

"That's why the computer failed to find a match! He was just uploaded into the system," Officer Burney said.

"Well let's run him through now and see what comes up," Detective Folier declared!

Officer Burney went back on the computer and typed in the information to determine if the samples matched Andrew. The computer took a matter of seconds to determine that Andrew was a definite match to the samples on file, therefore the officers high fived each other knowing that they had the evidence to prove that Andrew raped Robin. Rather than simply filing his report, Detective Folier brought his evidence over to the prosecution building to speak with the lawyers in charge of prosecuting Andrew Woolrey. It was important to the detective that rape charges be laid amid the vast number of charges already piled on the church shooter, therefore Folier presented his finding in person. When the prosecutors realized that the detective's discovery contradicted Andrew's narrative, they decided to add the rape charges onto the stack of others.

The most anticipated event that Monday did not transpire, which was the arraignment of Andrew Woolrey. Contrary to the accused shooter getting officially charged, the town of Dominion City became the focal point for demonstrators, who showed up from all over to express their grief. The Black Lives Matter, Anit-Racism, Ever Child Matter, and other signs were all on display, as many nationalities of people participated in the march. The organizers of the event planned to start a walk from the beginning of Dominion City, along Waddell Avenue down to Centennial Drive on which the church was located. Once they reached the church there were a few public speakers lined up to address the crowd, along with a few artists to perform. The demonstration was scheduled to begin at 1:00 PM and the organizers expected at least five hundred people to attend.

Following the failure review the Dakota Ojibwe Police Services received from their handling of the first protest in Dominion City, they made sure they were prepared for the next. There were adequate officers all along the expected protest route to ensure that the crowd remained peaceful. The entire street had been blocked off for the demonstrators, with a cruiser parked at each intersection. School officials learnt of the protest from the night prior and canceled all programs that day. By 12:30 the crowd had exceeded the expected amount, with more participants joining by the minute. Many of the demonstrators came with their signs already prepared, but before the proceeding got on the way there were people scrambling to find cardboard to make plaques. At 12:57, Zaphir Mullins who was one of the female organizers got on a loud-speak to fire up the crowd, which had reached nearly five thousand people.

"Ladies and gentlemen, boys, and girls, we would like to thank you all for showing up here today to let your voices be heard, so people from inside the government to the private sector will see, that we will no longer tolerate racism in our communities and our country! For those who have never done this before, we will be walking to the D.C United Church, and along the way we will just be express what we feel about racism and this terrible massacre that has happened! So, a round of applause for those who are here and let's go!"

Everyone began applauding and cheering, as Zaphir passed the loudspeaker to her colleague Samira James.

"No more racism," Samira shouted!

"No more racism," shouted the crowd as they began marching!

"No more mass shootings!"

"No more mass shootings!"

"No more hate crimes!"

"No more hate crimes!"

"Ban all assault rifles!"

"Ban all assault rifles!"

"No more racism!"

"No more racism!"

There were reporters and cameramen among the crowd recording the demonstration and speaking with the participants. Many reporters were surprised to uncover there were several protesters from the United States, who made the trip to voice their opinions. Many Canadians had been keeping eyes on the escalating massacres and hate crimes across the border and did not wish to see an increase of these crimes back at home. As a result, people were there from all parts of the country to express their sentiments on assault rifles, mass killings, and to denounce the recent tragedy.

The protesters marched slowly as they shouted their anti hate slogans until they reached the church. There was a stage assembled on the lawn of the United Church for the speakers, poets, and musical artists to perform. The crowd was treated to a delightful event, wherein they demonstrated and expressed their beliefs, before they enjoyed some quality entertainment. Although there were some angered residents who complained about the loud noises, the demonstration was overall peaceful and ended at 8:00 PM.

The spectacle that the everyone expected to happen that Monday at the courthouse, was moved to the following day. There were so many passionate people over the issues in question, that representatives from both supporters of assault rifles and those who wanted them banned, showed up to protest. Andrew was not scheduled to get arraigned until the early afternoon, yet there were people camped out in front the courthouse from 5:00 AM to demonstrate.

The Canadian Prime Minister was asked about his thoughts on the massacre at a fundraiser party the evening prior and he mentioned that "His thoughts and prayers were with those killed and their families; and his government would consider looking into banning certain types of weapons." The Prime Minister's comment angered gun producers and gun owners alike, who showed up outside the courthouse to support their rights to bare arms. With news of the protest all over television, gun owners had to express their thoughts and used the biggest ongoing stage to do so. When asked how they felt about the massacre, most of those who supported the gun laws were saddened by the killings, but they were only there to defend their guns. The massacre revived the gun argument overnight, therefore the leader of the N.D.P fired back at the Prime Minister that morning and said, "The Prime Minister had not gone far enough to keep Canadians safe!" The leader of the Quebec Party also fired off at the Prime Minister's comment and said, "They supported Canadians who wanted their weapons and would fight for them!" The other ministers failed to comment on the issue, yet it became evident that gun laws would become a sticking point in the coming election.

There was a bit of overcast that morning which continued into the afternoon, so the skies appeared as though it might rain. When Jacquelin and Thomas showed up at the Emerson Court House that afternoon they were mobbed by reporters as they made their way to the entrance. While Thomas chose to remain silent and not get rattled by the hounds, his wife's tongue was fiery and ready for the nagging reporters. The parents were surprised at the political ambiance their son created, which forced the police to not only increase their presence, but to also set up metal barriers to keep the protesters separated. There was a wide corridor for the people attending court to walk through; before they reached the front door and had to pass through a metal detector device. On the right side of the barrier were people with signs that supported assault rifles, who shouted at their opposers across the courtyard. The people holding up signs on the left side of the courtyard, represented everyone from anti weapons protesters to Black Lives Matter supporters. Both sides of the barriers were yelling all sorts of insults and profanity at the other, as if they wanted to rip each other apart.

"Mrs. Woolrey, with two new bodies added to the list of those killed by your son, what does your family hope will happen," a female reporter asked?

"We want the truth to come out about what made my son do this! Because we know that those church people must have interfered with him, or he never would have done this," Jacquelin answered!

"So, what of his two latest victims," the reporter asked?

"Again, whenever the transcripts come out you will see that those people harassed my boy," Jacquelin stated!

"By those people, I presume you are referring to the black church attendants at the United Church," the reporter continued?

"Yes, of course I am! Their church is not even a godly church anyways, for them to be provoking my son," Jacquelin stated as they stormed pass security!

Andrew was still feeling like the man of the century, when they brought him into the courthouse. The guards had to keep him separated from the other detainees due to his charges, hence he mouthed off at the others who were cramped into two cells. The accused mass shooter kept boasting that 'his brother must be so proud of him' as he walked around solitary inside his bullpen. When the guards finally brought Andrew into the courtroom, he entered shouting "White power" before he saw the serious look on his father's face and remained quiet throughout the remainder of the proceedings. Jacquelin signaled her son to call her when they made eye contact, then blew him a kiss to assure him that she was in his corner. Thomas and Jacquelin thought they were aware of all the legal counts laid against their son, until they were blindsided by an additional rape charge.

Following the arraignment, the parents spoke with Andrew's lawyer, who explained that their office only learnt of the rape charge the day prior. It was only the first process of the trial; therefore, the prosecution had no obligation to mention the rape victim's name, thus nobody had any idea who that person was. The province provided attorney told Thomas and Jacquelin that the prosecution's case versus their son was basically impenetrable, therefore their only option may be to throw themselves at the mercy of the Crown.

Chapter 46

Aaron had only received legal mail since he got incarcerated again, so when his name got called during mail announcement, he was rather surprised. The stamp on the envelope showed it was sent from Morris General Hospital in Manitoba, which puzzled the accused killer. When he received the mail on the Wednesday before the 4:00 PM lock down for prisoners' head count, he casually shoved it into his pocket to read during lock down. Although he reacted as if he wasn't excited to receive an actual correspondence, Aaron quickly opened the envelope once the guards locked the doors. It wasn't until he unfolded the paper that he realized it was from Mrs. Shirley Devers, a name he had not heard since he left Dominion City. Still, with excitement he started reading every word on the page, which quickly got difficult to get through.

Miss Shirley told him that after he stole her daughter away, his childish stupidity made him not only lose a decent wife, but Celine also left him pregnant and never told him. He could feel Miss Shirley's emotions pouring out when she spoke of how Andrew raping Robin affected her and drove her to attempting suicide. There was nothing withheld by Miss Shirley, who told Aaron about the pregnancy and abortion, which she thought would drive her granddaughter mad. The letter went through the positive things that were happening for Celine, before his brother Andrew snatched away her life. The grandmother spoke of where she was, and the prayers that were being said for Celine's son, who was also injured by his brother. The final comment the grandmother made was to tell Aaron that she forgave him; and wished the Lord blessed him, however, his challenging the courts in his trial was not only a slap in the face to Celine, but to their daughter Robin who was raised by another man. The plain white paper was soaked with drops of tears at the end of his reading; therefore, he crushed it in his palm and threw it in the corner.

Aaron laid back on his bunk with tears running from his eyes. Had he not influenced his brother into violence none of what transpired would have, therefore he blamed himself for all the tragedy that Andrew caused.

"Why didn't you tell me," Aaron said out loud?

"Tell you what man," his cellmate asked?

"I, I wasn't talking to you G," Aaron answered.

"Are you crying man," his cellmate enquired?

"Mind your own business G! I just got news my grandmother died," Aaron lied.

"Ah, my condolences man," his cellmate said!

As soon as they got allowed back into the general pod area, Aaron went to the phone and first contacted his lawyer's office. Monsieur McGill had left the office for the day, but the off-shift secretary accepted the phone charges. Most of his co-defendants who were involved in the robbery where he shot and killed Lloyd Walker, had gotten sentenced and sent to other prisons to do their time, except for the prosecution's key witness.

"Yes, good evening," the secretary answered!

"Yes, my name is Aaron Adams and I want you to let my attorney know that I have decided to plead guilty on all the charges laid against me," Aaron explained!

"OK, Mr. Ah, Adams, what would your lawyer's name be," the secretary asked?

"Christophe McGill, I believe! Listen, just let him know it's over man! I killed Lloyd Walker! Thank him for the help and all, but I killed Mister Walker in that convenience store! So, I'm changing my plea to guilty," Aaron exclaimed then disconnected the call.

The disgruntled detainee then phoned his mother, who was at home making supper with Viveen. Thomas was watching the news inside the living room, but he had been in a snobbish mood from they left the courthouse. To avoid worsening their problems, Jacquelin left Viveen stirring the meat sauce while she answered the phone and went into her bathroom to talk. She quickly pressed the button to accept the call and lowered her voice to alert Thomas she was on the phone.

"Yes, Aaron how are you," Jacquelin asked?

Aaron turned away from the other jailers so no one could see in case he started crying. "Hi, mom I'm fine! I just learned some things from Celine's mother that I believe I must tell you!"

"What is wrong with you? Why do you sound like that," Jacquelin enquired?

"Mom, Celine's daughter is mine," Aaron exclaimed!

"What did you just say," Jacquelin demanded?

"I said, that little girl Robin who your son Andrew raped is my daughter," Aaron stated as tears again began flowing!

"Oh, my Sweet Jesus," Jacquelin said as she sat on her bed with tears gushing from her eyes! "No," she then screamed and smashed the phone against the wall!

～ ～ ～

Celine and Julious' parents all had excellent life insurance coverages that allowed for their relatives to have a seamless process during their times of retirement. A lawyer from the Bennett's Legal Firm who represented Celine's assets, contacted Robin and Miss Shirley, and arranged a meeting after all the burial proceedings had ended. As a protective mother, Celine had created a legal binding will in which she left everything she owned to her children. The will gave her legal team the right to protect all her assets for her children, therefore the lawyer was to update them further during their meeting.

Throughout the next two weeks, those who knew the deceased adherents went to several nine nights functions and life celebrations. Robin spent most of her time at the hospital by her brother's side reading, singing, and talking to him, to help him awaken from his comatose state. Miss Shirley also spent a grave amount of time at the hospital by her grandson's side, but she also had three funeral plans to incorporate into one grand event. Coy and Julious went by the hospital a few times and tried to enlighten Julien, who continued sleeping as if he just needed someone to nudge him awake.

The town had quieted down a bit, but there were still reporters capturing the funeral services and sadness across Dominion City. On the day of the viewing for Celine, Evelin, and Gary, Miss Shirley had to trade places with Robin at the hospital for her to go and look at the bodies. Robin wanted someone by Julien's side twenty-four, seven, in case he awoke. She did not want him to panic due to the tubes inserted into his mouth, or because he did not recognize where he was, so someone had to be always present. Due to the number of bodies scheduled for viewing at the church, each family was given a specific day and a timeline of two hours for them to spend with their deceased loved ones. The tight viewing window gave Miss Shirley only forty minutes to spend at the viewing, before Coy drove her to the hospital and brought back Robin, who also got to spend forty minutes with her mother.

Coy had to walk his niece up to Celine's casket, after her feet wobbled while she approached. When Robin looked at her mother laying peacefully, she stretched into the casket and gave her a kiss on her forehead. Robin felt the need to speak with her mother, therefore she moved to the opposite side of the casket to allow other viewers to continue passing. It was incredibly hard for the teenage girl, who lost her father not even a year prior in a similar murderous faction. The mourners who went by all had something spectacular to say about Celine, who was in the midst of changing the town through exercise. The tributes for their mother were so dynamic, that Robin positioned her phone and recorded many of them to show Julien, whenever he awoke.

Julious had lost his entire world; therefore, he stood on the opposite side of their caskets while the viewers passed and gave their condolences. From the handler opened his parents' caskets Julious stood by them both and spoke to them. Pastor Roundtree prayed for them and extended a place for Julious to stay if he ever needed somewhere to go. The mourning young man stood by the caskets for the duration of time, until the handler re-closed them for transfer back to the morgue. There was another viewing about to get on the way after the triple viewing of Celine, Evelin, and Gary, so almost everyone who paid their respects were still there.

Robin hugged Julious and again offered her condolences, before she exited the church. Coy and Julious had become close buddies since he began staying by Miss Shirley's house, hence the mechanic offered to hire him full time at the garage. Julious had gone by his house and taken his father's Dodge Ram 4X4, therefore he had his own wheels around town. There was only one place Robin wanted to be and if she had to walk there, she would, so Coy brought his niece right back to the hospital. While at Morris General Hospital, Coy received an emergency call to fix an overheated motor for a stranded family. To avoid leaving his mother and Robin carless at the hospital, Coy asked Julious to pick him up and bring him to the shop. It had been a few days since Coy opened his garage, so it felt good coming back if even for a quick repair.

Lorna telephoned Miss Shirley and told her they had to visit Celine's gym. Through all the madness that had unfolded the last thing any of them thought about was peoples' fitness. Miss Shirley and Robin had been at the hospital for two days, so she telephoned Coy and had him come child sit. Robin thought they were only driving home to get some fresh personal items before they went back to the hospital, but her grandmother drove to a little boutique they had in town. The old lady who owned the store, helped them to find a dress for Robin to wear to the funeral, instead of having to travel to the big city to purchase one.

After Robin and her grandmother left the boutique, they drove to the gym to see what Lorna insisted they look at. When they pulled up in the parking lot, both females started crying when they saw the memorial tribute which the members left for Celine. At the sight of the love shown to Celine, with all the teddy bears, flowers, cards, letters, balloons, and bottles of wine, Miss Shirley vowed to continue the business her daughter started. Robin took several pictures of the tribute and posted them on her social media page, to express how cherished her mother was in their community.

When they returned to the house, Robin forgot Julious was still staying there and walked into her mother's bedroom without knocking. Julious had two 9mm handguns on the bed beside his clothes and was listening to music through his headphones, so he did not hear when the ladies walked into the house. Robin quickly closed the door behind herself and walked over to Julious, then shoved him in the back.

"What is up with all this? Suppose grandma walked in here and saw all that shit," Robin argued!

"Don't worry about, that," Julious said!

"What are you doing with these anyways," Robin asked as she picked up one of the guns and pointed it as if she knew how to shoot?

"I can't tell, you that," Julious stated!

"OK that's cool! Keep your little secret then! Me and grandma only came by to get some stuff, so we'll be leaving in a few minutes," Robin declared as she put down the gun and took some clothing from Julien's drawers!

Julious walked out of the bedroom behind Robin and told Miss Shirley "Hello"! When the grandmother emerged from her bedroom she gave the young man a warm hug, as if she understood exactly what he had been going through. Within minutes the ladies were in and through the door, and thus left Julious feeling that void of not having his mother. As she went through the door Robin looked back at Julious and shook her head, as if she knew what his intentions were.

Andrew telephoned his mother who sounded like she was just crawling out of bed. Following her last conversation with Aaron, which ended abruptly when she threw the phone against the wall and broke it, she got into a terrible fight with Thomas. After her husband rushed into the bedroom and enquired what happened, she told him what she had learned from Aaron about his fathering Robin. Thomas went berserk when he heard that his son raped and impregnated a female of mixed breed, which was something he had warned against. The argument escalated to the point where Thomas confessed that he had gotten fired following Andrew's massacre, therefore he had endured enough humiliation and wanted a divorce. Despite Viveen crying and pleading for her father to stay, Thomas packed his suitcase, and walked away from his marriage.

"Hey honey, how is it going in there," Jacquelin greeted!?

"I'm great so far! Is everything OK at home," Andrew stated?

"Well, your father wants to get a divorce. But aside from that, all is well," Jacquelin said.

"Why would dad want to leave you and Viveen," Andrew exclaimed?

"It's OK, calm down! It's not the end of the world! He wasn't your father anyways," Jacquelin answered!

"What do you mean by he wasn't..." Andrew remarked?

"Stop pretending as if you're some child suddenly! Your brother Aaron said that little girl you raped was his daughter, then you turned right around and killed her mother and son," Jacquelin declared!

"But Aaron doesn't have a daughter," Andrew quarrelled!

"Not according to him," Jacquelin said!

"Tell him I'm sorry! I was just trying to make him proud of me," Andrew stated!

"I don't think he wants to have anything to do with you ever again," Jacquelin warned!

"What, what! Not my Bro! He didn't mean that," Andrew said before he disconnected the call and began knocking himself on the head!

The guard who went to transfer Andrew back to his cell did not expect to get attacked. When the guard brought the detainee to use the telephone, he was rather calm yet excited, but following his conversation with his mother he completely changed. Andrew was walking ahead of the guard when he unexpectedly turned and began punching the corrections employee several times. The guard tried defending himself, but Andrew overpowered him and kept beating him until his comrades intervened and stopped him. A few of the guards roughed up the detainee as they brought him back to his cell, where they threw him inside.

"I just want to die! I just want to die..." Andrew continued repeating so one of the guards threw a nylon belt into his cell!

Nobody checked on Andrew until five hours later, when a female guard found him strung up hanging by the belt. The guard called for help and entered the cell when her backup officers arrived, to lower the detainee and remove the noose from around his neck. The jailhouse doctor was called in and Andrew was pronounced dead on the spot, after an examination was done. Jacquelin received a notification call from the jail an hour after her son was pronounced dead, to inform her that 'he had chosen to hang himself'. The caller had no further information except to offer her condolences and advised Jacquelin that someone would get in touch with her about the proceedings.

On the morning of Celine, Evelin, and Gary's funeral, Robin showered and got dressed at the hospital inside Julien's bathroom. After she emerged from the bathroom in her dress, she noticed the news reporters showing pictures of Andrew Woolrey on the screen. Robin grabbed the TV remote and turned up the volume to hear what they were saying, only to realize that her rapist had hanged himself.

"Karma; is a bitch they say Jules," Robin stated as she continued getting ready!

Pastor Roundtree had several burial services to minister over that day, so their funeral was scheduled from 9:00 to 11:00 AM. They had a nurse's aide worker scheduled to sit with Julien from 8:30 AM until someone returned from the funerals to relieve her. Robin made sure she recorded as much of the event as she could for Julien to watch whenever he awoke. With so many bodies to get buried in the local cemetery, space was of the utmost importance, therefore Evelin and her husband Gary were to be buried in the same grave next to Celine. The graves closeness gave Pastor Roundtree the opportunity to perform one ceremony for both families at the graveyard, therefore with all the attendants gathered inside the church he began the procession precisely at 9:00 AM.

It was a beautiful Saturday morning, and the sun was beaming in the sky. A news crew was on the scene capturing the procession from a slight distance to award the mourners their privacy. The attendance for the three funerals far exceeded all the other funerals, as people attended to show the appreciation. There was a larger contingency of Caucasians gathered to bury both ladies, who served people of all creed at their employments. Pastor Roundtree was deeply hurt by the deaths of the two women they were laying to rest, because they were both black business owners.

"Good morning, everyone and thank you all for attending these burials services this morning, for Celine Devers Walker, Evelin Simms, and Gary Simms! We will begin with the singing of Amazing Grace, followed by a prayer," Pastor Roundtree said!

Everyone joined their voices and sang loudly as if they had been taught the hymn previously. Following the hymn, the pastor delivered a heartwarming prayer, before he began calling up the speakers. The eulogies were delivered by family members and church adherents, who spoke warmly of each deceased. Those who appreciated the services provided by the murdered hair stylist and the gym owner, were drawn to tears by the magnificent things said about them. There have been a lot of negativities mentioned about his church since the shooting, yet the pastor saw the good in his community to overlook those comments and spoke of unity in his speech. The pastor again led the audience in singing, Here I Am, Lord, before he said one final prayer. With ten minutes remaining before the first hour expired, Pastor Roundtree allowed the families a few last minutes to see their loved ones before the caskets got closed.

The entire procession then slowly made its way over to the graveyard, where people stacked the grounds to pay their final respects. With the bodies positioned over the graves for burial, Pastor Roundtree again took center stage and led the crowd in singing, 'The Lord Is My Shepherd'. Following the hymn, the pastor prayed for those present before he dived into his next topic, which was about getting into the kingdom of God. The grave handlers began lowering Gary's body while the attendants sang, 'Abide With Me', before they positioned Evelin's casket for descent also. Those who wished to cast the first bit of dirt on the casket were allowed to come forward, then given a shovel to perform the task.

With Gary's burial complete, Pastor Roundtree led the crowd in singing, 'All Things Bright And Beautiful', before he spoke of the greatness that Evelin and Celine created and left behind. The pastor's speech was meant to inspire everyone, especially the youth in the crowd, but the more Robin listened to him speak was the more she felt her mother was envied. Coy and her grandmother were standing next to her holding her hands, but as she looked around all she saw were strange faces. Robin began thinking all sorts of weird thoughts, such as Julien and Celine were holding her hands and the people around her were inside the coffins.

Pastor Roundtree then asked everyone to bend their heads in prayer, while he said one final word for Celine and Evelin. As soon as the pastor finished his prayer he led the crowd into their final hymn, which was, 'Nearer My God To Thee', while the grave handlers descended the two coffins. Robin felt as though her stomach was sinking beneath the earth, while watching her mother's casket descend into the grave. She looked at Julious behind the dark shades and expected to see tears rolling down his face, but the artistic young man's heart had hardened to his situation. With both his parents' coffins lowered into the grave, Julious stood there and watched the entire burial process, until nearly everyone including the workers finished and went away. When Julious thought that everyone had abandoned him, he looked across at Celine's coffin and saw Robin standing there. Miss Shirley returned to the hospital to relieve Julien's sitter and left Coy to bring Robin home. The grandmother wanted Robin to relax in her bed and chat with her friends for the night, without having to worry about her brother.

Coy did as instructed by his mother and returned home with Robin. By the time they reached home it was a little past midday, so Robin made them sandwiches for lunch. She had been living on hospital food for the past few days and felt for a decent meal, so she decided to prepare supper. Julious came home from the funeral a few minutes later and went directly to his room and closed the door. Robin had started making spaghetti, so she chopped up the vegetables to add to the mince meat, while the noodles boiled in the pot. When she started cooking the mince meat and added all her herbs, vegetables, and spices, Julious slowly emerged from the bedroom to see what was cooking.

"You want some of this to eat," Robin asked?

"OK, I will take, some," Julious answered!

"Sorry, this is for supper! You go have to fix yourself a sandwich, like we did," Robin teased!

Julious looked over at Coy who was playing video games inside the living room.

"What you looking at me for? I had a sandwich, don't you think I'd prefer the spaghetti," Coy stated!

Julious angrily went and looked inside the fridge, where he withdrew a loaf of bread, with peanut butter and jam. As he walked to the counter to make himself a sandwich, all Robin heard was Julious grumbling to himself.

"You have something to say," Robin asked?

"No, I did not, say anything," Julious responded!

"Oh! I thought so," Robin replied!

Coy laughed from inside the living room. "You two sound like an old married couple!"

They all hung out laughing and teasing each other, while Coy continued playing his video games. Robin contacted her grandmother and enquired about Julien, whose condition had not changed. She at first disagreed with her grandmother's decision to send her home, but the more she laughed was the more she realized how much she needed to unwind. Later that evening they all ate supper together, which to Robin felt like the old days with Lloyd at the table. Julious on the other hand imagined being with Evander and his mother, considering his father used to always be on the road. The thought of his deceased siblings placed Julious in a depress mood, wherein he fought to appear as though he was content.

Sandra telephoned Coy a short while after they finished eating and invited him over. Moments after he spoke with his girlfriend, Coy departed through the door without mentioning when he would return. When Coy vanished and left them alone, Julious went back into his room where he began loading bullets into extra magazines he had. Robin walked into the room and again picked up a firearm off the bed, but Julious quickly took it from her and wiped the handle clean.

"I'm not going to stop asking what these guns are for until you tell me," Robin asked?

"I don't want, your fingerprints, on them so, stop touching the, guns," Julious stated!

"I'm not going to stop touching them until you tell me what you plan on doing with them," Robin stated?

"OK, OK! Stop! I am going, to get revenge, for my parents," Julious said!

"What do you mean? Are you thinking of shooting up those white people's church," Robin asked?

Julious was at first hesitant to respond until he said, "They did it, to my church, so I'm going, to do it, to them!"

"No, they didn't Julious! Some crazy white man decided to do that on his own," Robin reasoned!

"Them I'm the, crazy black man, just like him," Julious declared!

"But we are better than that Julious! We don't need to stoop to their level to prove a point," Robin remarked!

"Then maybe it's, time we do! Let them feel, what it's like, to get their, mothers and fathers, taken away," Julious declared with tears falling from his eyes and a stern facial expression!

"Julious you are a lover of God, you go to church! You are not a murderer! The bible says to forgive your fellow man," Robin argued!

"That guy who, raped you went, to church too! Yet still he, killed my parents," Julious stated!

"I understand, but you are not racist," Robin lamented!

Julious took a weapon and selected a bullet into the firing chamber. "Exactly! But it seems, like this is, the only thing, that will make, those hateful bastards, understand that I, am built different!"

"You are really serious about doing this aren't you," Robin said?

"Nothing is going, to stop me," Julious exclaimed with that same stern look on his face!

Robin stood there watching Julious load bullets into his 9mm magazines. She thought long and hard about her parents and what losing Julious would mean to her; before she joined him and began loading bullets into a cartridge.

"I told you, I don't want, your fingerprints, on the weapons," Julious repeated!

"I guess it doesn't matter if I'm coming with you, does it," Robin stated as she looked Julious in the eyes?

Julious stood up and held onto Robin's biceps as if he was about to profusely disagree. As he stared into her eyes they then fell into each other's arms and began passionately kissing. There was no rushing the intimacy as beginners, so they slowly did what felt natural to them. After being violated and raped, being intimate with a man was not a sensation Robin thought she would ever experience again, yet she was voluntarily giving herself to Julious. Knowing that his partner had been raped, Julious did not want to appear forceful, so he allowed Robin to lead and followed at her pace.

They had been respectful of each other's feelings since they met, but if they were to die the following day, they had to make love at least once. Robin began undressing Julious while they continued kissing, however his inactivity was beginning to concern her. To make sure her partner realized that he had the red light to fondle her, Robin took one of his hands and placed it on her waist. After Julious realized she consented fully, he began caressing her and rubbing his hands all over her body: before he located the zipper for her dress and slid it down. With their passion mounting, Julious shoved all the weapons onto the floor to clear the bed for their antics. From the instant they locked lips, they kissed as if they never intended to separate, while they fondled with each other's bodies.

Julious and Robin were like magnets attached to each other, as they continued kissing and caressing while they slid onto the bed. It was the young man's first time being with a female and he wanted the experience to be as memorable for her as it would be for him. Robin had led the way thus far, so as impatient as Julious felt to insert himself, he thought it best to wait until she gave him a hint. Having a nude female pressed against his naked body was the most enticing feeling he had ever felt, thus he began questioning his decision. When Robin maneuvered beneath him then spread her legs apart for him to enter, Julious had no doubt she wanted him to proceed, hence he slid into her. Rather than taking off like a bunny rabbit, the artistic Romeo slowly worked himself in while his partner reached her comfort level. Julious had been fantasizing about squeezing and caressing his partner's entire body since the moment he saw her. Therefore, given the opportunity, he ran his fingers through her hair, gently touched her face, massaged her breasts, and wherever his hands could reach, while he placed several hickies over her neck and chest area.

With his lover professing her emotions by sinking her fingers into his skin at the height of her climax, Julious was abled to decipher the power of their connection. Robin felt as though she was gliding among the clouds although she was laying flat on her back. The thrust and recoil motions of her lover felt so dynamic, that she wished they had been loving each other from day one. No matter what her partner did felt incredible, therefore she was willing to do whatever he wanted to please him. The sensation was such that Julious wished he could prolong for the entire night, but as he began getting overly excited, he felt his body temperature exceeding its limit, until he could no longer resist the urge to ejaculate. The thought that a female would surrender her life with him was immeasurable, therefore even after they finished engaging in coitus, Julious could not stop kissing Robin.

Chapter 47

Pastor Hemming would customarily greet his members at the building's entrance when they arrived at church, then bid them farewell from the same location whenever they left. Because of this, he would always be the last to enter the building unless there were late attendants. When Pastor Hemming was getting ready to close the doors to commence his Sunday service, he saw Pastor Roundtree and his wife driving by, therefore he waved at them. Pastor Roundtree sounded his horn and waved as they went by to prep their church hall for the day's services. Contrary to what most people thought, the two pastors had mutual respect as leaders of their churches. In fact, following the massacre Pastor Hemming telephoned Pastor Roundtree and offered his condolences. The Catholic pastor also offered the use of their building for church services, if the United Church building was inhabitable for any period.

There was a constant police presence throughout the town of Dominion City since the shooting, which felt weird to the locals who in the past went months at times without seeing any members of law enforcement. The Dakota Ojibwe Police Department had a large territory to cover, so they could only spare one officer to patrol the small town and its close surroundings. The officer on duty that morning was Officer Gilmore, and his closest backup was at the station seven minutes away. The patrolling officer's wife and children were attending church; therefore, he circled the block more often than he normally would.

Since his friend Officer Pedward got arrested, there had been numerous changes at the precinct due to the insertion of a new Police Chief. The department's new chief threatened to dismiss all officers who failed to do their jobs as trained. Nevertheless, it was business as usual for Officer Gilmore and most of the veteran officers, who knew how to effectively do their jobs. Neither Officer Gilmore nor his wife Malory had spoken to Rochelle, so none of them had any idea what became of her since. The Pedward's house was up for sale, but no one knew if she still lived there or moved away. Even though Grey could not attend Ray's arraignment due to his work schedule, he had distanced himself from the former officer and no longer accepted his communications.

The day prior was bright and sunny across the province of Manitoba, but that Sunday was a complete temperature reversal. There was no rain in the forecast, yet the skies were dark and hazy. When Julious awoke that morning and looked over at the clock, the time read 8:03. Robin was under the covers beside him naked, therefore he lifted the sheet and admired her body. He kissed her gently on her shoulder, her neck, and her lips, before he snuck out of bed. As he stood over Robin admiring her beauty, he began rethinking his decision to carry her along. Julious began quietly picking up his clothes, weapons, and ammunition, which he placed into his bag. He had brought a Walter PPQ-M2 9mm handgun that he could not find anywhere, so he decided to leave with the pair of Taurus GX4 Micro-Compact handguns.

"Bam," sounded the Walter PPQ-M2 which startled Julious who froze as a result! The bullet struck the door frame and tore into the wood.

"Are you crazy," Julious exclaimed?

"Don't play with me boy! I love you, but I will shoot you! I already told you I was coming," Robin threatened!

"I just did, not want to, wake you as, yet," Julious declared.

"Stop lying, you were trying to sneak out without me," Robin stated!

Robin got out the bed and pulled a sheet around herself to cover up. She walked toward Julious who had not moved, nevertheless, she carried the handgun for assurance. As she went by him, she paused and slapped him on the buttocks, then gave him a kiss on the cheek and proceeded. The young man had gotten the message and realized which weapon Robin preferred. Julious looked at the smaller micro-compact handguns inside his bag, then shook his head as he watched Robin modeling the bigger Walter PPQ-M2. Robin used the bathroom then went into her bedroom to get dressed, before they went to the kitchen and ate cereal. Miss Shirley kept a note pad with a pen attached by the telephone, so while they ate Robin wrote three letters to Julien, Coy, and her grandmother.

Coy had still not returned from Sandra's house and they wanted to leave before he got home, so they hurried and exited the house thereafter. When the revenge seekers reached St. Luke Catholic Church, Julious decided to cruise by and case the area before they made their move. Officer Gilmore had just turned off Centennial Drive onto the second block which was Waddell Avenue, as Julious drove around to the front of the church. Julious expected to see a police cruiser stationed somewhere along the roadway, so when he saw there was no deterrence, he turned onto the first side street which was O'Brien Avenue East and parked.

"You ready to, do this," Julious asked?

"Let's go," Robin stated as they kissed each other then hopped from the 4X4 and walked back to the church!

Robin was dressed for church in a sleek skin-tight black dress, with black heels, while Julious was casually dressed in a Thermo black shirt, with grey jeans, and his Air Jordan sneakers. The temperature was nineteen-degree-Celsius despite the clouds blocking out the sun and making it appeared rainy. Neither of the revenge seekers concealed their weapon, as the walked up the steps to the church door. Before they entered the church they paused and looked at each other, then stormed in blasting everyone in sight.

Old man Tully was heading to the grocery store to pick up a few essentials. As he approached the corner at Centennial Drive and Taylor Avenue by the church, he noticed the two shooters entering the building armed. The old man drove around the corner and parked away from danger, before he used his cell phone and dialed 911. Officer Gilmore was four blocks away circling the town when the emergency alert came through his radio. The officer immediately thought of his wife and children and threw on his siren as he sped to the location. While speeding to the church, Grey felt angered knowing he had just drove by the building.

Pastor Roundtree opened the front door for some air to blow through the hall. As he began walking to the rear of his church, he overheard the blasts from bullets being fired.

"Oh, my Lord that's gunfire," Pastor Roundtree said to his wife as he cautiously moved to the front door to decipher where it was coming from!

When Pastor Roundtree reached the front door and listened carefully, he realized the sounds were emanating from inside the Catholic Church. The pastor instructed his wife to contact emergency services and alert them, as he cautiously walked out and began heading to the Catholic Church. Officer Gilmore burst around the corner onto Centennial Drive at that same time and came to a screeching halt outside the church. Rather than taking up tactical position behind his cruiser, the officer pulled his sidearm and raced up the steps to the church door. There were no other officers on the scene at the time, but Grey believed his family members were in danger and refused to wait for backup.

As the gunshots rang out inside the church there were Christians sprinting through an exit door. Robin walked in behind Julious whose eyes were watery with hate. While Julious was blasting away at every adult he saw, Robin had to envision Andrew's face on individuals before she could squeeze the trigger. Julious did not have the greatest aim, therefore he was shooting and connecting yet missing targets. The shooters made their way down the center isle toward the alter, blasting away at innocent worshipers who were lovers of God.

Jacquelin and Viveen were seated along the sixth row of chairs from the back. When all the screaming and hysteria began, Jacquelin grabbed Viveen's hand and ran toward the corner isles for them to escape through a rear exit. Once

Robin spotted Jacquelin, there was no need for her to imagine that the woman resembled Andrew, after seeing her on television always supporting her venomous son. Robin aimed the Walter PPQ-M2 at the fleeing woman, before she realized she was dragging Viveen along. Watching the fleeing mother and her daughter reminded Robin of Celine with her when she was younger. She also remembered Viveen's face from school, therefore she withheld firing.

Julious' weapons had to get reloaded, so he paused shooting and started changing his magazines. As Robin turned away from Jacquelin, she caught sight of an armed male positioning himself to shoot Julious. Robin immediately squeezed the trigger and shot the male who dropped dead, for which Julious nodded his head and was grateful. When Julious got ready to recommence shooting, he noticed a little girl crouched and crying in the isle ahead of him. The little girl caused his mind to think about Julien, so Julious looked back at Robin and started shaking his head. The silence of his weapons allowed him to hear the screams and crying of victims, therefore he dropped the guns and went to pick up the little girl.

Julious started picking up the little girl who had injured her leg, when Officer Gilmore opened fire from the back of the church. The officer had snuck in the entrance and thought the massacre was still ongoing, so he shot Julious four times from behind. Robin began spinning around to see who was shooting, when the officer shot her once in the upper right shoulder and grazed her forehead with his second shot. The female avenger fell to the ground and bumped her head on the floor, as her weapon went flying across the floor. She could hear someone yelling instructions, but she had no idea what they were saying. There was a female screaming so loudly that her voice echoed inside the church. As Robin looked over at Julious, she noticed he was bleeding and not moving, hence she feared he might had been killed. The little girl who Julious was picking up was also bleeding and lifeless on the floor, as Robin slowly blanked out.

Miss Shirley was inside Julien's room when a nurse barged in and told her to turn on the television to the local news. The nurse had tears running down her face and was very shaken, so Miss Shirley hurried and turned on the television. When the screen came on and she saw the area with all the ambulances and emergency responders, she threw both her hands over her mouth. There was a huge crowd behind the police yellow tape line, among which Miss Shirley saw her pastor and many of her church adherents. The reporter came on after the cameraman showed the St. Luke Church building with all the excitement ongoing.

"As we have reported, we have no motive to say why these two young people have chosen to enter this church this morning, but they have killed eleven people and injured two others! One of the gunmen was also killed, while the other was shot multiple times and taken to the hospital, I was told! This is just a tragic, tragic situation here at St. Luke Catholic Church, in Dominion City, which had been plagued over these past months with racial issues! If you remember, only two weeks ago a white gunman entered the United Church building just down the way here; and killed twenty-four members with an assault rifle. Now, some people I have spoken to say why was there no police presence here, but I was told by officers that there was an officer in the area, who had just driven by the church before this sad incident happened. As expected, people are very angry, they want this stuff gone away from their community and they say its time for them to unite! There is a late-night vigil planned here for mourners this evening; and a silent demonstration planned for this Tuesday. I must say that I have uncovered a bit of information about the young lady who was shot and taken to the hospital. Though I can not mention her name at this point, she was a minor who lived in this neighborhood and her accomplice was also from this town, and only a few years older than her..."

Coy began calling her cellular while she listened to the reporter, hence she answered the call and placed the phone by her ears. "Mom, these cops are at the door saying that Robin was shot and taken to the hospital!"

The nurse hugged the grandmother who had begun crying. "Oh, my Lord, not my Robin!"

"I will go and check if they brought her here! If not, I will find out which hospital they brought Robin and what her stat..." the nurse began explaining, when Julien opened his eyes and took a huge breath!

➤ ➤ ➤

When the paramedic technician awoke Robin, she was inside an ambulance heading to the hospital handcuffed to the bed. Robin had questions she needed answered, but as she looked around, she would have to wait for those responses. There was a male officer on-board with the paramedics, who served as extra security for the high-profile prisoner. At the hospital doctors took X-rays of the wound before Robin was taken into surgery, where they removed the bullet and stitched her up. It did not take the injured detainee very long to realize that certain nationalities of people supported what Julious and she did, while some Caucasians were highly upset. The black nurses and doctor who treated her at the hospital were all pleasant and kind, but the bigots went by and gave her the dirtiest stares. The nurse who they assigned to dress her head wound was the first person who answered some of her questions.

"Hello, my name is Taejah! I'm here to clean and dress your head wound! How are you," the nurse asked?

"I'm in a bit of pain, can I get some medication for it," Robin said?

"No problem, I will get the doctor to provide you with something as soon as he is done with his patient! But can you tell me, why did you and your boyfriend do it," the nurse asked?

"What," Robin asked?

"Why did you guys shoot all those people," the nurse enquired?

359

"How many people got shot," Robin remarked?

"Thirteen in total according to the news; make that fourteen with your boyfriend," the nurse answered!

"It was all revenge," Robin answered then turned her head to the side and began crying!

Immediately after Robin got patched up, she was transferred to RCMP lockup facility on Portage Avenue in Winnipeg. As an under-aged high-profile prisoner, she was assigned to the Protective Care Unit for her safety, while the government began prosecution proceeding against her for the church massacre. Miss Shirley and Coy found a top-notch attorney and hired him to represent Robin, therefore six hours following her transfer to the RCMP lockup, her Attorney Joe Debrinka went to speak with her. Robin's sixteenth birthday was upcoming in two weeks, so the government wanted to charge her as an adult. Mr. Debrinka was not abled to sit with Robin in a room, but the facility allowed them to speak through a phone, behind a plexiglass in a booth.

➤ ➤ ➤

When the United Church held their candle vigil, there were mostly colored individuals there from the community, but everyone felt the need to come together and heal after their recent act of violence. Pastor Hemming and Pastor Roundtree joined in prayer for their community and held the largest candle vigil ever held across the territory. Mayor Bathurst was again present to mourn with her community, as they grappled with yet another tragedy. The residents showed their heartbreak by creating another tribute post, filled with cards, letters, teddy bears, and sentimental objects.

At the silent demonstration a few days later, the community again came out in massive numbers to denounce gun violence and signaled the need for gun law changes. One of the people at the front of the demonstration was Miss Shirley, who walked hand in hand with her dear Caucasian friends Mrs. Michelle Zap, Miss Mutty, and others. There were thousands of people involved the march, who all came together to reclaim their community and their lives. Coy kept Julien's company at the hospital as his little nephew watched and re-watched the videos his sister recorded for him. The police department once again faced scrutiny for Officer Gilmore's action, which resulted in the death of his own daughter. The officer was given the opportunity to retire due to his years of service, for not following protocol and wait for backup in the Catholic Church massacre. Officer Gilmore chose to retire rather than getting fired, as the Dakota Ojibwe Police Department continued to strive for perfection.

Chapter 48

The arraignment process was done via satellite, wherein Robin was locked in a video room and popped up a monitor with the judge, the prosecution, and her attorney. Robin did not understand much of the technicalities that transpired, but her lawyer arranged their trial dates for them to argue against the government's case. When Attorney Debrinka heard Robin's story he was moved to find a compassionate defense, to show the courts the emotional anguish the female was under.

Robin spent two days locked in a cell going bored out of her mind, with only reading materials at her disposal. After the second day she asked the sergeant if she could get transferred to the regular population. The sergeant absolutely refused, knowing that should anything happened to Robin it might cost her career, but the newcomer kept requesting. When she saw the sergeant would not budge on her answer, Robin asked Lieutenant Gill for permission, and he approved her transfer. Most of the guards believed it would be a stupid idea to put a minor in a pod with female adult prisoners, but Robin was no regular teenager. Lieutenant Gill thought that after a few ladies slapped her around, she would be pleading to return to the PC unit for her own protection. The guards moved her into A-Pod the following morning and kept her under close observation. There were two other new detainees being send into A-Pod, so the guards thought no one who realize who Robin was if she entered with the new girls.

Each new detainee entered the pod with a plastic bin that held all their personal and other items. The newcomers were all assigned rooms and were expected to make their bunks immediately after they entered their new cells. Robin walked in with her bin and headed for cell number seven on the bottom floor. There was no one inside the room when she entered and began making her top bunk. Six Caucasian females who were standing beside the showers walked to the cell and blocked the entrance. Their leader Big Liz went into the cell and stood by the door, while Robin continued fixing her bed. Robin did not hear any of the ladies enter, but when she spun and saw them, she was rather friendly.

"Hello, are you my new cellmate? Hi, I'm Robin!"

"You think you're going to get away for running into a Catholic Church and killing white folks, bitch," Big Liz stated!

Robin was trapped with nowhere to go and had some monster ladies to fend off. There were five black ladies at a table playing cards, who noticed the invasion. They got up and walked over and stood behind the white ladies blocking the door.

"Excuse me y'all, but why are you bitches in my cell," Erica demanded?

The Caucasian ladies spun around and saw Erica and her friends behind them. Erica walked right through the ladies at the door and into the cell, where she stood up and faced Big Liz.

"This is not your cell Erica! What are you looking for trouble," Big Liz declared?

"You right this isn't my house, but my new home girl just moved in, so that makes this our place," Erica stated!

Big Liz was furious and wanted to smash Robin, but she had no choice but to walk out and leave. Robin was beyond grateful for the help, after she expected to get pounded by the Caucasian females.

"Huh, thank you ladies for saving me," Robin stated!

"You that chick they been talking about on the news, who started some new revolution," Denise stated!

"Could be," Robin stated! "Are you, my cellmate?"

"No, she went to court this morning. I'm Erica, she is Denise, Faith, Jackey, and Helen!"

"Nice to meet you ladies! I'm Robin!"

"Hey guys come look at the news," a female detainee called out to the group of colored ladies.

They went over and began watching the news, where a reporter featured a mourning black father in Ohio, United States, who searched for the address of the mass shooter's parents who killed his wife and daughter, then went to their residence and killed them. The second story featured a black woman in Colorado, who also tracked down the parents of the teenager who went into her son's school and killed eight people. The woman then went to their house and killed everyone at the residence and left a note blaming them for being awful parents. The reporter sighted that incident such as those were happening all across the country due to the revenge seekers in Canada. For insights on what some black Americans thought of the attacks, the reporter asked several random people off the street, "What they thought about the incidents?"

"If those mass shooters are going to target African Americans, then they need to feel what loss feels like," one woman stated!

"Black people aren't going to just keep taking that shit after hundreds of years of slavery," one man stated!

"I think that is a little extreme for people to do! I mean that's why we have the police," another man said!

"Racism must stop! That's it," said a female!

Two weeks later Robin was laying on her bunk, when she climbed down quickly, bent over the toilet, and started vomiting. Tara her Caucasian cellmate was reading a magazine and asked if she was, OK? Robin mentioned that it was probably a bug and went back to doing what they were doing. The next morning, she vomited again, yet she overlooked it and went about her day. When she vomited for the third day in a row, Tara suggested she went to the infirmary. Following a few tests, the doctors determined that Robin was a few weeks pregnant. After she was forced to miss Julious' funeral it seemed like destiny for her to conceive his child and prolonged the Simms family name.

When Robin contacted her grandmother and gave her the news, Miss Shirley was stunned. Contrary to her rape situation, Robin felt honored to carry the developing child in her womb. Because her granddaughter wholeheartedly wanted to keep her unborn baby, Miss Shirley felt delighted and promised to raise the child throughout her incarceration. Coy hated the idea of her being there, yet he encouraged her and told her to remain strong. Julien and Robin had a great conversation wherein she advised him that he was about to become an uncle. The little boy was back home and recovering well, therefore he was delighted to hear about the new family addition.

Coy and Miss Shirley never missed a day of Robin's trial and sat in the front row directly behind the defense bench each court date. By the time her trial ended Robin was a few weeks from delivering her baby, therefore despite the circumstances everyone was overjoyed. The prosecution wanted her to get up to twenty years in prison, but Attorney Debrinka argued an excellent case for the defense. The judge in the case listened to both sides' arguments and noted all the evidence entered; before she deliberated to consider the case and rendered her verdict. When Judge June Simmons recalled the court two days later, everyone was anxious to hear her decision. After she carefully considered all the evidence, Judge Simmons awarded Robin five years for her involvement in the church shooting.

The defense accepted the judge's ruling considering she was quite lenient and could have given her a much longer sentence. Following the trial Robin, Miss Shirley, and Coy thanked Attorney Debrinka for his great work, which they thought was money well spent. They hugged and said goodbyes as Robin got brought back to finish serving the remainder of her sentence. A week later Miss

Shirley received notification that Robin had delivered her baby boy, who they went and collected at the hospital. Robin decided to call her son Julious Simms Jr after his father and handed him over to her grandmother to look after until her release.

---

18 Months Later

As Robin looked at the soldiers to the left and right of her, their intensity increased her energy to fight. The battlefield was about to get bloody, and her comrades dressed in their all-black tactical uniforms were prepared for the challenge. The two armies standing across from each other were made up of volunteers, one being the infamous Ku Klux Klan versus The Black Coalition. Both armies were well armed with high powered rifles and other dangerous weaponry. All the verbal dialog was over, and the two sides were ready to settle their differences once and for all. The swatch patches on the bigots' jackets proved their disdain for their colored opponents, whose intentions were to trample white supremacy. As a people strong and resilient, Robin's associates would not back down from any race war, because that was a battle they had to win for their existence. The black soldiers listen to the fuel of hate the racist leaders spilt to their fighters, while they patiently waited for the charge to sound to kill them all. The leader who Robin and the Black Coalition army followed understood that surrender and defeat were no options, therefore they would fight until their racist opponents were wiped out.

As Robin stood behind their leader waiting for the battle cry to sound, the prison guard banged on her door and woke her from her dream. "Pack your stuff Walker, be ready to go in ten minutes!"

It was an emotional morning for Robin who was going home after she was granted parole for good behavior. She would have to stay out of trouble and sign in at a probation office once each week until her sentence was complete, but at lease she was free to be with her son. As she left the pod everyone wished her the best and cried with her after such a challenging journey. All the ladies had an amazing time with Robin, who would hold commissary parties, where she bought all the goodies from the prison store for the entire A-pod. Even the guards wished her the best on her way out, knowing the growth she had made over the past few months.

When she reached outside the facility her entire family were there to pick her up. Young Julious Jr. was happy to see his mother and gave her the greatest hugs. It was a delight to see and hold her brother who had grown and was almost as tall as her. Robin was delighted being back with her family, but she had an unexpected surprise. Rather than returning to Dominion City, she asked Coy to drive her to the airport, as she planned on starting a new life in a fresh environment. Miss Shirley completely understood her granddaughter's decision, knowing how difficult it would have been for her to be around families whom she had scarred deeply.

The family was separating for a short while, but they were content after all they had been through. Robin left for Toronto with her child to spend time with Lloyd's father and finish her schooling. The revenge seeking that Julious and she started had caused a significant decline in mass murders, with shooters a bit more conscious of retaliations. After recognizing the effects of how potent Julious' actions have proven to be against white supremacy, Robin was invited to speak at a black rally in Queen's Park before thousands. With her grandfather and son in the audience to support her, Robin waved at them as she waited to deliver her speech. When introduced at the function Robin stepped to the mic and began her speech by saying, "I have a dream!"

THE END

www.ingramcontent.com/pod-product-compliance
Lightning Source LLC
Chambersburg PA
CBHW070902120626
46546CB00001B/102